T0166092

MUSLIM-CHRISTIAN RELATIONS
IN THE NEW ORDER INDONESIA

MUSLIM-CHRISTIAN RELATIONS IN THE NEW ORDER INDONESIA

The Exclusivist and Inclusivist Muslims' Perspectives

Fatimah Husein

mizan

Muslim-Christian Relations In the New Order Indonesia:
The Exclusivist and Inclusivist Muslims' Perspectives
Copyright © Fatimah Husein 2005

Published by
Mizan Pustaka
Jalan Yodkali 16
Bandung 40124
Indonesia
Ph. +62-22-7200931
Fax. +62-22-7207038
http://www.mizan.com

ISBN 979-433-385-9

No part of this book may be reproduced in any form without the prior permission of the publisher. All rights reserved.

Cover design by Andreas Kusumahadi

Distributed by
Mizan Media Utama (MMU)
Jln. Cinambo (Cisaranten Wetan) No. 146
Ujungberung, Bandung 40294
Ph. 62-22-7815500 – Fax. 62-22-7802288
e-mail: mizanmu@bdg.centrin.net.id

Table of Contents

Preface — 9
Acknowledgments — 11
Notes on Translation and Transliteration — 15
List of Abbreviations — 17
Glossary — 23

1   Introduction — 27
    Defining Some Key Terms — 28
        Exclusivist Muslims — 29
        Inclusivist Muslims Christians — 31
        Christians — 31
    The Position of Muhammadiyah and Nahdhatul Ulama — 32
    Objective of the Study — 34
    Organisation of the Study — 35
    Data Collection — 37

2   Muslim-Christian Relations in Classical Islam
        and in the 20ᵗʰ Century — 38
    Introduction — 38
    Theological Perception of the Christian 'Other' in Classical
        Islam — 39
    The Religious 'Other' in Classical Islamic Law — 43
        Rights and Obligations of *Ahl al-Dhimma* — 43
        Marriage between a Muslim and an *Ahl Kitāb* — 48
        Greeting Jews and Christians — 49

Interfaith Dialogue in the 20th Century: A Survey of the
   International Discourse — 51
Concluding Remarks — 57

3   An Overview of Muslim–Christian Relations in Indonesian
   until 1965 — 59
Introduction — 59
Dutch Colonial Policy on Muslims and Christian — 60
Depiction of Christianity and Islam in Early 20th Century
   Indonesia — 68
Muslim–Christian Relations in the Old Order (1945–1965) — 71
      Regional Rebellions of DI/TII and PRRI — 78
      Christianisation Issues and Muslim Writings on
         Christianity — 82
      Sukarno and Islam — 87
Concluding Remarks — 90

4   The New Order and Muslim–Christian Relations
   (1965–1998) — 92
Introduction — 92
Soeharto's SARA Policy and Muslim–Christian Relations — 93
      'Othering' the Ethnic Chinese — 94
      Weakening Islamic Political Power — 99
Muslims, Abangan and Christians in the New Order
   Bureaucracy — 116
Other Sources of Muslim Animosity towards Christians — 120
      Conversion to Christianity — 120
      Social Services Owned by Christians — 122
State-Sponsored Efforts for Inter-religious Dialogue — 127
      Inter-Religions Consultation Forum — 127
      Ministry of Religious Affairs on Inter-religious
         Dialogue — 130
      Majelis Ulama Indonesia and Some Fatāwā on
         Muslim-Christian Relations — 135
Concluding Remarks — 141

5   **The Exclusivist Muslims' Perceptions of Christians** — 143
Introduction — 143
The Exclusivist Muslim Organisations — 144
    Dewan Dakwah Islamiyah Indonesia — 144
    Komite Indonesia untuk Solidaritas Dunia Islam — 149
    Front Pembela Islam — 151
    Laskar Jihad — 154
A Brief Theological Account of the Christian 'Other' — 157
    The Perspective on *Ahl al-Kitāb* — 157
    The Distortion of Christianity — 160
    Christians as Colonialists — 163
Attempts at Reviving the Jakarta Charter and Establishing an
    Islamic State — 166
Issue of Christianisation — 180
    Inter-religious Consultation Forum — 185
    The Issue of Church Buildings in Relation to Decree
        No. 01/BER/MDN-MAG/1969, Decree No. 70/1978,
        and Decree No. 77/1978 — 189
    The 1973 Marriage Bill and the Issue of Inter-religious
        Marriage — 198
    Participation in Christmas Celebrations and Imitating
        Muslim Traditions — 205
    The Religious Judicature Act Bill — 208
    Christianisation through Education — 213
A Brief Account of the Ambon Conflicts and Muslim–Christian
    Relations — 216
    The Exclusivists' Perspectives on the Ambon
        Conflicts — 217
    The Inflammatory Rhetoric of the Laskar Jihad — 220
Concluding Remarks — 225

6   **The Inclusivist Muslims' Viewpoints on the Religious**
    'Other' — 226
Introduction — 226

The Birth of Inclusive Thought in Indonesia — 227
    Background of the Renewal of Islamic Thought — 228
    Nurcholish Madjid: Key Figure of the Renewal of Islamic
        Thought — 231
    Neo-modernism and Renewal of Islamic Thought in
        Indonesia — 237
The Inclusivists on the Image of the Religious 'Other' — 241
    The Issue of Religious Pluralism — 241
    The Concept of Ahl al-Kitāb — 252
    On Inter-regious Marriage — 259
Christianisation and Roots of Disharmony between Muslims
   and Christians — 263
    On Christianisation — 264
    Roots of Disharmony — 267
The Role of the Inclusivists in Indonesian Society — 270
    Non-Goverment Organisations on Interfaith
        Dialogue — 270
    State Institute of Islamic Studies (IAIN) — 276
Concluding Remarks — 278

7   **Mutual Critiques between the Exclusivists and
        Inclusivist** — 280
Introduction — 280
Exclusivists' Perspectives on the Inclusivists — 281
    The Renewal Movement and Inclusivist Theological
        Perspectives — 281
    Ahl al-Kitāb — 289
Inclusivists' Responses to the Exclusivists' Perspectives — 293
Concluding Remarks — 297

8   **Conclusion** — 298

Selected Bibliography — 305
Appendices — 331
Index — 351

Preface

Some chapters of the thesis have been presented at seminars or adapted as journal articles. Chapter Four "The New Order and Muslim-Christian Relations (1965-1998)" was adapted into an article entitled "Dry Leaves and Grass: Muslim-Christian relations in Indonesia" and published in *Interface* 4/1 (May 2001): 11-31. With some modifications, part of Chapter Four has also been published as "Hubungan Muslim-Kristen dan Pemerintah Orde Baru Indonesia: Perspektif Sejarah" in *Antologi Studi Islam: Teori & Metodologi*, edited by Amin Abdullah et al. (Yogyakarta: IAIN Sunan Kalijaga Press, 2000), 69-84. Chapter Five "The Exclusivist Muslims' Perspectives on the Religious 'Other'" was presented at the seminar on "Religion and Modernity: Asian Perspectives" at the National University of Singapore on 17-18 May 2002 as "The Exclusivist Muslims' Responses to the New Order's Project of Modernisation and Secularisation". With some modifications, this chapter was presented as "Muhammadiyah and Exclusivist Muslims: Perspectives on Christianisation", at the Melbourne Indonesia Consortium Conference "The Dynamics of Political Islam" on 11-12 July 2003; and as "Muslim-Christian Relations in Indonesia:

The Exclusivist Muslims' Perspectives", at the seminar "Indonesia and Christian–Muslim Relations: Paradigms and Perspectives", at the University of Auckland and at Waikato University, New Zealand, on 19 and 21 August 2003, respectively.[]

Acknowledgments

This study owes much to the help and contribution of a great many people. Sincere gratitude is firstly due to my thesis supervisors Associate Professor Abdullah Saeed and Professor Arief Budiman. Associate Professor Abdullah Saeed gave constructive criticism and penetrating comments to my drafts so that I was able to complete the best possible result. In addition, Prof Budiman always encouraged to persist through challenging periods during completion of this PhD program. To these two supervisors I acknowledge my profound indebtedness. I would also like to thank Professor Merle Ricklefs of Melbourne University for reading parts of my draft and for his invaluable advice.

There are some institutions that have significantly contributed to the completion of this study: the Australian Agency for International Development (AusAID) for awarding me a doctoral scholarship; the Melbourne Institute of Asian Languages and Society (MIALS), which provided me with generous funds for my field research and attending conferences; the University of Melbourne for awarding me the Melbourne University Travelling Scholarship and MA Bartlett

Special Travel Grant-id-aid; the Research School of Pacific and Asian Studies (RSPAS) of the Australian National University (ANU) Canberra that granted me generous funding through the National Visiting Scholarship Scheme (NVSS) and enabled me to stay in Canberra for one month and to use the ANU and National Library collections.

My sincere thanks are due to Professor A.H. Johns and Dr Greg Fealy of the ANU for the discussions we had and for their constructive comments on some parts of my early thesis draft. I would also thank Professor Gavin Jones and Professor Terence Hull of the ANU for providing me with some important materials, and Aline Scott-Maxwell of Monash University for her help in assisting me in finding some materials at Monash libraries.

I also wish to thank some special friends Ariel Heryanto, Yanti Heryanto, Justin Wejak, Elly Erawaty, Titi Sukriyah, Miranda Francis, Luthfi Assyaukanie, Syafi'i Anwar, Redha Ameur, Tahmina Rashid, and Emenda Sembiring for the friendships we made during my stay in Melbourne. I would also thank all postgraduate students who often come to MIALS, especially Dale Chia-Ching Lin, for bitter and sweet memories of our lovely postgraduate room. Also to MIALS staff members, especially Mary Kidd, Robyn Borg, Tonia Eckfeld, and Sachiyo Sekiguchi, for making MIALS feel like a home away from home.

I would like to express my debt and gratitude to my family. First is my husband, Ugi, who has always supported me and understood my commitment to my studies. We had to 'sacrifice' two good years of our married life to being separated from each other. We realise how difficult it is to be away from the one we love and therefore we have made a commitment that upon the completion of this thesis we will make the best possible efforts to stay together, *inshaallah*. For my mother (Nur Segaf Basri), father (Husein Djufri), two brothers (Muhammad Amin and Hasan Lutfi), and cousins (Fathiyah Basri, Mustafa Anis and Memet Hadi), I say thank you for your help, patience and encouragement, without which this study would not have been possible. I always take Mum's questions 'Are you going to ever stop studying?' and 'When are you coming back home for good?' as her expression of missing her only daughter who has been away from her for quite a long time. To her I dedicate this thesis.[]

Notes on Translation and Transliteration

In dealing with the variations of the spelling of Indonesian names and terms, the study has adopted the following system: titles of books and articles are rendered according to their original spellings; Indonesian words, terms and place-names not in quotations are written according to the *Ejaan Baru Bahasa Indonesia* (1972), and proper names are spelled in the way used by the individual him/herself (the majority of Indonesian call themselves by their first names). If there is no certainty on how an Indonesian person's name is spelled, his/her full name will be cited.

Some names, such as Prophet Muhammad, Caliph Uthman, or Ibn Hazm, are already widely used in English and therefore will not be transliterated, except when it was first quoted in the footnotes or in direct quotations.

For the translation of the Qur'ān, the study utilises the works of Abdullah Yusuf Ali and Muhammad Asad. The following is the transliteration from Arabic to English.

English	Arabic
th	ث
ḥ	ح
kh	خ
ḍ	د
dh	ذ
sh	ش
ṣ	ص
d	ض
ṭ	ط
ẓ	ظ
c	ع
gh	غ
'	ء

The long vowels of ا, و, ي are typed using a macron above characters: ā, ī, ū.

In the case of *tā' marbūṭah* (ة) *h* is omitted.

List of Abbreviation

ABRI	:	Armed Forces of the Republic of Indonesia (Angkatan Bersenjata Republik Indonesia)
Bakin	:	National Intelligent Coordinative Body (Badan Koordinasi Intelejen Negara)
Bappenas	:	National Development Planning Agency (Badan Perencanaan Pembangunan Nasional)
BKAM	:	Coordinating Institution of Muslim Groups (Badan Koordinasi Amal Muslimin)
BMI	:	Islamic Bank of Indonesia (Bank Muamalat Indonesia)
BPS	:	Central Statistics Bureau (Biro Pusat Statistik)
BPUPKI	:	Investigating Committee for Preparatory Work for Indonesian Independence (Badan Usaha Penyelidik Persiapan Kemerdekaan Indonesia)
CSIS	:	Centre for Strategic and International Studies
DDII	:	Indonesian Islamic Preaching Council (Dewan Dakwah Islamiyah Indonesia)

DGI   :   Council of Indonesian Churches (Dewan Gereja-gereja Indonesia). Since 1984 DGI changed its name into PGI

DI   :   Darul Islam (from Arabic *dār al-Islām*, territory or house of Islam)

DPR   :   People's Representative Council (Dewan Perwakilan Rakyat)

FKM   :   Front of Moluccas Sovereignity (Front Kedaulatan Maluku)

FPI   :   Front of Defenders of Islam (Front Pembela Islam)

G 30 S   :   The September 30th Affair (Gerakan Tigapuluh September)

GBHN   :   Broad Outlines of the State Policy (Garis-garis Besar Haluan Negara)

GGBI   :   The Indonesian Baptist Churches (Gabungan Gereja-gereja Baptis Indonesia)

GMII   :   Indonesian Islamic Youth (Generasi Muda Islam Indonesia)

Golkar   :   Functional Group (Golongan Karya)

GPII   :   Islamic Youth Movement of Indonesia (Gerakan Pemuda Islam Indonesia)

GPPI   :   Renewal of Islamic thought (Gerakan Pembaruan Pemikiran Islam)

HMI   :   Muslim Students Association (Himpunan Mahasiswa Islam)

IAIN   :   State Institute of Islamic Studies (Institut Agama Islam Negeri)

ICMI   :   Association of Indonesian Muslim Intellectuals (Ikatan Cendekiawan Muslim Indonesia)

JIL   :   Islamic Liberal Network (Jaringan Islam Liberal)

KAMI : Action-Committee of Indonesian Students (Komite Aksi Mahasiswa Indonesia)

KAP Gestapu : Action Front to Crush the Thirtieth of September Movement (Kesatuan Aksi Pengganyangan Gerakan September Tigapuluh)

KISDI : Indonesian Committee for Solidarity with the Islamic World (Komite Indonesia untuk Solidaritas Dunia Islam)

Komnas HAM : National Committee of Human Rights (Komisi Nasional Hak Asasi Manusia)

Kopkamtib : Operational Command for the Restoration of Security and Order (Komando Pemulihan Keamanan dan Ketertiban)

Kostrad : Army Strategic Reserve Command (Komando Cadangan Strategis Angkatan Darat)

KTP : Residential Card (Kartu Tanda Penduduk)

KWI : Indonesian Catholic Bishops' Conference (Konferensi Waligereja Indonesia)

LIPIA : The Institute of Islamic and Arabic Studies (Lembaga Ilmu Pengetahuan Islam dan Arab)

MAWI : Indonesian Council of Bishops (Mejelis Agung Waligereja Indonesia). Since November 1986 MAWI changed its name into KWI

Masyumi : Consultative Council of Indonesian Muslims (Majelis Syuro Muslimin Indonesia)

MIAI : The Supreme Indonesian Council of Islam (Majlisul Islamil A'laa Indonesia)

MPPB : Master Plan for the Development of the Nation (Master Plan Pembangunan Bangsa)

MPR : People's Consultative Assembly (Majelis Permusyawaratan Rakyat)

MUI : Council of the *ʿUlamā'* of Indonesia (Majelis Ulama Indonesia)

NIFCON : Network for Interfaith Concerns

NII : Indonesian Islamic State (Negara Islam Indonesia)

NU : Nahdhatul Ulama

Parkindo : Indonesian Protestant Party (Partai Kristen Indonesia)

Parmusi : Indonesian Muslim Party (Partai Muslimin Indonesia)

PCID : Pontifical Council for Inter-religious Dialogue

PDI : Indonesian Democratic Party (Partai Demokrasi Indonesia)

Pemda : Local government (Pemerintah Daerah)

PHDP : Association of Indonesian Hindu Dharma (Parisada Hindu Dharma Pusat)

PGI : The Communion of Churches in Indonesia (Persatuan Gereja-gereja di Indonesia)

PII : Indonesian Islamic Students (Pelajar Islam Indonesia)

PKI : Indonesian Communist Party (Partai Komunis Indonesia)

PMKRI : Indonesian Catholic Student Association (Perhimpunan Mahasiswa Katolik Republik Indonesia)

PNI : Indonesian Nationalist Party (Partai Nasionalis Indonesia)

PPKI : Committee for the Preparation of Indonesia's Independence (Panitia Persiapan Kemerdekaan Indonesia)

PPP : United Development Party (Partai Persatuan Pembangunan)

PRRI : Revolutionary Government of the Indonesian Republic (Pemerintah Revolusioner Republik Indonesia)

PSI : Indonesian Socialist Party (Partai Sosialis Indonesia)

PSII	:	Islamic Political Association of Indonesia (Partai Sarikat Islam Indonesia)
Repelita	:	Five-Year Plan for Development (Rencana Pembangunan Lima Tahun)
RMS	:	Republic of South Maluku (Republik Maluku Selatan)
RUUP	:	Marriage Bill (Rencana Undang-Undang Perkawinan)
RUU-PA	:	Religious Judicature Act (Rencana Undang-Undang Peradilan Agama)
SARA	:	Ethnicity, Religion, Race, and Inter-group relations (Suku, Agama, Ras, Antar-golongan)
Sekber Golkar	:	Joint Secretariat of Functional Groups (Sekretariat Bersama Golongan Karya)
TII	:	Indonesian Islamic Army (Tentara Islam Indonesia)
UUDS	:	Temporary Constitution (Undang-Undang Dasar Sementara)
Walubi	:	Council of Indonesian Buddhist (Perwalian Umat Buddha Indonesia)
WCC	:	World Council of Churches
WCRP	:	World Conference on Religion and Peace
WFDD	:	World Faiths Development Dialogue

Glossary

All terms are in Arabic unless otherwise stated

abangan : (Javanese) Muslims who have nominal commitment to Islam and who do not care in practising the Islamic ritual duties

ahl al-dhimma/ dhimmīs : non-Muslim protected minorities who lived under the Islamic rule, including Christians

ahl al-kitāb: People of the Book, i.e. the Qur'ānic expression used to describe people to whom a Holy Book has been revealed (including the Jews and Christians)

ahl al-sunna wa al-jamāʿa : People of the *sunna*, i.e. those who uphold customs based on the practice and authority of the Prophet Muhammad and his companions

ahadīth/ ḥadīths : pl. of *ḥadīth*

amar al-maʿrūf wa al-nahy al-munkar : enjoining good and preventing evil

ᶜibāda : worship, obedience to rituals including ablutions, prayer, fasting, pilgrimage

ᶜIed al-Fiṭr : celebration of the end of the *Ramaḍān* fasting month

bidᶜa : heresy; deviation from Islamic tradition

daᶜwa : propagation of Islamic faith, Islamic mission

fatwā : legal opinion concerning Islamic Law

fatwās or fatāwā: pl. of *fatwā*

fiqh : Islamic jurisprudence; science of the *sharīᶜa*

fuqahā' : Muslim jurists; experts on Islamic law

ḥadīth : reports on the sayings and the traditions of Prophet Muhammad or what he witnessed and approved

ḥalal : something that is lawful and permitted in Islam

ḥarām : something which is unlawful or prohibited in Islam

hizbullah : army of Allah; corps of the Muslims formatted during the Japanese period (1942–1945)

ḥudūd : the limits ordained by Allah. This includes the punishment for crimes

ijtihād : individual inquiry to establish the ruling of Islamic law upon a given point

imām : leader of Muslim community in prayer or in intellectual thought

Injīl : Gospel

jizya : protection tax paid by the *dhimmīs* to the state where they lived

jundi : the FPI members who received semi-military training and were active at combating immoral activities

khalaf : the later generations of Muslims, i.e. the Muslims who lived at the period after the Prophet Muhammad and his acquaintances kharaj : land tax paid by the *dhimmīs* to the state where they lived. This tax still applied even though they later converted into Islam

khurafāt : superstitions

madhhab : a system of *fiqh*, or Muslim school of law. There are four schools accepted as legitimate by the Sunnis, namely the Ḥanafī, Malikī, Shāfiʿī, and Ḥanbalī

mafsadah : harm

maslahah : benefits

mufassir : Qur'ānic interpreter

mushrik : one who is worshipping more than one God; polytheist.

mushrikūn : pl. of *mushrik*

najis : impure according to the Islamic teaching

Pancasila : (Sanskrit) the Five Principles, namely: belief in one God, humanity, nationalism, mutual deliberation, and social justice

pesantren : (Indonesian) Islamic boarding school

pribumi : (Indonesian) The indigenous population of Indonesia

rajam : death by stoning

ramaḍān : the ninth month of the Islamic calendar, the month of annual fasting

salafȳ : the followers of the first generations of Muslims, i.e. the Prophet Muhammad and his acquaintances. Because of their proximity to the Prophet Muhammad, their beliefs and practice are considered authoritative

santri : (Indonesian) devout Muslims who have serious commitment to Islam and who are practising the Islamic ritual duties

sharīʿa : the path to be followed; Islamic law, the totality of the Islamic way of life; revealed Islamic code of conduct; the outer path *shirk*   : envisaging a partner for the Divinity and therefore of compromising God's inviolable Unity

sunna   : the practice of the Prophet and the early community which becomes for all Muslims an authoritative example of the correct way to live a Muslim life

sunni   : those who accept the *sunna* and the succession of the Caliphs, the majority of the Muslim community in Indonesia

tabliġ akbar : mass religious gatherings to remind people of doing good and preventing evil

taḥrīf   : falsifications, corruptions or changes towards Scriptures

tathlīth   : the Trinity

tawḥīd   : unity, the oneness of God's being and the unity of the mystic with the divine being

ᶜulamā'   : the collective term for religious scholars of Islam

umma   : Islamic community

uṣūl al-fiqh : 'roots' or principles of Islamic jurisprudence, sources of Islamic law (Qur'ān, *sunna* of Prophet, consensus (*ijmāʾ*), analogical reasoning (*qiyās*)

al-yaum al-qiyāma : end of the world

zakāt   : tax levied on Muslims

1

Introduction

The relationship between Muslims and Christians in Indonesia's New Order (1965–1998) deserves special focus. First, as is known, Muslims constitute the Indonesian majority with more than 85% of the total population. However, there is a commonly held view that they did not play an important role initially in Indonesian politics, especially during the first 20 years of the Soeharto government. In contrast, although Christians, both Catholics and Protestants, represent only around 9% of the total population they appear to have played an important role in Indonesia, especially in the economic domain. Therefore, the relationship between Muslims and Christians is more significant to analyse as compared to the interactions between other religious groups within Indonesian society. Second, although Muslim–Christian relations during the New Order period were at times harmonious, it was these two groups more than any other religious groups who were often involved in tensions and misperceptions. Third, the relations between Muslims and Christians in present day Indonesia are to a great extent connected to various policies and regulations issued by the New Order government, which may have derived these policies from different experiences in the past.

The views of 'exclusivist' and 'inclusivist' Muslims on Muslim–Christian relations in Indonesia's New Order are equally important. Firstly, at discourse level, the complexity of Muslim–Christian relations is not fully understood. Secondly, exploration of the perspectives of 'exclusivists' and 'inclusivists' on Muslim–Christian relations may unveil the reasons why the attitudes of 'exclusivists' towards Christians differ from those of 'inclusivists'. It is hoped this understanding will facilitate better relations between the two religious groups. Three key terms used in the study will be defined, namely: 'exclusivists', 'inclusivists', and Christians. Other related terminologies and concepts used in the study are briefly explained in the Glossary.

Defining Some Key Terms

This study is not the first attempt to label Indonesian Muslims as 'exclusivist' or 'inclusivist'. Among the works that have been written on this issue is Liddle's '*Media Dakwah* Scripturalism: One Form of Islamic Political Thought and Action in New Order Indonesia', in which he designated the groups as 'substantialist' and 'scripturalist'.[1] Another typology to label these groups is used by Shepard in 'Secularists, Traditionalists and Islamists in Southeast Asia: A Paradigm Revisited'. He labels such groups as 'radical Islamist' and 'neo-modernist'.[2] The typology in this study is to a significant extent influenced by Saeed's classification of 'legalist-exclusivists' and 'contextualist-inclusivists' in his unpublished paper 'Religious Reconciliation in Indonesia: "Legalist-Exclusivists" vs "Contextualist-Inclusivists"'.

---

[1] Published in Mark R. Woodward, ed., *Toward a New Paradigm: Recent Developments in Indonesian Islamic Thought* (Tempe: Arizona State University, Program for Southeast Asian Studies, 1996), 323-356.

[2] A paper presented at the conference 'Islam, Civil Society and Development in Southeast Asia', University of Melbourne, 11-12 July 1998.

There are some risks in labelling certain groups as 'exclusivists' or 'inclusivists'. First, the labels could be easily interpreted as value judgements. Second, to designate a certain group with a particular label could face the risk of lumping together several phenomena. Third, certain people that are put together in one group might not agree with the label designated to them.[3] Nevertheless, in discussing a vast Muslim society such as Indonesia, especially in regard to the issue of Indonesian Muslims' perspectives on Muslim-Christian relations, applying labels is unavoidable.

The study will discuss 'exclusivist' and 'inclusivist' Muslims as groups which are tied by common ideas. However, the terms 'exclusivists' and 'inclusivists' here will be placed on a continuum, because within each group the degree of 'exclusiveness' or 'inclusiveness' varies. As the study will show, it is even possible that someone could be an 'inclusivist' at certain points and be 'exclusivist' at others. Nevertheless, each group's essential perspectives will be identified.

Exclusivist Muslims

The term 'exclusivist' Muslims is used in this study to identify a group of Muslims who appear to have these characteristics in common:

(1) They apply a literal approach in understanding the foundation texts of Islam, namely the Qur'ān and the sunna of the Prophet, and are past-oriented. As this approach emphasises the literal meaning of the texts, the role of ijtihād (individual inquiry to establish the ruling of Islamic law upon a given point) is not central in their frame of thought.

---

[3] For example, in an interview, Adian Husaini, who in this study would be categorised as an exclusivist, rejected the label attributed to him, arguing that 'the term is not appropriate as it only emphasises the theological outlook of the group'. As an alternative he suggested the label 'comprehensive Muslims' as opposed to the 'reductionist Muslims'. Adian Husaini, interview by author, Jakarta, 29 January 2002.

(2) They hold the view that salvation can only be achieved through the religion of Islam. For them, Islam is the final religion, which came to correct other religions; therefore they question the validity of scriptures and religions other than Islam. This attitude is translated into the rejection of other religions as well as other religious believers. Although the exclusivists differ in the degree of intolerance towards the non-Muslim 'other', one of their markers is their often incisive rhetoric, especially towards Christians.

(3) They emphasise the notion that there should be no separation between Islam and the state (*Islām dīn wa dawla*), and that all aspects of life should ideally be governed by Islamic principles. Within the Indonesian context, an exclusivist would like very much to see the *sharīʿa* (Islamic law), which is perceived as a set of rules, implemented in day to day life; thus, they are opposed to any government rules or regulations that are seen as contradicting the *sharīʿa*. Moreover, they are also critical towards any perceived attempts, especially from Christians, to prevent the implementation of the *sharīʿa* within the Indonesian law. Nevertheless, it is important to note that they vary in their arguments that Indonesia should become an Islamic state. Even among those who support the transformation of Indonesia to an Islamic state, they differ in their activism.

(4) They believe that there is a conspiracy between the Indonesian government and Christians to weaken Islamic political power. More globally, this alleged conspiracy is often perceived as part of the grand scenario of certain Western countries, especially the United States, to discredit Islam. Even though not all of the exclusivists tend to be suspicious of Christians, many of them claim to have abundant 'proof' of efforts to convert Muslims to Christianity in different areas of Indonesia.

Inclusivist Muslims

The term 'inclusivist' Muslims is used in this study to identify a group of Muslims who appear to have these characteristics in common:

(1) As they perceive Islam as an evolving religion they apply a contextual reading to the Qur'ān and *sunna*. This approach advocates reinterpreting the foundation texts of Islam. In this context, the role of *ijtihād* is central in their thinking.

(2) Unlike the pluralists, who tend to claim that all religions are the same, the inclusivists hold that Islam is the best religion for them. Nevertheless, they believe that salvation is also possible outside Islam, and therefore tend to be more tolerant of the faith of the 'other'. Within the inclusivists' writings, one will scarcely find harsh expressions directed towards other religious believers, more specifically Christians.

(3) They argue for the separation of Islam and the state. For them, the present structure of the Indonesian state is adequate. They acknowledge the validity of the Indonesian constitution, although it may seem secular to the exclusivist Muslims in that it does not clearly say that the state is responsible for religious matters in the society. The inclusivists hold that within the Indonesian state both Muslims and non-Muslims should enjoy the same rights. In addition, they do not support the effort to implement the *sharīʿa* in day to day life, as they do not perceive it as a set of rules but rather as moral guidance.

Christians

The writings and statements of the exclusivist and inclusivist Muslims generally refer to 'the Christians' as one group without differentiating between Catholics and Protestants. Therefore, in general, the term 'Christians' is used in this study to refer to both Catholics and Protestants, unless otherwise specified.

The Position of Muhammadiyah and Nahdhatul Ulama

One question that may arise from the above classification of the exclusivists and inclusivists is the position of Muhammadiyah and Nahdhatul Ulama within these categories. A brief description of both organisations is needed before their positions are discussed in this study.

The Indonesian mass organisation most associated with modernism is Muhammadiyah, which was founded in 1912 by Ahmad Dahlan (d.1923). It aimed at purifying Islamic practices from *bid'a* (innovation) and *khurafāt* (superstition) along the lines advocated by Muhammad Abduh of Egypt (d. 1905).[4] It was thought that by preventing Muslims from *bid'a* and by placing Islam as a fundamental reference for various problems, Muslims would be able to respond to demands of the modern world. Muhammadiyah gathers its members, estimated at around 25–30 million, mainly from urban commercial communities and the better educated. Among its programs are education and welfare activities.

One may argue that among the Muhammadiyah members there is a tendency of not being tolerant towards the Christians. This can be explained in several ways. First, it is true that Muhammadiyah and other modernist organisations emerged as a response to the intellectual and cultural impact of the West and therefore tried to take up certain issues that had become important in the West, such as democracy and human rights. Nevertheless, as part of its attempt to purify Islamic practices, Muhammadiyah is quite literal in interpreting the Islamic teachings, including on the issue of the religious 'other'. Second, in urban areas, Christians have built many social services, including education and health, which are believed by some Muslims (as

---

[4] Herbert Feith and Lance Castles, eds., *Indonesian Political Thinking 1945-1965* (Ithaca and London: Cornell University Press, 1970), 201.

will be discussed in Chapter Four) to be part of Christianisation efforts. Therefore, as people who live in urban areas, some Muhammadiyah members may feel the tensions between themselves and Christians, as they feel that they have to compete with the latter.

The Nahdhatul Ulama (NU) was established in 1926 by Wahab Chasbullah (d. 1971) with the support of Hasjim Asj'ari (d. 1947). The organisation was formed because its leaders realised that their interests of the Shafi'i school of law might be ignored with the growing number of Muhammadiyah followers.[5] They also wanted to defend their religious belief, which was blended with Javanese practices that they had held for centuries, against Muhammadiyah attack.[6] Members of this organisation, estimated at around 35 million, come from more traditionalist religious scholars (*°ulamā*) and teachers (*kyais*), and are mainly from Islamic schools in rural East and Central Java. Like Muhammadiyah, NU is concerned with education as well as economic development for the poor.

One may argue that the tendency among the Nahdhatul Ulama members is tolerant towards Christians.[7] This can be supported by examining NU's geographic background. In contrast to the urban areas, tensions between Muslims and Christians are not widely felt in rural areas. Social services provided by Christians in the rural areas are scarcely found in the villages where most NU members live, thereby reducing competitive ambitions and potential conflicts.

The tendencies of Muhammadiyah and Nahdhatul Ulama members towards Christians might lead one to conclude that, on the issue of

---

[5] Merle C. Ricklefs, *A History of Modern Indonesia since c. 1200*, 3rd ed. (Stanford, California: Stanford University Press, 2001), 223.

[6] Allan Samson, 'Islam in Indonesian Politics', *Asian Survey* 8, no. 12 (December 1968): 1011.

[7] This is not to neglect the fact that there were few exceptions. In 1967, for example, during the Inter-religious Consultation Forum (will be discussed in Chapter Four), Christians objected to K.H.M. Dachlan (The Minister of Religious Affair and also an NU)'s suggestion that each religious community must not attempt at converting another religious community. NU palpably stated that the forum was failed and accused non-Muslims (especially Christians) as not having enough religious tolerance. Quoted from *Duta Masyarakat*, 21 December 1967 by Andrée Feillard, *NU vis-à-vis Negara: Pencarian Isi, Bentuk dan Makna* (Yogyakarta: LKiS, 1999), 143.

Muslim–Christian relations, the former are exclusivists and the latter inclusivists. That is not always the case. Within Muhammadiyah and NU there are people with exclusivist and inclusivist tendencies, and within the exclusivist and inclusivist groups there may be people with Muhammadiyah and NU backgrounds. More importantly, one cannot speak about the perspectives of Muhammadiyah and NU without considering the period and leadership within which such perspectives arose. Different leaders of Muhammadiyah, for example, may have different perspectives on a certain issue.[8] It is also important to note that the figures of the exclusivists and inclusivists discussed in this study have little connections with the Muhammadiyah and NU. Therefore, positions or opinions on Muslim–Christian relations posited by Muhammadiyah or NU figures or people associated with these groups will be presented in the study but will not be dealt with separately.

Objective of the Study

The main focus of this study is the exclusivist and inclusivist Muslims' perspectives on Muslim–Christian relations in Indonesia's New Order (1967–1998). The discussion on relations here includes harmonious interaction, tension, misperception, or conflict involving Indonesian Muslims and Christians. Its chief objective is to identify how some exclusivist groups perceive Muslim–Christian relations and Christianity. It is important to emphasise that the study does not explore a specific conflict in Indonesia. However, as the relations between Muslims and Christians are to a significant extent coloured by disharmony and conflict, this issue will of necessity come to the fore and highlighted in the study. In addition, the study does not focus on general inter-faith issues or the Christians' perspectives on Muslim–Christian relations. This study will also question the assumption that disharmonious relations between certain Muslims and Christians, as

---

[8]For example, Syafii Ma'arif (the current leader of Muhammadiyah) refused the re-inclusion of the Jakarta Charter within the amendment of the 1945 Constitution, which could be interpreted as his concern for the fate of non-Muslims (including Christians) were Indonesia to be transformed into an Islamic State. See Chapter Five for discussion of this issue.

well as certain conflicts in various areas of Indonesia, are purely religious in nature. In doing so, the study will:

(1) discuss briefly some relevant classical legal and theological texts on Muslim–Christian relations in order to understand the debates in that era and to analyse the degree to which exclusivist and inclusivist Muslim perceptions were influenced by those texts analyse;

(2) investigate the social, economic, political and religious backgrounds during the New Order period within which the exclusivists' and inclusivists' perspectives on Muslim" Christian relations developed;

(3) explore the central concerns and perspectives of exclusivist and inclusivist Muslims regarding the issue of Muslim–Christian relations.

Organisation of the Study

To facilitate the investigation, the study will be divided into eight chapters. Chapter 2 examines briefly the issue of Muslim–Christian relations in the classical period of Islam as expressed in some theological and legal texts. It will also provide a survey of the development of the issue in the 20th century, focusing on the emergence of some inter-faith dialogue institutions.

Chapter 3 will first discuss Muslim–Christian relations under Dutch colonialism. The discussion will focus on some policies that were introduced by the Dutch and which influenced Muslim–Christian relations. The chapter will then briefly discuss the depiction of Christianity and Islam in early 20th century Indonesia. The last section of this chapter explores the issue under the Old Order period (1945–1965), focusing on government attitudes and policies.

Chapter 4 scrutinises the issues surrounding Muslim–Christian relations within the New Order period (1965–1998) to analyse how these issues shaped the relations between the two religious groups. Issues discussed here include SARA policy, the role of Muslims and Christians in the New Order bureaucracy, sources of Muslim animosity towards Christians, and state-sponsored efforts for inter-religious dialogues.

Chapter 5 examines the perspectives of the exclusivist Muslims on Muslim–Christian relations. There are four main exclusivist institutions discussed here: the Dewan Dakwah Islamiyah Indonesia (DDII), the Komite Indonesia untuk Solidaritas Dunia Islam (KISDI), the Front Pembela Islam (FPI), and the Laskar Jihad. These major groups are significant in the context of Muslim–Christian relations. A thematic approach will be applied to discussing key issues that have become the concerns of the group and how these issues have affected the exclusivist Muslims' relations with Christians. Issues discussed are the theological perspectives of the Christian 'other' on the part of exclusivist organisations, the relations between religion and the state, Christianisation, and the Ambon conflicts. The inclusion of figures such as Ja'far Thalib and Rizieq Shihab, who gained their reputations after the fall of Soeharto, within the exclusivist group is relevant because, as will be seen in this Chapter, the views of these figures on Muslim–Christian relations have to a significant extent been influenced by certain New Order Policies. In addition, the inclusion of the Ambon conflicts, firstly occurred in 1999, which were involving Muslims and Christians were to some extent influenced by New Order policies which makes this issue relevant in the discussion of Muslim–Christian relations and the New Order.

Chapter 6 explores inclusivist Muslims' perspectives on the religious 'other', with an emphasis on Christians. It will first discuss the birth of inclusive thought in Indonesia. It will also examine thematically issues related to Muslim–Christian relations that have become concerns of the inclusivist Muslims. The chapter will then explore the issue of Christianisation with an examination of the inclusivists' perspectives on the roots of disharmonious relations between Muslims and Christians. The last section of this chapter examines the roles of the inclusivists in the society by discussing some key institutions that support their perspectives.

Chapter 7 analyses how exclusivists and inclusivists perceive the issues and critiques put forward respectively on Muslim-Christian relations.

Chapter 8 provides a conclusion and some recommendations for further research.

Data Collection

The main resources for this study are documentary data, including books, articles and papers, written by exclusivist and inclusivist Muslims, as well as by Christians, related to the issue of Muslim-Christian relations in Indonesia. Materials published by the exclusivist and inclusivist organisations, such as books, papers, guidelines, reports, and official websites also constitute essential sources for the study. In addition, writings produced by other people on the issue of Muslim-Christian relations in Indonesia and in different parts of the world are also taken into account.

Another important source of the study is interviews. Ideas of exclusivists and inclusivists, which are not specifically articulated in their writings, were gathered from in-depth, open-ended interviews. Key figures of DDII, KISDI, FPI, and Laskar Jihad, such as Hussein Umar, Adian Husaini, and Rizieq Shihab, as well as prominent intellectuals characterised as the inclusivists, including Nurcholish Madjid, Azyumardi Azra and Zainun Kamal, were interviewed. The reason for choosing these organisations and individuals was based on their significant concerns in the context of Muslim-Christian relations. Furthermore, the study uses participant observation in which notes were taken from discussions, lectures or seminars held by exclusivist and inclusivist Muslims, to reveal perspectives on Muslim-Christian relations.[]

2

Muslim–Christian Relations in Classical Islam and in the 20ᵗʰ Century

Introduction

Although the debates on Muslim–Christian relations during the New Order period (1965-1998) and in contemporary Indonesia might lack the range which characterised those of classical times, they still to a significant extent reflect the image of Christians and Christianity which was prevalent in the classical period. For that reason, the portrayal of Christianity in some classical texts is examined in this chapter to provide a basis for analysing the degree to which exclusivist and inclusivist Muslim perceptions were influenced by certain classical Islamic texts (see Chapters Five and Six). In addition, the discourse on Muslim–Christian relations in the 20ᵗʰ century is also important to understanding the range of issues and any linkage between those issues and the concerns of exclusivist and inclusivist Muslims (see Chapters Five and Six).

This chapter provides an overview of some theological and legal perceptions and attitudes to Christians and Christianity in classical Islam and the discourse on Muslim–Christian relations in the 20ᵗʰ century.

Section one briefly examines the views of the Christian 'other' prevalent in some Islamic theological texts of the classical period. Two main points in this section are the Christian Scripture and the concept of the Trinity. Section two briefly examines the legal position of Christians within certain classical Islamic texts in regard to rights and obligations, and inter-religious marriage. Section three highlights the development of Muslim–Christian relations in the 20th century by discussing the emergence of some inter-faith dialogue institutions at the international level. This chapter will not discuss contemporary discourse or new interpretation of some classical concepts as it aims to trace possible roots of the issue of Muslim–Christian relations during the New Order period within the relevant classical Islamic texts. Chapters Five and Six will discuss how these classical texts are interpreted by the exclusivists and inclusivists in light of new circumstances in Indonesia.

Theological Perceptions of the Christian 'Other' in Classical Islam

The Qur'ān repeatedly confirms previous revelations, in particular the Torah and *Injīl* (Gospel). However, Muslims have found it difficult to accept the Old and New Testaments because several key issues that are mentioned in the Qur'ān contradict these Jewish and Christian Holy Books. Muslims' doubt towards the validity of the Jewish and Christian Scriptures is supported by several Qur'ānic verses that explicitly or implicitly accuse the *ahl al-kitāb* of concealing some parts of their Scriptures. To take one example, the Qur'ān 4:44 states:

> Among those of the Jewish faith there are some who distort (*yuḥarrifūna*) the meaning of the [revealed] words, taking them out of their context and saying, [as it were,] 'We have heard, but we disobey', and, 'Hear without hearkening', and, 'Hearken thou unto us, [O Muhammad]'—thus making a play with their tongues, and implying that the [true] Faith is false.

In discussing this, classical theological Islamic texts generally argued that both Scriptures were corrupted. Different theologians placed different emphases on the reason for this charge, but most centred on two main issues: the alleged alterations and changes in the Torah and *Injil*, and the concept of the Trinity. Two notable Muslim theologians of the classical period who wrote important treatises on the subject were Ibn Taymiyya (d. 1328) and Ibn Hazm (d. 1064).

Ibn Taymiyya wrote his *Al-Jawāb al-Ṣaḥīḥ li man Baddala Dīn al-Masīḥ* (The Correct Reply to Those Who Have Altered the Religion of Christ) in response to some books which contained arguments, among others, that Prophet Muhammad was not sent to the Christians but to those who were ignorant amongst the Arabs, that Christians were monotheists, and that the doctrine of the Trinity was consistent with reason and religious principles.[1] The Syrian and Egyptian milieu within which Ibn Taymiyya lived was characterised by religious pluralism. Muslims, Christians and Jews lived together and their relationship was often marked with enmity. It was within such a milieu that his work was written.[2]

Ibn Taymiyya maintained that the Torah and *Injil* had undergone some changes to their meanings (*taḥrīf*) and some alterations to their wordings (*tabdīl*) before the time of Prophet Muhammad. For Ibn Taymiyya, who was a Hanbalite with a strong tradition of ḥadīth,[3] the Torah and *Injil* had come down to their followers by non-valid transmission. He further stated that the *Injil* was not written by Isa (*lam yaktubuhu al-masīḥ ʿalaihi al-salām*); instead it was composed by his two disciples Matthew and John. For him, the claim that Mark and Luke also transmitted the *Injil* to the community was not valid as these two persons did not meet Prophet Isa (or Jesus in Christian understanding).[4]

---

[1] Taqī al-Dīn Abī al-ʿAbbās Aḥmad Ibn Taymiyya, *Al-Jawāb al-Ṣaḥīḥ li man Baddala Dīn al-Masīḥ*, ed. Majdī Qāsim, vol. 1 (Jeddah: Maktabat al-Balad al-Amīn, 1993), 21–22.

[2] Nancy R. Roberts, 'Reopening the Muslim–Christian Dialogue of the 13–14th Centuries: Critical Reflections on Ibn Taymiyyah's Response to Christianity in *Al-Jawāb al-Ṣaḥīḥ li man Baddala Dīn al-Masīḥ*', *Muslim World* 86, nos. 3–4 (July–October 1996): 343–345.

[3] This tradition was established by Ahmad bin Hanbal (780–855), and was one of the four Sunni legal schools (the others being the Hanafi, Maliki, and Shafii). It was renowned for its traditional approach to the Islamic foundation texts, especially the Qur'ān, and put a heavy emphasis on the ḥadīth. Against this background, Ibn Taymiyya classified the information he gathered on Torah and Injil based on the chain of transmission.

[4] Ibn Taymiyya, *Al-Jawāb al-Ṣaḥīḥ*, vol. 1, 387, 393.

In a similar line, Ibn Hazm (d. 1064) severely criticised the Gospels by demonstrating that there was no assurance that they were revealed text.[5] In his *Al-Fiṣal fi al-Milal wa-al-Ahwā' wa-al-Niḥal*, Ibn Hazm examined the Christian doctrine of the Trinity and different concepts of prophecy in Judaism and Christianity. He argued that the Torah and *Injīl* contained contradictions (*munāqaḍat*) and untruths (*akādhīb*) because some of their verses were in contradiction to Islamic belief as stated in the Qur'ān. Ibn Hazm then listed some forty examples of these contradictions in the Torah including the wrong account of the length of stay of *Banī Isrā'īl* in Egypt, the statements that Adam was a deity (*al-ilāh*), and that the Prophet Lot was accused of sleeping with his daughter.[6]

Ibn Hazm further argued that contradictions were also apparent within the *Injīl*. One example was the story of the genealogy of Isa, which was described in various versions. For Ibn Hazm, this showed that the *Injīl* had undergone some changes and alterations, as the claim that Isa had a father contradicted the Qur'ānic statement that Isa was a human being who was created by God within the womb of Maryam without having a father. In addition, Ibn Hazm maintained that the *Injīl* contradicted some historical facts. For example, it was mentioned that Yahya was a prophet as well as a king. For him, this contradicted the Qur'ānic statement that Yahya was only a prophet.[7] Another contradiction within the Gospels highlighted by Ibn Hazm was the different accounts of the call of Andrew and Simon given by John, and by Matthew, Mark and Luke. [8]

---

[5] Bernard Lewis et al., eds., *The Encyclopaedia of Islam*, new ed. (Leiden: E.J. Brill, 1971), s.v. 'Ibn Ḥazm', by R. Arnaldez.

[6] Abī Muḥammad ʿAlī ibn Aḥmad al-Maʿrūf Ibn Ḥazm, Al-Fiṣal fi al-Milal wa-al-Ahwā' wa-al-Niḥal, vol. 1 (Bayrut: Dār al-Kutub al-ʿIlmiyyah, 1996), 144-159.

[7] Ibn Hazm, *Al-Fiṣal*, vol. 1, 265.

[8] R. Arnaldez, *Grammaire et théologie chez Ibn Hazm de Cordoue* (Paris, 1956), 305-313, as quoted by Neal Robinson, *Christ in Islam and Christianity: The Representation of Jesus in the Qur'ān and the Classical Muslim Commentaries* (London: Macmillan, 1991), 46.

On the question of the Trinity, most classical Muslim theologians held the view that the doctrine was against Islamic teachings and that Isa was not the son of God. This doctrine was also used by theologians to show that Christianity was not a valid religion. Ibn Taymiyya was aware of the widely conflicting ideas among Christians on certain aspects of Christianity, such as the Incarnation. He, however, held the view that Christians agreed upon one point that 'Christ is God, and also the Son of God. [9] The doctrine of the Trinity was severely castigated by Ibn Taymiyya who argued that it was irreconcilable with sound reason. Ibn Taymiyya further stated that the word 'tathlīth' (Trinity) was an odd term. He maintained that none of the prophets used the word to mean 'Trinity' as understood by Christians. What Christians claimed to be the meaning of the term 'Trinity' was based on their own invention (mimmā ibtadaᶜūhu), not on any religious doctrine (sharᶜun) or sound reason (ᶜaqlun).[10] He further addressed Christians with the following questions:

> Why do you not leave Christ's words as they are rather than distorting them in this way [i.e., by taking them to mean that God is Three in One]...? Well spoke the virtuous one who said, 'If you were to ask a Christian, his son, and his grandson what they believe, each one would relate to you a doctrine which contradicted those of the others'... If you adhered to the straightforward meaning of this verse, you would not go astray...[11]

Expressing a similar idea, Ibn Hazm firmly stated that Isa was not God or son of God; instead, he was a human being who was born of a woman (wa innamā huwa insānun wulida min imra'atin min al-bashr). Unlike Ibn Taymiyya, however, Ibn Hazm held the view that not all Christians agreed on the concept of the Trinity. He stated that some

---

[9] Ibn Taymiyya, Tafsīr Sūrah al-Ikhlāṣ, quoted by Roberts, 'Reopening the Muslim-Christian Dialogue', 345.

[10] Ibn Taymiyya, Al-Jawāb al-Ṣaḥīḥ, vol. 2, 98.

[11] Ibn Taymiyya, Al-Jawāb al-Ṣaḥīḥ, vol. 3, 159 as quoted by Roberts, 'Reopening the Muslim-Christian Dialogue', 346.

Christians, who disagreed with the doctrine, supported the Islamic concepts of the Oneness of God, of prophecy, and of the revelation of Scripture. There were three groups of Christians, the al-Aryūsiyya, al-Maqdūniyya, and al-Būliqāniyya, who believed in Isa as only a prophet based on Isa's prayer: 'O, God, please send the Paraclete (al-Bāriqlīṭ) so that they [the Christians] will know that the son of a human being will only possibly be a human being'. However, they differed in their opinions on the matter of believing in some of God's prophets.[12]

The Religious 'Other' in Classical Islamic Law

The discussion below does not attempt to give a complete picture of the Christian 'other' in classical Islamic law. Rather, it aims at giving some examples of classical Islamic law texts in order to portray the common opinions on two important legal issues related to Christianity: namely the rights and obligations of *ahl al-dhimma* (non-Muslim protected minorities who lived under Islamic rule, including Christians), and marriage between a Muslim and an *ahl al-kitāb*.

Rights and Obligations of the Ahl al-Dhimma

Before discussing the rights and obligations of the *ahl al-dhimma*, it is important to note that the term or concept 'citizenship' only existed from the 18th century C.E. and is thus quite novel. Before that, within every community, there were categorisations based on different groupings. Within the Islamic state, the principal category used to define a community was religion. Therefore, there were Muslim and non-Muslim communities, who enjoyed different rights and obligations.

The position of non-Muslim protected minorities (*ahl al-dhimma* or *dhimmīs*) within the traditional Islamic law was clear in that the law had positioned Muslims above them in several key areas.[13] There were obligations and rights for the *dhimmīs* as outlined by the ʿulamāʾ.

---

[12] Ibn Hazm, *Al-Fisal*, vol. 1, 117, 133.

[13] Abdullah Saeed, 'Rethinking Citizenship Rights of Non-Muslims in an Islamic State: Rashīd al-Ghannūshī's Contribution to the Evolving Debate', *Islam and Christian-Muslim Relations* 10, no. 3 (1999): 307.

Al-Mawardi (d. 1058) listed six compulsory obligations for the *dhimmīs*: they must respect the Qur'ān; they must respect God's prophets; they must not talk about Islam in insulting language; they must not commit adultery or marry Muslim women; they must not preach their religions to Muslims or assault Islam; and they must not help enemies of Islam. These points were included in a protection agreement between Muslim rulers and the *dhimmīs*, who had to observe these requirements.[14]

In addition, Al-Mawardi noted six desirable conditions that were expected from the *dhimmīs*, even though these were not included in the protection agreement. The six points were: they should distinguish their appearance from Muslims by wearing different clothes; they should not build higher buildings than those of Muslims; they should not recite their Scripture or ring their church bells in such a tone that would be heard by Muslims; they should not display their drinking, crosses or pigs in front of Muslims; they should bury their dead discreetly; and they should not ride horses but could ride mules or donkeys.[15] These expected behaviours of the *dhimmīs* were also put forward by Ibn Qayyim al-Jawziyya (d. 1350), who stated that a distinctive sign (*ghiyar*) should be imposed on the *dhimmīs* so that Muslims would be able to detect them and therefore would refrain from addressing the *dhimmīs* as *brother* or *master*, from calling them as witnesses, or from giving them religious or legal books concerning Islam.[16]

Besides the obligations to the *dhimmīs* listed by Al-Mawardi, Ibn Taymiyya added that the closing down and destruction of *dhimmī* places of worship by Muslim rulers was not unjust. Ibn Taymiyya gave this answer to a question put to him when some churches and syna-

---

[14] ʿAlī ibn Muḥammad al-Māwardī, *Al-Aḥkām al-Sulṭāniyya wa al-Wilāyāt al-Dīniyya* (Cairo: Maṭbaʿah Musṭafā al-Bābī al-Halabī wa Aulādah, 1973), 145.

[15] Al-Mawardi, *Al-Aḥkām al-Sulṭāniyya*, 145.

[16] Bat Ye'or, *The Dhimmi: Jews and Christians under Islam* (Rutherford, N.J: Fairleigh Dickinson, 1985), 197.

gogues in Cairo were closed down at the beginning of the 14th century. He further argued that the Muslims of the four schools of law and some other *ᶜulamāʾ* had unanimously agreed that if Muslim rulers wished to destroy all churches and synagogues in the Muslim lands they could not be charged with injustice and people were obliged to obey their decision.[17]

However, the *dhimmīs* received only one right as compared to the obligations they had. Their right was to protection in terms of their life and property, which did not come free as the *dhimmīs* had to pay the protection tax called *jizya* (tribute) to the state. Al-Mawardi further underlined that among non-Muslims, only women, children, the insane and slaves were exempted from *jizya*. In addition to *jizya*, non-believers were also charged *kharaj* (land tax) on the conquered lands of the *dhimmīs* which were now owned by the community. However, there were three differences between *jizya* and *kharaj*: firstly, *jizya* was stipulated by the Qurʾān while *kharaj* was regulated by the ruler; secondly, the minimum amount of *jizya* was regulated by legal decree and the maximum was decided by the *ijtihād* of the *ᶜulamāʾ*, whereas the minimum and maximum amounts of *kharaj* were decided by the *ᶜulamāʾ*; thirdly, *jizya* was only applicable to the *dhimmīs* while land tax was taken even if they later converted to Islam.[18]

The obligation of the *dhimmīs* to pay *jizya* could be compared with Muslims' responsibility to pay *zakāt* (tax levied on Muslims). In the field of *zakāt*, the *fuqahāʾ* (Muslim jurists) were very firm in determining that *zakāt* was only obligatory for Muslims and that non-Muslims were obliged to pay *jizya*. It seems that the Muslim jurists were quite flexible in defining the term *ahl al-dhimma*. Sometimes it referred to the *ahl al-kitāb* and the Magians, and sometimes it included the *mushrik* (one who worships more than one God). Malik ibn Anas (d. 795) in his *al-Muwaṭṭaʾ*, for example, provided a reason why the

---

[17] Ye'or, *The Dhimmi*, 195.

[18] Al-Mawardi, *Al-Aḥkām al-Sulṭāniyya*, 144.

ahl al-dhimma and the Magians did not have to pay *zakāt*. He stated that this was because:

> *zakat* is imposed on the Muslims to purify them and to be given back to their poor, whereas *jizya* is imposed on the People of the Book to humble them. As long as they are in the country they have agreed to live in, they do not have to pay anything on their property except the *jizya*.[19]

However, if non-Muslims had to travel in and out of places under Muslim rule on business, they had to pay a tenth of what they invested in such business every time they did so. Malik further stated that Caliph Umar ibn Khattab imposed a *jizya* of four *dinars* for those who lived in a region where gold was the currency, and forty *dirhams* for those who lived in a region where silver was the currency. In addition, they had to receive Muslims as guests and provide them with accommodation for three days.[20]

Malik also reported that Prophet Muhammad 'took *jizya* from the Magians of Bahrain, that Umar ibn al-Khattab took it from the Magians of Persia and that Uthman ibn Affan took it from the Berbers'.[21] Malik further reported that he had heard the same ḥadīth, which was related from ᶜAbd al-Rahman ibn ᶜAwf quoted above. Thus it is clear that Malik held the view that the Magians were obliged to pay the *jizya*. As stated, *jizya* was only paid by non-Muslims, and Malik further specified that among non-Muslims there was no *jizya* due from women or children of People of the Book, and that *jizya* was only taken from men who had reached puberty.[22]

Abū al-Walīd Muḥammad Ibn Rushd (d. 1198) stated that the *fuqahā'* agreed that *zakāt* was obligatory upon every Muslim who was free, had reached puberty (*bāligh*), was sane, and who owned

---

[19] Malik ibn Anas, *Al-Muwatta: The First Formulation of Islamic Law*, trans. Aisha Abdurrahman Bewley (London and New York: Kegan Paul International, 1989), 108.

[20] Malik ibn Anas, *Al-Muwatta*, 108.

[21] Malik ibn Anas, *Al-Muwatta*, 107.

[22] Malik ibn Anas, *Al-Muwatta*, 108.

wealth that had reached a prescribed scale (*niṣāb*). Nevertheless, the Muslim jurists disagreed about the *zakāt* of orphans, the insane, slaves, the *ahl al-dhimma*, and anyone with deficient ownership, such as a person who was in debt.[23] Ibn Rushd further maintained that most of the *fuqahā'* agreed that there was no *zakāt* on all categories of the *ahl al-dhimma*, 'except what is related by a group about the imposition of *zakāt* for the Arab Christians of Banū Taghlab'. Ibn Rushd explained that he meant, for example, that 'an amount should be taken from them equal to what is taken from the Muslims on all things'. He emphasised that among those who supported this view were al-Shafii, Abu Hanifa, Ahmad, and al-Thawri.[24] Ibn Rushd then explored different opinions regarding the annual amount due for *jizya*. He quoted al-Shafii, who said that the minimum amount was fixed at one *dinar* but the maximum was not fixed and depended on negotiation. Ibn Rushd also stated that a group of Muslim jurists said that there was no determination on the amount and this was left to the *ijtihād* of the *ʿulamā'*.[25]

It is quite difficult to relate the issue of *zakāt* as discussed within the classical Islamic texts quoted above to the contemporary situation between Indonesian Muslims and Christians, as the circumstances are different. However, it would be interesting and important to analyse the treatment of the *ahl al-kitāb* and the *ahl al-dhimma* within classical texts in relation to the way Indonesian Muslims treat their fellow Christians (see Chapters Five and Six of the thesis).

---

[23] Abu al-Walīd Muḥammad Ibn Rushd, *The Distinguished Jurist's Primer: A Translation of Bidāyat al-Mujtahid*, trans. Imran A.K. Nyazee, vol. 1 (Reading, UK: Centre for Muslim Contribution to Civilization, 1994), 283.

[24] Ibn Rushd, *The Distinguished Jurist's Primer*, vol. 1, 284.

[25] Ibn Rushd, *The Distinguished Jurist's Primer*, vol. 1, 484. A.S. Tritton mentioned that according to Abu Hanifa, the *jizya* was fixed at 12, 24, and 48 dirhams; whereas Ahmad ibn Hanbal said that it was not fixed but depended on the ruler. A.S. Tritton, *The Caliphs and Their Non-Muslim Subjects: A Critical Study of the Covenant of ʿUmar*, 2nd ed. (London: Frank Cass and Co., 1970), 216.

Marriage between a Muslim and an Ahl al-Kitāb

Generally speaking, classical Islamic legal texts did not explore the question whether a Muslim man could marry an *ahl al-kitāb* woman, because based on their readings of the Qur'ānic texts and the practice of Prophet Muhammad the *ʿulamāʾ* believed that such a practice was permissible (*halāl*). What dominated the discussion on marriage in the classical legal writings was, for instance, the question whether a free *ahl al-kitāb* and a slave *ahl al-kitāb* woman had the same rights to marry a Muslim man. Similarly, the issue of the status of Muslim women's marriage in time of war and that of temporary marriage dominated the discussion on marriage within *fiqh* (science of the *sharīʿa*) texts.

Imam Malik in his *al-Muwaṭṭaʾ*, for example, stated 'It is not *halal* to marry a Christian or Jewish slave-girl' based on the Qur'ān 5:5: 'And [lawful to you are], in wedlock, women from among those who believe [in this divine writ], and in wedlock, women from among those who have been vouchsafed revelation before your time'. Malik further said, 'In our opinion, Allah made marriage to believing slave-girls *halal*, and He did not make *halal* marriage to Christian and Jewish slave-girls from the People of the Book'.[26]

In discussing the issue of marriage, Ibn Rushd in his *Bidāyat al-Mujtahid* briefly stated that the majority of the *fuqahāʾ* agreed that a Muslim man might marry a free *ahl al-kitāb* woman.[27] He then went into detail in examining different opinions regarding marriage between a Muslim man and a slave *ahl al-kitāb* woman. Some *fuqahāʾ* stated that such a marriage was permissible and some said it was not. Ibn Rushd also discussed the status of marriage in time of war by posing the question whether imprisonment of a married enslaved *ahl al-kitāb* woman during war negated her marriage. He posited Abu Hanifa's opinion that if the couple were imprisoned together their marriage

---

[26] Mālik ibn Anas, *Al-Muwatta*, 216.

[27] Ibn Rushd, *The Distinguished Jurist's Primer*, trans. Imran A.K. Nyazee, vol. 2 (Reading, UK: Centre for Muslim Contribution to Civilization, 1996), 51.

was not annulled, but that if they were imprisoned separately their marriage was annulled.[28]

As mentioned, an exploration of the notion of marriage between a Muslim man and an *ahl al-kitāb* woman was lacking within the body of classical Islamic legal texts, as the *fuqahā'* did not consider it a controversial issue. Furthermore, the issue of marriage between a Muslim woman and an *ahl al-kitāb* man seemed to be lacking in the classical Islamic legal texts. This void could possibly be explained by referring to the Qur'ān 5:5 quoted above, which seemed to be interpreted as only granting permission for a Muslim man to marry an *ahl al-kitāb* woman. Therefore, the *fuqahā'* seemed to think that the opposite circumstance, namely marriage between a Muslim woman and an *ahl al-kitāb* man, was unthinkable at this period.

As will become more obvious in the following chapters, the issue of inter-religious marriage in present day Indonesia has gone beyond the classical legal texts quoted above, because marriage between a Muslim woman and an *ahl al-kitāb* man is now debated. However, it is important to explore possible links between marriage as it appeared in the body of classical *fiqh* and marriage between Muslims and non-Muslims, especially the *ahl al-kitāb*, in contemporary Indonesia. This issue will be explored in Chapters Five and Six.

Greeting Jews and Christians

The greeting *assalāmu ᶜalaykum* (May God bless your happiness and prosperity) in Islam was different from a mere greeting as it had religious connotation. Therefore, the issue of greetings was discussed within some Islamic law texts and concerned Muslim jurists, as it was important to decide whether Muslims were permitted or not permitted (*harām*) to greet non-Muslims, especially the Jews and Christians.

---

[28] Ibn Rushd, *The Distinguished Jurist's Primer*, vol. 2, 51-52.

Al-Ṣanʿānī quoted a ḥadīth from Abū Hurayra stating 'lā tabda'ū al-yahūda wa al-naṣārā bi al-salām' (Do not be first in greeting the Jews and the Christians). The ḥadīth continued that if a Muslim met a Jew or Christian on the street, the Muslim should obstruct their way. Al-Ṣanʿānī, however, also reported that Ibn Abbas stated that it was permissible for Muslims to greet Jews and Christians, and that was also the opinion of some Shafiite ʿulamā'. They based their argument on the Qur'ānic verse: 'wa qūlū li al-nāsi ḥusnan' (and you shall speak unto all people in a kindly way), and other ḥadīths that permitted such a greeting.[29] Nevertheless, al-Ṣanʿānī also stated that some ʿulamā' argued that the permissibility of greeting Jews and Christians was only valid provided they were walking together with Muslims. If, however, they were not walking with Muslims, Jews and Christians were not allowed to be greeted. Al-Ṣanʿānī also narrated that another ḥadīth stated that if Muslims were greeted first by the ahl al-kitāb they could respond with the expression wa ʿalaykum (and upon you too) and not wa ʿalaykum salām (may happiness and prosperity be blessed upon you too). However, Muslims could not initiate the greeting towards Jews and Christians.[30]

In a similar line, Ibn Taymiyya stated that if a Jew or Christian greeted a Muslim, the latter should reply 'and upon you' without mentioning the word 'peace'. This would countervail any intended curse that Jews and Christian might possess in their minds when they greeted Muslims.[31] In addition, Imam Malik reported a ḥadīth that the Prophet said 'innal yahūda idhā sallamū ʿalaykum yaqūlu ahaduhum as-sāmu ʿalaykum faqūlū wa ʿalayk' (When a Jew greets you and says, 'Poison to you', say, 'And to you').[32]

The issue of greeting non-Muslims, which at first glance seem irrelevant for the contemporary circumstances, is in fact quite signifi-

---

[29] Al-Ṣanʿānī, Subul al-Salām: Sharh Bulūgh al-Marām min Jamīʿ Adillat al-Aḥkām, vol. 4 (Beirūt: Dār al-Jīl, 1982), 1377.

[30] Al-Ṣanʿānī, Subul al-Salām, vol. 4, 1378.

[31] Ye'or, The Dhimmi, 197.

[32] Malik ibn Anas, Al-Muwatta, 404.

cant as this also becomes the concern of Indonesian exclusivist Muslims. Therefore, the above discussion on the issue of greeting non-Muslims is also scrutinised in explaining the relations between Muslims and Christians in Indonesia (see Chapter Five).

Interfaith Dialogue in the 20th Century: A Survey of the International Discourse

Muslim–Christian relations in the 20th century changed dramatically as compared to those of the classical period. Some issues that were of significance during those classical times are no longer relevant because citizens are no longer categorised based on religion. Within Islam and Christianity, issues concerning relationships between people of different faiths are seriously discussed and some religious-oriented organisations have been established as a result.

Within Catholic communities, attempts at interfaith dialogue can be traced back to the appointment of Angelo Giuseppe Cardinal Roncalli (Pope John XXIII) in 1958. Pope John astounded Catholics when, some three months after his accession to the papal throne, he called for a general council of the Roman Catholic Church to be held in 1962. In his formal convocation of the Council, Pope John expressed his firm belief in the need of the Catholic Church to engage in dialogue with other Christian churches as well as other traditions and ideologies outside Christianity. He led the first session of the council in 1962, which determined the directions of the interfaith dialogue project. When Pope John died in 1963, the project was continued by Cardinal Montini (Paul VI). It was during his papacy that the council produced an excellent collection of documents on interfaith dialogue.[33]

The five important texts produced were: *Lumen Gentium* (Lights of the Nations), *Nostra Aetate* (In Our Times), *Dei Verbum* (On Divine Revelation), *Gaudium et Spes* (Joy and Hope), *Ad Gentes Divinitus* (the Universal Sacrament of Salvation) and *Dignitatis Humanae* (Dig-

---

[33] Gregory A. Schissel, 'The Quest for Common Ground: The Roman Catholic Church and Islam after the Second Vatican Council', (Ph.D. diss., Harvard University, 1998), 59–62.

nity of the Human Person). Part of these texts said of Islam: 'The plan of salvation also includes those who acknowledge the Creator. In the first place among these are the Mohamedans, who, professing to hold the faith of Abraham, along with us adore the one and merciful God, who on the last day will judge mankind.'[34] Furthermore, one part of *Nostra Aetate* reads:

> The Church regards with esteem also the Moslems. They adore the one God, living and subsisting in Himself; merciful and all-powerful, the Creator of heaven and earth, who has spoken to men; they take pains to submit wholeheartedly to even His inscrutable decrees, just as Abraham, with whom the faith of Islam takes pleasure in linking itself, submitted to God. Though they do not acknowledge Jesus as God, they revere Him as a prophet. They also honor Mary, His virgin Mother; at times they even call on her with devotion. In addition, they await the day of judgment when God will render their deserts to all those who have been raised up from the dead. Finally, they value the moral life and worship God especially through prayer, almsgiving and fasting.[35]

Some people, however, were critical of the fact that 'none of these texts contains highly developed concepts of inter-religious dialogue', nor 'refers explicitly to Islam.'[36] Others argued that even though the texts indicated a change of attitude of Roman Catholicism towards Islam, they failed to discuss the issue of the status of Muhammad *vis-à-vis*

---

[34] Paul VI, Lumen Gentium, chapter 2, no.16 [online]; available from http://www. vatican.va/archive/hist_councils/ii_vatican_council/documents/vat-ii_const_19641121_ lumen-gentium_en.html; accessed 29 March 2003.

[35] Paul VI, Nostra Aetate, no. 3 [online], available from http://www. vatican.va/archive/hist_councils/ii_vatican_council/documents/vat-ii_decl_19651028_nostra-aetate_en.html; accessed 29 March 2003.

[36] See, among others, Ataullah Siddiqui, *Christian-Muslim Dialogue in the Twentieth Century* (London: Macmillan Press Ltd, 1997), 34.

Christians,[37] and to suggest that 'Islam in and of itself is a proper and valid way to God'.[38] Apart from the acknowledgment and criticism of the texts of the Second Vatican Council, the tension between 'mission' and 'dialogue' remained unresolved. In order to clarify this dispute, the document, *The Attitude of the Church towards the Followers of Other Religions: Reflections on Dialogue and Mission in 1984* was issued by the Church's dialogue office. Two other important documents, '*Dialogue and Proclamation*' and '*Redemptoris Missio 1991*' were published with the same purpose.

When Pope John Paul II acceded to the papal throne in 1978, efforts for interfaith dialogue continued. The Pope's concern with dialogue, especially between Muslims and Christians, could be discerned from his various addresses to Muslims on different occasions or to bishops residing in Muslim countries. An example of this was his remarks to a group of bishops from North Africa:

> It is, in effect, *one of the essential characteristics of the life of the Church in the Maghreb that it is invited to enter into a constructive dialogue between Christianity and Islam.* I hold it very important to encourage you to proceed upon this difficult road which, if conflicts may be many, hope is always stronger. In order to maintain it, Christian conviction must be very temperate.[39]

This positive attitude towards Islam, however, came under question when *Crossing the Threshold of Hope* was published in 1994. On the issue of Muslims' rejection of Jesus' divinity, for example, Pope John II argued that in Islam God had appeared as a distant deity, 'ultimately a God outside of the world, a God who is only Majesty, never

---

[37] See for example G. Anawati, 'Christian-Islamic Dialogue', in *The Vatican, Islam, and the Middle East*, ed. Kail C. Ellis (Syracuse: Syracuse University Press, 1987), 51-68. See also Siddiquis' critique on the Council's reluctance to accept the Qur'ānic revelation and the prophecy of Muhammad, in Siddiqui, *Christian-Muslim Dialogue*, 37-39.

[38] See, Schissel, 'The Quest for Common Ground', 72.

[39] Quoted in Schissel, 'The Quest for Common Ground', 114. Italics are original.

Emmanuel, God-with-us'.[40] He further compared Christianity and Islam, arguing that the latter was theologically and anthropologically 'very distant from Christianity'.[41] It appeared that the Pope, as a person, had an ambivalent attitude towards Islam.

Another important institution for dialogue was the Pontifical Council for Inter-religious Dialogue (PCID).[42] Due to the increasing need of the Vatican to discuss the relationship of the Catholic Church with other religions, a Vatican Secretariat for Non-Christian Religions was established on 19 May 1964. Since March 1989, this institution has been known as the PCID. The question whether salvation was possible outside Christianity remained an important point behind the establishment of this institute. After a period of ambiguity concerning the direction of its work, especially when faced with the issue of the purpose of dialogue, the PCID focused its efforts on Muslims through a special commission for Islam, and through a publication, *Guidelines for a Dialogue between Muslims and Christians,*[43] which aimed to provide a basic instrument for dialogue between religious believers.

The Anglican Communion started to include the discussion on interfaith dialogue in the 1968 Archive for Resolutions from Lambeth Conferences of Anglican Bishops. This once-a-decade worldwide conference was a gathering of bishops under the presidency of the Archbishop of Canterbury in London.[44] While in the previous years the resolutions from the conferences paid more attention to internal issues within the Anglican churches, for example deepening the quality of Bible study or seeking to live by the teaching and example of

---

[40] John Paul II, *Crossing the Threshold of Hope*, trans. Jenny and Martha McPhee (New York: Alfred A. Knopf Publisher,1994), 91.

[41] John Paul II, *Crossing the Threshold of Hope*, 93.

[42] For a complete discussion of the institute see Schissel, 'The Quest for Common Ground', 138-196.

[43] Secretariatus Pro Non-Christianis, *Guidelines for a Dialogue between Muslims and Christians* (Rome: Secretariat for Non-Christians, 1969).

[44] There have been thirteen conferences to date. The first conference was held in 1867, and the most recent was in 1998. The data below on the Anglican Communion was from its website (http://www.anglicancommunion.org); accessed 15 July 2003.

Jesus Christ, the 1968 Conference issued two resolutions on religious dialogue. Resolution 11 urged Christian churches to undertake positive relationships with different religious believers in the fields of economic, social, and moral action. In addition, Resolution 12 recommended 'a renewed and vigorous implementation of the task of inter-religious dialogue' and urged Anglican Churches to support it 'both in the seconding of personnel and in the provision of money.'

The 1978 Lambeth Conference decided upon Resolution 37 which, among others, recommended an open exchange of thought and experience with people of other faiths. The Anglican Churches were aware that they were involved in some activities, including evangelisation, in areas where Hinduism, Buddhism, Taoism, Confucianism and Islam were dominant. For that reason, the Conference urged the whole Anglican Communion to support people of different faiths by understanding, prayer, and where appropriate, by partnership with them. The next conference, held in 1988, produced more substantial recommendations on interfaith dialogue, especially between Christians, Muslims and Jews. Resolution 20 recommended that dialogues with people of different faiths should be held with an understanding that exchange of ideas depended upon mutual understanding, mutual respect and mutual trust. Moreover, the resolution urged the Churches of the Anglican Communion to contribute towards helping other religious believers to make 'common cause in resolving issues of peacemaking, social justice and religious liberty'. Resolution 21 of the same conference recommended the Churches to engage in dialogue with Jews and Muslims on the basis of understanding. In addition, it urged the Anglican Consultative Council to set up an interfaith committee, which would work in close co-operation with the Inter-Faith Dialogue Committee of the World Council of Churches.[45]

---

[45] Within the Christian communities, efforts to undertake dialogues between people of different faiths could be found as early as the formation of The World Council of Churches (WCC) on 23 August 1948. In line with the changing social and political climate following World Wars I and II, some new emerging countries had sought their identities independently of Western authority. Christian thinkers, therefore, were forced to relate to people of different faiths and traditions. This was the point when the WCC exercised its role.

Following these resolutions of 1988, the Network for Interfaith Concerns (NIFCON) of the Anglican Communion was established in 1993 and was one of several networks working with Anglican structures. NIFCON, through networking, meeting, and publication, encouraged open and loving relationships between Christians and people of other faiths; exchange of news, information, ideas and resources relating to inter faith concerns between provinces of the Anglican Communion; sensitive witness and evangelism where appropriate; prayerful and urgent action with all involved in tension and conflict; and local contextual and wider theological reflection. NIFCON also had an important task, which was charged by the 1998 Lambeth Conference, to study and evaluate Muslim-Christian relations and report regularly to the Anglican Consultative Council.

On the Islamic side, the *Mu'tamar al-ᶜĀlam al-Islāmī* (World Muslim Congress) was established in Mecca, Saudi Arabia, in 1926.[46] Even though the aims of this institution were focused more on political and social issues and not directly related to Muslim-Christian dialogue, in 1969, its secretary general, Inamullah Khan, addressed the area of religious dialogue, especially with Christianity. In 1982, against the background of the occupation of Afghanistan by the Soviet Union, the institution took part in a dialogue with the World Council of Churches. Dialogue with other religions is now part of *Mu'tamar's* programs.

Another Islamic institution concerned with dialogue is *Rābiṭat al-ᶜĀlam al-Islāmī* (Muslim World League), established in 1962. It aims to explain Islam to different religious believers so that misconceptions about Islam can be minimised. In responding particularly to the Second Vatican Council's statement on other religions (*Nostra Aetate*), *Rābiṭat* was very optimistic. *Jamᶜiyya al-Daᶜwa al-Islāmiyya al-ᶜĀlamiyyah* (the World Islamic Call Society) is another important organisation that has addressed the issue of Muslim-Christian relations. Launched in

---

[46] The information on these Islamic institutions was taken from Siddiqui, *Christian-Muslim Dialogue*, 173-189. He conducted extensive interviews of key people of these organisations so that he could gather information that was not available in print.

Libya in 1982, this organisation, under its previous name, Association of the Islamic Convocation, established contact with Christian institutions such as the Vatican and Pontifical Council for Inter-Religious Dialogue. The two main aims of this dialogue were to overcome atheism and Zionism, and to present Islam in a better way.

By the end of the 20th century and the early 21st century, Muslim–Christian dialogue and interfaith dialogue had been extended to cover broader subjects. Two examples are quoted here. Firstly, the World Conference on Religion and Peace (WCRP) was established in 1970 in Kyoto, Japan. More than 1,000 religious leaders from different countries gathered and addressed the need for people of different faiths to take action towards achieving peace. The WCRP's concerns included conflict transformation, children's rights, security issues, human rights, and peace education, which were translated into various programs.[47] Secondly, in 1998, a project jointly sponsored by the World Bank and leaders of the world religions, called World Faiths Development Dialogue (WFDD), was launched. The main interest of this project, which was chaired by Rev. Michael Taylor, was to promote the participation of religious communities in poverty and development. Its programs included workshops on faith and development and a seminar series on alternatives to global capitalism.[48]

Concluding Remarks

Some classical theological texts pictured Christianity as a corrupted religion because it was believed to have undergone some substantial changes and alterations. In addition, the concept of the Trinity (*tathlīth*) was seen as contradicting the doctrine of *tawḥīd*. Similarly, within certain classical legal texts, Christians were not seen as equal to Mus-

---

[47] Information on this organisation is available from http://www.wcrp.org/; accessed 15 July 2003.

[48] Information on this organisation is available from http://www.wfdd.org.uk/; accessed 15 July 2003. See also, Michael H. Taylor, 'The Role of Religion in Society', in *Christians and Muslims in the Commonwealth*, eds. Anthony O'Mahony and Ataullah Siddiqui (London: Altajir World of Islam Trust, 2001), 51.

lims and as a consequence did not enjoy equal rights with their fellow Muslims. Christians, as well as other *dhimmīs*, had many obligations to fulfil but had one principle right: to be protected in their life and property. However, with the 20th and 21st centuries, the discourse on Muslim–Christian relations changed significantly. Different organisations, religious-and non-religious-based, offered more cooperative work involving people of different faiths. Their main concern was to promote fairness, equality, and respect for life; the values that were deeply rooted within every belief system. It is important to analyse (see Chapters Five and Six) how this discourse on Muslim–Christian relations in classical Islam and in the contemporary period might have influenced exclusivist and inclusivist Muslims' perspectives on Muslim–Christian relations in Indonesia.[]

3

An Overview of Muslim–Christian Relations in Indonesia until 1965

Introduction

Muslim-Christian relations in contemporary Indonesia have been through a long historical process. Therefore, to discuss this issue, one must trace back, at least, to the Dutch colonial period (1596–1942), when policies were implemented that affected community relations. Furthermore, it is important to discuss the depictions of Christianity and Islam during the early 20th century to better understand the types of discourse on Muslim-Christian relations that existed during that period. More importantly, we cannot discuss relations between Muslims and Christians in the New Order period without taking into consideration the developments in the years following Indonesian independence in 1945.

The aim of the present chapter is to provide a historical background to the issue of Muslim-Christian relations in Indonesia. This will be done in three sections. The first section explores Muslim-Christian relations during the colonial period. It highlights Dutch policies on Muslims and Christians at different periods of colonialism. The second section briefly discusses the depiction of Christianity and Islam during early 20th century Indonesia. The third section deals with Muslim–Christian relations under the Old Order and is centred on four main issues: the debates on the Jakarta Charter; the regional rebellions; Christianisation and Muslim writings on Christianity; and Sukarno's policies in the area of Muslim–Christian relations.

Dutch Colonial Policy on Muslims and Christians

It is not the intention here to discuss extensively Dutch colonialism and its relations with Islam in Indonesia as much has already been written in the area.[1] Rather, this section highlights Dutch policies towards Muslims and Christians at different periods of colonialism, leading to a later analysis of the connection between these policies and Muslim–Christian relations in the New Order period. To this end, the study utilises Karel Steenbrink's account of Dutch colonial policy towards Indonesian Muslims, which provides substantial details on the issue.[2]

Focusing on Dutch perceptions of Indonesian Islam, Karel Steenbrink discerned four major attitudes during the long period 1596-1940. Although the policies which emerged from Dutch perceptions were explicitly directed towards the Muslims, they were to a significant extent related to Indonesian Christians, and were therefore relevant to the question of Muslim–Christian relations. One attitude depicted the Muslims as 'respected heretics'.[3] This attitude developed mainly amongst the Dutch traders who came to the Dutch East Indies (now called

---

[1] See, for example, Karel Steenbrink, *Dutch Colonialism and Indonesian Islam: Contacts and Conflicts 1596-1950*, trans. J. Steenbrink and H. Jansen (Amsterdam: Rodopy, 1993); Harry J. Benda, 'Indonesian Islam and the Foundations of Dutch Islamic Policy', in his *The Crescent and the Rising Sun: Indonesian Islam under the Japanese Occupation 1942-1945* (The Hague and Bandung: W. van Hoeve, 1958), 9-31; Aqib Suminto, *Politik Islam Hindia Belanda* (Jakarta: LP3ES, 1985); Hamid Algadri, *Dutch Policy against Islam and Indonesians of Arab Descent in Indonesia* (Jakarta: LP3ES, 1994); and Alwi Shihab, 'Kebijakan Pemerintah Belanda terhadap Islam', in his *Membendung Arus: Respon Gerakan Muhammadiyah terhadap Penetrasi Misi Kristen di Indonesia* (Bandung: Mizan, 1998), 61-91.

[2] Steenbrink, *Dutch Colonialism and Indonesian Islam*.

[3] Steenbrink, *Dutch Colonialism and Indonesian Islam*, 25.

Indonesia) in the 16th century and was based on their personal observations as well as preconceived opinions brought from their home country regarding Islam and Muslims. The preconceived opinion of Islam as heresy was rooted, according to Olaf Schumann, in the Christian doctrine on salvation 'extra ecclesia nulla salus' (there is no salvation outside the church).[4] Within this pattern, the Dutch held to a fusion of contradictory attitudes: respect for the Muslims' steadfastness in their faith; and denunciation of Islamic teachings such as the practice of circumcision and the prohibition against eating pork. However, the early colonisers portrayed the Muslims with less prejudice compared with their successors.[5]

The second attitude, held mainly by Dutch travellers and missionaries from 1600–1800, considered the Muslims as 'detestable heretics'. This attitude portrayed Islam as a superstitious and heretical religion and was rooted in the 17th century theology of the Netherlands.[6] Chief amongst scholars who held this opinion was Gisbertus Voetius (d. 1676), who defined Islam as 'complete denial of the true God and the covenant of the gospel, a denial of the theological doctrine of redemption and the doctrine of morality'.[7]

The third trend was a development of the second attitude by the colonial government in Indonesia: Islam was regarded as a 'natural hostility' and Muslims as 'untrustworthy and fanatics'. According to Steenbrink, it was Jan Pieterszoon Coen (d. 1629) who excluded Muslims from various alliances with the Dutch.[8] Although religion seemed to be the justification for Coen and others like him to behave

---

[4] Olaf Schumann, 'Christian–Muslim Encounter in Indonesia', in *Christian–Muslim Encounters*, eds. Yvonne Yazbeck Haddad and Wadi Z. Haddad (Gainesville: University of Florida, 1988), 285-287.

[5] Steenbrink, *Dutch Colonialism and Indonesian Islam*, 26-27.

[6] According to Steenbrink this pattern combined 'crusader ideals with [Martin] Luther's politically biased rejection of Islam in connection with the expansion of the Ottoman Empire'. See his *Dutch Colonialism and Indonesian Islam*, 24.

[7] Steenbrink, *Dutch Colonialism and Indonesian Islam*, 50.

[8] Steenbrink, *Dutch Colonialism and Indonesian Islam*, 60-61.

inconsiderately to Muslims, he did not support plans to Christianise the Muslims, as he realised that such attempts might provoke protest. For Coen and like-minded people, Islam was perceived as a threat to the existence of the Dutch in Indonesia.[9] In 1651 the Dutch government in Batavia (now called Jakarta) banned any 'public or secret meetings for practising their evil and Mahometan religion...'. One of the main reasons for such a ban was the Dutch's fear that the native (Indonesian) Christians, converted from Islam, would revert to what the Dutch termed 'the Moorish religion'[10] once they learnt more about Islam.

The fourth attitude viewed Muslims as 'members of a backward religion'. This attitude developed during the period 1850–1940 when the Dutch had pursued their prime concern of acquiring territory rather than simply pursuing commercial interests, and when Dutch power had been firmly established in Indonesia.[11] The Dutch no longer perceived Islam as 'a powerful heretical religion in competition with Christianity' but as a 'weak and backward' religion. Despite the fact that Islam was viewed as a backward religion, it was perceived nonetheless as a threat.[12] To fight this threat, the Dutch realised that Islam should not be confronted directly but its development should be curtailed. At this stage, the colonial powers wanted to act as 'tutors' for the Muslims by applying a modern method of education in order to limit the spread of Islamic teachings through traditional religious schools. Through this system of education, Dutch

---

[9] Some other scholars hold the same opinion that it was the political motives to maintain the colonial power in Indonesia that determined such an attitude to the Muslims. See, for instance, Stephen Neill, *History of Christian Missions* (Harmondsworth, Middlesex: Penguin, 1964), 224. Cf. Steenbrink, *Dutch Colonialism and Indonesian Islam*, 63–64.

[10] Steenbrink, *Dutch Colonialism and Indonesian Islam*, 70.

[11] Islam also changed dramatically in this period. It became more aggressive and more anti-colonial. Therefore, Islam was more of a threat to the Dutch, even sometimes resistant and rebellious; see Ricklefs, *A History of Modern Indonesia*, 169–170.

[12] Steenbrink, *Dutch Colonialism and Indonesian Islam*, 76.

missionary activities were also carried out.[13] One of the most important figures in implementing this policy was Snouck Hurgronje (d. 1936).

Being an expert on Indonesian Islam, Snouck Hurgronje was appointed as the Dutch adviser for native affairs (*Adviseur voor Inlandsche Zaken*) and came to Indonesia in 1889. He argued that Indonesian Muslims were different from their co-religionists in the Middle East in terms of their Islamic fanaticism. To him, many Indonesian Muslims, especially in Java, were nominal Muslims only. However, he believed that they should not be underestimated as a religious and political force, since Muslims considered Islam to be a bond that united them against the 'other'. Together with the idea, prevalent among Muslims, that the Dutch wanted to Christianise Indonesia, this bond had the potential to arouse the fighting spirit of the followers of Islam.[14] In this context, Snouck Hurgronje suggested that the Dutch educate and train Indonesian Muslims without alluding to Christianisation. He also emphasised that the colonial government should maintain a policy of religious neutrality and suppress any political ambitions on the part of Muslims.[15]

Even before Snouck Hurgronje was appointed an adviser, this security issue had actually prevented the colonial government from favouring Christian proselytising efforts. Certain strongly Muslim areas, such as Aceh in North Sumatra, were prohibited areas for Christian missionaries. In addition, the colonial administration had set a difficult precondition for these missionaries to enter other areas

---

[13] Steenbrink, *Dutch Colonialism and Indonesian Islam*, 76-77.

[14] Snouck Hurgronje, *Nederland en de Islam* (Leiden: Brill, 1911), 59, as quoted by Steenbrink, *Dutch Colonialism and Indonesian Islam*, 87-88.

[15] H.J. Benda, 'Christian Snouck Hurgronje and the Foundations of Dutch Islamic Policy in Indonesia', in *Continuity and Change in Southeast Asia: Collected Journal Articles of Harry J. Benda*, ed. A. Suddard (New Haven, Connecticut: Yale University Southeast Asia Studies, 1972), 83-92. See also a similar explanation in another of Benda's works *The Crescent and the Rising Sun*, 20-31.

with large Muslim populations.[16] The official policy on religious neutrality was stated, for instance, by Colonial Minister Charles Ferdinand Pahud in 1854:

> The government has to state ... the Netherlands is not a Christian state. The king, the administrators and the nation may be Christians, but when it is concerned with protection in general, and especially as in this case, [protection of] a population who for a greater part do not embrace the Christian doctrine, then gentlemen, impartiality and caution should be emphasised.[17]

This statement was in line with article 199 of the *Regeeringsreglement* (Government Regulation) of 1885 which stated that the Dutch government 'recognized freedom of religion and adopted a neutral attitude toward it ...'.[18]

The claim that the Dutch maintained a policy of religious neutrality is also supported by some scholars. Samuel Zwemer, for example, confirmed Gottfried Simon's argument that what hindered the Christianisation process in some areas of Indonesia was the colonial policy of religious neutrality.[19] Expressing a similar idea, Fred von der Mehden argued that the Dutch position of official neutrality towards religion was manifested in limiting permission for Christian missionary activities.[20]

This policy of religious neutrality might be correct to the extent that not all Dutch government officials favoured Christianity or were truly eager to convert Muslims to Christianity. Samuel E. Harthoorn (d. 1883), for example, was quite liberal in his theological outlook and criticised the missionary strategy of talking behind the Muslims'

---

[16] M.P.M. Muskens, *Partner in Nation Building: The Catholic Church in Indonesia* (Aachen: Missio Aktuell Verlag, 1979), 93.

[17] Quoted in Deliar Noer, *The Modernist Muslim Movement in Indonesia 1900–1942* (London and New York: Oxford University Press, 1973), 165–166.

[18] Quoted in Noer, *The Modernist Muslim Movement*, 166.

[19] Samuel M. Zwemer, *Across the World of Islam* (New York: F.H. Revell, 1929), 268–269.

[20] Fred R. von der Mehden, *Religion and Nationalism in Southeast Asia* (Madison: University of Wisconsin, 1963), 172.

backs. Steenbrink pointed out that for Harthoorn education was 'no longer simply a means to the goal of conversion but as the most important goal itself'.[21] Another Dutch scholar who tried to be neutral in terms of religious affairs was Godard Arend Hazeu (d. 1929). One example of this was his involvement in the conflict between Islamic and Christian missions in Northern Sumatra. In 1903 the Dutch government dismissed a village chief in the Angkola area on the border of North and South Tapanuli who had converted to Islam because he was viewed as a possible means of Islamisation in the area. The chief's son, Saikh Ibrahim, registered a protest with Hazeu, who later appealed to the government to abolish the obstruction of Islamisation. After several attempts Hazeu was successful and Ibrahim was elected chief by the people of Angkola, who were mainly Christians.[22]

However, the above-mentioned examples were the few exceptions. In practice, the Dutch often violated their policy of religious neutrality, and the missionaries continued their Christianisation efforts. In the Royal address of 1901, it was stated:

> As a Christian nation the Netherlands have a duty to improve the condition of native Christians in the Indian archipelago, to give Christian missionary activity more aid and to inform the entire administration that the Netherlands have a moral obligation to fulfill as regards the population of those regions.[23]

An example of the violation of this policy was the *Algemeene Bepaling van Wetgeving* (General Rule of Enactment) issued in 1849 which stated that native Christians were given the same legal rights and privileges as the Dutch, therefore grouping Muslims with others

---

[21] Steenbrink, *Dutch Colonialism and Indonesian Islam*, 101.

[22] Steenbrink, *Dutch Colonialism and Indonesian Islam*, 93–94.

[23] Quoted in Justus Maria van der Kroef, '*Dutch Colonial Policy in Indonesia 1900–1941*', (Ph.D. diss., Columbia University, 1950), 53.

in another less-respected category.[24] It is true that the rule was abrogated in 1854, yet the Christians continued to enjoy special treatment by the government through some of its policies.[25] Another case in point was the decree known as *goeroe ordonnantie* (teacher ordinance). First introduced in 1905, it stipulated that Islamic schools in Java, but not Christian schools, should obtain written permission from the authorities before delivering religious instruction to their students, and keep lists of their pupils. In 1925 another *goeroe ordonnantie* was imposed on all Islamic schools in Indonesia, albeit in a milder way, as only the standard forms of student lists and curriculum details were required.[26] Although the Dutch claimed that both ordinances were intended to advance the quality of Islamic education, for some Muslims including A.R. Fachruddin of the Muhammadiyah this was perceived as colonial control of the spread of Islam in Indonesia.[27]

Another example of Dutch favouritism towards Christians was the generous subsidies given to Christian missionary schools, churches, hospitals and orphanages, as well as various tax exemptions. In 1936 the subsidies received by the Protestants amounted to f. 686,100, the Catholics received f. 286,500, but the Muslims only f. 7,500. This amount increased rapidly in 1939 to f. 844,000 to the Protestants, f. 335,700 to the Catholics, but only rose very slightly to f. 7,600 for the Muslims.[28]

---

[24] This is not so much a case of prejudice of a modern, racist kind, but rather of the pretty universal idea that religion is one of the primary marks of human identity. Islam has the same views. Therefore, an Indonesian who becomes Christian is of course someone different, as is a Christian who becomes a Muslim.

[25] Noer, *The Modernist Muslim Movement*, 8.

[26] Ricklefs, *A History of Modern Indonesia*, 223-224.

[27] Noer, *The Modernist Muslim Movement*, 176. In the second *goeroe ordonnatie*,Taman Siswa Shcool (Garden of Pupils), which was a combination of modern education and traditional Javanese arts set up by Ki Hadjar Dewantara in Yogyakarta in 1922, also felt that the ordinance interfered with indigenous or nationalist schools, not just Islamic schools; see Ricklefs, *A History of Modern Indonesia*, 254.

[28] Quoted from Staatsblad, 1936: No. 355: 25, 26; 1937: No. 410: 25, 26; 1938: No. 511: 27, 28;1939: No. 593: 32, in Noer, *The Modernist Muslim Movement*, 170. See also Benda, *The Crescent and the Rising Sun*, 223, n. 57.

Another illustration is the comparison between the subsidies given to the Muslims to build mosques and to the Christians to build churches. In 1868 the amount given for the building of mosques was f. 4,500, whereas for Catholic Church buildings it was f. 50,000. Similarly, in 1928, the Christians received subsidies of f. 1,666,300 for church officials, priests and teachers. In comparison, Muslims received only f. 3,950.[29] About 70 years later, the imbalance in subsidies received by the Muslims and the Christians had not shown a dramatic change. During 1940, the number of Muslim primary schools receiving subsidies was 115 in comparison to 2,470 Christian (Protestant and Catholic) primary schools.[30]

In the case of the Ambonese, the Dutch recruited many Christians for the colonial armed forces, especially from the 1870s onwards. To encourage these Christians to become soldiers, the army differentiated between the 'Ambonese', who were defined as Christian natives coming from the Moluccan islands, and 'Malays', who were non-Christians. The Ambonese received higher pay than the Malays. Within this system, very few Muslims were recruited. Furthermore, Muslims were reluctant to join the armed forces since supporting the colonial government was considered *harām*.[31]

The four attitudinal trends discussed above show that the prevailing depiction by the Dutch of the Muslims was negative. In contrast, the Christians enjoyed a good relationship with the Dutch. This understanding was held deeply by Muslims, who identified the Dutch and the Christians as two sides of the same coin. The Muslim experiences during this colonial period left a deep wound in the Muslim memory regarding the Dutch as well as the Christians, and in turn provided the potential to ignite the flame of hatred within Muslim thinking.

---

[29] Suminto, *Politik Islam Hindia Belanda*, 33-36.

[30] Benda, *The Crescent and the Rising Sun*, 22, n. 55.

[31] Richard Chauvel, *Nationalists, Soldiers and Separatists: The Ambonese Islands from Colonialism to Revolt 1880-1950* (Leiden: KITLV Press, 1990), 39-40.

Depiction of Christianity and Islam in Early 20ᵗʰ Century Indonesia

At the level of society, it is important to examine briefly what kind of perceptions of Christianity and Islam existed during the early 20ᵗʰ century before Indonesian independence in 1945, as reflected in various writings. The discussion is not exhaustive as it serves as background information only. A few examples reveal that many Muslim works were composed as responses to literature by Christians, mainly missionaries, on Islam. Literature produced by Christians on Islam and by Muslims on Christianity was mainly apologetic and polemic, and had quite inflammatory rhetoric.

Among early writings on Christians and Christianity was A.D. Haanie's *Islam Menentang Kraemer* (Islam against Kraemer), which was published in 1929.[32] A prominent Muhammadiyah leader, Haanie felt obliged to respond to Kraemer's *Agama Islam* (The Religion of Islam),[33] which according to Haanie contained numerous mistakes. Kraemer, a Christian missionary activist, stated that his book was designed as an explanation for Christian teachers and to enhance Christians' knowledge of Islam. Kraemer added that, although the book was not written by a Muslim, its intention was to describe Islam as accurately as possible. However, the book contained some controversial ideas, especially on the Prophet Muhammad.

Haanie criticised Kraemer's statement that 'Before Muhammad was appointed as a prophet, he often went quite far away from his home to trade. It was very unlikely that a person who did not know how to read and write could perform such a difficult job'.[34] For Haanie, this statement had a very serious consequence, in that Kramer was arguing that the Qur'ān was not God's words but the words of Muhammad, and so it was important to state that Muhammad was literate. Haanie further maintained that it was the tradition of the

---

[32] A.D. Haanie, *Islam Menentang Kraemer* (Yogyakarta and Pekalongan: Penyiaran Islam, 1929).

[33] Hendrik Kraemer, *Agama Islam*, 3rd ed. (Jakarta: Badan Penerbit Kristen, 1952). The first edition of this book was published in 1928.

[34] Kraemer, *Agama Islam*, 17.

Christians to interpret an assumption as a fact.[35] Another point that Kraemer raised was Muhammad's human weakness shown by the fact that the Prophet altered the direction of prayers from Jerusalem to Mecca only because he hated the Jews. Kraemer explained that because Muhammad was insulted by the Jews and was told that the religious teachings he brought were not in accordance with the Torah, the prophet was angry with the Jews.[36] Haanie was irritated and stated that Kraemer 'was unjust, fanatical, and had made this statement just for the sake of having something to say'. For Haanie, Kraemer stressed Muhammad's human weakness because of his intention 'to strengthen his religion that never gained victory from Islam'.[37]

One important issue that Haanie dealt with was the 'satanic verses' affair. This referred to an event in which Muhammad was reported as accepting, as deities next to Allah, three Meccan idols: *al-Lāt, al-ᶜUzza,* and *al-Manat,* as a result of Satan's temptation. Kramer explained that, according to history books written by early Muslims, the context of this event was Muhammad's background in Mecca where he and his followers were insulted by the Meccan community. Muhammad reportedly thought that it was better to negotiate with the Meccan community and so acknowledged the three idols, yet later rejected his acknowledgment and regretted his deeds.[38] Haanie maintained that Kraemer had been led astray in believing the story and argued that Kramer's intention in quoting it was to discredit the authority of the Prophet as the bearer of Islam. Haanie stated that it was true that the affair was mentioned in some history books written by early Muslims, but the story was not correct and was rejected by many *ᶜulamā'.* He attributed the story to the *zindiq,* persons who pretended to be Muslims but were not. Haanie quoted

---

[35] Haanie, *Islam Menentang Kraemer,* 14, 49.

[36] Kraemer, *Agama Islam,* 31.

[37] Haanie, *Islam Menentang Kraemer,* 56, 60.

[38] Kraemer, *Agama Islam,* 25-26.

some ḥadīths which explained that the pagans (*mushrikūn*) prayed together with the Prophet not because he had acknowledged their deities but because the Prophet had recited some Qur'ānic verses.[39]

Another example of writings produced to respond to Dutch anti-Islamic apologetics was Mohammad Natsir's articles, which appeared from 1930 onwards in the periodical *Pembela Islam* (Defender of Islam). Natsir was a prominent member of *Persatuan Islam* in Bandung, West Java, and the *Pembela Islam* was published by this organisation. In 1931, J.J. Ten Berg, a Jesuit Priest based in Muntilan, Central Java, published two articles on the Qur'ān in the Journal *Studiën*. These were also circulated in Indonesia. In his second article, he quoted the Qur'ān 5:79, which states: 'The Christ, son of Mary, was but an apostle: all [other] apostles had passed away before him; and his mother was one who never deviated from the truth; and they both ate food [like other mortals].' Ten Berg then commented on this verse:

> One can see that according to Mohammed Christians conceive of a father and a mother and a son in a sexual sense. How would it have been possible for him, the anthropomorphist, the ignorant Arab, the gross sensualist, who was in the habit of sleeping with women, to conceive of a different and more elevated conception of Fatherhood![40]

In response to Ten Berg's writing, Natsir wrote an article arguing that such a description of the Prophet Muhammad should not have been uttered by an educated person like Ten Berg. More importantly, Natsir utilised the affair to criticise the general assault on Islam, arguing that the religion had at times been the target of the politics of religious neutrality by the colonial government.[41] For Natsir, the policy of religious neutrality had been proven to be wrong.[42]

---

[39] Haanie, *Islam Menentang Kraemer*, 53–54.

[40] As quoted by Steenbrink, *Dutch Colonialism and Indonesian Islam*, 118.

[41] See above for the explanation on the Dutch policy of religious neutrality.

[42] Mohammad Natsir, 'Islam, Katholiek, Pemerintah', *Pembela Islam* 33 (1931). Reprinted in his *Islam dan Kristen di Indonesia* (Jakarta: Media Dakwah, 1980), 37–43.

The colonial government, in response to Muslim denunciation, criticised Ten Berg's statements. This, however, caused unease for the Catholic community, which argued that the government's critique was a 'completely unjustified and imprudent statement'.[43] Responding to this, Natsir became very angry and questioned why Catholics were furious when their priest was criticised but did not consider how Muslims felt when their prophet was insulted.[44]

Muslim–Christian Relations in the Old Order (1945–1965)

The discussion on Muslim–Christian relations under the Old Order will centre on four main issues. First, it will survey the debates on the philosophical basis of the Indonesian State, which gained its Independence on 17 August 1945. This debate was central not only between Muslims and Christians, but also between the Islamic group (*kelompok Islam*) on the one hand, and the nationalist group (*kelompok nasionalis*) including Christians, nationalists, and nominal Muslims/ *abangan*[45] on the other. The second issue concerns some regional rebellions by Muslims in their attempt to reject the central authority. Third, Christianisation is also of great importance, and also includes Muslim writings on Christianity. The fourth issue is the policies of Sukarno (d. 1970) in managing Muslim–Christian relations, in particular some of his statements. As in the analysis of the Dutch period, the exploration here is meant as a basis for understanding the extent to which the attitudes of the Old Order government towards Muslim–Christian relations were connected to the New Order's policy on the same matters.

---

[43] Steenbrink, *Dutch Colonialism and Indonesian Islam*, 120.

[44] Natsir, *Islam dan Kristen di Indonesia*, 40–42.

[45] Indonesian, more specifically Javanese society, was classified by Clifford Geertz into three variants: santri (devout Muslim), abangan (nominal Muslim), and priyayi (aristocrats). Although several scholars have criticised this classification it is still widely used. Clifford Geertz, *Religion of Java* (Chicago: University of Chicago Press, 1960). The term abangan is used here to refer to Muslims who have nominal commitment to Islam and who do not practise the Islamic ritual duties.

The Jakarta Charter Debate

The exploration of the Jakarta Charter debate cannot be detached from the role of the Japanese (1942-1945) in substantiating the position of Islam in Indonesia. When the Japanese came to colonise Indonesia in March 1942, they made more concessions to the Muslims than to the nationalists (including some Christians from North Sulawesi and nominal Muslims).[46] The new colonial regime attracted the Muslims by giving them more positions within the government (as compared with their positions during the Dutch period) and by administratively eliminating 'attitudes of discrimination towards them'.[47] Some of these new policies were the reopening of religious schools, the creation of the Office for Religious Affairs, the formation of the Masyumi, and the formation of a corps of Muslims (*Hizbullah*/Army of Allah).[48] The last three will be discussed or referred to later in this section.

One reason why the Japanese favoured the Muslims was the fact that the Muslims, especially the Nahdhatul Ulama people, had links into the rural population which gave the Japanese potential avenues for control and mobilisation.[49] Another possible reason was Japanese suspicion of the nationalists, who during the Dutch era 'expressed disagreement with and condemnation of Fascism on many occasions, even warning the people of the danger of the Fascists, whom they considered more suppressive than the Dutch colonizers'.[50] Even though, towards the end of its power, the Japanese gave parallel support to the nationalists, Benda argued that at that time, however, 'Indonesian Islam had been allowed to gain a position of unprecedented strength from which it could no longer be easily displaced by the nationalist leadership'.[51]

---

[46] B.J. Boland, *The Struggle of Islam in Modern Indonesia* (The Hague: Martinus Nijhoff, 1982), 8.

[47] Deliar Noer, *Administration of Islam in Indonesia* (Ithaca, New York: Cornell University Monograph Series, 1978), 9. See also Benda, The Crescent and the Rising Sun, 132-149.

[48] Muhammad Abdul Aziz, *Japan's Colonialism and Indonesia* (The Hague: Martinus Nijhoff, 1955), 200-208. See also Aiko Kurasawa, *Mobilisasi dan Kontrol: Studi tentang Perubahan Sosial di Pedesaan Jawa 1942-1954* (Jakarta: Rasindo, 1993), 273-285.

[49] Ricklefs, *A History of Modern Indonesia*, 253.

[50] Noer, *Administration of Islam in Indonesia*, 9-10.

[51] Benda, *The Crescent and the Rising Sun*, 202.

In March 1945, the Japanese established an Investigating Committee for Preparatory Work for Indonesian Independence (Badan Usaha Penyelidik Persiapan Kemerdekaan Indonesia/BPUPKI). This organisation nominated 62 people from different ideological backgrounds, who were inaugurated on 28 May 1945, to draft the foundation of the Indonesian state. Whether Indonesia should be an Islamic or a secular state was heatedly disputed.[52] On 1 June 1945 Sukarno delivered a speech before the BPUPKI meeting in which he offered Pancasila (the Five Principles: belief in one God, humanity, nationalism, mutual deliberation, and social justice) as a middle way to accommodate both parties and lead Indonesia neither to an Islamic state nor to a secular one.[53] This offer, however, did not solve the problem, as the Muslims believed that they deserved more privileges and also wanted Islamic law to be implemented in Indonesia.

Sukarno later chose nine prominent political leaders from Islamic and nationalist groups[54] from the 62 people mentioned above in order to settle the dispute. These two groups engaged in a heated debate, but on 22 June 1945 arrived at a compromise on what was intended to be the 'Preamble' of the Constitution, and which is known as the Piagam Jakarta (Jakarta Charter). Part the document reads: '... National independence is hereby expressed in a Constitution of the Indonesian state which is moulded in the form of the Republic of Indonesia, resting upon the people's sovereignty and founded on [the following principles]: the Belief in God (ke-Tuhanan), with the obligation for adherents of Islam to practise Islamic law ...'.[55] This phrase 'with the obligation for

---

[52] The discussion on the political situation during this period in this study is not meant to be exhaustive. Many studies have been conducted in regard to this very issue. See, for example, Endang Saifuddin Anshari, *Piagam Jakarta 22 Juni 1945* (Jakarta: Rajawali, 1981).

[53] Muhammad Yamin, *Naskah Persiapan Undang-Undang Dasar 1945*, vol. 1 (Jakarta: Yayasan Prapantja, 1959), 61-81. This book is on the three volumes of Yamin's essential work, which includes texts of speeches and minutes of meetings surrounding the conception of the 1945 Constitution.

[54] The nine signatories were (in alphabetical order): A.A. Maramis, Achmad Subardjo, Abdul Kahar Muzakkir, Abikusno Tjokrosujoso, Agus Salim, Mohammad Hatta, Mohammad Yamin, Sukarno, and Wahid Hasjim.

[55] The English expression quoted above was taken from Boland, *The Struggle of Islam*, 26.

adherents of Islam to practise Islamic law' (known in Indonesian language as '*tujuh kata*' or seven words) was also to be included within the article of the Constitution on religion.

From 10 to 16 July 1945, the committee of 62 held several meetings focusing on the issues of the structure of the state and the Constitution. Within the Committee for the Constitution some disagreements appeared. These disagreements were expressed by, for instance, Latuharhary (d. 1959), a Protestant, who objected to the 'seven words' by predicting the consequences for other religious believers.[56] However, it is important to note that it was not only Christians who objected to the seven words. Wongsonegoro (a liberal Javanese, born in 1897) and Husein Djajadiningrat (a Muslim born in 1886, the first head of the Office for Religious Affairs) also disapproved of the phrase, arguing that the seven words could create fanaticism as they would be interpreted as giving the state authority to force (*memaksa*) Muslims to keep *sharīʿa*.[57] Wahid Hasjim (d. 1953) of the Nahdhatul Ulama denied the possible interpretation of compulsion because the state would be established on the basis of *permusyawaratan* (mutual deliberation). At this very moment Sukarno, the chairman of the Committee, reminded its members that the deletion of the seven words would be 'unacceptable to Muslims'.[58] The Committee finally accepted the draft.

At the next meeting, Wahid Hasjim promoted a further idea by suggesting a stipulation within the Constitution that the president and vice-president of Indonesia should be Muslims. Further, he argued that the article of the Constitution on religion should read: 'The religion of the state is Islam, with the guarantee of freedom for adherents of other religions to profess their own religion...'.[59] Moreover, Ki Bagus Hadikusumo (b. 1890), the Muhammadiyah leader, proposed the omission of the words 'for adherents of Islam' in the 'seven words' so that the

---

[56] Yamin, *Naskah Persiapan Undang-Undang Dasar 1945*, vol. 1, 259.

[57] Yamin, *Naskah Persiapan Undang-Undang Dasar 1945*, vol. 1, 262.

[58] Yamin, *Naskah Persiapan Undang-Undang Dasar 1945*, vol. 1, 259.

[59] Yamin, *Naskah Persiapan Undang-Undang Dasar 1945*, vol. 1, 262.

article would read: 'The state is founded on Belief in God, with the obligation to practise Islamic law'. He reasoned that to preserve the formula as it was would create double regulations, one for Muslims and another for non-Muslims.[60] After some debate at the meeting on 16 July 1945, Sukarno asked the nationalist group, especially Latuharhary and A.A. Maramis (b. 1897), who were non-Muslims, to make a sacrifice by allowing the Constitution to include the articles 'The President of the Republic of Indonesia must be a born Indonesian who is a Muslim', and that 'The State is founded on Belief in God, with the obligation for adherents of Islam to practise Islamic law'. The meeting ended with the acceptance of the proposed Constitution.[61]

BPUPKI was later dissolved and a similar institution named PPKI (Panitia Persiapan Kemerdekaan Indonesia/Committee for the Preparation of Indonesia's Independence), under the coordination of Sukarno, was established on 14 or 15 August 1945.[62] On 17 August 1945 Indonesia declared its independence. The next morning an informal discussion took place between Muhammad Hatta (d. 1980) and some representatives of the Islamic group, including Ki Bagus Hadikusumo and Wahid Hasjim. This meeting agreed to remove any Islamic formula within the Constitution, a change that implied that the seven words had to be deleted from both the Preamble and the Constitutional article on religion.[63] A further implication was that the requirement that the president was a Muslim had to be altered to 'The president is a native Indonesian'. In addition, the word *Muqaddimah* (derived from Arabic) had to be changed to *Pembukaan* (both words have the same meaning as Preamble).[64]

---

[60] Yamin, *Naskah Persiapan Undang-Undang Dasar 1945*, vol. 1, 282. See also, Anshari, *Piagam Jakarta 22 Juni 1945*, 36–38.

[61] Yamin, *Naskah Persiapan Undang-Undang Dasar 1945*, vol. 1, 392–393.

[62] Boland did not state the reason why the date of the creation of the new Preparatory Committee was either 14 or 15 August 1945. See Boland, *The Struggle of Islam*, 34.

[63] This decision to remove the Islamic formula was evident because the Japanese said that Christian areas of Indonesia would not support the Preamble unless such passages were deleted.

[64] Yamin, *Naskah Persiapan Undang-Undang Dasar 1945*, vol. 1, 401–403.

In the official meeting of PPKI that followed, Sukarno stated that a proposal for some changes to the Constitution had been received and, requesting the members of PPKI not to enter into another debate, asked Hatta to read the proposed alterations. These changes caused disappointment among the majority of Muslims even though they accepted these alterations for the sake of the unity of the Indonesian nation.[65] There were various arguments concerning these essential omissions. One of the most significant reasons was given by Muhammad Hatta that the Christians would prefer a separate state if the Constitution was accepted as it was.[66]

The Muslims' acceptance of the alterations mentioned above did not automatically please non-Muslims, especially those who resided outside Java and perceived that the Republic was dominated by the Javanese and Muslims. In April 1950 a demand to form the East Indonesia government was met by the Indonesian Republic and was meant as a temporary government that would later merge into a unitary Indonesia. Nevertheless, Dr. Soumokil, an Ambonese who served as the Minister of Justice in the East Indonesia government, proclaimed a Republic of South Maluku (Republik Maluku Selatan/RMS) in Ambon on 25 April 1950. This was defeated by Republican soldiers in November of the same year.[67] The RMS was seen as Christian treason against the Indonesian Republic.

Without going into detail, suffice it to say that, within the Constituent Assembly Sessions of 1957–1959, the debates over the issue of the basis of the state re-appeared. This was because, when the Islamic group accepted the essential changes proposed by Hatta on 18 August 1945, they believed Sukarno's promise that the Constitution (now including the alterations) was only 'a temporary Constitution' (Undang-Undang Dasar Sementara).[68] In the Assembly meeting on 4 May

---

[65] Anshari, *Piagam Jakarta 22 Juni 1945*, 53.

[66] Mohammad Hatta, *Sekitar Proklamasi 17 Agustus 1945* (Jakarta: Tintamas, 1970), 57–59.

[67] Ricklefs, *A History of Modern Indonesia*, 285.

[68] Yamin, *Naskah Persiapan Undang-Undang Dasar 1945*, vol. 1, 410.

1959, Saifuddin Zuhri of the Nahdhatul Ulama argued that the Jakarta Charter of 1945 was not only to be recognised as a historical document but had legal significance according to the 1945 Constitution. He further asked for the government's agreement that the Charter had legal significance and could be used as a source of law.[69] In contrast, at the meeting the next day, B. Mang Reng Say, the representative of the Catholic Party, argued that for his party the Jakarta Charter was an historical document but with an understanding that it would not be used as a means to discriminate against other religions and would not lessen freedom of religion. He further added that the Charter should not and could not be the source of law (*welbron van recht*).[70] After this long debate, Sukarno, under military pressure, dissolved the Constituent Assembly on 5 July 1959. He issued a Presidential decree and said that the Jakarta Charter was 'a historical document which inspired the whole of the constitution but was not itself a legal part of it'.[71]

Also closely related to the issue of the Jakarta Charter was the creation of the Office of Religious Affairs. As has been stated, the Muslims received some essential support from the Japanese, and amongst the concessions the Japanese gave them was the creation of an Office for Religious Affairs (Kantor Urusan Agama).[72] In the hope that the establishment of the Office for Religious Affairs would win Muslim support and fulfil their wishes, the Japanese appointed a Muslim scholar, Professor Husein Djajadiningrat, as the head of the Office on 1 October 1943. He was later, on 1 August 1944, succeeded by an *ᶜulamā'*, K.H. Hasjim Asj'ari, the head of the traditional Tebu Ireng *Pesantren*

---

[69] Yamin, *Naskah Persiapan Undang-Undang Dasar 1945*, vol. 2, (Jakarta: Yayasan Prapanjta, 1960), 406.

[70] Yamin, *Naskah Persiapan Undang-Undang Dasar 1945*, vol. 2, 473, 475–476.

[71] Ricklefs, *A History of Modern Indonesia*, 321–322. Until now the Jakarta Charter has never been included in the Constitution and the debates over this issue have been quoted to explain the roots of Muslim–Christian disharmonious relations in Indonesia.

[72] This Office also functioned to control and monitor Muslims. It was also in part of a successor to the Colonial Office for Nature Affairs (Kantoor voor Inlandsche Zaken).

(Islamic boarding school) in East Java.[73] Against this background, when Indonesia gained its independence, many Muslims proposed the establishment of the Ministry of Religious Affairs.

At a meeting of the Committee for the Preparation of Indonesia's Independence on 19 August 1945, an establishment of the Ministry of Religious Affairs was proposed. The meeting rejected the proposal. At this very point, the question of Muslim–Christian relations in Indonesia came to fore. Latuharhary, a Christian from Maluku, argued that the establishment of such a ministry would create 'uneasy feelings'. He further maintained that if the Minister of Religious Affairs was a Christian the Muslim community would be dissatisfied, while if the Minister was a Muslim the Christian community would not be happy. Latuharhary suggested that religious affairs be grouped with educational affairs.[74] It is interesting to note that Muslims as well as Christians rejected the proposal. For instance, Abdul Abbas, a Muslim representative from Lampung, South Sumatra, supported Latuharhary's idea that religious affairs be handled by the Ministry of Education, Training and Religion.[75] However, some Muslims perceived the Christians' insistence on refusing the establishment of such a ministry as another attempt at distancing Islam from the state. In spite of all criticism, the Ministry of Religious Affairs was finally created on 3 January 1946.

Regional Rebellions of DI/TII and PRRI

The regional rebellions of the Darul Islam (from Arabic *dār al-Islām*, territory or house of Islam/DI) organisation and its army, Tentara Islam Indonesia (Indonesian Islamic Army/TII), and the Revolutionary Government of the Indonesian Republic (Pemerintah Revolusioner Republik Indonesia/PRRI) are significant for two reasons. First, it is

---

[73] Benda, *The Crescent and the Rising Sun*, 126, 201. See also Noer, *Administration of Islam in Indonesia*, 11, and Aziz, *Japan's Colonialism and Indonesia*, 200-201.

[74] Yamin, *Naskah Persiapan Undang-Undang Dasar 1945*, vol. 1, 457.

[75] Yamin, *Naskah Persiapan Undang-Undang Dasar 1945*, vol. 1, 457.

important to examine Sukarno's attitude towards these two rebellions, both of which involved Muslims. Second, the issue of DI/TII and PRRI is interconnected with the discussion on the New Order's policy towards Muslims in the next chapter.

The Darul Islam movement was one of the greatest fears of the Sukarno government. Its leader, Sekarmadji Maridjan Kartosuwirjo (d. 1962), a Javanese mystic, was associated with the Partai Sarikat Islam Indonesia (Islamic Political Association of Indonesia/ PSII), first as its General Secretary in 1931, and then as its Vice President in 1936. Kartosuwirjo belonged to the PSII until 1939, when he was expelled as his ideas were not in line with those of the organisation. In 1940, he established the Suffah Institute, a kind of *pesantren* in Malangbong, West Java, which later became the centre for the training of the Islamic army (*Hizbullah*).[76] It is important to note that when Masyumi became a party in November 1945 Kartosuwirjo was one of the members of its Executive Board.[77]

When the Renville Agreement between the Netherlands and the Republic was achieved on 1 August 1949, Kartosuwirjo refused to accept it. The DI/TII continued its guerrilla campaign and by then had become anti-Republican. Efforts to negotiate with the DI/TII leaders were conducted several times. Under the Muhammad Natsir cabinet (September 1950 to March 1951), contacts and negotiations took place with Kartosuwirjo, who constantly rejected the idea of giving up his Negara Islam Indonesia (Indonesian Islamic State/ NII, commonly referred to as Darul Islam). The DI/TII did not hesitate to adopt a violent strategy in achieving their idea of the Islamic state. It was reported that on one occasion some members of the Darul Islam said to a villager in West Java: 'If you are for Sukarno, then go to Jogjakarta. If you are pro-Dutch, go to Bandung. In either case, be gone by tomorrow, or you will die. If you are for us, then prove it by putting yourself and your

---

[76] Ricklefs, *A History of Modern Indonesia*, 278.

[77] Boland, *The Struggle of Islam*, 42, 57. The establishment of the Masyumi will be discussed below.

possessions at our disposal'.[78] Kartosuwirjo decided to extend his territory to include the whole of Indonesia. The official proclamation of the NII was published on 7 August 1949 with him as its *imām* (leader) and Kamran as the army commander. With the cabinet change from Natsir to Sukiman, attempts to suppress the DI/TII movement were intensified, and by 1960 the movement had weakened. Kartosuwirjo was captured on 24 April 1962 and was sentenced to death sometime in September 1962.[79]

Another regional rebellion was by the PRRI. However, before discussing this movement, the formation of the Masyumi (Majelis Syuro Muslimin Indonesia/Consultative Council of Indonesian Muslims) must be explained briefly, as the master minds of the PRRI were among the members of Masyumi. It has been mentioned that another benefit from the Japanese to the Muslims was the formation of the Masyumi, which was the successor to the MIAI (Majlisul Islamil A'laa Indonesia/the Supreme Indonesian Council of Islam, established in 1937. (The more religious) MIAI was re-organised and named Masyumi (which was more political) in October 1943 as part of the Japanese Islamic policy for Indonesia, which perceived the former organisation as holding anti-foreign sentiments.[80] The Masyumi was transformed into a political party on 7 November 1945 in Yogyakarta, and shifted its orientation to embrace individual members as well as non-political organisations including Muhammadiyah, Nahdhatul Ulama, and some regional organisations in West Java.[81] The PSII, which had been banned by the Japanese, also fused into the Masyumi without liquidating itself as an organisation.[82] While on the one hand the Masyumi had to agree with

---

[78] C.A.O. van Nieuwenhuijze, *Aspects of Islam in Post-Colonial Indonesia* (The Hague: W. van Hoeve, 1958), 165, 173.

[79] Boland, *The Struggle of Islam*, 60–61.

[80] See Benda, *The Crescent and the Rising Sun*, 151–152; Boland, *The Struggle of Islam*, 10–11; and C.A.O. van Nieuwenhuijze, *Aspects of Islam*, 152–153.

[81] K.E. Ward, *The Foundation of the Partai Muslimin Indonesia* (Ithaca, New York: Cornell University Press, 1970), 9–16.

[82] George McTurnan Kahin, *Nationalism and Revolution in Indonesia* (Ithaca: Cornell University Press, 1952), 209 n. 103.

the Pancasila as the philosophical basis for the state, on the other hand it wanted to implement Islamic principles within the state and society. What distinguished the Masyumi from the DI/TII, however, was that the former wanted to struggle for the implementation of these principles in a democratic way.[83]

After the split of PSII (in 1948) and NU (in 1952) from the Masyumi, factions occurred between Muhammad Natsir (d. 1993) and Sukiman Wirjosandjojo (b. 1896). The Natsir wing was more representative of the Outer Islands and was sympathetic with the regionalist demand for greater autonomy, whereas Sukiman was more inclined to the Javanese interest. In December 1957, three of the national leaders of Masyumi, namely Muhammad Natsir, Burhanuddin Harahap (b. 1917), and Syafruddin Prawiranegara (d. 1989),[84] left for Padang, West Sumatra, to join the Sumatran Army to fight against the central government. Amongst the essential reasons for this rebellion was the introduction of the concept of Guided Democracy and the growing prominence that Sukarno had given to the Communist Party.[85] While Sukarno was overseas, the Pemerintah Revolusioner Republik Indonesia/PRRI was proclaimed in Padang on 15 February 1958, and Syafruddin Prawiranegara was appointed its Prime Minister. Jakarta responded to this coup attempt very quickly, and by mid 1958 had succeeded in crushing the rebels. Based on the involvement of Masyumi figures within the PRRI, the party was banned in August 1960 by Sukarno, and some of its prominent figures, including Muhammad Natsir, Burhanuddin Harahap, and Syafruddin Prawiranegara, were sentenced to gaol.[86] The DI/TII and PRII rebellions, as well as

---

[83] Boland, *The Struggle of Islam*, 43. See also, Nieuwenhuijze, *Aspects of Islam*, 164–165.

[84] All three leaders had previously been heads of government. Muhammad Natsir served as Prime Minister from September 1950–March 1951, Burhanuddin Harahap (August 1955–March 1956), and Syafruddin Prawiranegara was proclaimed Prime Minister of PRRI (1958–1961). These three leaders received significant support from the PSI (Indonesian Socialist Party, formed in 1948).

[85] Herbert Feith, 'The End of the Indonesian Rebellion', *Pacific Affairs 36*, 1 (Spring, 1963): 34–35.

[86] For a detailed account of the rebellion, see, among others, Feith, 'The End of the Indonesian Rebellion'. See also Ricklefs, *A History of Modern Indonesia*, 317–320.

the banning of the Masyumi, had a clear connection with the New Order's policy towards Muslims, which will be discussed in the next chapter.

Christianisation Issues and Muslim Writings on Christianity

The third important issue is Christianisation. In the years following independence, religiously speaking Christians enjoyed the same rights as other religious believers, as stated in article 29 of the Constitution: 'The state guarantees the freedom of its population to embrace their own religion and to practise their own religious teachings'. This implied that the above-mentioned restrictions that were imposed by the Dutch on the Christian missionaries were revoked by the Sukarno government. In 1950, for example, the Catholic Church started to expand its missionary activities to areas that had been closed to it during the colonial era, including South Kalimantan, North Maluku, and the territory of the Torajas in South Sulawesi.[87]

In the same year, 27 Protestant churches established the Council of Indonesian Churches (Dewan Gereja-Gereja di Indonesia/DGI), whose aim was, among others, 'to assist member churches in particular program areas, especially in witness and service, in gathering and distributing the fruits of study and research, and in developing resources, particularly personnel and facilities'.[88] Also, on 3 January 1961, Pope John XXIII initiated a Catholic ecclesiastical hierarchy in Indonesia consisting of 31 dioceses and 2 prefectures. This marked the beginning of the coordination of activities of the Catholic Church under the Majelis Wali Gereja Indonesia (Indonesian Council of Bishops/MAWI).[89] The Christian side claimed that the 1960s had witnessed the revival of Christianity. A.T. Willis, for example, stated that membership of the Indonesian Baptist Churches (Gabungan Gereja-Gereja

---

[87] Muskens, *Partner in Nation Building*, 93-94.

[88] Frank L. Cooley, *Indonesia: Church & Society* (New York: Friendship Press, 1968), 110.

[89] Pro Mundi Vita, 'Indigenous and Foreign Religions in Indonesia' (Belgium: PMV, Centrum Informationis, No. 35, 1971), 5-6, as quoted by Rifyal Ka'bah, *Christian Presence in Indonesia: A View of Christian–Muslim Relations* (Leicester: The Islamic Foundation, 1985), 12.

Baptis Indonesia or GGBI) increased rapidly from 1,317 in 1960 to 3,391 in 1965.[90] It was also recorded that during July–August 1966 the East Java Christian Church baptised nearly 10,000 persons. Moreover, the Karo Batak Protestant Church baptised over 26,000 persons in 1966-1967.[91]

In the early 1960s, a brochure about Christianisation in Java was circulated among Muslims. It stated that a join conference of Catholics and Protestants was held in 1963 in Malang, East Java, in which a plan was outlined to Christianise the Javanese within 20 years and all other Indonesians within 50 years. Among the programs were said to be open seminaries in areas with a Muslim majority, and support for male Christians to marry female Muslims with the purpose of converting them to Christianity.[92] It is difficult to trace the origin of this rumour and to examine the validity of the argument that the conference was ever held. However, for some Muslims, it did not matter whether the meeting was ever held, as they believed that the programs mentioned in the pamphlet fitted well with guides written for the Christian missionaries.[93] This pamphlet created tension between Christians and Muslims, as could be seen in some Islamic publications. The *Panji Masjarakat* Journal, for example, exclusively reported the pamphlet in one of its editions and denounced it as an effort to re-colonise Indonesia under the guise of religion.[94]

The freedom to spread religion enjoyed by the Christians following independence, and Christian missionary activities, seemed to give an impetus to Muslim writings unsympathetic to Christianity.

---

[90] A.T. Willis, *Indonesian Revival: Why Two Million Came to Christ* (California: William Carey Library, 1977), 180.

[91] David B Barret, ed., *World Christian Encyclopedia: A Comparative Study of Churches and Religions in the Modern World AD 1900-2000* (Nairobi: Oxford University Press, 1982), 384.

[92] Umar Hasyim, *Toleransi dan Kemerdekaan dalam Islam Sebagai Dasar Menuju Dialog dan Kerukunan Antar Agama* (Surabaya: Bina Ilmu, 1977), 270. See also Ismatu Ropi, 'Depicting the Other Faith: A Bibliographical Survey of Indonesian Muslim Polemics on Christianity', *Studia Islamika 6*, no. 1 (1999): 97-98. Boland had a different date for the alleged conference, namely 1962; see Boland, *The Struggle of Islam*, 227.

[93] Hasyim, *Toleransi dan Kemerdekaan dalam Islam*, 271-272.

Within this context, some writings on Christianity were characterised by Biblical criticism (critically examining the Bible), and were composed by educated Muslims who were familiar with modern study on comparative religion. Some of these writings were also composed as rebuttals of Christian works on Islam.

In the 1950s, one of several Muslim works on Christianity was Hasbullah Bakry's *Nabi Isa dalam al-Qur'ān dan Nabi Muhammad dalam Bijbel* (Jesus Christ in the Qur'ān and Muhamad in the Bible).[95] Hasbullah was the former lecturer in comparative religion at the Sekolah Pendidikan Hakim Islam Negeri (school for educating judges in Islamic law) in Yogyakarta. The book was first published in 1959 as a response to F.L. Bakker's *Tuhan Yesus dalam Agama Islam* (Lord Jesus in Islam).[96] Hasbullah clearly stated that the aim of his book was primarily to help Muslim parents to keep their children away from Christian teachings and Christian efforts to convert Muslims to Christianity. Indeed, as Hasbullah noted, he wrote the book because, when leadership of churches and missions was handed over from foreign authority to Indonesian Christians, thousands of young Muslims had converted to Christianity. In addition, although the book was internally circulated among Muslims, it was intended as an encouragement to Jews and Christians to embrace Islam. Hasbullah's approach in his book was a combination of a critical reading of Christian teachings and references to Qur'ānic notions on Christians and Christianity.[97]

Amongst important issues discussed by Hasbullah Bakry were the alterations or changes allegedly made by Christians to the Bible (or alternatively known as *taḥrīf*), and the notion of the Trinity in Christianity. On the first issue, Hasbullah maintained that until the 2nd century C.E. the Christians had not possessed an official canoni-

---

[94] *Panji Masjarakat* 17, 1967, 4.

[95] Hasbullah Bakry, *Nabi Isa dalam al-Qur'an dan Nabi Muhammad dalam Bijbel*, 4th ed. (Jakarta: Melati Offset, 1974). The first edition of this book was published in Solo by Siti Syamsiah in 1959.

[96] F.L. Bakker, *Tuhan Yesus dalam Agama Islam* (Jakarta: BPK Gunung Mulia, 1957).

[97] Bakry, *Nabi Isa dalam al-Qur'an*, 187-189. See also Bolland, *The Struggle of Islam*, 228.

cal Holy Book. What they did have was only the Old Testament of the Jews. However, the Christians at that period had some notes on the teachings of Isa (Jesus in Christian terms), which were held by different Christian communities in various places. Hasbullah argued that in the early 2nd century C.E., some Christian leaders wanted to codify all the notes into a canonical New Testament for all Christian communities. The codification process took a long time and it was only in the 4th century C.E. that it was definitively finalised. Commenting on the four Gospels (Injīl) of the New Testament, namely Matthew, Mark, Luke, and John, Hasbullah argued that the Gospels had contradictory content; hence, for him, they could not be considered as original revelations.[98] Moreover, he maintained that, according to the Qur'ān, the content of the Gospels was not in accordance with the principle of the Oneness of God (tawḥīd).[99]

On the issue of the Trinity and the divinity of Jesus, Hasbullah first argued that Jesus was sent only to the Israelites, by referring to some Qur'ānic verses as well as the New Testament. He maintained that the call to non-Israelites happened only after Jesus had separated from his followers, and was especially pioneered by Paul, a convert from Judaism. Hasbullah also stated that the doctrine of the Trinity was not Jesus' teaching but was first introduced by early Christian councils who had led Christians astray.[100] Hasbullah was at pains to criticise the concept of the Trinity in Christianity, as in Islam this doctrine was considered as a serious deviation from tawḥīd. He further argued that even amongst Christian leaders, the concept of the Trinity was considered as, to borrow Van Onck's term, 'a tricky theological concept' (theologisch spitsvondige theorieen).[101] Boland acknowledged Hasbullah's work mentioned above as 'a somewhat more

---

[98] Bakry, *Nabi Isa dalam al-Qur'an*, 35–37.

[99] Bakry, *Nabi Isa dalam al-Qur'an*, 47.

[100] Bakry, *Nabi Isa dalam al-Qur'an*, 58, 69.

[101] Van Onck, *Islam de Kracht die de Wereld der Moslims beweegt*, no publication details; see, Bakry, *Nabi Isa dalam al-Qur'an*, 87.

important book'[102] in comparison to polemic publications or pamphlets by Muslims such as Bisjron Wardy's *Memahami Kegiatan Nasrani* (Understanding the Activities of Christians).[103]

Boland's compliment to Hasbullah's work would also be better understood if one compares the latter's book with the work of Djarnawi Hadikusuma, one of the Muhammadiyah leaders and the first chairman of the Partai Muslimin Indonesia (Indonesian Muslim Party/Parmusi)[104] on a similar topic. In his book *Sekitar Perjanjian Lama dan Perjanjian Baru* (The Old and New Testament), Djarnawi sought to explain the origin of the Bible.[105] Djarnawi's examination of the history of the Old Testament, which allegedly had undergone several changes over a long period of time before it was codified, led him to conclude that the book contained several contradictions. In addition, Djarnawi maintained that research on the history of the writing of the Old Testament could not be historically proven.[106] On the New Testament, he stated that it was more important for Christians than the Old Testament. Towards the end of his book, Djarnawi examined some perceived controversies within the four Gospels of the New Testament, namely on the lineage of Jesus, the notion that Jesus was the Son of God, the claim that Jesus had the same essence (*haqīqah*) as God, and the crucifixion of Jesus.[107]

In his attempts at examining the Old and New Testaments, Djarnawi, like Hasbullah, used a lot of Biblical materials. In explaining the controversies within the New Testament, for example, Djarnawi compared the above-mentioned issues within the Gospels of Matthew, Mark, Luke and John, and quoted Arnold Toynbee's *A Study of*

---

[102] Boland, *The Struggle of Islam*, 227-228.

[103] Bisjron A. Wardy, *Memahami Kegiatan Nasrani* (Yogyakarta: Muhammadiyah, 1964).

[104] The discussion on Parmusi is provided in Chapter Four.

[105] Djarnawi Hadikusuma, *Sekitar Perjanjian Lama dan Perjanjian Baru*, 4th ed. (Yogyakarta: Pimpinan Pusat Muhammadiyah, no date).

[106] Hadikusuma, *Sekitar Perjanjian Lama*, 14.

[107] Hadikusuma, *Sekitar Perjanjian Lama*, 55-70.

History.[108] Nevertheless, Boland was correct in criticising the method that Djarnawi applied in quoting his sources. For example, Djarnawi deemed the book *New Heavens and a New Earth* (published by the International Bible Students' Association at Brooklyn, New York), on its dates and authors of the Old Testament, and Toynbee's *A Study of History*, on its account of the New Testament, as equally authoritative.[109]

Sukarno and Islam

The three issues discussed above, namely the Jakarta Charter, the regional rebellions, and Christianisation, lead to the last issue in Sukarno's policies in managing relations between followers of different religions in general, and Muslims and Christians in particular. It has been stated above that when the dispute regarding the basis of the state emerged, Sukarno offered *Pancasila* to lead Indonesia neither to an Islamic state nor a secular state. In a speech that he delivered on 1 June 1945 to mark the birth of *Pancasila*, he stated:

> If we really are a Muslim people, let us work as hard as possible so that most of the seats in the people's representative body which we will create, are occupied by Muslim delegates. If the Indonesian people really are a people who are for the greater part Muslim, and if it is true that Islam here is a religion which is alive in the hearts of the masses, let us leaders move every one of the people to mobilize as many Muslim delegates as possible for this representative body.[110]

At first glance, the above-quoted statement could be interpreted as Sukarno's support for Muslims or, even further, for the establishment of an Islamic state. This interpretation could also be strengthened by his approval, amid protests from some Christians and na-

---

[108] Hadikusuma, *Sekitar Perjanjian Lama*, 57.

[109] Boland argued that the book *New Heavens and a New Earth*, which was a translation from the Dutch *Nieuwe Hemelen en een Nieuwe Aarde*, was 'obviously an old publication of the Jehovah's Witness'. Boland, *The Struggle of Islam*, 226.

[110] Yamin, *Naskah Persiapan Undang-Undang Dasar 1945*, vol. 1, 74. The English translation quoted above was taken from Feith and Castles, eds., *Indonesian Political Thinking*, 45.

tionalists, of the creation of the Ministry of Religious Affairs discussed above. However, both his speech and his policy on the creation of such a ministry can be understood as efforts only to satisfy Muslims. Boland was probably correct in stating that Sukarno's speech quoted above was to 'only soothe the Muslims'.[111] Similarly, Noer argued that his approval for the creation of the Ministry of Religious Affairs was given when the government was considering the need to gain support from Muslims in the face of Dutch attempts to re-colonise Indonesia. By satisfying the Muslims, the Sukarno government hoped to win their support.[112]

A closer scrutiny will call into question the argument that Sukarno had given his full support to the Muslims. This is clear from his statement in a different part of the same speech quoted above:

> Within the people's representative body, Muslims and Christians will work as hard as possible. If, for instance, Christians desire every letter of the regulations of the Indonesian state to conform with the Bible, then let them work themselves to death in order that the greater part of the delegates who enter the Indonesian representative body are Christians. That is just— fair play![113]

This point is further strengthened by Sukarno's speech delivered at Amuntai, a strongly Muslim area in South Kalimantan, on 27 January 1953, in which his firm opposition to the idea of establishing an Islamic state can be clearly observed:

> The state we want is a national state consisting of all Indonesia. If we establish a state based on Islam, many areas whose population is not Islamic, such as the Moluccas, Bali, Flores, Timor, the Kai Island, and Sulawesi, will secede. And West

---

[111] Boland, *The Struggle of Islam*, 127.

[112] Noer, *Administration of Islam in Indonesia*, 13.

[113] Yamin, *Naskah Persiapan Undang-Undang Dasar 1945*, vol. 1, 75. The English translation quoted above was taken from Feith and Castles, eds., *Indonesian Political Thinking*, 46.

Irian, which has not yet become part of the territory of Indonesia, will not want to be part of the Republic.[114]

This speech instigated strong protests from Muslims. A number of Muslim organisations, including the Nahdhatul Ulama and Gerakan Pemuda Islam Indonesia/GPII (Islamic Youth Movement of Indonesia), stated that the President 'had exceeded his constitutional limitations'. These Muslims perceived Sukarno's speech as favouring ideology that opposed Islam. On the contrary, members of the Partai Nasionalis Indonesia (Indonesian Nationalist Party/PNI) supported the President's statement, arguing that the speech was the special prerogative of the President.[115]

It is clear from the above that Sukarno was very careful in dealing with the Muslims. His numerous statements and speeches, some of which are quoted above, seemed to show that Sukarno was trying to lead the newly established country into a direction that would not irritate certain religious or ethnic groups, especially the Muslims as the majority of the population. However, Sukarno's support for a secularist philosophical basis of the state, as opposed to a religious philosophical basis, was apparent. This had much to do with Sukarno's *abangan* background.

It is clear as well that what occupied Sukarno's mind during and after independence was the political issue of the newly-born state. Issues such as the Constitution and national integration were central in Sukarno's agenda. Therefore, it is understandable that other issues, such as missionary activities in the context of Muslim–Christian relations, did not attract his attention. Moreover, Muslim disappointment in the failure to implement Islamic teachings within the Indonesian state and in Christian missionary activities was not translated into physical conflict with Christians which would require Sukarno's particular

---

[114] Herbert Feith, *The Decline of Constitutional Democracy in Indonesia* (Ithaca and London: Cornell University Press, 1962), 281.

[115] Feith, *The Decline of Constitutional Democracy*, 281-282.

attention. Nevertheless there was a government decree (*Ketetapan Presiden*) No. 1/1965 on the Prevention of the Mistreatment of Religion. This decree was issued in response to some events that happened during early 1965, in which some spiritual organisations (*aliran kepercayaan*) in various areas of Indonesia attempted to interpret certain religious teachings from their own perspectives.[116] These events created uneasy feelings among religious believers but had no direct bearing on the issue of Muslim–Christian relations.

In September 1965, Indonesia witnessed the so-called 'Communist' coup, also known as the September 30th Affair or G 30 S/PKI, in which the Indonesian Communist Party (Partai Komunis Indonesia/PKI) was blamed as the master mind behind the coup.[117] On 1 October 1965, Major-General Soeharto (b. 1921), who held a position at Army Strategic Reserve Command (Komando Cadangan Strategis Angkatan Darat/Kostrad), took command of the army in the absence of A.H. Nasution (Minister of Defence and Security, d. 2000) and Achmad Yani (Chief of Staff of the Armed Forces, d. 1965). From there Soeharto, with the support of the army, built his power, especially in the period 1965–1967, until he was finally named Acting President in March 1967.

Concluding Remarks

The Dutch discriminatory treatment towards Muslims left animosity within Muslim feelings. Muslims began to learn to identify the colonists with the Christians. At the societal level, this was shown by, for example, the writings produced in the early 20th century by both Muslims and Christians, which were mainly quite inflammatory. When Indonesia

---

[116] Sudjangi, *Kompilasi Peraturan Perundang-undangan Kerukunan Hidup Umat Beragama* (Jakarta: Departemen Agama RI, 1997/1998), 87-94.

[117] The October 1 1965 coup has been a subject of dispute. Some argue that it was a Communist coup. Others believe that it was prepared by the Indonesian Army to topple Sukarno's presidency; see for example Benedict Anderson and Ruth T. McVey, *A Preliminary Analysis of the October 1, 1965, Coup in Indonesia* (Ithaca, N.Y.: Modern Indonesia Project, Cornell University, 1971). Merle Ricklefs, however, proposed a more reasonable argument that, due to the intricacies of the political situation at that time, it seemed impossible that the event was masterminded by a single person or organisation; see Ricklefs, *A History of Modern Indonesia*, 338.

was preparing for independence, some key figures (including Muslims and Christians) were in dispute over the philosophical basis of the state. Muslims attempted to impose Islamic law as the basis of the state, considering Islam as the religion of the majority of Indonesians. Nevertheless, Islam was not adopted as the basis of the state, and at state level the problem was seen as solved. However, for Muslims, the matter was incomplete, and they felt obliged to make other attempts to implement Islamic law. More importantly, Muslims saw that Christianisation effort was ongoing and were alarmed with the growing number of Christians, especially at the end of the first half of the 1960s. The Muslims' worries did not seem to concern Sukarno, who was heavily occupied with problems within the newly-born state. Even though he did not support the idea of adopting Islam as the basis of the state, weakening Islamic political power was not an agenda within Sukarno's government as it had been for the Dutch government. This was to change in the New Order period; this is discussed in the next chapter.[]

4

The New Order
and Muslim–Christian
Relations (1965–1998)

Introduction

With the shift of presidency from Sukarno to Soeharto, Muslim–Christian relations underwent some substantial changes. These changes stemmed from one major policy issued by Soeharto's New Order government (1965–1998): the policy of SARA (*Suku, Agama, Ras, Antargolongan*/Ethnicity, Religion, Race, and Inter-group relations). This chapter discusses the New Order's policies, which exacerbated tensions between Muslims and Christians. The chapter has four sections. Section one examines Soeharto's SARA policy of 'othering' the ethnic Chinese, who are mainly Christians, and of weakening Islamic political power. It will include a discussion on Soeharto's different attitude towards Muslims in the early 1990s. The role of Muslims, *abangan* and Christians in the New Order bureaucracy will be discussed in section two. Section three analyses other sources of Muslim animosity towards Christians. Section four explores government-sponsored efforts for inter-religious dialogue. The focus of this section is to explore these efforts in order to later examine the extent to which they were genuinely aimed at promoting religious tolerance between different believers.

It is important to underline that the discussion on the New Order here is not meant to provide a complete picture of the regime's political outlook. Many studies have been conducted and provided sufficient details of the New Order's politics during its 32-year reign. Much has also been done on the New Order's attitude towards Islam in its connection to various issues. Therefore, this chapter will only look at a few essential cases in which the New Order policies had an effect on Muslim-Christian relations in Indonesia.

Soeharto's SARA Policy and Muslim-Christian Relations

Soeharto's New Order Policy was based on SARA. The government banned discussions on ethnicity, religion, race, and inter-group relations. People were frightened to talk about SARA issues. The reason given for the banning was that discussions on SARA issues might lead to conflicts and destabilise the unity of the Indonesian nation. Relating to that, the New Order government defined four major problems within Indonesian society that should be overcome: the 'ethnic Chinese',[1] 'fundamentalist Islam',[2] Communism, and the West.[3] With regard to the theme of the thesis, the first two will be examined, with the aim of exploring the extent to which the SARA policy towards Chinese and Islam or Muslims influenced relations between Muslims and Christians. In presenting each issue, the policy is first discussed and then analysed in its connection to Muslim-Christian relations.

---

[1] The term 'ethnic Chinese' here refers to the Indonesians of Chinese descent (in Indonesian: orang Cina, or keturunan Cina, or orang Tionghoa). Hereafter it will be cited as the Chinese.

[2] The term 'fundamentalist Islam' or 'fundamentalist Muslims' was used by the New Order government to refer to Muslims who were active in advocating the establishment of an Islamic State or were eager to see Islamic teachings officially implemented in Indonesia.

[3] Ariel Heryanto, 'Ethnic Identities and Erasure: Chinese Indonesians in Public Culture', in *Southeast Asian Identities*, ed. J.S. Kahn (Singapore: ISEAS, 1998), 97. An army seminar held in Bandung, West Java, from 25 to 31 August 1966 declared that Indonesia's main enemies were Nekolim, an abbreviation for 'neo-colonialist imperialists' (including Western countries and the Chinese), the PKI and their followers; see Leo Suryadinata, *The Chinese Minority in Indonesia* (Singapore: Chopmen Enterprises, 1978), 122.

'Othering' the Ethnic Chinese

The discussion on the Chinese within the scheme of the New Order's SARA policy is important in relation to Muslim–Christian relations in so far as their religious identity, Christianity, is concerned. The claim that the majority of the Chinese were Christians is not easy to support with comprehensive data because the proportion of Chinese who were Christians was a politically sensitive subject during the New Order period. However, this difficulty did not obliterate the perception amongst Muslims that the Chinese were mainly Christians, based on the assumed alliance between the Chinese and the Dutch, who were mainly Christians.

During the colonial period the Chinese were given a special status and were seen as companions of the Dutch. It is true that in 1884, the *Algemene Bepalingen van Wetgeving* (General Regulation on Legislative Principles) divided the people of Indonesia based on their religious orientations into two categories, namely the Europeans (persons of the Christian faith) and the Natives (all non-Christians), and the Chinese were not given a special status. Nor were they given a special status when, in 1855, article 109 of the *Regerings Reglement* (Government Regulation) divided the population based not on religion but on race. Three racial groups were defined: Europeans (*Europeanen*), Natives (Inlanders), and Foreign Orientals (*Vreemde Oosterlingen*), which included the Chinese, Arab and Indian inhabitants. However, in 1926, article 163 and 131 of the *Indische Staatsregeling* (Dutch Constitution) defined who belonged to what group and regulated the law in force for each group.[4] At this stage, the Chinese enjoyed a special privilege as they were subject to almost the entire European Civil and Commercial Codes according to the Regulation on Chinese Private Law. This special status was given by the Dutch, as the Chinese traders often served as middlemen between European

---

[4] Sudargo Gautama and R.N. Hornick, *An Introduction to Indonesian Law: Unity and Diversity* (Bandung: Alumni, 1974), 3–4.

firms and indigenous traders.[5] As a consequence of this privilege, to many Indonesians 'the Chinese personify the evils of the colonial system as much as do the Dutch'.[6] With regard to the Muslims' perception discussed in the previous chapter that Dutch meant Christians, this close relationship between the Chinese and the Dutch also categorised the Sino-Indonesians as Christians.

The assumption that many of the Chinese were Christians was not totally erroneous. Even though there were attempts from the Chinese side to embrace Islam, as it was seen as a speedy way towards assimilation with the Indonesian majority, conversion did not always mean a warm welcome for the Chinese to join the Muslim community. At times there was suspicion amongst the Muslims in regard to the motives for conversion. As a result, many Chinese turn away from their traditions by, for instance, embracing Christianity. In the late 1950s and early 1960s in Semarang, Central Java, for example, the Chinese population who were Christians constituted almost 10% of the total Chinese in the area, which was a significant increase compared to previous years.[7] In addition, the second half of the 1960s witnessed a growing increase in the number of Chinese converts to Christianity. In 1967, for example, the percentage of the Chinese in Java who were Catholics was 28.1% of the Catholic population in that area.[8] It was also noted that the large number of converts to Christianity, estimated at over 2.5 million between 1965 and 1980, were mainly nominal Muslims, animists, Hindus, and Chinese.[9]

Within the framework of SARA, Soeharto's New Order state had maximised the exploitation of the Chinese by various means. On the one hand, under the banner of the 'Assimilation Program' the government

---

[5] Gautama and Hornick, *An Introduction to Indonesian Law*, 1.

[6] Mary F. Somers, *Peranakan Chinese Politics in Indonesia* (Ithaca: Cornell University, 1964), 51.

[7] Donald E. Willmott, *The National Status of the Chinese in Indonesia*, revised ed. (Ithaca, N.Y.: Cornell University, 1961), 105.

[8] Charles Coppel, *Indonesian Chinese in Crisis* (Kuala Lumpur and Melbourne: Oxford University Press, 1983), 108–109.

[9] David B. Barrett, George T. Kurian, and Todd M. Johnson, *World Christian Encyclopedia: A Comparative Survey of Churches and Religions in the Modern World*, vol. 1, 2nd ed. (Nairobi: Oxford University Press, 2001), 372.

promulgated laws obliging the Chinese to abandon their ethnic identities by adopting Indonesian names, eliminating the Chinese language, prohibiting *Imlek* (New Year) celebrations, closing down Chinese schools, and dissolving their socio-political organisations. On the other hand, the state produced a special numbering system on the Indonesian Chinese residential cards in an attempt at 'othering' them from the rest of the indigenous population (*pribumi*). At first glance, one may argue that this policy proved Soeharto's inconsistency towards Chinese. While the banning of anything 'Chinese' could be interpreted as his 'good' intention to integrate them into the *pribumi* majority, by distinguishing their identity cards it was clear that Soeharto did not intend to treat the Chinese as equal with *pribumi*.[10] Upon closer examination, Soeharto's purpose becomes clearer. The military-backed 'Assimilation Program' was based on a belief in the incompatibility of Chinese identity with the national personality. Through this program, the government wanted to emphasise that the dichotomy of *pribumi* and non-*pribumi* was something natural and primordial. This label was found to be very useful in the process of 'othering' the ethnic Chinese.[11]

Another means of Chinese exploitation that Soeharto used within the scheme of SARA was their role in the economic sector. In line with the government's policy in developing the Indonesian economy, Soeharto chose the Chinese to build mutually beneficial economic activity. While the government provided the protection that was needed by the Chinese, exempted them from various taxes, and supported them with state bank subsidies, they in return offered the regime new investments and supplied, especially to the military, generous funding. The result was striking; during the early years of the New Order the Chinese, who constituted around 3 percent of the Indonesian population,

---

[10] Leo Suryadinata, *The Ethnic Chinese Issue and National Integration in Indonesia* (Singapore: ISEAS, 1999), 5.

[11] Ariel Heryanto, 'Ethnic Identities and Erasure', 103. Coppel holds a different view, arguing that the replacement of the word '*asli*' by the word '*pribumi*' (both mean indigenous) reflected the New Order's accommodation of Chinese sensitivities since the word '*pribumi*' lacks the sense of 'genuine' or 'authentic'. See Coppel, *Indonesian Chinese in Crisis*, 158.

were widely believed to control 70 percent of the Indonesian economy. By the 1980s, Chinese firms were playing a decisive role in the Indonesian economy. In March 1984, for example, the government invited around 400 businessmen for a workshop in Jakarta in which several Chinese conglomerates, including Liem Sioe Liong, William Soerjadjaya, and The Nan King, were expected to invest a huge amount of money for national development. During the fourth Five-Year Plan (1984–1989),[12] these Chinese businessmen were expected to invest almost half of the total national budget.[13]

However, the economic activity that seemed to satisfy both the government and the Chinese was not in fact mutually beneficial. Soeharto was as clever as ever in concealing business cooperation with the Chinese from the public.[14] Therefore, in his effort to distance himself from involvement with these businessmen, Soeharto skilfully manipulated Chinese dependency on the government in the political field. Often when Indonesians criticised his rule, Soeharto turned the criticism on the Chinese by pointing to their greed in monopolising the Indonesian business sector. One example can be cited here. In the beginning of March 1990, Soeharto invited 30 of Indonesia's top businessmen, mainly Chinese, to his cattle ranch in Bogor, West Java. At the meeting, he requested them to thank God for their wealth by promoting social equality in the Indonesian population. Soeharto's proposed method was for the Chinese to sell up to 25 per cent of their shares to co-operatives (koperasi). More importantly, Soeharto emphasised that the social inequality that was happening could lead to possible social unrest, unless these Chinese businessmen responded to the society's need.[15] The message that Soeharto wanted to spread was clear.

---

[12] The New Order government set the plan to develop Indonesia as the 'Five-Year Plan for Development' (Rencana Pembangunan Lima Tahun/Repelita) starting from 1969.

[13] 'Dicari Partner Bonafide', Tempo, 14 March 1991, 68.

[14] Attempts at publishing brief profiles of Indonesian businessmen, many of whom were of Chinese descent, by Expo and Fokus magazines were banned by the government; see John Bresnan, Managing Indonesia: The Modern Political Economy (New York: Columbia University Press, 1993), 256.

[15] 'Tak Cukup dengan Ucapan Terima Kasih', Tempo, 10 March 1990, 22-23.

He let the Indonesians know that he himself had no favour towards the Chinese and that he had criticised these businessmen for their greediness and requested them to take care of their fellow Indonesians. Soeharto played his role perfectly as a hero for the Indonesian majority. At this point the issue of *pribumi* and non-*pribumi* reappeared.

One must be suspicious of the intentions underlying the New Order's perception that the existence of *pribumi* and non-*pribumi* was something given and beyond question. The formation of an ethnic group is very subjective.[16] In fact, it is this subjectivity that differentiates ethnic groups from kinship groups. Kahn makes a good point in describing a similar situation in Malaysia. While arguing that the definition of 'Malay' is very subjective, the classification of a Muslim, Christian, Buddhist, Hindu, or animist in Malaysia is somewhat arbitrary. Whilst cultural characteristics such as language, dress, domestic architecture or religion are used to identify specific ethnic groups, the conversion of a Malaysian Chinese to Islam, the religion of most Malays, does not change that person to a Malay.[17] The definition of what is a Malay person, or what precisely is a Muslim, is very arbitrary.

As a consequence of the New Order's propaganda of 'othering' and manipulating the ethnic Chinese, *pribumi* placed themselves above Chinese in the belief that the Chinese would contaminate the Indonesian 'authentic self'. This reasoning included perceptions that ethnic Chinese were 'outsiders', followed other religious and cultural traditions, were very rich, and had possible Communist leanings.[18] It is true that the anti-Chinese feeling or the violent actions directed towards the Chinese were not solely a matter of religious differences. The assumption that the Chinese were Christians did not automatically lead to

[16] Max Weber, *Economy and Society: An Outline of Interpretive Sociology*, eds., G. Roth and C. Wittich, vol. 1 (Berkeley and Los Angeles: University of California Press, 1978), 389.

[17] Joel S. Kahn, 'Class, Ethnicity and Diversity: Some Remarks on Malay Culture in Malaysia', in *Fragmented Vision: Culture and Politics in Contemporary Malaysia*, eds. Joel S. Kahn and F. Loh Kok Wah (Sydney: Allen & Unwin, 1992), 162.

[18] Ariel Heryanto, 'Ethnic Identities and Erasure', 97–98.

hostile attitudes towards them, albeit various anti-Chinese demonstrations were characterised by religious (especially Islamic) expressions. As has been discussed, the SARA policy gave the Chinese a significant role in the economic sector, which in turn helped to increase hatred amongst the Muslim majority. Therefore, the issue of Chinese relations with the *pribumi*, especially the Muslims, is complicated by religious, economic and political factors. In any case, the SARA policy of 'othering' the ethnic Chinese led to further resentment among Muslims and had its logical consequence. It is not surprising that, in any rebellion, people believe it was natural to humiliate the Chinese, and saw themselves as 'heroes' by debasing them.

Weakening Islamic Political Power

The weakening of Muslims within the frame of SARA policy is also important in explaining the relationship between Muslims and Christians in the New Order period, as some of its methodology involved Christians. As mentioned, the September 30 Affair attempted to exterminate Communism and Communist party members. At first, Muslim hopes flourished with the success of the extermination of the Communists, which was perceived as a Muslim victory. When Sukarno relinquished the presidency to Soeharto, Muslim hopes grew even bigger. They believed that then-General Soeharto would agree with them that the spiritual vacuum left empty by the Communists should be filled by Islam.[19]

It is true that Muslims, together with other civilian alliances including Christian groups and civil servants, supported the political role of the military (known in Indonesia as ABRI Angkatan Bersenjata Republik Indonesia/Armed Forces of the Republic of Indonesia) in maintaining security and providing economic stability.[20] However, Muslims sustained their hopes with two agendas: establishing an Islamic

---

[19] Boland, *The Struggle of Islam*, 158.

[20] Allan Samson, 'Indonesia 1972: The Solidification of Military Control', *Asian Survey* 13, no. 2 (February 1973): 127.

State and rehabilitating the Masyumi. In regard to their old agenda of reviving the Jakarta Charter, two examples can be cited here. First, during the June–July Sessions of the People's Congress of 1966, Muslims wanted to include discussion on the Jakarta Charter on the agenda. This was prevented because ABRI would not allow such a debate. Second, in March 1967, when Sukarno was deposed and Soeharto appointed Acting President, Muslims demanded that the President must be a Muslim and the state should be based on Islam. For the second time, this was rejected by the military.[21]

Efforts to rehabilitate the Masyumi faced the same fate. In 16 December 1965, 16 Islamic organisations, which were previously associated with the Masyumi, established Badan Koordinasi Amal Muslimin (Coordinating Institution of Muslim Groups/BKAM). One of its purposes was to lay down the foundation for the return of the Masyumi.[22] During the first half of 1966, BKAM members and supporters urged the government to rehabilitate the party banned by Sukarno. Various attempts were made through informal contacts with friends of Masyumi men within the army.[23] In May 1966, some ex-Masyumi figures, including Prawoto Mangkusasmito, Muhammad Natsir and Mohamad Roem (b. 1908), were released from confinement. By the end of 1966, the rehabilitation of the Masyumi was expected to occur very shortly. However, in playing its role as defender of Pancasila, the army gave a clear sign that they had no intentions of rehabilitating the Masyumi, which was perceived as a political party with a negative record of betraying the integration of Indonesia due to the involvement of some of its leaders in the PRRI. At the time when the Muslims wanted the rehabilitation to occur, the regional commanders of the Armed Forces issued a statement on 21 December 1966:

---

[21] Boland, *The Struggle of Islam*, 159.

[22] Samson, 'Islam in Indonesian Politics', 1004.

[23] Samson, 'Islam in Indonesian Politics', 1004–1005. See also, Ward, *The Foundation*, 21, 25.

[that it] would take firm steps against anyone, whichever side, whatever group which will deviate from Pantja Sila and the 1945 Constitution as which has already been done by the Communist Party Revolt in Madiun, Gestapu, Darul Islam/Islamic Army of Indonesia ... and Masjumi-Socialist Party of Indonesia ...[24]

Stunned by this statement, Prawoto Mangkusasmito, the former General Chairman of the Masyumi, published a denial stating that it was 'a great irony that Masjumi, which always invoked us to remain loyal to the Constitution, has now been grouped with those who have deviated from it'.[25] In his reply on 6 January 1967, Soeharto made it clear that the Armed Forces thought that the Masyumi could not be rehabilitated.[26] Realising this situation, the ex-Masyumi members and supporters devoted their energy to creating a new party that would have the same orientation as the Masyumi. Without going into detail, it is enough to state that on 7 May 1967 the BKAM formed a Committee of seven, which comprised six ex-Masyumi leaders and one leader of a supporter organisation, to establish a new Islamic party named Partai Muslimin. Indonesia (Indonesian Muslim Party/PMI).[27]

The Committee met with the military advisors to Soeharto on 20 June 1967 to discuss the formation of the party. After several debates within the organisations under the BKAM, PMI agreed not to give any ex-Masyumi figures an active role within the new party, but to place a number of them on the Executive Board.[28] Therefore, when the representatives of the supporter organisations of BKAM met Soeharto on 5 February 1968, they were astonished to hear that none of the ex-Masyumi figures would be allowed to occupy a position of central leadership. The new party could not be legalised, as a large number

---

[24] Cited in Samson, 'Islam in Indonesia Politics', 1005.

[25] Ward, *The Foundation*, 25.

[26] Solichin Salam, *Partai Muslimin Indonesia* (Jakarta: Lembaga Penyelidikan Islam, 1970), 12.

[27] Both Salam and Ward had 7 May 1967 as the date of the BKAM meeting to form the Committee of seven. However, Samson had 7 April 1967 for the meeting date. See Salam, *Partai Muslimin Indonesia*, 15; Samson, 'Islam in Indonesian Politics', 1006; and Ward, *The Foundation*, 30.

[28] Samson, 'Islam in Indonesian Politics', 1008.

of ex-Masyumi leaders were to be on its proposed Executive Board. Soeharto further stated that, for some groups of people (especially the military), the establishment of the PMI would be interpreted as the rehabilitation of the Masyumi. Therefore he asked that no ex-Masyumi figures who had been prominent when the party was dissolved be included within the leadership of the new party.[29] By removing all the Masyumi leaders from the new party leadership, the PMI was established.[30]

When the Partai Muslimin Indonesia was finally established on 20 February 1968, a week before the appointment of Soeharto as President, dissatisfaction was felt among Muslims that the new party, which was originally meant as the carrier of the Masyumi spirit, had no ex-Masyumi members in its leadership positions. More importantly, some thought that Partai Muslimin Indonesia was not fulfilling the needs of the Islamic community as it only served Soeharto's interests.[31] With Soeharto's promise that in the long run, when the Partai Muslimin Indonesia held its congress and elected ex-Masyumi members as leaders for the new party, he would not interfere with their decisions, the party council planned a congress in Malang, East Java, in the first week of November 1968. It was clear that the congress would elect some ex-Masyumi leaders. Nevertheless, another disappointment could not be avoided when Soeharto stated at the meeting on 28 October 1968 that 'It would be better not to have any change in the party leadership'. The congress went on and chose Muhammad Roem, an ex-Masyumi figure, as the General Chairman of the Partai Muslimin Indonesia.[32] The government was not pleased with this decision. In 1971, the chairmanship of the Partai Muslimin Indonesia was taken over by H.M. Safaat Mintaredja (b. 1921), the Minister of Social Affairs at that time, and

---

[29] For the minutes of this meeting, see Salam, *Partai Muslimin Indonesia*, 19-21. See also Ward, The Foundation, 36.

[30] Salam, *Partai Muslimin Indonesia*, 23-28; Samson, 'Islam in Indonesian Politics', 1008-1009.

[31] Samson, 'Islam in Indonesian Politics', 1009-1010.

[32] Ward, *The Foundation*, 51, 53.

Jailani Naro, a lawyer. Both leaders, who did not have enough ground in party politics, received full support from the government.

It is clear from the above that Soeharto's position towards Islam contradicted Muslim hopes. The perception that the Masyumi members were part of the rebellious group involved in DI/TII and PRRI convinced the New Order regime that the Muslims might destabilise Soeharto's power.[33] Compared to Sukarno, Soeharto showed a more constant resistance towards Islamic political power. This to a significant extent was related to Soeharto's personal *kebatinan* (Javanese mysticism) roots, in which Islam 'exists only in its more esoteric form and religious legalism has little force'.[34] In the years that followed, it became more obvious that the New Order government, especially in its first 20 years, had a clear agenda of depoliticising Muslim activities. Attempts at suppressing political Islam and favouring cultural Islam, as is discussed below, show a striking resemblance to the policy adopted by the Dutch.

The next move of the state anti-Islamic forces were the efforts to fuse the Islamic parties in 1973, and to force all social-political organisations to declare Pancasila as their sole ideology in 1984. The initiative of amalgamating the Islamic parties had begun with the 1955 election held in the Old Order period in which nine political parties were involved. The Indonesian Nationalist Party (Partai Nasionalis Indonesia/PNI) won the biggest vote with 22.3% of the total. Two of the Islamic parties, Masyumi (20.9% of the vote) and Nahdhatul Ulama (18.4%), came second and third. The fourth party was the Indonesian Communist Party (Partai Komunis Indonesia/PKI) with 16.4%. Other participants turned out to have become small parties. The Protestant party

---

[33] Whereas the involvement of the ex-Masyumi members in the PRRI/Permesta was direct, their association with the Darul Islam movement was less so. Feith argued that even though the Masyumi's position did not approve the method of violence that was applied by the Darul Islam members, it maintained that a political and religious approach 'was necessary to win away the rebels' popular support'. In contrast, the military did not support any negotiation with the Darul Islam leaders and perceived that the Masyumi members were somehow connected with the rebels; Feith, *The Decline of Constitutional Democracy*, 211.

[34] Ricklefs, *A History of Modern Indonesia*, 345.

(Partai Kristen Indonesia/Parkindo) and the Catholic party (Partai Katholik) won 2.6% and 2.0% respectively. The other two Islamic parties were PSII (Partai Sarikat Islam Indonesia) with 2.9% and Perti (Persatuan Tarbiyah Islamiyah) with 1.3%. The Socialist party (Partai Sosialis Indonesia/PSI) won 2.0% of the total vote.

This election result had created much discontent for the Islamic parties as they had pinned their hopes on receiving enormous support from the Muslim majority. In contrast, the New Order government interpreted the 1955 election result as a potential strength within the Islamic parties that could threat the government, especially with the collapse of Communism in 1965. Before the New Order government would consent to a first general election, it wanted to make sure that neither the Old Order nor other parties would win. Therefore, as early as 1968, Soeharto had suggested to Ali Moertopo, of Soeharto's private staff (Staf Pribadi/SPri, d. 1984), to use Sekretariat Bersama Golongan Karya (Joint Secretariat of Functional Groups/ Sekber Golkar), the government-sponsored 'non-party' established in 1964, as an electoral organisation.[35] The result was striking. In the 1971 election, Golkar won a decisive victory by receiving 62.8% of the total votes. It is true that the government should have predicted its victory because the election was not free from government manipulation and pressure. Nevertheless, the government was surprised to see how high the Golkar vote was.[36] NU was able to maintain its voting strength with over 18%. The 1971 election result gave Soeharto the confidence to take the final step in dismantling the old parties. Therefore, in approaching the 1977 election, the second to be held during the New Order period, the government proposed an electoral reform. The reform included several components, two of which were noteworthy as they were related to the issue of depoliticising Muslim

[35] K.E. Ward, *The 1971 Election in Indonesia: An East Java Case Study* (Clayton, Australia: Centre on Southeast Asian Studies Monash University, 1974), 10.

[36] Ricklefs, *A History of Modern Indonesia*, 360.

activities: the consolidation of Golongan Karya (Golkar) as the regime party, and the fusion of the existing political parties.

The first component was the consolidation of Golkar as the government party. Understanding Golkar's activities makes it clear that the party served the government's interest. Golkar's top leaders were dominated by the military personnel, chief amongst them being Generals Soemitro (d. 1998) and Darjatmo of the Ministry of Defence, Major General Amir Mahmud of the Ministry of Home Affairs, and Brigadier General Ali Moertopo.[37] In fact, Golkar was an amalgam of the military and the civilian bureaucracy. It continued to mobilise government officials to pressure regional officials and village heads to vote for Golkar. Golkar also developed a mechanism to ensure that all civil servants did not vote for any other party, and made them swear their 'singular loyalty' (monoloyalitas) to Golkar. Sanctions such as dismissal, if a person was caught not for voting for Golkar, were common. The Muslims too were not exempt. For example, those who worked at the Department of Religious Affairs, commonly recruited from various Islamic parties, were given a year and a half's grace (1973–1974) to be members of political parties other than Golkar, but yet were subject to the principle of monoloyalitas after that period.[38] It was not surprising that in the elections of 1977, 1982, and 1987 Golkar was victorious (see Table 1).

The second component of the electoral reform was the fusion of the existing parties. Ali Moertopo urged the New Order government to take direct action to control the Islamic parties to stop them reaping the benefits from the fall of the Communist party. More importantly, Ali Moertopo suggested that the effective way to weaken the Islamic parties was to fuse the modernist (as represented by Masyumi) and traditionalist (represented by NU) leaders into one political group, as the two would

[37] R. William Liddle, 'Participation and the Political Parties', in *Political Power and Communications in Indonesia*, eds. Karl D. Jackson and Lucian W. Pye (Los Angeles: University of California Press, 1978), 182–183.

[38] Robert Hefner, *Civil Islam: Muslims and Democratization in Indonesia* (Princeton and Oxford: Princeton University Press, 2000), 101.

have difficulties in dealing with each other.[39] Soeharto shared Ali Moertopo's belief that the fusion of several existing parties would make them more manageable to control.

Table 1: 1971, 1977, 1982, and 1987 Election Result[40]

	1971[41]	1977	1982	1987
Golkar	62.8%	62.1%	64.3%	73.2%
PPP	27.1%	29.3%	27.8%	16.0%
PDI	10.1%	8.6%	7.9%	10.9%
Totals	100.0%	100.0%	100.0%	100%

In 1973 the fusion was forced upon the existing parties by government edict. The Islamic parties were amalgamated into Partai Persatuan Pembangunan (United Development Party/PPP), which was not permitted to adopt an Islamic name. The Partai Demokrasi Indonesia (Indonesian Democratic Party/PDI) was formed by merging the nationalist parties and two Christian parties. After the 1977 election, the PPP was forced to change its Islamic symbol from the *ka^ba* (toward which the Islamic prayer is directed) to a star.[42] Some scholars argue that the fusion was a deliberate attempt to control NU as it was the only major party that was capable of maintaining its voting strength. Liddle, for example, argued that 'NU has been the govern-

---

[39] Hefner, *Civil Islam*, 100–101.

[40] For election results of 1971, 1977, and 1982, see Leo Suryadinata, *Political Parties and the 1982 General Elections in Indonesia* (Singapore: ISEAS, 1982); for 1987, R. William Liddle, 'Indonesia in 1987: The New Order at the Height of Its Power', *Asian Survey* 28, no. 2 (February 1988): 182.

[41] PPP percentage in this column is the total votes of the Islamic parties which became the PPP in 1973, whereas the percentage for PDI in this column is the total votes of the parties that were fused into PDI in the same year.

[42] See, among others, R. William Liddle, 'Regime: The New Order', in *Indonesia Beyond Suharto*, ed. Donald K. Emerson (Armonk, New York: M.E. Sharpe, 1999), 41–42.

ment's most vocal, persistent, and powerful critic, the closest thing there has been to a genuine opposition'.[43]

Ali Moertopo's calculation that the modernist and traditionalist leaders would not be able to work together was proven by the withdrawal of NU from PPP in 1984. NU declared its organisation to be non-political and socially oriented, even though in fact it remained active in the political arena. It is important to note that in 1987 some prominent NU figures took several trips around Indonesia to persuade their members and supporters that 'a vote for PPP is not required, for Golkar not prohibited, for PDI not a crime' (*Tak wajib nyoblos PPP, tak haram nyoblos Golkar, tak jahat nyoblos PDI*). As a result of this campaign millions of NU voters voted for Golkar.[44]

The next step after fusing and controlling parties other than Golkar was to enforce the acceptance of Pancasila by all social-political organisations (including the Council of Churches as well as Islamic and Christian organisations) as their sole ideology (*asas tunggal*). The PPP, which had to have Islam as their ideological foundation, was not exempted from this requirement as stated in the Law on Social and Political Organisations. In 1984 the PPP accepted Pancasila as its *asas tunggal* and became officially an open party.[45]

The foundation of the Partai Muslimin Indonesia and the government's attempt to control it, the efforts to fuse the Islamic parties, the pressure to vote for Golkar and to accept Pancasila as the *asas-tunggal*, which reflected SARA policy on depoliticising Muslims, were not directly related to the issue of Muslim–Christian relations. However, these have been perceived by Muslims as serial defeats following on from the battles to decide the philosophical basis of the state during the years 1945–1959. This disappointment, coupled with some other

---

[43] Liddle, 'Indonesia in 1987', 184. See also, Karl D. Jackson, 'Bureaucratic Polity: A Theoretical Framework for the Analysis of Power and Communications in Indonesia', in *Political Power and Communications in Indonesia*, 12.

[44] Liddle, 'Indonesia in 1987', 184.

[45] See, among others, Adam Schwarz, *A Nation in Waiting: Indonesia in the 1990s* (New South Wales, Australia: Allen & Unwin, 1994), 36.

government policies that will be discussed below, provided fertile ground for disharmonious relations between Muslims and Christians.

Amongst the policies that involved Christians and could be interpreted as a move to weaken political Islam was the introduction of the Marriage Bill (Rencana Undang-Undang Perkawinan/RUUP) in 1973. The debate over the Marriage Bill can be traced back to the years 1967 and 1968 when, in order to fulfil Muslim demands to see some elements of the Islamic law regulated by the government, Soeharto appointed a committee to draft a complete Marriage Law. Two Marriage Bills, namely the Marriage Bill for Indonesian Muslims (RUU Pernikahan Umat Islam) and the Marriage Bill on basic principles of marriage applicable to all religious groups (RUU Pokok-Pokok Perkawinan) were submitted in 1967 and 1968 respectively to the former People's Representative Council (Dewan Perwakilan Rakyat Gotong Royong/ DPRGR). Both bills, which accredited a separate marriage rule for Muslims and non-Muslims, were debated in Parliament during 1967–1970 and produced no result.[46] Amongst the arguments objecting to the Bills was the lack of an alternative possibility for a 'secular' wedding, namely a wedding that would not be conducted according to a certain religious law. The Christians too objected to the Bills as they thought that the Bills were reflecting the 'separation between citizens' (pengkotak-kotakan warga negara).[47] The Christians favoured a more general Bill that would accord with their marriage rules and would lessen Islamic influence.[48] More importantly, the Christians feared that the separate Marriage Bill that would be granted to Muslims might lead the latter to demand more autonomy in other areas of social, political, and economic life,

---

[46] Azyumardi Azra, 'The Indonesian Marriage Law of 1974: An Institutionalization of the Shari'a for Social Changes', in *Shari'a and Politics in Modern Indonesia*, eds. Arskal Salim and Azyumardi Azra (Singapore: ISEAS, 2003), 81-82.

[47] Boland, *The Struggle of Islam*, 168.

[48] June S. Katz and Ronald S. Katz, 'The New Indonesian Marriage Law: A Mirror of Indonesia's Political, Cultural, and Legal System', *The American Journal of Comparative Law* 23 (1975): 660.

which in turn would put the Christians' interests at risk.[49] The proposed draft was finally withdrawn by the government to be revised.

The debate re-emerged when the new Marriage Bill was proposed in 1973. The new Bill contained secular precepts and was perceived by many Muslims as contradicting the *sharīʿa*. The Muslims were infuriated because neither the Ministry of Religious Affairs nor any key Muslim leaders were consulted when the Bill was drafted.[50] Among several issues that concerned the Muslims were article 2 (1), which stated 'Civil registration was necessary for the validity of Muslim marriage', and article 11 (2), which stated 'The differences in nationality, ethnicity, country of origin, place of origin, religion, faith and ancestry should not constitute an impediment to marriage'.[51] Some Muslims rallied to the parliament building demanding that the Bill be annulled. Later, due to several protests from the Muslim side and to accommodate the Islamic perspective, the Bill was revised and was codified as Marriage Law No. 1/1974. The new formulation of the Bill included a stipulation that 'A marriage is valid only if it satisfies the religious law of the spouses'. This new formulation triggered disappointment among Catholics and Protestants.[52]

The night of 12 September 1984 also witnessed another measure of the New Order government in justifying any reason to suppress Muslim political activities. The event at Tanjung Priok Jakarta on that night had started a few days before when Hermanu, a village security officer at the district of South Koja, Jakarta, came to a local prayer house (*muṣolla*) in an attempt to remove posters that were believed capable of inciting hostility. The posters echoed Muslim protests against government pressure for all social organisations to accept Pancasila as their sole

---

[49] Daniel S. Lev, *Islamic Courts in Indonesia: A Study in the Political Bases of Legal Institution* (Berkeley: University of California Press, 1972), 139-140. The debates between Muslims and Christians over this Marriage Bill will be discussed in Chapter Five.

[50] Katz and Katz, 'The New Indonesian Marriage Law', 657.

[51] 'RUU Perkawinan: Aksi dan Reaksi', *Tempo*, 8 September 1973, 10.

[52] 'Dan Lahirlah UU Itu dengan Afdruk Kilat', *Tempo*, 29 December 1973, 5-8. See Chapter Five for more discussion on this issue.

ideology. What created the problem was Hermanu's attempt to remove the posters with drain water, which was considered *najis* (impure) in Islam. Shortly after, a local crowd gathered in front of the prayer house and rumours were spread alleging Hermanu was a Christian. In an attempt to demand Hermanu to apologise, the crowd became emotional and burnt his motor cycle.[53]

Four local people were arrested and the following days witnessed a more serious problem as speeches insulting to the government were given by mosque activists. The speeches expressed, for example, certain Muslims' disappointment at the government edict that required all social-political organisations to accept Pancasila as their sole ideology, and their discontent that the PPP had agreed.[54] After the speeches, the crowd marched to the police station in the Tanjung Priok area attempting to release the detainees, but was met by heavy-handed soldiers. Bresnan quoted that it was estimated that 63 people were killed by the military and more than 100 were severely injured. Some others were arrested and sentenced to gaol on charges of subversion.[55] This number was in contrast to the official number given by the government: 9 killed and 53 injured.[56] Even though, in its official press release, the then-Armed Forces Major-General L.B. Murdani did not name a certain religious community as responsible, in its brutal response to these Muslims the New Order regime sent a strong message of what those critical of the government's SARA policy could expect.

In addition to the New Order's anti-Islamic agenda, in the mid 1970s Soeharto was surrounded by a 'core group' including, among others, Lieutenant-General Ali Moertopo, deputy head of National Intelligence Coordinative Body (Badan Koordinasi Intelejen Negara/Bakin), Major-General Leonardus Benny Murdani (b. 1932), assistant for

---

[53] 'Huru-Hara di Tanjung Priok', *Tempo*, 22 September 1984,1215.

[54] 'Dari Perkara Priok dan Bom BCA', *Tempo*, 19 January 1985, 12-13.

[55] See, Bresnan, *Managing Indonesia*, 223.

[56] 'Huru-Hara di Tanjung Priok', 13.

intelligence to the Minister of Defence, and Admiral Sudomo (b. 1926), chief of staff of Operational Command for the Restoration of Security and Order (Komando Pemulihan Keamanan dan Ketertiban/Kopkam- tib). This group had very close access to the President and exercised decisive power in the government. In addition, Major-General Sudjono Humardani (d. 1986), who had a background in army finance and had served as Soeharto's staff when the latter was commander of the Central Java Diponegoro military region in the late 1950s, was appointed to the President's private staff.[57] These people had to a significant extent supported the government's anti-Islamic agenda. Ali Moertopo was known as one of 'the regime's main anti-Islamic figures',[58] and Benny Murdani and Sudomo were Javanese Catholics. In addition, both Ali Moertopo and Sudjono Humardani, who was also the Presi- dent's mystical guide, were the key persons in the establishment of the Centre for Strategic and International Studies (CSIS) on 1 September 1971. This was a private organisation predominantly operated by Catho- lics and *abangan*, and funded by Indonesian Chinese businessmen, which made it relevant to the issue of Muslim–Christian relations.

CSIS stated that its main activities were 'to undertake policy- oriented studies on both domestic and international affairs'. However, its main activities as a research body came under question when a study claimed that, in the late 1970s, CSIS completed an ambitious blue print called Master Plan Pembangunan Bangsa (Master Plan for the Development of the Nation), led by Liem Bian Kie (Sofyan Wanandi), an Indonesian Christian of Chinese descent.[59] This was supposed to be a long-term project to develop Indonesia, with a basic assumption that Islamic values were the factors that had hindered the national devel-

---

[57] David Jenkins, *Suharto and His Generals: Indonesian Military Politics 1975-1983* (Ithaca: Cornell Modern Indonesia Project, 1984), 20-23.

[58] Ricklefs, *A History of Modern Indonesia*, 361-362.

[59] The study was conducted by Oey Hong Lee, *Indonesia Facing the 1980s: A Political Analysis* (Hull, England: Published for South-East Asia Research Group by Europress, [pref. 1979]), 216- 217. Lee stated that the information regarding the Master Plan Pembangunan Bangsa was gathered from his 'contact person close to the PPP [Partai Persatuan Pembangunan]'.

opment and hence should be eradicated. One of its immediate plans was said to be replacing religious teachings by *Budi Pekerti* (character building), which was more secular in character. In addition, in 1982, religious-based political parties were to be prohibited, as they contradicted the secular nature of a 'political' party. In contrast, increased funding was to be given to enhance personal religious piety, such as facilitating the building of prayer houses. It was through the mediation of Ali Moertopo that this 'plan' was believed to have been sent to Soeharto for consideration.[60]

It is not easy to trace the origin of Master Plan Pembangunan Bangsa (MPPB), and it is understandable that if it existed, it was not meant for public knowledge as it would have upset Muslim.[61] However, it was clear that the intention of the CSIS intellectuals was to replace Communism and Islamic ideologies in Indonesian politics with economic development, as stated by Ali Moertopo in his various publications. For instance, Ali Moertopo's perspective on the national political strategy, written in 1974 and published by the CSIS, showed some similarities to the alleged MPPB. It stated that, until the end of the 1960s, 'The New Order government had successfully toppled any attempts both from the Communists and the Muslims to deviate Pancasila'.[62] Although the tone of his writing was descriptive, its message that he supported the replacement of Communism and Islam as the two obstacles to development was clear.

Ali Moertopo's other statement also demonstrated a similar point with the so-called MPPB. On the issue of political parties he argued that ideology-based political parties that had been introduced in the

---

[60] Lee, *Indonesia Facing the 1980s*, 217–218.

[61] Hadi Soesastro, the current Executive Director of CSIS, argued that the Master Plan never really existed. What existed was a mail with a one page attachment of a document claimed to be written by the CSIS. Hadi stated that it was this very document that was used by Oey Hong Lee as his sources for the Master Plan. Hadi further explained that he had met Lee, who promised Hadi that he would correct the information on MPPB. However, Hong Lee never corrected his information on the subject. (This information was based on an email correspondence with Hadi Soesastro conducted for this study July–August 2003).

[62] Ali Moertopo, *Strategi Politik Nasional* (Jakarta: CSIS, 1974), 17–18.

rural areas had caused excessive problems for the villagers as they tended to be involved in the political parties and neglected their daily necessities. As a solution, Ali Moertopo introduced a concept of 'floating mass', in which people in the rural areas were depoliticised.[63] This was similar to the MPPB, which urged the religious-based political parties to be prohibited, even though the prohibition he proposed here was more specific. However, what might strike one the most about the resemblance between the alleged MPPB and the CSIS intellectuals' views was Ali Moertopo's speech during the opening ceremony of Nurul Iman mosque in Jakarta on 11 July 1980. He stated that were Islam to win support to establish an Islamic state in Indonesia serious conflicts between fellow Indonesians would occur. This was so, he continued, because the disputes between the Muslims in regard to their schools of law were very sharp. Ali Moertopo concluded that Pancasila would be the best foundation for the Indonesian state, much better in comparison to Islam.[64] Hence, it is conceivable that many Muslims thought that the Chinese/Catholic Indonesians of the CSIS had conspired against them.

The last three cases discussed above, namely the Marriage Bill, the Tanjung Priok event and the role that the CSIS played in the Indonesian government, were the result of the SARA policy on suppressing any tendency of political Islam. As these cases involved or were perceived to involve Christians, Muslims believed that the Christians had been working with the government to eradicate Islamic political power. This heightened Muslim-Christian tensions.

However, by the end of the 1980s and the early 1990s, Soeharto's attitude to the Muslims changed. This alteration can be traced to Soeharto's different relationship with the army. As mentioned, Benny Murdani was Soeharto's most reliable person within the Armed Forces until 1987, when he risked his position by urging Soeharto to plan for the presidential succession and by criticising the greediness of

---

[63] Ali Moertopo, *Strategi Pembangunan Nasional* (Jakarta: CSIS, 1981), 97-99.

[64] Ali Moertopo, *Agama Bukan untuk Dipolitikkan* (Jakarta: Departemen Penerangan RI, 1980),79.

the president's children in various business activities. Soeharto appeared to be offended by Benny Murdani's advice, and sacked him from his position as the Armed Forces Commander to be replaced by General Try Sutrisno. Benny Murdani was then appointed Minister of Defence and Security (1988–1993), which was much less influential than his former position. In addition, during the Assembly meetings of 1988 to elect the vice president, some people, both military and civilian, protested Lieutenant General Sudharmono's candidacy, which was promoted by Soeharto.[65] Towards the end of the 1980s, especially after the election of Sudharmono as vice president, several important factions within the Indonesian military indicated their displeasure with Soeharto for his failure to promote them.[66] At this point, Soeharto needed to counterbalance the influence of the military. There was no question of ending the military's role as the regime was unthinkable without it. Nevertheless, Soeharto needed more room to manoeuvre, which required that the overwhelming weight of the military be counterbalanced in some way.

In 1990 Soeharto saw an opportunity to gain support from Muslims when he agreed to the establishment of Ikatan Cendekiawan Muslim Indonesia (Association of Indonesian Muslim Intellectuals/ ICMI). Soeharto's agreement to this establishment was important for Muslims because ICMI was the first indication that Soeharto might allow some organised Islamic political influence. The role of B.J. Habibie (b. 1936), Soeharto's protégé who became the third President of Indonesia, was central in linking the government with Islamic circles through ICMI. Himself a devout Muslim and an intellectual, he made Islamic intellectuals trust him to be the head of the new organisation. Among the key intellectuals in the founding of ICMI were Dawam Rahardjo (b. 1942), Nurcholish Madjid (b. 1939), and Imaduddin Abdulrahim (he was

---

[65] Salim Said, 'Suharto's Armed Forces: Building a Power Base in New Order Indonesia, 1966–1998', *Asian Survey* 38, no. 6 (June 1998): 541.

[66] See, among others, The Editors, 'Current Data on the Indonesian Military Elite: July 1, 1989–January 1, 1992', *Indonesia* 53 (April 1992): 93–136; and Benedict Anderson, 'Current Data on the Indonesian Military Elite', *Indonesia* 48 (October 1989): 65-96.

detained on several occasions in the early 1970s and was denounced as a 'fundamentalist' by security forces). While on the one hand the establishment of ICMI has been perceived by many as a new phase in the relationship between the government and Islam, it could be seen as marking the emergence of sectarianism in Indonesia. Shortly after its establishment, there emerged the Forum for Indonesian Hindu Scholars (Forum Cendekiawan Hindu Indonesia/FCHI) and the Association of Indonesian Buddhist Scholars (Keluarga Cendekiawan Buddhis Indonesia/KCBI), and two long established but non-active Christian organisations (Persatuan Inteligensia Kristen Indonesia/PIKI and Ikatan Sarjana Katolik Indonesia/ISKA) re-emerged. This situation concerned some Indonesian intellectuals, including Deliar Noer (b. 1926), Djohan Effendi, and Abdurrahman Wahid, who refused to join ICMI. This also provided an impetus for the creation of a forum in which democracy was the main framework. The establishment of Forum Demokrasi, with Abdurrahman Wahid (b. 1940) as its leader, was meant to counter the above-mentioned religious-oriented associations.[67] It is not difficult to see that the government was very restrictive towards Forum Demokrasi's activities and its members.

In June 1991 Soeharto and some of his family members went to Mecca to perform *hajj* (pilgrimage). This was the 70-year-old Soeharto's first *hajj*. Muslims differed in their opinions on the true intention of this pilgrimage. Some thought that he was merely performing his religious duty and did not see any reason to suspect Soeharto's intention. In various Friday prayers, numerous *ᶜulama'* expressed their happiness at this event as it erased doubts in their minds about the Islamic quality of Soeharto's family. However, others maintained that it was a political *hajj*, especially when considering its timing, as the general election would be held shortly in the following year. Not only were Indonesians

---

[67] For account on Forum Demokrasi, see for instance, Herdi SRS, 'Forum Demokrasi (Democratic Forum): An Intellectuals' Response to the State and Political Islam', *Studia Islamika*, 2, no. 4 (1995): 161-182.

suspicious of Soeharto's intention, but also some foreign scholars connected this pilgrimage with the coming election.[68]

In November 1991 Soeharto inaugurated the establishment of an Islamic Bank (Bank Muamalat Indonesia/BMI). The mobilisation of the funding for the new bank was held at the government palace in Bogor, West Java, and was attended by many Muslim businessmen including Aburizal Bakrie, Fahmi Idris, and Fadel Muhammad, as well as some Muslim religious figures such as Hasan Basri (of the Council of the the *ʿUlamā'* of Indonesia/Majelis Ulama Indonesia), Achmad Azhar Basyir (Muhammadiyah) and Ali Yafie (NU). From this meeting, the BMI collected more than 110 million rupiah as capital. It is worth questioning why the establishment of an Islamic bank, which was proposed in 1973, was only achieved in 1991. One may argue that it should be understood within the president's efforts to woo the Muslims before the general election of 1992. However, the MUI leader, Hasan Basri, rejected this argument, stating that the idea of establishing the BMI came from the MUI.[69]

Soeharto's favouring of the Muslims as discussed above did not automatically ease the tense relations between Muslims and Christians. Firstly, Muslims were not sure whether Soeharto was sincerely supporting Islam or was only 'playing the Muslim card'. Secondly, as was shown in the case of ICMI, his attitude to Islam created another tense relationship between Islam on the one hand and the four other religious groups on the other.

Muslims, *abangan*, and Christians in the New Order Bureaucracy

It is difficult to provide an exact figure on the number of Muslims (*abangan* and *santri*) and Christians within the Soeharto government, as the role of different religious believers within the bureauc-

---

[68] Michael Leifer, 'Suharto's Pilgrimage to Mecca: Is There a Subplot?' *International Herald Tribune*, 21 June 1991; and Margaret Scott, 'Suharto Writes His Last Chapter', *The New York Times Magazine*, 2 June 1991.

[69] 'Bank dengan Agunan Amanah,' *Tempo*, 9 November 1991, 22.

racy was a taboo under the SARA policy discussed above. However, looking back at the essential role that the military played in paving the way for Soeharto's power, it is not surprising that the military held major strategic bureaucratic positions within the New Order government. What can be observed from much research that has been conducted on the role of the military, especially the army (Angkatan Darat), in Soeharto's government is the army's policy in recruiting its staff as far as religion is concerned. In addition, one can also survey the number of Muslims and Christians within the cabinet portfolios. To serve the purpose of this study, this section examines a few important examples to depict the role of the *abangan, santri* and Christians within the New Order government, especially from the 1970s to the early 1990s.

As soon as Soeharto assumed power, active and retired military personnel controlled the higher central bureaucracy not only by dominating various leading positions in the Department of Defence and Security, but also by gaining increasing power in other departments within the New Order government. For example, within the Department of Home Affairs, the military penetration increased significantly from 29 percent of the leading positions in 1966 to 71 percent in 1971, and 89 percent in 1982. The military also held leading positions within the Departments of Information, Social Affairs, Religion, Foreign Affairs and Justice. More significantly, within the Third Development Cabinet (1979–1983), active and retired military officers occupied 50 percent of the 145 positions within the higher central bureaucracy,[70] and continued to hold various important ranks in the subsequent years. At this point, the issue of Muslim–Christian relations comes to fore, as these high-ranking officers were dominated by *abangan* and Christians.

As mentioned, within the military it was General Leonardus Benny Murdani, a Catholic, who was trusted by Soeharto to control the armed forces from the mid-1970s until the late 1980s. In 1978 he was named deputy head of Bakin, and constructed an extensive military intelligence

---

[70] John A. Macdougall, 'Patterns of Military Control in the Indonesian Higher Central Bureaucracy', *Indonesia 33* (April 1982): 89–90, 96.

network. He gained more power when, in 1983, he was appointed Armed Forces Commander. Benny Murdani had built a prominent support group of non-Muslims in the military and civilian sectors.[71] Moreover, he had surrounded himself with military officers from *abangan*, Christian and other religious minority backgrounds, thus excluding many *santri* within the army from numerous leading positions.[72] At the point of recruitment, most of the *santri* were screened out by various ways.[73] For those *santri* Muslims already in the army, it was very difficult to get promotion or to achieve the top positions. For example, Hartono Mardjono, a Muslim politician and former member of Parliament stated:

> [I]n the recruitment of officers of the army's elite troops, from 20 candidates admitted, 16 were Christians. The rest were two Muslims, one Hindu and one Buddhist. The recruitment tests were held during Friday prayers, when Muslims had to be in the mosque. Because of that the Muslim candidates lost their chance. This was one of their methods to corner the Muslims.[74]

In addition to the military domination by *abangan* and non-Muslims, especially Christians, the portfolios of economic affairs within the New Order cabinet were also dominated by Christians. In the Fourth Development Cabinet (1984–1988), for example, Radius Prawiro (a Protestant) was appointed Minister of Finance, and Johannes Sumarlin (a Catholic) Minister of State for National Development Planning and Chairman of National Development Planning Agency (Badan Perencanaan Pem-

[71] Said, 'Suharto's Armed Forces', 543–544.

[72] R. William Liddle, 'The Islamic Turn in Indonesia: A Political Explanation', *The Journal of Asian Studies 55*, no. 3 (August 1996): 628–629. Even before the Soeharto period, the tendency of the army to distrust Muslims, as a result of the DI/TII rebellions, was apparent. McVey stated that as a result of DI/TII, 'The santri officer became a rare bird, and, even when the army later entered into alliance with the Muslim forces in the anti-Communist campaigns surrounding the 1965 coup, it showed a notable concern to prevent its Islamic collaborators from acquiring any real access to power'. Ruth McVey, 'The Post-Revolutionary Transformation of the Indonesian Army', *Indonesia* 11 (April 1971): 139.

[73] Robert Lowry, *The Armed Forces of Indonesia* (New South Wales, Australia: Allen & Unwin, 1996), 199.

[74] *Republika*, 3 January 1997. Quoted in Said, 'Suharto's Armed Forces', 544.

bangunan Nasional/Bappenas). In the next cabinet structure (1988–1993), Radius Prawiro was Coordinating Minister for the Economy, Finance and Industry, Johannes Sumarlin was Minister for Finance, and Adrianus Mooy (a Protestant) was Central Bank Governor.

The elimination of the *santri* from the bureaucracy and especially from the military was due to a number of reasons. First, there was a fear on the side of the government that these Muslims would revive their idea of establishing an Islamic state provided they gained increasing power. Second, the *abangan*-dominated military officers who backed the Soeharto's regime viewed Islamic teachings as hostile to their syncretic tradition.[75] These discriminatory attitudes towards the *santri* Muslims within the bureaucracy became a point of tension, especially between the *santri* on the one hand and the *abangan* and the Christians on the other, because there was a perception that somehow the *santri* Muslims were neglected.

Another possible explanation of the elimination of the *santri* from key positions within the army and bureaucracy may be found by revealing the military-bureaucracy-Christian-education links. One major point here is that Christians tended to have higher educational qualifications in the 1970s. In a research that was based on the 1971 census data, it was apparent that Christians received better education than Muslims. All over Indonesia, 41.5% of Muslims had no education at all, whereas Christians with no education were about half of this number (22.4%). The number of Christians who completed high school was three times higher (17.0%) than that of Muslims (5.5%), and four times higher (1.2%) than Muslims (0.3%) at tertiary level.[76] This situation allowed the Christians to be over-represented in positions requiring educational qualifications.

---

[75] Nawaz B. Mody, *Indonesia under Suharto* (New York: APT Books Inc., 1987), 151.

[76] Gavin Jones, 'Religion and Education in Indonesia', *Indonesia* 22 (October 1976): 52–53.

Other Sources of Muslim Animosity towards Christians

It has been mentioned above that Muslims believed that Christians were to some extent involved in implementing the SARA policy practised by the New Order government. It has also been shown that, in several cases, Christians were indeed involved in marginalising the role of Muslims in the Indonesian state. The issue of conversion to Christianity in the aftermath of the 1965 coup heightened Muslim animosity towards Christians. Furthermore, there were several Christian-owned social services which were of a higher standard than the ones owned by Muslims. Some Muslims believed that these social services were conducting Christian missionary activities, which added to their hatred towards the Christians.

Conversion to Christianity

Closely related to the coup of 1965 was Christianisation. The attempts at exterminating Communism and Communist party members had caused a significant number of Indonesians, including some PKI members and *abangan*, to embrace Christianity. One report stated that in a period of six years (1965–1971), more than two million Javanese were converted to Christianity. During July–August 1966, some 10,000 persons were baptised at the East Java Christian Church, and in 1966-1967 the Karo Batak Protestant Church baptised over 26,000. Similarly, the number of Catholics in Indonesia rose from 2.2 million in 1969 to 2,538,000 in 1972.[77] Moreover, the shift in population in so far as religions are concerned was also shown by the increase in the Catholic population from just 275,000 in 1923 to almost 8 million in 2000.[78] Table 2 gives the comparative numbers of Muslims and Christians in 1971 and 1990.

---

[77] Barrett, Kurian, and Johnson, *World Christian Encyclopedia*, vol. 1, 374-375.

[78] *New Catholic Encyclopedia* (Detroit: Thomson/Gale; Washington, D.C.: Catholic University of America, 2002-2003), 430.

Table 2: Comparative Number of Muslims and Christians in 1971 and 1990[79]

	1971	Percentage of the total population	1990	Percentage of the total population
Muslims	103,579,496	87.5%	156,318,610	87.2%
Christians (Catholics and Protestants)	8,741,706	7.5%	17,232,563	9.6%

Some reasons can be put forward here to explain these conversions. Firstly, in the aftermath of the killings, it was the Christians, and not the Muslims, who were more willing to accept the ex-Communists. Various stories from the Communist side illustrated Muslim-Communist relations at that time. In one interview about the ex-Communists, who had embraced Christianity, it was stated that their reason not to embrace Islam was the Muslims' harsh treatment of them. The interviewee stated that 'The situation did not allow me to worship, because every day I heard slander, felt pressures, and heard threats to those of us who had been communists'.[80] Hence, at the moment when these ex-Communists needed a new identity, it was the Christians, and not the Muslims, who were ready to give them shelter and to embrace them as part of their community.

Secondly, ex-Communists and nominal Muslims found it hard to follow the Islamic precepts (such as prayer five times a day and fasting) and to avoid the prohibitions (such as on eating pork). Moreover, the fact that the Muslims had to use the Arabic language in their prayers was perceived by the ex-Communists as the failure of Islam to communicate its belief in a language that they understand. They cited two reasons. First, the ex-Communists thought that extra effort was needed

---

[79] *Sensus Penduduk 1971* (Jakarta: BPS, March 1975), and *Hasil Sensus Penduduk 1990* (Jakarta: BPS, 1990).

[80] Willis, *Indonesian Revival,* 50.

to memorise the words. Second, even if they could memorise them, more effort was needed to understand the meanings.[81] Therefore, Christianity was more attractive to them in comparison to Islam, as the former offered an easier way to practise religious teachings, such as reciting prayers in the Indonesian language.

That the government had become more tolerant towards Christian missionary activities and Christians had utilised this chance to gain more followers created tense feelings among Muslims. Moreover, apart from the Muslims' 'faults' in neglecting the ex-Communists, the fact that the Christians claimed a great number of new converts angered the Muslims and worsened Muslim–Christian relations. Nevertheless, this did not mean that there was no personal cooperation between Muslims and Christians, especially in 1965. For instance, it was Z.E. Subchan, a unique figure within the Nahdhatul Ulama, who after the 1965 coup worked together with Harry Tjan Silalahi of the Catholic party and Mar'ie Muhammad of the Himpunan Mahasiswa Islam (Muslim Student Association/HMI) to bring Sukarno down. These three people pioneered the foundation of an anti Communist action group named Kesatuan Aksi Pengganyangan Gerakan September Tigapuluh (Action Front to Crush the Thirtieth of September Movement/KAP Gestapu).[82]

Social Services Owned by Christians

In the field of medicine, Christian hospitals in different parts of Indonesia are well known for their services. To name a few, there are St. Carolus Hospital in Jakarta, Bethesda and Panti Rapih Hospitals in Yogyakarta, Advent Hospital in Bandung, Charitas Hospital in Palembang (South Sumatra), and Gunung Maria Hospital in Tomohon (North Sulawesi). In addition, the Protestant churches reported in 1971 that medical facilities operated by 23 churches included 23 hospitals,

---

[81] Boland, *The Struggle of Islam*, 232. See also, Willis, *Indonesian Revival*, 49.

[82] Harold Crouch, *The Army and Politics in Indonesia*, revised ed. (Ithaca and London: Cornell University Press, 1978), 141.

10 clinics, 7 dispensaries, 8 maternity hospitals, 8 maternity clinics, 7 health centres, 41 family planning clinics and 3 leprosaria. These numbers increased significantly in 1975, when the division of health of the Council of Indonesian Churches coordinated 27 hospitals and 148 clinics staffed by 62 physicians, 385 nurses, 76 midwives and 335 other staff.[83] Similarly, it was reported that, in 1980, Catholic hospitals provided 6,302 beds, and took care of 183,000 patients. It is worth noting that more than 60 percent of the patients treated at Catholic hospitals in Indonesia in 1980 came from poor families.[84] This apparently worried some Muslims, as the medical service could be used as a means of converting Muslims to Christianity.

Another field of Christian social service is education. As in the medical field, Christian schools and universities have provided one of the best education systems in the country. Stella Duce and De Britto High Schools in Yogyakarta, Kanisius and St Ursula High Schools in Jakarta, Santo Thomas Catholic High School in Medan, South Sumatra, Satya Wacana Christian University in Salatiga, Central Java, Sanata Dharma Catholic University in Yogyakarta, and Petra Christian University in Surabaya, East Java, are a few examples. The Protestant churches are heavily involved in the field of education. In 1971 it was reported that these churches were involved in 230 kindergartens, 2,158 elementary schools, 75 junior and 62 senior high schools, as well as 75 junior and 78 senior trade and vocational schools. Similarly, in 1972, the Catholic church operated 381 kindergartens, 2,823 elementary schools, 610 junior high schools, 137 senior high schools and 275 vocational schools.[85]

Closely related to the Christian education system was the National Education System Law (Undang-Undang Sistem Pendidikan Nasional) No. 2/1989. Article 28 no. 2 of this law stated 'In order to be

---

[83] Barrett, ed., *World Christian Encyclopedia*, 384.

[84] A. Hauken SJ, *Ensiklopedi Populer tentang Gereja Katolik di Indonesia* (Jakarta: Yayasan Cipta Loka Caraka, 1989), 348-349.

[85] Barrett, ed., *World Christian Encyclopedia*, 384.

appointed as teachers, persons have to believe in God, comprehend Pancasila and the 1945 Constitution, and meet all the qualifications'. However, the explanation of this article created debate, especially among Christians, as it ran as follows: 'Teachers who teach religious studies have to have the same religion as the subject she or he is teaching'. Father Widjojo, a Catholic priest, argued that in the case of private schools that were religious (*sekolah swasta yang bercirikan agama*), such as the Catholic High School, it would be very difficult to provide teachers for five recognised religions (Islam, Catholicism, Protestantism, Hinduism and Buddhism). He further asserted that under this law there would be no legal guarantee to maintain the characteristic of such a school.[86] In reality, the teaching of religions other than Catholicism is not offered at Catholic institutions. The Indonesian Council of Bishops does not allow such teaching because the school orientation cannot be detached from a good understanding of Christianity. Therefore, non-Catholic students, although permitted to observe their own religion, are urged to understand Christianity.[87] Muslims have perceived the Christian insistence on not providing religious studies other than Christianity in Christian schools as efforts at Christianisation.

Publishing houses and mass media are two other high standard services offered by the Christians. In 1975, 27 publishing houses belonged to Protestants and 22 to Catholics. One of the most important Protestant publishing houses is Badan Penerbit Kristen Gunung Mulia (BPK). BPK's publications include non-religious knowledge such as medicines, psychology, sex education, and household management, in the form of pamphlets, magazines and books. Although the publications do not contain obvious Christian propaganda, the vision of BPK to proclaim the Christian message by spreading love and educating human beings has clearly coloured its publications. Since 1965 its

---

[86] S. Widjojo, 'UU Sistem Pendidikan Nasional Ditandatangani', *Hidup* 5 March 1989, 24-25.
[87] Hauken, *Ensiklopedi Populer*, 314.

production has increased to 40 to 50 titles annually, written by both Indonesians and Dutch Christians (especially theological books). [88]

The Catholic publishing houses include Cipta Loka Caraka, Dioma, Kanisius, and Obor, which put a heavy emphasis on religious publications. Cipta Loka Caraka (CRC), for example, is a continuing project of Christian Life Communities, which since 1970 has written, translated and published brochures and books in pocket size on Christian teachings. Similarly, Obor has published religious books and documents of the Council of Bishops of Indonesia since 1979.[89] In line with its aim to distribute Catholic books to all areas of Indonesia, Obor has successfully sold about 30,000 copies annually of a textbook entitled *Reading*, which heavily subsidised by the Catholic Mission in Indonesia.[90]

In addition, *Kompas*, which was born as the daily voice of Partai Katolik Indonesia (Indonesian Catholic Party) on 28 June 1965, is one of the leading newspapers in Indonesia. It started with 4,800 copies and its circulation increased rapidly every year to reach 600,000 daily in 1999. Considering its origin, some thought that the name *Kompas* was an abbreviation for *Komando Pastor* (Priest's Command). *Kompas* is one of several publications owned by Christians under the Kelompok Kompas Gramedia (Kompas Gramedia Group/ KKG), which was perceived by Muslims as the publishing house serving as the voice of Christian missionaries. This perception seemed to gain popularity when a poll carried out by KKG's weekly *Monitor* and published on 15 October 1990 ranked the Prophet Muhammad as 11th in a list of popular figures. Arswendo Atmowiloto, a Christian and Chief Editor of the weekly magazine, and the head office of KKG became targets of anger. What angered the Muslims the most was their belief that the concept of prophecy was very important within the

---

[88] Zubaidah Isa, 'Printing and Publishing in Indonesia: 1602-1970', (Ph.D. diss., Indiana University, 1972), 112.

[89] Hauken, *Ensiklopedi Populer*, 55-56 and 282-283.

[90] Isa, 'Printing and Publishing in Indonesia', 111.

Islamic faith and the poll had insulted the honoured position of the Prophet Muhammad. A large number of Islamic organisations, including Pemuda Muhammadiyah (the youth member of Muhammadiyah) and some student organisations, protested against the poll and demanded that the magazine be banned and that Arswendo be brought to justice. He was sentenced to gaol for two years. The fact that the weekly magazine was owned by the Christian media company was a point of tension for Muslim–Christian relations.[91]

As mentioned, social services conducted by Christians added ammunition to the hatred on the part of the Muslims. Another case is briefly discussed here as one example of the tensions between Muslims and Christians in daily life relationship. In early 1988, a sensitive issue arose within the Muslim community based on the claim that certain foods contained *lemak babi* (the pork fat), prohibited (*harām*) for Muslims. The issue started from a study conducted by some researchers from Brawijaya University in Malang, East Java, on the ingredients of certain food products. Tri Susanto, a lecturer on food technology, with the help of some of his students published his research listing 34 food products that contained gelatine, shortening, and lard, all of which could contain pork fat. Soon the rumour spread through the Muslim community that the products listed by Tri Susanto, and another 29 other products that were added to the list from an unknown source, were prohibited to them.[92] Muslims did not directly accuse the Chinese Christians, owners of the major food industries whose products were under suspicion, of deliberately selling the *harām* products to them, but expressed regret that these industries were not respecting consumers' beliefs. This too was a source of tension between Muslims and Christians.

---

[91] 'Arswendo' and 'Setelah "Kagum 5 Juta" Itu Diumumkan', *Tempo*, 27 October 1990, 27-30.
[92] 'Babi atau Bukan Itulah Soalnya', *Tempo*, 5 November 1988, 72-75.

State-Sponsored Efforts for Inter-Religious Dialogue

The government was one of the main supporters of inter-religious cooperation and dialogue. The state-sponsored dialogues involved followers of five religions recognised by the state mentioned above. At first glance, these efforts contradicted the SARA policy, especially on Chinese and Muslim, which had to a significant extent worsened the relationships between Muslims and Christians. It would become clear in the following that, besides some genuine intentions for promoting inter-religious dialogues, the state had its own agenda in facilitating these dialogues.

Inter-Religious Consultation Forum

After the fight for freedom, the conflicts involving Muslims, nationalists, and Christians arose within the debates over the philosophical basis of the state and other issues. During the 1950s and the first half of the 1960s, the Communists came on the scene of the conflict, as they enjoyed powerful support from Sukarno. After the demise of Communism in 1965, the Christian churches were flooded with new converts. While these converts constituted good news for the Christians, the assumption that the church had given a shelter to Communist members and supporters caused tension between Muslims and Christians.

In June 1967, it was reported that a church in Meulaboh, West Aceh in North Sumatra was burnt down by local Muslims. The building of this church had been sponsored by, among others, newly converted Chinese residents. The Muslims' anger was stimulated by the fact that the building of this new church took place inside the Muslim compound, which had few Christian residents. On 1 October 1967, another violent event took place. After the night prayer, some Muslim youths in Makassar, South Sulawesi, destroyed about twenty Protestant and Christian churches and schools and burnt some Bibles. Some sources reported that the event was instigated by a Protestant teacher named Mangunbahan, who, when was asked by some Muslim students to define the Christian view of polygamy, argued that

the concept (of polygamy) was considered adultery. This was understood by the Muslim students as an insult to the polygamous marriage
practised by the Prophet Muhammad, who during his life married
nine wives.[93] Another magazine cited a more provocative statement by
Mangunbahan, in which he pronounced that Muhammad 'was only
married to nine of his wives and lived in adultery with the others'.[94]

After the Makassar event, on 17 October 1967, the Action Committee of Indonesian Students (Komite Aksi Mahasiswa Indonesia/
KAMI) sent an open letter to Acting President Soeharto urging the
government to stop the spread of religious conflict by establishing a
consultative body to discuss religious tolerance. In addition, Mar'ie
Muhammad, the KAMI leader, urged the government to advise the
press not to expose the religious conflict that happened in Makassar,
and to issue rules that regulated state officials in commenting on religious matters to the press. Soeharto, in responding to this violent event,
reminded all religious groups to maintain high alert at the Partai Komunis
Indonesia's attempt at disuniting the Indonesian community.[95] As in
the case of other conflicts, it is difficult to draw a clear boundary as to
whether the background of the Makassar event was religiously-based
or socio-economically rooted.

About four weeks after the incident, the Indonesian Council of
Churches held its 6th Triennial Congress in Makassar. Soeharto had
urged them to go ahead with their plan despite the violent event. Through
this meeting the government hoped to show the Indonesian community as well as people outside Indonesia that peace had been restored
in Makassar. At the meeting, the Council stated that the Christians had
to make efforts to establish the free and peaceful practice of religion
throughout Indonesia. However, once it came to the question of spreading God's word, the Council's position was clear, as can be seen in

---

[93] 'The Incident of Makassar on October 1, 1967: Attempts to Repair the Crack in the Indonesian
Image of Tolerance?', *Review of Indonesian and Malayan Affairs 1*, no. 4 (December 1967): 20.

[94] See *Pandji Masjarakat*, October 1967, 25.

[95] *Djakarta Times*, 16/10/1967 and 19/10/1967, as quoted in *Review of Indonesian and
Malayan Affairs 1*, no. 4 (December 1967): 25, 29.

some of their statements: 'We must proclaim the gospel ... we must be prepared to face the consequences of our faithfulness to the Lord who commands us'.[96]

Against these backdrops, on 30 November 1967, the Inter-religious Consultation Forum (Musyawarah Antar Agama) was held in Jakarta at the initiative of the government. The meeting was chaired by the Minister of Religion at that time, K.H.M. Dachlan, and included some 20 distinguished Muslim, Protestant and Catholic leaders. In his speech, Soeharto clearly stated that the meeting was in response to religious tensions and conflicts in various areas of Indonesia. He re-emphasised his previous statement regarding attempts by the remaining followers of the Communists to disunite the Indonesian community, and about the fundamental principles of religious freedom which were guaranteed by the 1945 Constitution. Soeharto further argued that no religious community should attempt to convert another religious community. He therefore urged the leaders of the different religions to prevent any attempt at distributing religious messages which would lead to conflict, especially when they were directed at persons who had embraced a certain religion. In a similar tone, the Minister of Religious Affairs appealed for tolerance between followers of different religions. He emphasised that this tolerance constituted the most important prerequisite for the stability of economic and political life in Indonesia. Nevertheless, the meeting did not reach an agreement on the proposal that missionary activities must not target other religious believers.[97]

From that time the government, through the Department of Religious Affairs, introduced additional regulations regarding inter-religious harmony. In 1969, the ministers for both Internal and Religious Affairs signed a joint decree (No. 01/BER/MDN-MAG/1969) on the implementation of government mandates for ensuring law and order

---

[96] 'The Incident of Makassar on October 1, 1967', 28.

[97] Sudjangi, *Pembinaan Kerukunan Hidup Umat Beragama: 50 Tahun Kemerdekaan Republik Indonesia* (Jakarta: Departemen Agama RI, 1995/1996), 43-52. The Muslim and Christian views on this proposal will be discussed in Chapter Five.

and the effective administration of religious development and worship by religious followers. This decree was issued based on, for instance, the thought that the State had to ensure the freedom of every citizen to follow her/his own religion and to conduct worship according to that religion and faith. Amongst the important regulations was that the District Head (*Kepala Daerah*) had to monitor the propagation and worship of religions by their followers in order that such activities did not incite conflicts among religious followers. In addition, these activities could not be accompanied by intimidation, bribes, force, or threats of any kind, and could not violate the law or public peace and order. More importantly, the decree determined that the establishment of any place of worship would require permission of the governor of the province or a government official, who was appointed to deal with such a matter.[98]

Ministry of Religious Affairs on Inter-religious Dialogue

The government firmly underlined through its policies and regulations that religious policies of the New Order were to create a religious society instead of a political society. This was conducted through significant religious activity, including facilitating of religious worship in different government offices and the publication of Scriptures. Among the government institutions responsible for implementing religious policy was the Ministry of Religious Affairs. Mukti Ali, a Muslim scholar who had devoted a great deal of attention to inter-religious dialogue, was Minister for Religious Affairs from 1971–1978.

Mukti Ali's concept of inter-religious dialogue may be found in his writings on comparative religion; indeed, he has been named as one of the founding fathers of comparative religious studies in Indonesia. Mukti Ali emphasised that comparative religion was a method of understanding the relations between God and history, and that one of its benefits was to improve the methods of research in social sciences which in turn may guide one to overcome prejudice towards other religions. Boland pointed out that Mukti Ali advocated inter-religious dialogue on a high level through comparative religion.[99]

In this context, a criticism was directed towards Mukti Ali's concept of inter-religious tolerance that it 'Only touched the political and psychological sphere of those religious communities'.[100] Nevertheless, this claim was not totally correct. Probably at the discourse level, Mukti Ali offered a concept of inter-religious dialogue that would only benefit certain aspects of a religious community. At the level of practice, however, through various activities on religious tolerance by the Department of Religious Affairs during his ministry, Mukti Ali proposed some practicable steps. While these activities involved not just Muslims and Christians, special attention was given to these two groups. For instance, in 1977, Mukti Ali's department conducted the Cooperative Social Program (*Program Kerja Sama Sosial Kemasyarakatan*) in Jakarta and Medan, North Sumatra. Some 10 students of the Institut Agama Islam Negeri (State Institute of Islamic Studies/IAIN), 10 students of Sekolah Tinggi Teologi (Institute of Theology, a Protestant institution) and 10 students of Sekolah Tinggi Filsafat Driyarkara (Driyarkara Institute of Philosophy, a Catholic institution) were involved in panel discussions on religious issues and followed up this activity with a social program of helping local communities on practical matters.[101]

Alamsyah Ratu Prawiranegara, an army general, held the post of Minister of Religious Affairs from 1978–1982 as Mukti Ali's successor. As a political figure, he was concerned with national stability and it was in this context that, in 1978, his ministry issued two decrees (SK 70/1978 and SK 77/1978), which were strengthened by the

---

[98] Sudjangi, *Kompilasi Peraturan Perundang-undangan Kerukunan*, 102-105.

[99] Boland, *The Struggle of Islam*, 211.

[100] Ali Munhanif, 'Islam and the Struggle for Religious Pluralism in Indonesia; A Political Reading of the Religious Thought of Mukti Ali', *Studia Islamika 3*, no. 1 (1996): 108.

[101] Djohan Effendi, 'Dialog Antar-Agama: Bisakah Melahirkan Teologi Kerukunan?', in *Agama dan Tantangan Zaman: Pilihan Artikel Prisma 1975-1984* (Jakarta: LP3ES, 1985), 174. For other projects of the Department of Religious Affairs during this period, see also pages 168-174 of the same book.

joint decree of the ministers for Internal and Religious Affairs, No. 1/1979.[102] The first decree contained the guidance for religious propagation. Among the important points of this decree was the government regulation prohibiting the propagation of religion directed at people who were already of a certain faith. The decree turned the rejected proposal of the Inter-religious Consultation meeting of 1967 into a government rule. The SK 70/1978 also prohibited religious propagation carried out by the distribution of pamphlets, bulletins, magazines, books and the like in areas where the people already had another religion, or by approaching the private residences of people of another religion. This, however, does not mean that religious propagation was totally prohibited. In a speech delivered at the official meeting of the Department of Religious Affairs, Soeharto stated:

> ... preaching and religious mission (da^{c}wa) was not and could not be banned. However, there should be sincerity among us not to confuse the aims of the da^{c}wa with other goals. If one used the aims of da^{c}wa to achieve their own goals, especially when the methods applied to achieve their goals created instability within the community, then the government officials would take necessary action...[103]

The additional SK 77/1978 restricted foreign aid to religious institutions. The decree ruled that aid might only be carried out with the consent or recommendation of the Minister for Religious Affairs. In addition, for the sake of the development, propagation and leadership of religion in Indonesia, the decree ruled that the use of foreign personnel must be limited.[104] As the decree required all five religious institutions (all under the auspices of the Department of Religious Affairs) to implement this and to take any required action, it not only restricted the

---

[102] The decree No. 1/1979 on religious guidance for religious propagation and foreign aid to religious institutions was only an explanation of both decrees (SK 70/1978 and SK /77/1978) in more detail and therefore will not be separately discussed.

[103] Sudjangi, *Kompilasi Peraturan Perundang-undangan Kerukunan*, 32.

[104] Sudjangi, *Pembinaan Kerukunan Hidup Umat Beragama*, 149-154.

Christians, who received a large amount of foreign aid, but also had an impact on the Muslims, as the support they formerly received from Middle Eastern countries was to be controlled by the government. In general, however, Muslims were more supportive in accepting these decrees than Christians.[105]

During his ministry, Alamsyah Perwiranegara launched a threefold program of religious harmony: (a) internal harmony among various factions within a certain religion; (b) harmony between the various religions; (c) harmony between various religions and the government.[106] This program was a continuation of Mukti Ali's effort to develop some practicable activities involving people of different religions. The activities included a large number of meetings between religious leaders, cooperative work in daily life, and numerous publications. The message that the government seemed to emphasise through these programs was that tolerance and mutual understanding between religious communities could be achieved on the basis of common interest, such as economic development and environmental issues.

It was under Alamsyah Perwiranegara's ministry in 1980 that the Inter-religious Council (Wadah Musyawarah Antar Umat Beragama), first proposed in 1967, was established by decree No. 35/1980. Its programs were funded by the Ministry of Religious Affairs. The Council, which consisted of the leaders of MUI, MAW I, DGI, the Council of Indonesian Buddhist (Perwalian Umat Buddha Indonesia/Walubi), and the Association of Indonesian Hindu Dharma (Parisada Hindu Dharma Pusat/PHDP), agreed to sign a basic guideline for inter-religious relations.

The guidelines for the Council which were annexed to the decree required it to act as a forum for consultation and communication between religious leaders in Indonesia. The Council should also discuss mutual responsibility and co-operation amongst citizens of different

---

[105] For discussion on how Muslims and Christians responded to both decrees mentioned above, see Chapter Five.

[106] Karel Steenbrink, 'Muslim–Christian Relations in the Pancasila State of Indonesia', *Muslim World 88*, nos. 3-4 (July–October, 1998): 332.

religious, based on Pancasila and the 1945 Constitution. The decisions reached by the Council were agreements with a morally binding value and were to be taken as suggestions or recommendations for the government and society at large. In line with Pancasila, the Council agreed that any decisions reached were to be based on consultation (*musyawarah*) with the aim of achieving a consensus (*mufakat*). In the instance of a consensus not being reached, the issue in question was to be postponed and then re-discussed after allowing sufficient time to settle.[107]

The Wadah Musyawarah Antar Umat Beragama was active in responding to various events, especially those related to inter-religious relations in Indonesia. For example, in response to the incident of 12 November 1991 in which Indonesian troops fired upon a memorial procession to a cemetery in Santa Cruz, Dili (East Timor) and killed some 271 East Timorese, the Inter-religious Council issued a statement of concern and stated that the event had no connection with religious matters. This statement was meant to maintain calm, because the killing of some hundreds of East Timorese who were Christians might cause inter-religious conflict.[108]

Munawir Sjadzali took over Alamsyah Perwiranegara's post in 1982, and paid less attention than his predecessors to inter-religious dialogue. However, Tarmizi Taher, who held the post of Minister of Religious Affairs from 1993-1998, was very active in promoting Indonesian religious harmony to different parts of the world. In a paper presented in 1993, for example, he stated:

> In spite of religious pluralism in Indonesia, religious conflicts when they do occur, have never had the character of national coercion. The history of Indonesia portrays a story of religious tolerance. There is no conflict when Muslims go to mosque on Fridays and Christians go to church on Sundays. The same is

---

[107] Sudjangi, *Kompilasi Peraturan Perundang-undangan Kerukunan*, 118-122.
[108] Sudjangi, *Pembinaan Kerukunan Hidup Umat Beragama*, 131-133.

true for when the Hindus and Buddhists go to their temples. Things proceed peacefully as far as religious worship is concerned. For instance, in Ambon, Maluku, Muslims and Christians help each other in village reconstruction and even in building or renovating mosques and churches. In quite a number of large cities in Indonesia, churches and mosques stand side by side.[109]

However, the inter-religious relations in Indonesia in the years following Tarmizi's speech quoted above were not as peaceful as his depiction. Various conflicts involving Muslims and Christians happened in different parts of Indonesia, especially in the second half of the 1990s. Therefore, under his ministry, some regulations concerning inter-religious relations were issued. For instance, the decree of the Minister of Religious Affairs No. 84, 1996 on guidelines for overcoming the threat of inter-religious tolerance, listed types of religious activities that could incite tensions between different believers. Important among the elements listed were the construction of a new religious building within the compound of another religious community, religious propagation which was directed towards other believers, inter-religious marriages, and religious celebration that did not consider the neighbouring community.[110]

Majelis Ulama Indonesia and Some Fatāwā on Muslim–Christian Relations

In 1975 Soeharto proposed the establishment of the new Majelis Ulama Indonesia (MUI). This Council was first established in West Java on 12 July 1958 for security reasons due to the movement of the DI/TII. The ex-officio head of the West Java Council of the ᶜUlamā' was the regional military commander. The Central Council of the ᶜUlamā' was established in October 1962 but had no significant role

---

[109] Tarmizi Taher, 'Inter-Religious Harmony; Indonesian Experience', in his *Aspiring for the Middle Path: Religious Harmony in Indonesia* (Jakarta: CENSIS, 1997). This article was originally a paper presented at the Travelling Dialogue of the Indonesian Inter-Religious Forum to Singapore, 24-28 November 1993.

[110] Sudjangi, *Kompilasi Peraturan Perundang-undangan Kerukunan*, 176-190.

except to provide support to the government. After the 1965 event the council focused its task on missionary work (*da'wa*) and received less direction from the government. The council started to play its role as an institution for discussing religious and social matters depending on local conditions, as well as advisor to the government on the question on Muslim–Christian relations. However, their efforts were not always successful. For example, the West Sumatra Council of the *'Ulamā'* urged the provincial government to obstruct the Baptist Church's plan to build a hospital in Bukittinggi.[111] Moreover, in the case of the Meulaboh incident, before the destruction of the church occurred, the Majelis Ulama of Aceh had already reminded the local government to block the plan due to the resistance of the majority Muslim residents.[112]

When the new MUI was established both NU and Muhammadiyah *'ulamā'* were represented.[113] This was initiated by the government, which emphasised the need for a council of *'ulamā'* because 'the Catholic community is already organised through the Conference of Catholic Bishops of Indonesia, while the Protestants have a Council of Churches representing them. The Hindu and Buddhists communities also have their representations ...'.[114] However, some unwritten reasons for this establishment may be traced in the political situation of Indonesia during the years preceding 1975. As mentioned, in the 1971 election, the Islamic parties, except NU, won only a small proportion of votes, which created disappointment among their members. Secondly, when the 1973 Marriage law was initially introduced, the Muslims strongly reacted against it. These disappointments were seen by the government as a potential threat to Indonesian stability. From 1970, the government had attempted to urge on Muslims the establishment of the

---

[111] Noer, *Administration of Islam in Indonesia*, 65–68.

[112] Sudjangi, *Pembinaan Kerukunan Hidup Umat Beragama*, 29.

[113] NU *'ulamā'* had started issuing fatwā as early as 1926, and Muhammadiyah *'ulamā'* began to be concerned with fatwā in 1927; see Nadirsyah Hosen, '*Fatwa* and Politics in Indonesia', in *Shari'a and Politics in Modern Indonesia*, 168.

[114] Steenbrink, 'The Pancasila Ideology and an Indonesian Muslim Theology of Religions', in *Muslim Perceptions of Other Religions: A Historical Survey*, ed. J. Waardenburg (New York and Oxford: Oxford University Press, 1999), 285.

Council of *Ulamā'*, but was constantly repulsed by some of Muslims, who perceived the establishment of the MUI as Soeharto's effort to control them. Therefore, when Hamka (d. 1981) accepted the position of chairman of the MUI, some Muslims criticised him.[115]

The MUI played a role mainly as advisor to the government and to Muslims on religious matters and to provide *fatāwā* (pl. of *fatwā*), i.e. religious opinions on legal questions. It was not and could not be involved in practical matters such as the establishing of Islamic schools, hospitals or mosques. In its first meeting with Soeharto, the MUI expressed concern on the problem of Christianisation in Indonesia. Hamka explained to the President the interpretation of the Qur'ān 60:7–9 in order to illustrate the proselytising efforts by Christians to convert Muslims to their religion.[116] He also discussed with Soeharto the building of the Baptist Church, mentioned earlier, as an example of an obvious effort by Christians to convert Muslims through social services.[117]

In regard to Muslim–Christian relations, some examples of the MUI's *fatawā* are interesting. On 1 June 1980, a *fatwā* on inter-religious marriage was issued. It stated that a Muslim woman was prohibited (*harām*) from marrying a non-Muslim man, and that a Muslim man was forbidden (*harām*) to marry a non-Muslim woman. The interesting point of this *fatwā* was that it prohibited Muslim men from marrying non-Muslim women, an opinion that contradicted the Qur'ānic precept and classical Islamic legal texts, which give permission to a Muslim man to marry a woman of the *ahl al-kitāb*

---

[115] Rusydi Hamka, *Pribadi dan Martabat Buya Prof. Dr. Hamka* (Jakarta: Pustaka Panjimas, 1983), 192.

[116] The verses state: '[But] it may well be that God will bring about [mutual] affection between you [O believers] and some of those whom you [now] face as enemies: for, God is all-powerful and God is much-forgiving, a dispenser of grace. As for such [of the believers] as do not fight against you on account of [your] faith, and neither drive you forth from your homelands, God does not forbid you to show them kindness and to believe towards them with full equity: for, verily, God loves those who act equitably. God only forbids you to turn in friendship towards such as fight against you because of [your] faith, and drive you forth from your homelands, or aid [others] in driving you forth: and as for those [from among you] who turn towards them in friendship, it is they, they who are truly wrongdoers!'

[117] Rusydi Hamka, *Pribadi dan Martabat*, 194–195.

(People of the Book).[118] The argument of the MUI was that the harm (*mafsadah*) of such a marriage outweighed its benefits (*maslahah*).[119] This was strengthened by a statement issued by the Jakarta Council of *ʿUlamāʾ* dated 30 September 1986 urging Muslim men and women not to marry non-Muslims.[120] According to Atho Mudzhar, even though the terms 'non-Muslim' and *ahl al-kitāb* were used both in the *fatwā* of the MUI of 1980 and the statement by Majelis Ulama of Jakarta, it was obvious that these were referring to Christians, because the inter-religious marriage cases reported in the media were Muslim–Christian marriages. Hence the underlying reason for such a unique *fatwā* that contradicted the Qurʾānic notions can be found in the concerns of the *ʿulamāʾ* on the possible conversion of Muslims to Christianity. The *ʿulamāʾ* may have thought that the proselytising efforts of Christians to convert Muslims had reached a point that might endanger Muslims, so that any possibility of opening a way for conversion, in this case through inter-religious marriage, should be shut altogether.[121]

In 1992 the government appeared to challenge MUI's *fatwā* on inter-religious marriage when the Minister of Religious Affairs at that time, Munawir Sjadzali, suggested that, based on the religious heterogeneity of Indonesian society, a new formulation of the 1974 Marriage Law permitting couples of different religions to marry, should be promulgated. The MUI and other Islamic organisations, including Muhammadiyah, rejected this suggestion.[122]

---

[118] See, for example, Zakariyya al-Anshari, *Fath al-Wahhāb bī Sharh Tanqīh al-Lubab* (Beyrūt: Dār al-Kutub al-ʿIlmiyyah, 1998), 45.

[119] Majelis Ulama Indonesia, *Tuntunan Perkawinan Bagi Umat Islam Indonesia* (Jakarta: Sekretariat MUI, 1986), 71–77. However, it also possible that the MUI perceived that the Christians and Jews were no longer regarded as the *ahl al-kitāb* after the arrival of Prophet Muhammad because their religion had undergone substantial changes and alterations.

[120] Majelis Ulama DKI Jakarta, *Seruan Tentang Perkawinan Antar Agama* (Jakarta: MUI Jakarta, 1986), 1–19.

[121] Mohammad Atho Mudzhar, *Fatwas of the Council of Indonesia Ulama: A Study of Islamic Legal Thought in Indonesia 1975–1988* (Jakarta: INIS, 1993), 88–89.

[122] The debates on this issue in its relation to the 1974 Marriage Bill will be discussed in Chapter Five.

On 7 March 1981 the MUI signed a *fatwā* prohibiting Muslims from participating in Christmas celebrations because these were considered to be Christian prayers. The background of this *fatwā*, which was originally published in the MUI monthly bulletin no. 3/April 1981 and was intended for a limited audience, was the MUI's concern at seeing some Muslims actively taking part in Christmas celebrations.[123] Moreover, both Muslim society and the Department of Religious Affairs urged the MUI to issue such a *fatwā* to be used internally for Muslims who were sometimes reluctant to decline invitations to Christmas celebrations for fear of being accused of intolerance. However, an unknown source[124] disclosed the *fatwā* to various national newspapers and magazines and created a heated debate among Indonesians. Interestingly, one day after the publication of the *fatwā* in the newspapers, the MUI released a statement signed by Hamka and Burhani Tjokrohandoko (MUI secretary) withdrawing its circulation. It is important to note, however, that this statement did not revoke the *fatwā*, which still exists today. In the following days Hamka released his own opinion in national newspapers, explaining that the statement he signed did not affect the legal value of the *fatwā* itself; what was cancelled was only its circulation.[125] Within the next few months after this controversy, Hamka signed his resignation.

The statement issued by MUI following the circulation of the *fatwā* on Christmas celebrations was obviously influenced by the government. It had been a policy and common practice of the New Order government to attend *Perayaan Natal Bersama* (Christmas celebrations attended by key figures of different religions), which was seen as promoting religious harmony, and the *fatwā* was perceived as contradicting this policy. Therefore, soon after this contro-

---

[123] Majelis Ulama Indonesia, *Kumpulan Fatwa Majelis Ulama Indonesia* (Jakarta: Pustaka Panjimas,1984), 81-89.

[124] There was no evidence as to who disclosed the *fatwā* to the press. However, in the following days the MUI Secretary, Mas'udi, was fired by the Ministry of Religious Affairs as he was suspected of doing the deed. Rusydi Hamka, *Pribadi dan Martabat*, 218.

[125] 'Buya, Fatwa dan Kerukunan Beragama', *Tempo*, 30 May 1980, 12-14.

versy, the government felt obliged to intervene and forced the MUI to issue a statement explaining that, even though Muslims were not encouraged to participate in Christmas celebrations, their participation, in so far as it did not involve the ritual aspects, was not prohibited by Islam. As mentioned, the *fatwā* was never revoked by the MUI; yet the government's influence in pressuring the MUI to justify its policies was obvious from this case and others.[126]

In regard to the rivalry between Muslims and Christians in terms of proselytising, one *fatwā* and an MUI recommendation can be cited. The First was the issue of child adoption, on which a *fatwā* was issued in 1984. The *fatwā* stated that Islam would only recognise biological parenthood bound by legal marriage. Therefore, from the Islamic point of view, child adoption would not end the legal relationship between the child and her/his biological parents, and would not create a new legal relationship with the adoptive parents. The *fatwā* added that Islam supported the practice of child adoption that had no intention of changing the religion of the child or of ending the legal relationship between child and biological parents. The second was the sale of inherited lands, which produced a recommendation of the 1984 annual conference of the MUI. The MUI advised that inherited lands were to be shared by the inheritors. If, for some reasons, the land had to be sold, the MUI suggested that it be offered to other inheritors or to the owner of neighbouring land, or to other Muslim buyers from the same village.[127] The issuance of both the *fatwā* on child adoption and the recommendation cited above may again be understood within the context of tense Muslim–Christian relations. Atho Mudzhar rightly argued that the *fatwā* on child adoption was apparently issued in anticipation of the threat of Christianisation, as some Christians were believed to have practised child adoption to later convert children to Christianity, or even to educate them to become

---

[126] Another example that was not related to the issue of Muslim–Christian relations yet obviously reflected the government's influence on a fatwā was the family planning program. The MUI stated that such a program was mubah (permissible); Hosen, 'Fatwa and Politics in Indonesia', 174.

[127] Majelis Ulama Indonesia, *Kumpulan Fatwa*, 125-131.

Christian missionaries. A similar reason also urged the *ᶜulamā'* to issue their recommendation on inherited lands. The *ᶜulamā'* had apparently heard of rumours that certain Christian individuals and organisations were trying to build churches within Muslim compounds or to build houses which would function as prayer quarters.[128]

Concluding Remarks

Soeharto's role in suppressing the 1965 coup and the discourse on a 'Communist threat' were the formative bases of his New Order, within which he exercised his power for around 32 years. The relations between Islam and the state during the New Order period underwent a significant change as compared to the Old Order. During his presidency, especially until the late 1980s, Soeharto skilfully played 'Islamic and Christian cards' through his SARA policy by positioning the latter as scapegoats for policies unpopular to Muslims. This helped intensify Muslim animosity towards Christians, which had sat in Muslim consciousness since colonial times. Added to the fact of the increase of the Christian population and Christian-owned top-class social services in education, medicine and publishing, Muslim–Christian relations worsened during the New Order period.

State-sponsored efforts for inter-religious dialogue intended to ease tension between religious believers, especially Muslims and Christians, did not in fact contradict Soeharto's SARA policy, for at least two reasons. Firstly, these efforts to a significant extent served as a means for Soeharto to control his religious policy and distance religion from politics. Secondly, these efforts, such as the case of the *fatwā* on Christmas celebrations, were made to support the government's own end. It was obvious that Soeharto wanted to keep Muslim political activism at bay but at the same time to support cultural activities of Muslims. This shows a striking resemblance to the policy developed by Snouck Hurgronje discussed in Chapter Three. In the following two chapters,

---

[128] Mudzhar, *Fatwas of the Council,* 91-92.

the exclusivist and inclusivist Muslim perspectives on Muslim–Christian relations will be analysed against the theological and political backgrounds that were discussed in Chapters Two, Three and Four.[]

5

The Exclusivist Muslims'
Perceptions of Christians

Introduction

This chapter deals with the perspectives on Christians of exclusivist Muslims, as represented by Dewan Dakwah Islamiyah Indonesia (DDII), Komite Indonesia untuk Solidaritas Dunia Islam (KISDI), FPI and Laskar Jihad. Although these groups differ in terms of their background and concerns, and were not established just to address the issue of Muslim-Christian relations, they are the outspoken exclusivist groups on Muslim-Christian relations.

This chapter will be divided into five sections. It will first discuss the four exclusivist Muslim organisations and analyse the background to their emergence and interests. It will then explore the perspectives of these organisations on Muslim-Christian relations using a thematic approach. Section two briefly discusses the theological perspectives of exclusivist organisations on the Christian 'other', which to some extent have served as the basis of their attitudes on Muslim-Christian relations. The relations between religion and the state will be examined in section three. This discussion is relevant within the frame of Muslim–Christian relations because attempts by some Muslims at establishing an Islamic state would have bearing on the fate of Christians in Indonesia. Section four discusses Christianisation. As this issue has become the central concern of the exclusivist organisations, different aspects of Christianisation activities will be dealt with separately. The last section briefly analyses the conflicts in Ambon involving Muslims and Christians, with special attention to Laskar Jihad as that group was particularly active there.

The Exclusivist Muslim Organisations

A few important points need to be stated before discussing these exclusivist Muslim organisations. Firstly, in comparison to the other three groups, DDII is the oldest exclusivist Muslim organisation to give priority to the question of Muslim–Christian relations and was established partly to respond to the problems of Muslim–Christian relations. Therefore, we find more statements and programs on Muslim–Christian relations from DDII than from the other three groups. Secondly, as the emergence of each group discussed here was different, they have different emphases within their statements and programs, and argue on different aspects of Muslim–Christian relations in Indonesia.

Dewan Dakwah Islamiyah Indonesia

Dewan Dakwah Islamiyah Indonesia (Indonesian Islamic Preaching Council/DDII) was founded on 26 February 1967 at the al-Munawwarah mosque, Jakarta. The establishment was initiated by a *ḥalāl bi ḥalāl* gathering (celebration of the end of the *Ramaḍān* fasting month/ᶜ*Ied al-Fiṭr*), where some ᶜ*ulamā'* and former Masyumi leaders and activists gathered. Indeed, the establishment of DDII was sponsored by the former Masyumi activists who were concerned with the decline of morality in the *umma* (Islamic community) during the period of the Old Order.[1]

It has been discussed in Chapters Three and Four that efforts of the ex-Masyumi leaders to take part in the New Order political sphere were closely monitored and even circumscribed by the government. Realising that the government would not easily assist the former Masyumi activists to revive their political career, these Muslims directed their endeavour to *daʿwa* (mission).[2] This effort for *daʿwa* was significant in two ways. First, given the pressure from the New Order government, it was better for Muslims to concentrate on social activities rather than on political organisation. As leaders of the *umma*, the former Masyumi activists believed that they were responsible for conveying the Muslims' voices. The fact that these leaders could no longer express their voice through political institutions led them to think of an alternative. It was against such a background that DDII was founded and it was logical that its establishment took the form of *yayasan* (foundation), to be legalised only by a notary.[3] Even though the Yayasan Dewan Dakwah Islamiyah Indonesia had a sizable board, it did not have a formal membership and therefore consisted of some founders and supporters. Second, the choice of the word *dakwah* (*daʿwa*) carried special meaning. Although it could be simply translated as 'mission', the DDII founders understood the word in a broader sense of religious and social practices. However, this did not mean that the activities of DDII were detached from missionary activities.

The *ḥalāl bi ḥalāl* meeting chose Mohammad Natsir by acclamation as the leader of DDII, and he took the chair for 26 years (1967–1993). Indeed, Natsir was the most influential leader within the

---

[1] Buchari Tamam, *Laporan Kegiatan DDII Pusat Selama 24 Tahun pada Tasyakur 24 Tahun DDII* (Jakarta: Dewan Dakwah, 1991), 2-3. This section does not aim at explaining the complete history of DDII. A study of DDII has been conducted by, among others, Asna Husin, 'Philosophical and Sociological Aspects of Da'wah: A Study of Dewan Dakwah Islamiyah Indonesia' (Ph.D. diss., Columbia University, 1998).

[2] Lukman Hakiem, *Perjalanan Mencari Keadilan dan Persatuan: Biografi Dr. Anwar Harjono, SH* (Jakarta: Media Dakwah, 1993), 235. See also Buchari Tamam, *Laporan Kegiatan DDII*, 3.

[3] Tamam, *Laporan Kegiatan DDII*, 4.

organisation and who helped shape the direction of DDII. Born in West Sumatra on 17 July 1908, Natsir was educated at European schools and undertook informal religious studies in Bandung, West Java, under the supervision of Ahmad Hassan (the leader of *Persatuan Islam/ Persis*). Natsir was always actively involved in various Muslim movements. He was also active in politics and was appointed the first post-Revolutionary Prime Minister, although for a very short time, from 1950 to 1951.

When Mohammad Natsir passed away his position was taken by a team of leaders with Anwar Harjono as the executive director. Anwar Harjono (b. 1923) had been active in DDII since 1983 as its third director. Moreover, when Harjono was still the leader of Gerakan Pemuda Islam Indonesia (Islamic Youth Movement of Indonesia/GPII), he was appointed by the Masyumi congress as a member of the executive council of the party. After the banning of the Masyumi in 1960, Harjono continued his studies and wrote his doctoral thesis in the Faculty of Law, at the Islamic University Jakarta, on *Hukum Islam, Keluasan dan Keadilannya.* He completed his Ph.D. in 1968.[4]

Another important figure within DDII was H.M. Rasjidi (d.2001). After finishing his secondary schooling in Malang, East Java, in 1930, he pursued his studies at Al-Azhar University, Cairo. He completed his studies in 1937 and went back to Indonesia to later join the Partai Islam Indonesia (PII) at the Yogyakarta branch. After independence, during the period of Prime Minister Sjahrir (1945–1947), Rasjidi was appointed to the state ministry and later as the first Minister of Religious Affairs. When DDII was first established, Rasjidi was appointed its vice director and remained in this position until 1993. In the following years, when DDII was led by a team of leaders, Rasjidi was re-appointed as one of the leaders together with Yunan Nasution, Anwar Harjono, and Rusjad Nurdin.[5]

---

[4] For an account of Harjono's biography, see Hakiem, *Perjalanan Mencari Keadilan.*

[5] H. Soebagijo, I.N, 'Dari Saridi ke Rasjidi', in Endang Basri Ananda, ed., *70 Tahun Prof. Dr. H.M. Rasjidi* (Jakarta: Pelita, 1985), 3–92.

Hussein Umar was another key figure within DDII. He was enrolled at the Faculty of Law at the Universitas Sumatra Utara (University of North Sumatra/USU) but did not complete his studies. At the Muktamar Nasional XII (national meeting) of the Pelajar Islam Indonesia (Indonesian Islamic Students/PII) on August 1969 in Makassar, South Sulawesi, Umar was appointed leader and held the position until 1973. Since the early period of DDII, Hussein Umar was involved in its activities and was later appointed secretary to this organisation, a position he still holds. He was also one of KISDI's leaders.

As mentioned, when Natsir and other ex-Masyumi activists contended that there was no hope within the New Order government of reviving their political party, an alternative had to be found. For Natsir especially, the most important task that remained in front of Muslims was to improve mission (*daʿwa*). The focus on *daʿwa* was important, as for Natsir, '*Daʿwah* was a process of conscientation [sic], which led to the broader aspects of social life, including politics'. Moreover, in an interview with Yusril Ihza Mahendra in December 1991, Natsir jokingly stated that after the banning of the Masyumi 'We are no longer conducting *daʿwah* by means of politics, but engaging in political activities by means of *daʿwah*. The result will be the same'.[6]

At this point, one might ask whether DDII was a transformation of the Masyumi into another guise, and if so, why did the New Order government not ban the organisation? It was obvious from the very beginning that the ex-Masyumi leaders who were gathered at the *ḥalāl bi ḥalāl* meeting did not want to establish a mass-based political party. They had learned from their past experience of severe treatment by the New Order government. Although the connection between DDII and the Masyumi was very clear, the fact that the former did not choose to form a political party meant that the New Order government had no grounds to ban it.

---

[6] Yusril Ihza Mahendra, 'Combining Activism and Intellectualism: The Biography of Mohammad Natsir', *Studia Islamika* 2, no. 1 (1995): 129.

Natsir's view of *da'wa* was well translated into DDII's programs, including developing training for preachers and prospective preachers, conducting research for the benefit of preachers, and spreading information through publications to help improve the quality of *da'wa*.[7] In other words, DDII functioned as both a laboratory and consultation medium for the 'effective propagation of Islam in modern society'.[8] All these were placed within the frame of responding to the ongoing Christianisation efforts. Based on its philosophy that activities had to include both religious and social aspects, another important program within the organisation was the improvement of health facilities, especially for poor Muslims, in response to Christian welfare programs. Natsir and DDII supporters protested against the plan to build a hospital by the Baptist Church in Bukittinggi, West Sumatra (see Chapter Four). As an alternative to the proposed hospital, in September 1971 DDII laid the foundation of Ibnu Sina Islamic hospital in the same area.[9]

Furthermore, DDII was also concerned with education. It helped to provide library collections to some mosques and universities. In addition, the organisation attempted to standardise the curriculum of some Islamic boarding schools (*pesantren*). At this point one might notice a similarity between the education programs of DDII and other *da'wa* organisations, such as Muhammadiyah. In contrast to Muhammadiyah, however, the DDII founders were preoccupied with 'governmental policies that affected the Muslim community'.[10] As will become clear in the discussion below, for DDII leaders the fact that they concentrated on *da'wa* did not mean that they did not understand about politics. Hence their interest in the area of *da'wa* was religious politics.

---

[7] Dewan Dakwah Islamiyah Indonesia, *Anggaran Dasar & Perobahan dan Penambahan Akta* (Jakarta: DDII, 1967), 5.

[8] Muhammad Kamal Hassan, *Muslim Intellectual Responses to 'New Order' Modernization in Indonesia* (Kuala Lumpur: Dewan Bahasa dan Pustaka, 1982), 71.

[9] Hakiem, *Perjalanan Mencari Keadilan*, 237.

[10] R. Hefner, 'Print Islam: Mass Media and Ideological Rivalries among Indonesian Muslims', *Indonesia* 64 (October 1997): 84.

The discussion on DDII in relation to Muslim-Christian relations will focus on its official statements as well as opinions forwarded by persons who were associated with the organisations and which were in line with the views of DDII. These persons include Mohammad Natsir, H.M. Rasjidi, Anwar Harjono, and Hussein Umar, who produced a significant number of writings on the issue on Muslim-Christian relations.

Komite Indonesia untuk Solidaritas Dunia Islam

In 1987 DDII sponsored the formation of *Komite Indonesia untuk Solidaritas Dunia Islam* (Indonesian Committee for Solidarity with the Islamic World/KISDI), which was originally concerned with the Israeli attacks on Palestinian Muslims, and was launched by Mohammad Natsir. KISDI later developed its interests to campaign for Muslim rights and to help ease Muslim misery throughout the world, including Bosnia, Kashmir and Mindanao (the Philippines). However, in the early 1990s, in line with Soeharto's support for the establishment of ICMI, KISDI's members were actively involved in Indonesian politics, particularly in fighting for Indonesian Muslims which were seen to be marginalised by the government. KISDI was very active in conveying the fervour of its suspicions about Christians. In commenting on the Ambon conflict, for example, KISDI argued that the conflict was part of a larger scenario of a 'Muslim cleansing policy' in the eastern part of Indonesia. KISDI firmly reminded Christians to cease their involvement in the Ambon conflicts. Moreover, KISDI was very critical towards Christianisation.[11] In addition, KISDI barely concealed its anti-Semitism. Many of its statements harshly criticised Israel for its conflict with Palestine. In its various statements KISDI urged the

---

[11] KISDI, 'KISDI: Sikap Pihak Kristen Sudah Terlalu Jauh', in *KISDI Menggugat (2) Upaya Melawan Kezaliman dan Kemungkaran* (Jakarta: KISDI, 2002), 57. More on this issue will be discussed below.

government to cease diplomatic relations with Israel and countries supporting Israel, especially the USA.[12]

KISDI's first executive director was Ahmad Sumargono. He once actively participated in Himpunan Mahasiswa Islam (Muslim Students Association/HMI) when he was a student at the Economic Faculty of the Indonesian University (Universitas Indonesia/UI) in 1963. He was later appointed leader of Korps Mubalig Jakarta (Jakarta Preachers Association) and was also involved in some DDII activities. Sumargono's name was well known from his appointment as leader of KISDI in 1987 until he unofficially resigned on 10 July 2000.[13] He ceased being active in KISDI after he joined and then left the 'group of 16 rebellion' against Yusril Ihza Mahendra at the second Partai Bulan Bintang (Moon and Crescent Party/PBB) meeting (*Muktamar*).[14]

When Sumargono left KISDI, a key figure within this organisation was Adian Husaini (b. 1965). Adian has served as KISDI's secretary since 1997. His education was mainly in Islamic boarding schools. He also took an Arabic course at the Lembaga Ilmu Pengetahuan Islam dan Arab (Institute of Islamic and Arabic Studies/LIPIA), an institute that was funded by the Saudi government. When he finished his undergraduate degree at the Faculty of Veterinary Science at Bogor Institute of Agriculture, he pursued his Masters degree at the Jayabaya University where he wrote his thesis on 'The Pragmatism of Israel's International Politics'. At present he is pursuing doctoral studies at the International Institute of Islamic Thought and Civilization, Malaysia. Adian is a prolific writer and has published books and articles, especially on the issue on Islam versus non-Islam.

---

[12] KISDI, 'Kekejaman Zionis Israel Semakin Menjadi-jadi', *KISDI Menggugat* (2), 62-64.

[13] 'Ancaman Bagi yang Kafir dan yang Kufar', *Forum Keadilan*, 14 December 1998, 32-36.

[14] The first meeting was held on 24 April 2000 and chose Yusril Ihza Mahendra as the chairperson for PBB. On 5 May 2000, 16 key members of the party, including Hartono Mardjono, Fadli Zon, and Sumargono, held a second meeting and founded a new PBB with Hartono as the chairperson. It was after Sumargono's involvement in the 'Group of 16 rebellion' that other KISDI activists, especially Cholil Ridwan and Adian Husaini, did not want him involved at KISDI.

It has been mentioned that KISDI's establishment was sponsored by DDII. Moreover, KISDI's close relationship with DDII was shown by the involvement of some DDII supporters, such as Hussein Umar, in KISDI. In reverse, some KISDI activists, such as Soemargono, were also active in DDII although was never formally a DDII board member. Although KISDI did not exclusively pay attention to Muslim-Christian relations, some of its official statements related to the issue, as well as views of persons associated with organisations that mirrored the views of KISDI, will be analysed below.

Front Pembela Islam

Front Pembela Islam (Front of Defenders of Islam/FPI) was formed in Jakarta on 17 August 1998. Among its founders was Habieb Muhammad Rizieq Shihab (b. 1965), who was of Betawi-Arab descent. Rizieq studied at the Institute for Islamic and Arabic Studies (LIPIA) and then completed his study on *uṣūl al-fiqh* (Islamic legal theory) at King Muhammad ibn Saud University, Riyadh, Saudi Arabia, in 1990. Rizieq believed that Muslims should follow only the practice of the Prophet Muhammad and his Companions because this was the only 'pure' Islam. In this regard, he claimed his group to be the *Salafȳ*, i.e. the followers of the pious ancestors, meaning the Prophet Muhammad and his acquaintances.[15] The doctrine of *Salafȳ* developed by the FPI had a strong connection to Wahhabism, a movement developed by Muhammad ibn Abd al-Wahhab (d. 1787), which aimed at developing a 'pure' Islam by strictly and literally interpreting Islamic doctrines.[16]

FPI had branches in several provinces and claimed to have 50,000 members in Jakarta alone, mainly young urbanites, and 10 million members in 17 other provinces,[17] a figure that seems to be largely exaggerated. FPI members, named *jundi*, received semi-military train-

---

[15] Rizieq Shihab, interview by author, Jakarta, 6 February 2002.

[16] Noorhaidi Hasan, 'Faith and Politics: The Rise of the Laskar Jihad in the Era of Transition in Indonesia', *Indonesia* 73 (April 2003): 147.

[17] 'Polisi Moral di Rimba Metropolitan', *Tempo*, 23 January 2000, 44-45.

ing in which the most successful trainees could be promoted as *rois* or *amir* (commandant). These *jundis* did not receive any payment, yet in any rallies organised by FPI, people who sympathised with the organisation would pay for the transportation and daily needs of these *jundis*. There was an allegation that FPI was related to PAM Swakarsa (self security guards formed during Habibie's presidency to fight against student activists in Jakarta in November 1998), but Rizieq Shihab denied the charge.[18] Nevertheless, most scholars writing on this topic asserted the PAM Swakarsa and Army connection.[19] The link could be seen from semi-military training that FPI members received.

Islamic reform by imposing Islamic law in Indonesia constituted FPI's main agenda. This agenda emerged from their concern regarding the situation in Indonesia in this period where Islamic teachings and moral values were seen to be declining. Therefore, the organisation attempted to promote *al-amru bi al-maʿrūf wa al-nahyu ʿan al-munkar* (enjoining good and preventing evil) in all aspects of life. To realise this, FPI first attempted to conduct mass religious gatherings (*tabligh akbar*) to remind people to refrain from vice, and to publish a missionary bulletin named *Buletin Dakwah*. However, the FPI felt that these two methods were not successful. They then tried to instigate an 'anti-vice' campaign (*Gerakan Anti Maksiat*) at the national level by going into the streets. For example, on 13 December 2000, FPI went to the local government office of Jakarta (Pemda DKI) to demand the closure of places of 'sin', including nightclubs, massage parlours, discotheques, and bars during the fasting month of *Ramaḍān* and one week after the ʿIed al-Fiṭr. This visit to the Pemda DKI was the fourth within a period of two months. Their demand was finally met by Sutiyoso, the Governor of Jakarta, who was afraid that FPI might otherwise directly attack those

---

[18] 'Polisi Moral di Rimba Metropolitan', 45.

[19] International Crisis Group, 'Indonesia: Violence and Radical Muslims' [online], available from http://www.crisisweb.org/projects/asia/indonesia/reports/A400455_ 10102001.pdf; accessed 20 October 2001. The article argued that some observers claimed that the police often pretended that they did not know of the FPI attack and this in turn made the operators of the discotheques and casinos turn to the police or military for protection by paying substantial amounts of money.

places.[20] The governor's fear was reasonable, as FPI was believed to be the actor behind several attacks on discotheques, nightclubs and brothels in December 2000 (during the fasting month) in areas of Jakarta and Bogor (West Java).[21]

On 16 October 2002, Rizieq was arrested by the Jakarta District Police (Polda Metro Jaya) and was charged with violating article 160 of the Indonesian Criminal Code (Kitab Undang-Undang Hukum Pidana/ KUHP) on provocation (*penghasutan*) and article 170 on mass violation against persons or belongings. He was put under house arrest on 5 November 2002 and on 6 November 2002 FPI suspended (*membekukan*) its own activities for an indefinite period. The official reason given for this suspension was that FPI needed to clear the organisation of unidentified persons who had infiltrated it, and to evaluate its activities to be more effective in guarding the image of Islam. FPI's secretary argued that the suspension had nothing to do with the arrest of Rizieq.[22]

Two important things needed to be highlighted. First, Rizieq's arrest occurred four days after the Bali bombing. This must not have been a coincidence. The arrest and the suspension of FPI might well have been linked to the Bali bombing. The reason given by the Jakarta District Police seemed to be invented. The FPI had attacked a number of places before, but Rizieq had never been charged under that law before. Second, the reason given by the FPI official appeared to be groundless as well. The claim that FPI had been infiltrated by subversive elements seemed to be invented to conceal the true reason behind its closure.

---

[20] 'Polisi Moral di Rimba Metropolitan', 44.

[21] International Crisis Group, 'Indonesia: Violence and Radical Muslims'; accessed 20 October 2001.

[22] 'Laskar Front Pembela Islam Dibekukan' [online], available from http://www.kompas.com/kompas-cetak/0211/07/utama/clas01.htm; accessed 7 November 2002. The discussion on FPI's attitude to the Muslim-Christian relations below will only include the period which spanned its establishment until its suspension in November 2002.

Laskar Jihad

Laskar Jihad (Jihad Paramilitary Force) was formed by people of different professions and backgrounds, mainly recruited from various *pengajian* (religious discussion forums) and with mainly low socio-economic status. It was a paramilitary group of the Forum Komunikasi Ahlus Sunnah wal-Jama'ah (Communication Forum of Those Who Upheld Customs Based on the Practice and Authority of the Prophet Muhammad and his Companions/FKAWJ).[23] It claimed to have 10,000 members, many of whom were young men who were seeking moral assurance amidst the uncertainty of Indonesian political life, especially after the fall of Soeharto in 1998. Its leader, Ja'far Umar Thalib, united people of the same vision and mission to oppose the 'oppression and humiliation directed toward the Indonesian Muslim'.[24]

Ja'far Thalib was born in Malang, East Java, on 29 December 1961. His father, who was of Yemeni descent, was a veteran of the war of 10 November 1945 in Surabaya, East Java. This had provided a way for Ja'far to rise to semi-military training. After finishing his high school he went to the Pesantren Persatuan Islam (Persis) in East Java and then headed to Jakarta to study at the LIPIA, the same institution to which Rizieq went. At this institution, Ja'far felt unsatisfied and had a fierce argument with one of his lecturers. He later went to Pakistan to study at the Mawdudi Institute at Lahore. He stayed there for less than one year, and in 1987 he joined the *jihād* in Afghanistan against the Soviet Union for almost two years. In 1991 he flew to the Middle East to learn from several ᶜ*ulamās*, including Syaikh Muqbil ibn Hadi al-Wadi'i in North Yemen, who was known

---

[23] The doctrine promoted by the Laskar Jihad is not to be confused with the doctrine of *ahl al-sunna wa al-jama'a* developed by the Nahdhatul Ulama (NU). Within the NU, it meant that they followed one of the four Sunni schools of Islamic jurisprudence. As is mentioned below, Laskar Jihad disagreed with the understanding of Islam as developed by NU and Muhammadiyah; see Hasan, 'Faith and Politics', 146.

[24] Available from http://www.laskarjihad.or.id/english/article/ljtroopers.htm; accessed 18 May 2001.

for his links with the Salafi-Wahhabi movement in Yemen sponsored by the Saudi government.[25]

When he went back to Indonesia in 1993, he set up the Pesantren Ihya'us Sunnah in Yogyakarta, which was later well-known as the headquarters of Laskar Jihad *Ahlus Sunnah wal-Jama'ah.* The forum was formed to promote 'true Islamic values', and its doctrine was remarkable for 'its narrow Islamism and exclusivism'.[26] As is been widely known, many Islamic organisations in Indonesia, including Front Pembela Islam, claimed to be part of *ahlus sunnah wal jama'ah.* However, FKAWJ believed that 'only they can rightly use this ascription'. To them, other organisations, including Nahdhatul Ulama and Muhammadiyah, were corrupting the Islamic doctrines by adopting non-Islamic sources.[27]

The birth of Laskar Jihad owed much to the conflict involving Muslims and Christians in Ambon (Moluccas), which erupted on 19 January 1999 and will be discussed below. On 30 January 2000, which marked one year of conflict, there was a mass religious gathering in Yogyakarta to reflect on the Muslim condition in Ambon. Ja'far came up with a '*jihād*' (war) resolution with a three-month deadline. The deadline was given to the government to solve the problem in Ambon within the given period. Indeed, it was their view that the government was favouring the Christians in Ambon. After this deadline elapsed and there was no final solution to the problem, on 6 April 2000 Ja'far and a great number of his followers declared their intention to go to Ambon and to form Laskar Jihad; this was understood as 'a holy ibadah for Muslims'.[28]

Laskar Jihad was very active in promoting their thought through the buletin *Laskar Jihad,* the *Salafy̑* Magazine, and their website (www.

---

[25] Hasan, 'Faith and Politics', 153.

[26] Greg Fealy, 'Inside the Laskar Jihad: An Interview with the Leader of a New, Radical and Militant Sect', *Inside Indonesia* 65 (Januar–March 2001): 28–29.

[27] Fealy, 'Inside the Laskar Jihad', 28.

[28] Available from http://www.laskarjihad.or.id; accessed 18 May 2001.

Laskarjihad.or.id), before it dissolved itself on 5 October 2002. It is interesting to note that Laskar Jihad officially released the statement of its dispersal on 16 October 2002, a few days after the Bali bombing. However, Ja'far maintained that the closure of his organisation did not have any relation to the Bali bombing or government pressure. Laskar Jihad stated a few reasons for its disbanding, including its concern that some of the organisation's members tended to be involved in practical politics, which would distort the vision of the organisation.[29]

It could be true that, as was the case for the closure of the FPI, the disbanding of Laskar Jihad was somehow related to the Bali bombing. Nevertheless, a few other reasons are important to state. It appears to be correct that the FKAWJ held its final conference around two weeks before the Bali bombing and resolved to disband Laskar Jihad. Among the reasons relating to its dissolution could include the *fatwā* issued by some *ᶜulamās*, including Syaikh Rabi' ibn Hadi al-Madkhali, a *Salafȳ ᶜulamā* from Saudi Arabia, who suggested that Laskar Jihad should change its orientation to *daᶜwa*.[30] Another possible reason for its closure might also relate to the loss of military support. Even though Laskar Jihad officials did not and would not point to that reason, they indicated that a reason for the dissolution was financial problems.[31] This could well be linked to the loss of military support which appeared to provide financial help for Laskar Jihad. It was also probable that the closure of Laskar Jihad was related to the trial of Ja'far, who was charged with provoking and delivering deliberate

---

[29] 'Pembubaran Laskar Jihad Bukan Tekanan Pemerintah' [online], available from http://www .kompas.com/kompas-cetak/0210/17/daerah/pemb19.htm; accessed 9 November 2002. As in the case of FPI, the discussion on Laskar Jihad's attitudes on Muslim–Christian relations below will only include the period which spanned its establishment until its suspension on 16 October 2002.

[30] 'Alasan Pembubaran Laskar Jihad' [online], available from http://www.pikiran-rakyat.com/cetak/1002/17/0106; accessed 7 November 2002.

[31] 'Pembubaran Laskar Jihad Tak Terkait Bom Bali' [online], available from http://www.detik.com; accessed 7 November 2002.

enmity and hostility to the Indonesian president during the months proceeding the disbanding.[32]

A Brief Theological Account of the Christian 'Other'

It is important to note that all the exclusivist Muslim organisations discussed in this study were concerned more with practical matters of Muslim–Christian relations than with exercising the theological perspectives on Christianity. Therefore, it is not easy to trace the theological understandings of Christianity, especially on the part of Laskar Jihad and FPI. Nevertheless, there are some points on which these exclusivist organisations stated their views on Christianity or Christians, albeit briefly. The most important issues discussed were the concept of *ahl al-kitāb* (People of the Book) in Islam, the validity of Christianity as a religion, and the perception of Christians as colonialists. As will be seen below, even though the degree of negative feeling towards Christianity and Christians differed amongst the exclusivists, there was a generally disapproving attitude towards Christianity as a religion as well as towards Christians.

The Perspective on Ahl al-Kitāb

One of the focuses of DDII activities when it was first established was to respond to the large number of Muslim conversions following the mass killings in 1965–1967 (see Chapter Four).[33] It is important to note, however, that based on the Qur'ānic notion that 'there shall be no coercion in matters of faith'[34] DDII was more concerned to maintain and consolidate the existing Islamic community rather than forcing other religious believers, including Christians, to embrace Islam. This explains DDII's perspective on Christianity and *ahl al-kitāb*.

---

[32] More explanation of this issue appears below in the section on the Ambon conflicts.

[33] Tamam, Laporan Kegiatan DDII, 2–5.

[34] The Qur'ān 2:256.

In the Forum on Inter-religious Consultation held in Jakarta on 30 November 1967,[35] for example, Mohammad Natsir stated that, in Muslim eyes, Christians were regarded as the *ahl al-kitāb*, who had a special status within Islam,[36] by quoting the Qur'ānic verses below:

> I am bidden to bring about equity in your mutual views. God is our Sustainer as well as your Sustainer. To us shall be accounted our deeds, and to you, your deeds. Let there be no contention between us and you; God will bring us all together— for with Him is all journeys' end (Q.S. 42:15).

However, the Christians' status as *ahl al-kitāb* did not exempt them from being called to the right path. Natsir argued that based on the Qur'ānic teachings Muslims are compelled to call Christians to the truth:

> Say: 'O followers of earlier revelation![37] Come unto that tenet which we and you hold in common: that we shall worship none but God, and that we shall not ascribe divinity to aught beside Him, and that we shall not take human beings for our lords beside God'. And if they turn away, then say: 'Bear witness that it is we who have surrendered ourselves unto Him' (Q.S. 3:64).

---

[35] See Chapter Four for the discussion on the Forum on Inter-religious Consultation.

[36] Natsir, *Islam dan Kristen di Indonesia,* 213.

[37] Muhammad Asad used the phrase 'the followers of earlier revelation' or 'followers of the Bible' to translate the *ahl al-kitāb* in his The Message of the Qur'aɔn (Gibraltar: Dar al-Andalus, 1980). However, the common translation for *ahl al-kitāb* is 'People of the Book', see, for example, Abdullah Yusuf Ali, *The Holy Qur'an: Text, Translation and Commentary* (Beirut, Lebanon: Dar al-Arabia, 1938).

The DDII leaders believed that the call to Islam was a response to the underlying intention of the *ahl al-kitāb* to deny the truth and to bring Muslims to follow their religions, as stated in the Qur'ān:[38]

> Out of their selfish envy, many among the followers of earlier revelation would like to bring you back to denying the truth after you have attained to faith—[even] after the truth has become clear unto them. None the less, forgive and forbear, until God shall make manifest His will: behold, God has the power to will anything (Q.S. 2:109).

> For, never will the Jews be pleased with thee, nor yet the Christians, unless thou follow their own creeds. Say: 'Behold, God's guidance is the only true guidance'. And, indeed, if thou shouldst follow their errant views after all the knowledge that has come unto thee, thou wouldst have none to protect thee from God, and none to bring thee succour (Q.S. 2:120).

Natsir translated the phrase '*ᶜan la taᶜbudū illā-allāh*' in verse 3:64 as 'please do not worship other than Allah'. Therefore, this translation served as the basis to invite the *ahl al-kitāb* to follow the teachings of Islam, although there was no force to embrace the religion.[39] Nevertheless, Muhammad Asad argued that the word *illā-allāh* in the above verse should not be translated as 'none but Allah', even though it was directed towards both the Christians, who 'attribute divinity to Jesus and certain aspects of divinity to their saints', and the Jews, who 'assign a quasi-divine authority to Ezra and even to some of their great

---

[38] Arguments forwarded by the DDII leaders that the Christians had tried to convert Muslims to Christianity can be found in almost every edition of the DDII magazine, *Media Dakwah*. See also Hussein Umar, 'Intoleransi Kaum Nasrani terhadap Umat Islam', in Lukman Hakiem, ed., *Fakta & Data: Usaha-Usaha Kristenisasi di Indonesia* (Jakarta: Media Dakwah, 1991). Husein Umar's article was republished with some additional remarks under the same title in Adian Husaini, *Gereja-Gereja Dibakar: Membedah Akar Konflik SARA di Indonesia* (Jakarta: DEA Press, 2000), 1-24. This study refers to the latest publication.

[39] Natsir, *Islam dan Kristen di Indonesia*, 213.

Talmudic scholars'.[40] Instead, it should be translated as 'none but God'. Hence, in Natsir's understanding, the word '*allāh*' meant God who was worshiped by the Muslims, whereas the original meaning of the word *allāh* in Arabic was God.

The brief description of the *ahl al-kitāb* from the perspective of the DDII reveals two important things. On the one hand, the DDII believed that, as stated in the Qur'ān, Christians were regarded as the *ahl al-kitāb* and had a special status within Islam. On the other hand, it held the view that the Qur'ān reminded Muslims that the *ahl al-kitāb* had denied the truth and attempted to make the Muslims follow their religions. The seemingly contradictory notions of the Qur'ān to a significant extent influenced DDII's attitude towards Christians. In daily life, this was translated into not planning an organised agenda to convert Christians to Islam, even though a significant number of Christians did so.[41] DDII's policy of not having an organised plan to convert Christians to Islam could also be explained by the social condition of the Christians. As mentioned, during the New Order era, Christians enjoyed excellent privileges as compared to Muslims, which left the former better of financially and educationally. This situation made it difficult for Muslims, in this case DDII, to target them. Moreover, DDII severely criticised the Christians who did not want to obey the guide for propagating religions (SK 70/1978), and therefore it was unreasonable for DDII to target Christians as converts to Islam.

The Distortion of Christianity

Before discussing the exclusivists' perspectives on the perceived distortions contained within Christianity, it is important to underline that their views on this particular issue were not based on a thorough study of the Qur'ānic notion of *taḥrīf*, i.e. falsifications, corruptions or changes

---

[40] Asad, *The Message of the Qur'ān*, 76-77.
[41] Tamam, *Laporan Kegiatan DDII*, 8.

that had taken place within Scriptures.[42] Therefore, it is not surprising that critical examinations on the concept of *taḥrīf* did not exist in the literature of the exclusivists. What concerned the exclusivist Muslims more was the assumption that there were certain Christian teachings that were believed to be false based on the exclusivist textual reading of the Qur'ān.

The perception that Christianity had undergone alterations was clear in articles written by DDII leaders. One example was DDII's criticism directed towards Robert Paul Walean, a Protestant priest, in a dialogue conducted by DDII at Bekasi, Jakarta, in June 2001. Robert stated that there were no differences between Islam and Christianity, as both religions worshipped the same God. DDII supporters who were present at the meeting severely criticised this argument based on two reasons. First, from the Islamic perspective, Isa was considered a prophet, whereas he was believed to be God by Christians. Second, unlike the Qur'ān, the Bible as it exists now has been corrupted and altered by human beings and therefore is not as it was first revealed.[43]

Moreover, Laskar Jihad officials criticised the publication of books that were deemed responsible for weakening the belief of Muslims, as the writings gave the wrong impression that the Qur'ān validated the concept of God within Christianity. This was seen as endangering lay Muslim readers who might be easily influenced to accept Christianity. One example was a book titled *Isa Almasih di dalam al-Qur'an dan Hadits* (Isa Almasih in the Qur'ān and Ḥadīth), which was written by a person named Abd. Yadi.[44] He quoted some Qur'ānic verses and concluded that, according to the Islamic teachings, Jesus was God. Laskar Jihad officials maintained that even though Prophet Isa performed some miracles, in the perspective of Islam he was not God. They

---

[42] For a discussion on taḥrīf see Abdullah Saeed, 'The Charge of Distortion of Jewish and Christian Scriptures', *Muslim World* 92 (Fall 2002): 419–436.

[43] 'Dialog tentang Nabi Isa', *Media Dakwah*, June 2001, 57.

[44] This study had difficulty in finding the above-mentioned book as apparently it was published by an infamous publisher. Therefore, complete publication details could not be provided.

further argued that after the death of Prophet Isa, the originality of the *Injīl* was not maintained and therefore the Bible as it exists now is not authentic, an argument that was close to that of some classical Muslim theologians. On the contrary, Laskar Jihad emphasised that the Qur'ān had been preserving its originality and would be maintained until the end of the world (*al-yaum al-qiyāma*).[45]

On the concept of the Trinity in Christianity, Adian Husaini, for example, maintained that the God of Muslims was different from that of the Christians, because in Christianity God was described as having offspring. To support his argument, he referred to Matthew 3:17 'And a voice from heaven said, "This is my Son, the beloved, with whom I am well pleased"', and to Luke 4:41, which stated that 'Demons also came out of many, shouting, "You are the Son of God!" But he rebuked them and would not allow them to speak, because they knew that he was the Messiah'. Adian further argued that in the Islamic understanding Jesus was only a prophet and that Islam severely criticised the Christian perception on the divinity of Jesus as mentioned, for example, in verses 5:72-75. Adian emphasised that the Christian concept of the Trinity was considered by the Qur'ān to be polytheistic (*shirk*), and that God would not forgive those who committed polytheism.[46] In a similar line, some statements issued by KISDI also perceived Christianity as a corrupted religion. It criticised comments forwarded by various Muslim figures during the first half of 1999 that all religions were the same. Without clarifying who those figures were, KISDI leaders stated that with this concept of 'religious syncretism' (*penyamaan agama*), anybody who supported 'peace', 'justice', 'democracy', and 'human rights', would attain heaven. In this

---

[45] 'Buku Putih Sang Penginjil' [online], available from http://www.laskarjihad.or.id; accessed 19 March 2001.

[46] Adian Husaini, *Penyesatan Opini: Sebuah Rekayasa Mengubah Citra* (Jakarta: Gema Insani Press, 2002), 68-69.

context, KISDI maintained that there were some ʿulamāʾ who argued that the Jews and Christians were not kāfirūn.[47]

Christians as Colonialists

Adian Husaini maintained that some Muslims regarded Christians as colonialists and Christianisation efforts as part of colonialism. Therefore some ʿulamāʾ likened Christianisation to 'war' against Muslims. For him, therefore, the rules of war could be applied:[48]

> And fight in God's cause against those who wage war against you, but do not commit aggression—for, verily, God does not love aggressors. And slay them wherever you may come upon them, and drive them away from wherever they drove you away—for oppression [fitnah][49] is even worse than killing. And fight not against them near the Inviolable House of Worship unless they fight against you there first; but if they fight against you, slay them: such shall be the recompense of those who deny the truth (Q.S. 2:190–191).

To support his argument, Adian referred to Sayyid Qutb's tafsīr. In his Fī Dhilālil Qurʾān, Qutb indicated permission for Muslims to fight back if their belief was violated. While noting that Qutb did not state outright that Christianisation could be legally equated with physical attacks on Muslims, Adian put the question whether attacking ʿaqīdah (belief) through missionary activities was more dangerous than physically attacking Muslims. As he believed that ʿaqīdah was more important than the physical body, he then asked: 'Could the logic of qiyās awlawī [analogy based on the principle of priority][50] be applied in this

---

[47] KISDI, 'Mencermati Gerakan Kristenisasi: Dibalik Gerakan Sekularisme dan Sinkretisme', KISDI Menggugat (2), 14-22.

[48] Husaini, Gereja-Gereja Dibakar, 105.

[49] Asad translated the word 'finah' as 'oppression' arguing that this translation was justified 'by the application of this term to any affliction which may cause man to go astray and to lose his faith in spiritual values'; see Asad, The Message of the Qurʾān, 41, n. 168.

[50] See below for a clearer example of qiyās awlawī.

case that the punishment to the oppressor of ʿaqīdah should be more severe?' Even though Adian stated that only God knew the answers to those questions, he seemed to support his line of reasoning by arguing that, according to Q.S. 2:191 quoted above, *fitnah* was even worse than killing. More importantly, *fitnah* in this context was referred to by Adian as *shirk* (polytheism).[51]

A clear example of Adian's perspective on the above was the killing of Eric Constable. This happened in July 1974, when Indonesian and international politics were shocked by the death of Eric Constable, an Australian Anglican priest, who was killed by Hasyim Yahya in Surabaya, East Java. There was a dispute over the motive behind the killing. Police argued that the motive was purely criminal, as Hasyim had attempted to steal money from Constable. However, others disagreed, as Hasyim was considered a moderate and pious man. Adian seemed to support the latter argument, quoting Hasyim's explanation, according to which Constable was killed because Hasyim was 'practicing what was ruled by the Qur'ān'. Hasyim referred to Qur'ān 2:190–191, and argued that he had consulted some prominent ʿulamās in Indonesia. These ʿulamās, Hasyim added, asserted that Christianisation was the same as fighting against Muslims. Hasyim added that, during the 1970s, the Christianisation process was lively and that Muslim–Christian tension was heightened. In addition, among the New Order's support for Christians was the plan to hold the World Council of Churches Congress in Jakarta in 1975. Although some Muslims rejected this idea, the government went ahead. As a response to the whole situation, Hasyim decided to kill the foreign priest. Adian argued that Hasyim's perception that missionaries could be charged with the equivalent of physically attacking Muslims seemed to be based on *qiyās* (analogy). Therefore, some Muslims believed that Christian missionaries who were trying to proselytise Muslims could

---

[51] Husaini, *Gereja-Gereja Dibakar*, 105-106.

be attacked or killed. Nevertheless, Adian acknowledged that this kind of thinking was not mainstream to Indonesian Muslim thought.[52]

Two important points need to be highlighted here: first, Adian's reference to Qutb's *tafsīr*, and second, his remark on *qiyās awlawī*. First, in his *tafsīr* on the verses 2:190–191, Qutb was supportive of the idea of fighting in God's cause, yet underlined that the fight should be conducted without hatred and without excess (*walākin dūnā i'tidā'in*).[53] Moreover, as Adian himself admitted, there was no point at which Qutb likened Christianisation with physical attacks on Muslims. It is also important to note that the verse quoted above (Q.S. 2:190) started with the phrase '*wa qātilū*' and not '*waqtulū*'. The word *qātala* in Arabic means to kill each other, whereas the word *qatala* means to kill someone; hence it was clear that the context of the verse was the battle field, where killing is expected.

Second, it is worthy of note that Adian suggested comparing proselytising Muslims with physical attack within the context of *qiyās awlawī*, and also that the killing of Constable was based on *qiyās*. The term *qiyās awlawī* was referred to by some jurists, including Ibn al-Subkhi, as *qiyās jālī*. *Qiyās jālī*, as opposed to *qiyās khāfī*, was 'an analogy where the cause is only one, and which is established by certain evidence, allowing no other interpretation (*ta'wīl*)'. In addition, *qiyās jālī* or *qiyās awlawī* was 'an analogy where the parallel case is stronger than the original case'. To give an illustration, the Qur'ān verse 17:23 says that saying 'fie' or 'ugh!' to one's parents is forbidden. Therefore, beating or hurting them was '*a fortiori* forbidden'.[54] Even though Adian seemed to follow the logic of *qiyās awlawī*, his argument that *ʿaqīdah* was more important than the physical body was questionable. Moreover, even if the logic of *qiyās awlawī* were

---

[52] Husaini, *Gereja-Gereja Dibakar*, 113.

[53] Sayyid Qutb, *Fī Dhilālil Qur'ān*, vol. 1 (Beyrūt: Dār Al-Shuruq, 1993), 187.

[54] Ahmad Hasan, *Analogical Reasoning in Islamic Jurisprudence: A Study of the Juridical Principle of Qiyas* (Islamabad, Pakistan: Islamic Research Institute, 1986), 78–79 and 84.

applied to Christian missionaries in order to punish them for attempting to proselytise Muslims, does it mean that it is permissible to kill them? Neither Qutb nor Mawdudi, who appeared to be the sources of Adian's interpretations, read it that way.

These two points show that Adian applied faulty logic to support his view on Christians. His perspective on the Christian 'other' seemed to correspond to theological and legal perceptions of the Christian 'other' within some classical Islamic texts (see Chapter Two). However, as the exclusivists did not produce a comprehensive theological analysis of Christianity, it is difficult to see a more concrete connection between their perspectives on this issue and those of classical Islam. More importantly, other factors, including the New Order's policies towards Muslims and Christians should not be overlooked, as it was through these policies that exclusivist Muslims learnt to view Christians as their 'enemy'.

Attempts at Reviving the Jakarta Charter and Establishing an Islamic State

The question on the relationship between religion and the state has occupied Muslim thought since the 1920s. Chapter Three discussed how Muslim groups attempted to establish a formal link between Islam and the state by urging the Old Order government to, for example, include the Jakarta Charter in the Preamble of the 1945 Constitution. The failure to do this did not end Muslim efforts to revive the Charter, as it was perceived as the gateway to implementing Islamic law in Indonesia.

The discussion below on the exclusivists' attempts at reviving the Jakarta Charter and at establishing an Islamic state is related to Muslim–Christian relations in two main ways. Firstly, as seen in Chapter Three, the erasure of the Jakarta Charter from the Preamble was to a significant extent caused by some Christians who supported a separate state provided the Constitution was accepted as it stood. Secondly, and closely related to the first point, was the fate of

Christians in Indonesia were the country to be transformed into an Islamic state. Christians were afraid that their interests would be threatened. All four exclusivist groups discussed in this study held the view that the Jakarta Charter should be revived. This can be seen from their publications as well as the interviews conducted for this study. Nevertheless, they differed in their views as to whether this meant that Indonesia should be transformed into an Islamic state. In addition, as is seen below, not all the exclusivist groups discussed had a clear concept regarding the status of the Christian minority if the Jakarta Charter were revived and an Islamic state established.

As mentioned, the main agenda of FPI was to implement Islamic law in Indonesia and therefore it was the most active group in terms of mobilising people on to the streets to urge the revival of the Jakarta Charter. The reason behind this was FPI's belief that efforts to confront vice would be strengthened provided they had a legal base, and that this could be achieved through the enactment of Islamic law in Indonesia. Rizieq Shihab believed that the enactment of the *sharīʿa* in Indonesia was not the obligation of the FPI activists alone. By quoting some Qurʾānic verses, he argued that it was the obligation of all Muslims[55]:

> And [tell them that] I have not created the invisible beings and men to any end other than that they may [know and] worship Me (Q.S. 51:56).

> And, finally, [O Muhammad,] We have set thee on a way by which the purpose [of faith] may be fulfilled: so follow thou this [way], and follow not the likes and dislikes of those who do not know [the truth] (Q.S. 45:18).

---

[55] Rizieq Shihab, *Dialog Piagam Jakarta* (Jakarta: Pustaka Ibnu Sidah, 2000), 22-23.

Rizieq did not explain how the above verses related to the question of implementing the *sharīʿa* in Indonesia. As one might note, the first verse quoted above carries a general meaning referring to the purpose of the creation of human beings in the context of *ʿibāda* (worship). There is no specific reference to the *sharīʿa*. The second verse refers to the *sharīʿa*, and this was understood by Rizieq as a codification of law that needed to be implemented in Indonesia. The word *sharīʿa*, as well as other words such as *islām* and *manhaj*, has a complex meaning. These words are used in many different meanings, and finding these meanings entails looking at the context of the verse, the background of its revelation, and the relation between the verse and other verses with a similar context. At this point, the method of interpreting the Qur'ān known as *tafsīr bi al-ma'thūr* (especially *tafsīr* the Qur'ān with the Qur'ān) is very important in scrutinising the meaning of the word *sharīʿa*. Muhammad Asad, for example, interpreted the word as 'way'. There are also several verses in the Qur'ān that refer to the word *sharīʿa* as 'way', such as *sharīʿa* Nūḥ or *sharīʿa* Ibrāhīm. What was then the basis for FPI to interpret the word *sharīʿa* in the above quoted verse as the codification of law that needed to be implemented in Indonesia? This suggests that Rizieq quoted these verses only to justify his opinion on the need to implement the *sharīʿa* in Indonesia.

In August 2001, FPI supporters requested that the People's Representative Council (Dewan Perwakilan Rakyat/DPR) include a discussion on the implementation of Islamic law in Indonesia, as stated in the Jakarta Charter, at the annual meeting of the People's Consultative Assembly (Majelis Permusyawaratan Rakyat/MPR) 2001. The request was based on an argument that the elimination of the Charter was responsible for the lack of morality of Indonesian society, especially the Muslim majority. This argument stemmed from the perception that the exclusion of the Charter from the Preamble and the 1945 Constitution was a betrayal of Muslims, which according to Rizieq had left a 'deep wound' in the Muslim memory.[56]

At the annual meeting of the People's Consultative Assembly which started on 1 August 2002, FPI leaders and other Muslims figures including Abubakar Baasyir (co-founder of Ngruki Boarding School, Central Java, and commander of the Majelis Mujahidin Indonesia) urged for the inclusion of the clause on the implementation of the *sharīʿa* within the amendment of the 1945 Constitution. Rizieq stated that the inclusion of this clause in article 29 of the 1945 Constitution was to assure the uprightness of the entire Indonesian society. He added that Islam was a religion that carried benevolence to all human beings (*Islam raḥmatan li al-ʿālamīn*). He reasoned that the Jakarta Charter and the *sharīʿa*, which contained detail explanations on social interactions, were of benefit to those inside and outside Islam.[57] He defended his argument by claiming that he was once approached by some Christians groups from various areas in Indonesia, including Papua, supporting the inclusion of the clause on the *sharīʿa* into the Constitution. Rizieq further added that the minority would be assured of their safety provided the *sharīʿa* was implemented.[58]

Rizieq believed that the reference to the *sharīʿa* within the Preamble to the 1945 Constitution was reasonable considering that the majority of Indonesian were Muslims. 'This', he argued, 'concurs with just and rational principles'. In addition, Rizieq was confident that the implementation of the *sharīʿa* would not do any harm to non-Muslim minorities. On the contrary, non-Muslims would receive some benefits from this implementation, including the creation of a better moral sys-

---

[56] Shihab, *Dialog Piagam Jakarta*, 30-31. As is known, the Minister of Justice and Human Rights Prof. Yusril Ihza Mahendra stated on April 2002 that a Criminal Law Companion based on Islamic Law would soon be implemented in Indonesia. However, the discussion on the accommodation of Islamic Law within the Indonesian state needs a separate examination.

[57] Shihab, *Dialog Piagam Jakarta*, 51.

[58] 'Lagi, Syariat Islam Diusulkan Masuk Amandemen' [online], available from http://www.kompas.com/utama/news/0208/05/051643.htm; accessed 5 August 2002.

tem. Rizieq maintained that the implementation would not discriminate against non-Muslims, as the wording of the Jakarta Charter 'with
the obligation for adherents of Islam to practice Islamic law' would only
be applied to Muslims. He further reasoned that the *sharīʿa* would not
negate non-Muslim rights in Indonesia. In addition to the assurance
from the Muslim side that non-Muslims would be treated justly, Rizieq
emphasised that government institutions could play a role in controlling the implementation of the *sharīʿa*.[59]

Examining Rizieq's arguments regarding the implementation of
the *sharīʿa* raises questions. First, one might question his argument
that non-Muslims would be treated justly under the control of government institutions, as there was no assurance of this. Second, Rizieq's
statement that the majority of Indonesians would accept the implementation of the *sharīʿa* was also open to debate. In this context, it is
interesting to quote the finding of a comprehensive survey that was
conducted by the Centre for the Study of Islam and Society (Pusat
Pengkajian Islam dan Masyarakat/PPIM) of the IAIN Jakarta in 16
provinces.[60] The theme of the survey was 'Islam and the culture of good
governance'. Although 58 percent of the respondents affirmed that good
politics must be based on the *sharīʿa* and 61 percent said that the
government should oblige Muslims to follow the *sharīʿa*, only a small
number of them agreed with the enforcement of strict Islamic law.
For instance, only 10 percent of them maintained that police should
monitor whether Muslims performed their prayers and only 13 percent thought that a government agency should monitor whether Muslims fasted during the month of *Ramaḍān*. The survey concluded
that for the majority of Muslims, Islamic law was understood as

---

[59] Shihab, *Dialog Piagam Jakarta*, 17, 19.

[60] The sixteen provinces include all provinces in Java and Madura, Nusa Tenggara Barat,
West Sumatra, North Sumatra, South Sumatra, Lampung, Riau, Jambi, South Kalimantan,
East Kalimantan, and South Sulawesi. The variables of the survey included religious factors
on the one hand, and Islamic political culture and democratic political culture on the other.

'sacred', yet when it came to the criminal law (*ḥudūd*) the majority of Muslims were resistant to the implementation of the *sharīʿa*.[61]

The discussion on the demand to implement the *sharīʿa* led to the question whether this would also mean that the FPI would demand an Islamic state. Rizieq argued that the Jakarta Charter had come into existence in 1945 as the solution for two contradictory demands: to establish an Islamic state on the one hand or a secular state on the other. He further refuted the argument that the revival of the Jakarta Charter would be (mis)used by certain groups of Muslims to drastically change existing laws and force followers of different religions to follow the *sharīʿa*. There was some truth in Rizieq's remarks. It is true that the revival of the Jakarta Charter and the implementation of the *sharīʿa* would not make Indonesia an Islamic state. There are grounds for arguing this. First, the Jakarta Charter was only intended as an adjunct to the religiously neutral Pancasila. Second, the Charter would not have, of itself, led to Islamisation of the statutes as this would require Muslim majorities in the DPR. Third, the Charter did not propose that Islam become the 'state religion.' However, a closer examination of Rizieq's views on the Jakarta Charter reveals that he supported the idea of the establishment of an Islamic state even though he emphasised a clause 'in so far as the Indonesian citizens wanted to within the constitutional corridor'.[62]

Although it is clear from the above that it was the FPI that, from its establishment, was very active in campaigning for the enactment of Islamic law in Indonesia, Laskar Jihad also attempted to realise that goal. One case in point was the sentence of *rajam* (death by stoning) on

---

[61] Saiful Mujani, 'Syariah's OK, but Let's Wait before Cutting off Hands' [online], available from http://www.tempo.co.id; accessed 9 January 2002. To a significant extent this survey accurately portrayed the perspective of the majority of Muslims on the implementation of the sharīʿa in Indonesia. The survey was based on multistage random sampling of 2200 Muslims in those 16 provinces. Men and women were equally represented in the sample. This information was gathered from Saiful Mujani (the researcher who conducted this survey) in an email contact with him 25-27 July 2002.

[62] Shihab, *Dialog Piagam Jakarta*, 24-25, 84.

a person named Abdullah on 27 March 2001. The case started when Abdullah went to Ambon to join Laskar Jihad, leaving his two wives and two children, and committed adultery there. He reported this to Ja'far and chose to be stoned to death. Ja'far agreed with Abdullah's choice and implemented the *rajam* law on him. Ja'far was arrested by the police and charged with taking someone's life.[63] Amidst the controversy as to whether the *rajam* law could be applied in Indonesia, some newspapers, including *Saksi, Sabili, Media Dakwah* and *Suara Hidayatullah*, gave a certificate of honour to Abdullah's family on 21 May 2001 in recognition of his bravery in upholding Islamic law.[64]

Through this use of the *rajam* law, Ja'far attempted to reason that the implementation of the *sharī'a* was possible, at least in Ambon where the Muslim community had agreed to implement Islamic law in every case that emerged within their community. In the case of Abdullah, in addition to the agreement made by the Muslim community of Ambon on 27 March 2001 at the al-Fatah Mosque to implement the *sharī'a*, many references have been quoted from the Islamic foundation texts to support Laskar Jihad's decision to execute him. Moreover, Laskar Jihad members argued that Ambon was a war area where the Indonesian positive law could not be implemented and therefore an alternative law was needed.[65]

Regarding the question of the *rajam* law, in commenting on the case of Abdullah, Goenawan Mohamad (the chief editor of *Tempo* Magazine) contended that it was a *biadab* (barbaric or ill-mannered) action. Goenawan said:

> You might say, 'That was because you do not know what God ordained'. I would ask, as I have asked myself, 'But what is

---

[63] On 8 October 2001 Ja'far came to the Central Policy Office in Jakarta demanding that they issue the Surat Perintah Penghentian Penyidikan (letter of policy authority for stopping the investigation). The police authority suspends his case.

[64] 'Hukum Rajam Sah, Mengapa Dipersoalkan?', *Media Dakwah*, June 2001, 41–55.

[65] 'Hukum Rajam Sah, Mengapa Dipersoalkan?', 46–47.

the punishment really for? Is it for the sake of God—as if God really needed it?' Need is the sign of insufficiency, but do we not call Him the Most Perfect? I never imagined Him as the One whose needs must be has to be fulfilled, let alone with a body that was damaged and bleeding [because of the death by stoning].[66]

Ja'far's anger towards Goenawan's comments was obvious. Ja'far stressed that justice could only be achieved through God's laws (the *shari'a*), as other laws were unable to do this. This was so because the *shari'a* came from Allah, the Most Just, whereas other laws were created by human beings who were full of insufficiencies and mistakes.[67] Ja'far quoted the verses below:

> Hence, judge between the followers of earlier revelation in accordance with what God has bestowed from on high, and do not follow their errant views; and beware of them, lest they tempt thee away from aught that God has bestowed from on high upon thee. And if they turn away [from His commandments], then know that it is but God's will [thus] to afflict them for some of their sins: for, behold, a great many people are iniquitous indeed. Do they perchance, desire [to be ruled by] the law of pagan ignorance? But for people who have inner certainty, who could be a better law-giver than God? (Q.S. 5:49-50).

Moreover, Ja'far maintained that God's intention in ordaining the *shari'a* was stated in the following verses:

> God wills that you have ease, and does not will you to suffer hardship (Q.S. 2:185).

---

[66] Ja'far Umar Thalib, 'Goenawan Merajam Syariah', *Buletin Laskar Jihad Ahlus Sunnah Wal Jamaah* 13, 2002, 4-6.

[67] Ja'far Thalib's criticism to Goenawan Mohammad was published in 'Syariah Merajam Goenawan', *Buletin Laskar Jihad Ahlus Sunnah Wal Jamaah* 14, 2002, 5-6.

O Man! We did not bestow the Qur'an on thee from on high
to make thee unhappy, but only as an exhortation to all who
stand in awe [of God] (Q.S. 20:1-3).

The context of verse 2:185 was the fasting month of *Ramaḍān*. It
stated 'Whoever of you lives to see this month shall fast throughout it;
but he that is ill, or on a journey, [shall fast instead for the same] number
of other days'. It then followed with the part of the verse quoted by Ja'far
above: 'God wills that you shall have ease, and does not will you to suffer
hardship'. Indeed, the quoted verse was not completed as it continued to
read as follows: 'But [He desires] that you complete the number [of days
required], and that you extol God for His having guided you aright, and
that you render your thanks [unto Him]'. It is true that fasting was
part of the *sharīʿa*. However, to claim that verse 2:185 stated God's
intention in ordaining the *sharīʿa* was quite misleading.

Laskar Jihad's practice of upholding the *sharīʿa* led to a further
question as to whether it wanted to establish an Islamic state in
Indonesia or to transform Indonesia to an Islamic state. From the
speeches delivered by Laskar Jihad leaders or statements released
by this organisation, it is clear that the implementation of Islamic law
in Indonesia is central to their agenda. However, when it comes to
the discussion of the establishment of the Islamic State of Indonesia
there seems to be no firm intention amongst Laskar Jihad members
for such an establishment. Eko Rahardjo, the Public Relations officer
of Laskar Jihad, for example, argued 'We do not need an Islamic state
because as long as the Islamic teachings have been implemented in
Indonesia that will be enough'. He further maintained 'All that Muslims want is to be respected of their rights to conduct their religious
obligations'.[68]

The implementation of Islamic law also concerned KISDI figure
Adian Husaini, who argued that, at the beginning of Islam, the Prophet

---

[68] Eko Rahardjo (Public Relations of Laskar Jihad), interview by author, Jakarta, 5 February
2002.

Muhammad had a written constitution named the *Piagam Madinah* (Madina Charter), in which Islamic law was implemented. This meant that the state was responsible for the implementation of the *sharīʿa*. Therefore, for Adian, religion in Indonesia should not be detached from the state and the Jakarta Charter should be revived.[69] He further added that the implementation of the *sharīʿa* was declared in Qurʾān 4:65: 'But nay, by thy Sustainer! They do not [really] believe unless they make thee [O Prophet] a judge of all on which they disagree among themselves, and then find in their hearts no bar to an acceptance of thy decisions and give themselves up [to it] in utter self-surrender'. Therefore, Adian supported Jaʿfar's decision to agree to Abdullah's choice of the *rajam* law, arguing that the torture that Abdullah felt in this world would be much lighter as compared to the torture that he would feel in hell should he not have the *rajam* law implemented.[70]

Adian further maintained that a 'normal' Muslim would be willing to live in an Islamic state, within which life would be governed by Islamic rules. This was because Islamic teachings could only be essentially manifested within a formal Islamic state. Adian further questioned why many Indonesians were opposed to the implementation of Islamic law in daily life but at the same time felt oppressed by the current Indonesian (secular) law. For him, the discourse on the implementation of Islamic law in Indonesia was legal and normal, and Muslims should fight for it through political campaigns.[71] Adian, however, realised that the problem now was not whether it was right or wrong to establish an Islamic state; the problem was to find a leader who could manage the heterogeneity of the Indonesians. He argued that it was the lack of such a leader that had caused tensions and conflicts involving different religious believers in Indonesia.[72]

---

[69] Husaini, *Penyesatan Opini*, 95–98.

[70] Adian Husaini, 'Rajam, Siapa Takut?', *Media Dakwah*, June 2001, 41.

[71] Adian Husaini, interview by author, Jakarta, 29 January 2002.

[72] Adian Husaini, interview by author, Jakarta, 29 January 2002.

KISDI's support for the implementation of Islamic law was carried further by Ahmad Sumargono who supported the establishment of an Islamic state. In a debate in 1997 with Denny J.A., the executive director of Jayabaya University Foundation who was himself a Muslim, on the relation between religion and the state, Sumargono argued that the debate on the importance of a secular state stemmed from excessive fear of transforming Indonesia into an Islamic state. Taking Malaysia as an example of a state that had implemented Islamic law, Sumargono argued that there was nothing to fear from the establishment of an Islamic state. To support his argument, he claimed that non-Muslims in Malaysia did not protest the implementation of Islamic law. In addition, the *sharīʿa* did not prevent Malaysia from becoming a civilised and democratic country.[73] Sumargono disagreed with Denny's reasoning that the issue of Islam versus non-Islam, which arose after the fall of Soeharto in 1998, was engineered by supporters of Soeharto in order to achieve their political ends. On the contrary, Sumargono believed that there was a possibility that Soeharto's supporters and critics alike had adopted the issue of Islam versus non-Islam to achieve their political goals. He further underlined that the issue of religion should have its own place in politics.[74]

On 11 December 2000, KISDI officials were surprised when the *Republika* newspaper reported that Sumargono had resigned from KISDI and had formed another organisation named Gerakan Persaudaraan Muslim Indonesia (Association of Indonesian Muslim Brotherhood/GPMI). Sumargono missed two KISDI meetings before he sent his resignation letter. More surprisingly, in contrast to Sumargono's support for the establishment of an Islamic state, his unoffi-

---

[73] Ahmad Sumargono, 'Negara Sekuler: Tanggapan atas Tulisan Denny JA', in *Negara Sekuler: Sebuah Polemik*, ed. Saripudin (Jakarta: Putra Berdikari Bangsa, 2000), 25. Sumargono's claim that Malaysia is a democratic country is disputable. It is true that it has democratic elections but also authoritarian tendencies. The case of the imprisonment of Anwar Ibrahim by Mahathir Mohammad's regime was a clear example of authoritarian practice to overcome the political disputes between these two people.

[74] Ahmad Sumargono, 'Negara Sekuler', 46-47.

cial resignation was perceived by other KISDI leaders as being related to his earlier statements and position which might call into question his religiosity. One example was Sumargono's position in receiving funding that was suspected by other KISDI leaders to come from gamblers.[75]

Hussein Umar and DDII supporters in general were also concerned with the possibility of amending the 1945 Constitution. Hussein Umar argued that, during the colonial period, law related to ʿibāda/ rituals was enforced. After independence, hukum keluarga (family law) was put into practice. Therefore, 50% of Islamic law was in fact practised in Indonesia. He further emphasised that with the implementation of Islamic law in Indonesia any act that contradicted the sharīʿa could be legally prosecuted.[76]

In this context, Hussein Umar and the DDII first supported Abdullah's decision to uphold Islamic law (by choosing rajam) when some Muslims still feared the implementation of Islamic law in Indonesia. He also supported Ja'far's bravery in carrying out rajam law on Abdullah. Hussein Umar further questioned the arrest of Ja'far, which was perceived as the Christians' well-planned agenda to discredit Laskar Jihad.[77] Hussein Umar's perception reflected DDII's attitude towards the arrest of Ja'far. In a mass gathering held on 7 May 2001, DDII supporters protested the government's decision to arrest him and urged that Ja'far be freed.[78]

The above discussion on the implementation of the sharīʿa to a significant extent related to the Christians, who were widely perceived by exclusivist Muslims as the groups that would object to its implementation. However, Rizieq held a different view, stating that there were two groups of people objecting the implementation of the sharīʿa. According to him the first group was people who had a phobia towards

---

[75] KISDI, 'Maklumat KISDI tentang "Keluarnya Sumargono dari KISDI"', KISDI Menggugat (2), 71-74.

[76] Hussein Umar, 'Perjuangan Menegakkan Syariat Islam', Media Dakwah, July 2002, 6-7.

[77] 'Mengenang "Abdullah" Teladan dalam Kesadaran Hukum', Media Dakwah, June 2001, 6-7.

[78] 'Syariat Islam Diadili, Umat Islam Bergolak', Media Dakwah, June 2001, 50-51.

Islam even though they professed themselves to be Muslims. He believed that this group was not actually big in number but consisted of some key figures. The second group included people who did not actually comprehend the meaning of the implementation of the *sharīa*. This group was bigger than the first and was easier to persuade by popularising the idea of the *sharīa*. Without naming the two groups, Rizieq reasoned that it was wrong to believe that many of Indonesians rejected the implementation of the *sharīa*, and that this could be tested in a national referendum on the implementation of the *sharīa*.[79]

In this context, Adian shared Rizieq's argument that some Muslims were fearful of the implementation of the *sharīa*. Adian criticised a joint statement signed by three prominent Muslims, namely Hasyim Muzadi (the leader of the Nahdhatul Ulama), Syafii Ma'arif (the leader of Muhammadiyah), and Nurcholish Madjid (head of the Paramadina Foundation), on 10 August 2000, in which they refused the re-inclusion of the Jakarta Charter within the amendment of the 1945 Constitution.[80] The DDII was also disappointed with this statement, because it argued that including the *sharīa* within the Constitution would lead the state to intervene in personal faith. The DDII believed that the state had actually intervened in the practical religious issues of its community, such as in the law on marriage, the religious judicature act, and the law on Islamic banking.[81]

Rizieq realised that for some the revival of the Jakarta Charter could be interpreted as the intervention of the state within the area of religion. For him, however, this intervention was perceived as a logical consequence of adopting the leadership of the Prophet Muhammad. This was so as Muhammad implemented the *sharīa* in the name of the state. Rizieq quoted this verse:

---

[79] Rizieq Shihab, interview by author, Jakarta, 6 February 2002.
[80] Husaini, *Penyesatan Opini*, 92–93.
[81] 'Mengapa Takut Syariat Islam', *Media Dakwah*, July 2002, 42–43.

Verily, in the Apostle of God you have a good example for everyone who looks forward [with hope and awe] to God and the Last Day, and remembers God unceasingly (Q.S. 33:21).

In addition, Rizieq firmly believed that there was no single point that was not touched on or discussed by the *sharī'a*. However, there were some direct and lengthy explanations and some non-direct descriptions. The Qur'ān 17:12 said: 'For clearly, most clearly, have We spelt out everything!' [82]

The first verse quoted by Rizieq above to support his argument on the imposition of the *sharī'a* by the state seems out of context. Having the Prophet Muhammad as an example in life is one thing, and the imposition of the *sharī'a* by the state is another. Moreover, the second verse quoted to support his argument that the *sharī'a* covered every aspect of life is equally questionable. As Muhammad Asad explained, 'everything' in the verse meant 'everything that man may be in need of in the domain of ethics and religion'.[83] Therefore, to claim that everything was touched on or discussed by the *sharī'a* was inappropriate.

As mentioned, the erasure of the Jakarta Charter, which caused disappointment among the majority of Muslims, was to a significant extent caused by Christians. Even though attempts at reviving the Jakarta Charter and establishing an Islamic state were not specifically intended as revenge for what Christians had done to Muslims, it had an effect on Christians and Muslim–Christian relations. One might argue that the exclusivist Muslims' insistence on reviving the Charter and on establishing an Islamic state stemmed from their theological perspective that there should be no separation between state and religion (*Islām dīn wa dawla*). However, as their literature did not explain their theological reading of the Islamic concept of state, it is not

---

[82] Shihab, *Dialog Piagam Jakarta*, 31-32.
[83] Asad, *The Message of the Qur'ān*, 420.

easy to make such a claim. In this case, the role of the New Order government in weakening Islamic political power might go further to explain the exclusivists' insistence on the revival of the Jakarta Charter. The exclusivists might have thought that, with the implementation of the Charter, and more strongly with the establishment of an Islamic state, Muslims' religious and political rights would be better catered for.

Issue of Christianisation

The issue of Christianisation was the central concern during the interviews conducted for this study with key figures in exclusivist Muslim organisations. All exclusivist groups stated the view that it was the Christianisation activities that had torn the relationship between Muslims and Christians apart. Indeed, this issue was often put forward by Muslims following tensions or conflicts between Muslims and Christians as the reason behind the events.

In addition to the alleged brochure about the plan to Christianise Java (see Chapter Three), DDII in one of its publications quoted the policy of the DGI which was claimed to be issued in 1979 and to contain plans and targets for Christianising Indonesia. The detailed plans included efforts to decrease the number of Indonesian Muslims through family planning programs, to control mass media in order to confront Muslims by reporting their bad deeds, and to control education so that there would be fewer educated Muslims.[84] The exclusivists believed that Christians had a well-planned agenda, as part of the Christian international conspiracy, to discredit Islam.

Adian argued that Christianisation was the central issue behind the burning of several churches. In the case of conflict involving Muslims and Christians in Tasikmalaya and Rangkasdengklok (both are in West Java) in February 1997, for example, Adian quoted the findings

---

[84] 'Ini Rencana Mereka, Apa Jawab Kita? Program Jangka Panjang Kristenisasi di Indonesia', in *Fakta dan Data*, 53-59. This document was quoted by the DDII from *Crescent International*, 16-30 November, 1988 (published in Toronto, Canada), and was published in *Media Dakwah*, June 1990.

of the joint investigation team of KISDI and *Media Dakwah* which revealed several causes behind the conflicts. According to the findings, one of the serious causes was Christian efforts to convert people to Christianity with the support of the Indonesian Chinese and overseas aid. In Tasikmalaya, for instance, there were 18 churches surrounding a mosque. Adian considered this circumstance abnormal, as the total population of Christians in that area was only 3,800 compared to 1.5 million Muslims.[85]

Adian added that not all Christians were missionaries or evangelists; yet what created the problem was that there were evangelist Christians who were very aggressive in conducting their missions. For Adian, it was this aggressiveness that had become their trademark.[86] It is important to note that Adian pointed more to the Protestants than to the Catholics when he said, 'The PGI should remind these people of their aggressiveness as many cases such as the establishment of Institutes of Theology of Apostolos and Kalimatullah caused anxieties among Muslims'.[87] Adian strengthened his claim by referring to A.A. Yewangoe's (a Protestant) statement that the number of Indonesian Protestants was 16-17% or even 20% of the total Indonesian population due to the success of Christian missions. Yewangoe criticised the former Minister of Religious Affairs Tarmizi Taher, who stated that the Protestant population was only 5-6%. In Yewangoe's view, Tarmizi's statement was an attempt to show that Protestants were a minority in Indonesia. This would give the Protestants a minority mentality, which would later create a feeling of being second class citizens.[88]

---

[85] Husaini, *Gereja-Gereja Dibakar*, 140-141.

[86] Adian Husaini, interview by author, Jakarta, 29 January 2002.

[87] Adian Husaini, interview by author, Jakarta, 29 January 2002. Both Apostolos Institutes of Theology and Kalimatullah were Protestant-based. More discussion on these institutes will be given below.

[88] A.A. Yewangoe, 'Gereja di Era Reformasi', in *Gereja dan Reformasi*, ed. Victor Silaen (Jakarta: Yakoma PGI, 1999), 31-32.

Two issues arise here. First, Yewangoe's basis for the assumption that the number of Protestants was approaching 20% of the Indonesian population is questionable. It is probably true that the survey by the Central Statistics Bureau (Biro Pusat Statistik/BPS) in 1990, which showed that the Protestant population was 6%, was not perfect.[89] Nevertheless, so far there has been no better survey in Indonesia. Second, although Adian asserted that Yewangoe was too brave to make such a claim, the positive tone of Adian's comment suggests that Yewangoe's statement could be true. Adian's confirmatory tone regarding Yewangoe's claim deserves special mention. On one hand, when Adian and other exclusivist groups discussed in this study promoted the implementation of Islamic teachings or the establishment of an Islamic state, they often referred to the Muslims as the majority with more than 85% of the total population. On the other hand, when Christians claimed that the number of their followers was growing, the exclusivists tended to accept this claim and made a connection between the claim and the success of Christianisation programs. It seems that Adian's reference to this dubious figure was part of his attempt to find any information that would confirm the threat of Christianisation.

In addition to Adian's statement, KISDI commented on the issue of Christianisation as follows:

> We do not need to blame other people, but it is us who have to develop ourselves and our condition. We do not need to condemn the rights of our Christian friends to Christianise Indonesia since that is their religious duty. What we need to do is to strengthen our belief and our knowledge of Islam, and to enlighten our society so that they could be aware of any attempts launched by the devils (setan-setan) to lead our society array. We have to know that those devils never stop working.[90]

---

[89] It is important to note that the BPS applied a survey method, not a census based on a citizen's religion, in counting the Indonesian population by religion. The survey used sampling, thus did not count the whole Indonesian population.

[90] KISDI, 'Mencermati Gerakan Kristenisasi', 21-22.

The issue of Christianisation also concerned Rizieq Shihab and the FPI. His anger seemed not only directed towards the Protestants but also the Catholics, as he believed that both religious groups had the same intention to Christianise Muslims. 'It is true', he argued, 'that Protestantism has many sects, but the Catholic missionary is also very well organised'. Rizieq maintained that there should be a code of ethics between religious believers in terms of propagating their religions. To give an example, he stated that, in Bali, where Muslims were a minority, Muslims did not build mosques out of their wish to be tolerant of other believers. However, Rizieq argued that Christians had built churches everywhere without considering the number of Christians living in the area. In this context, he questioned why the Hindus and Buddhists were quite moderate in their interaction with the Muslims and why it was only the Christians who had problems with the Muslims. He suggested that the Christians should reflect on themselves.[91]

Rizieq's claim that it was only the Christians and not the Hindus and Buddhists who had problems with the Muslims, especially in building places of worship, is arguable. Rizieq, like other exclusivist Muslims, assumed that only Christians were vocal in criticising the joint decree of the Minister of Religious Affairs and the Minister of International Affairs in 1969 (SKB/1969), as this was seen as putting great limitations on Christian missionary activities. However, recent events suggested differently. For example, the director of Walubi, Hartati Murdaya, reasoned that the SKB/1969 was an obstacle for the development of the Buddhists. She argued that according to the decree a Buddhist temple could not be built if Buddhist followers did not reach a certain number. This situation forced them to go across island for their prayers. As a consequence, she demanded reconsideration of SKB/1969.[92] Another example was the debate over the revival of the Jakarta Charter in August

---

[91] Rizieq Shihab, interview by author, Jakarta, 6 February 2002.

[92] Rizki Ridyasmara, [online], available from http://www.sabili.co.id; accessed 22 June 2002.

1999. Contrary to the exclusivists' general assumption that it was only Christians who were anxious about any attempt at implementing the *sharīʿa*, in a meeting with Hamzah Haz, the Vice President of Indonesia at that time, Hartati Murdaya asked for an assurance from him that Indonesia would not be transformed into an Islamic state.[93]

FPI's animosity towards Christians generated accusations that this group was the actor behind several attacks in Jakarta and surrounding areas. FPI claimed that certain groups of people who named themselves 'anti-vice campaigners' had destroyed places which they considered centres of entertainment, such as discotheques and nightclubs. The members of this movement wore white robes imitating the uniform worn by FPI supporters, and therefore people swiftly associated them with FPI. In addition, FPI was blamed for the Ketapang incident involving Christian Moluccan gangsters in Jakarta and local Muslims,[94] and the burning of Doulos Institute of Theology in 1999.[95] However, Rizieq firmly denied any link to the riots but made some efforts to free the Muslims people who were gaoled over this case.[96] The charge against FPI was also probably due to Rizieq's remark that, although he condemned these destructive actions, he lent his support to any moral campaign. He believed that what the Muslims had done to the Christians was a mere reaction to what the Christians had done to the Muslims. Rizieq further explained that FPI supporters had never harassed churches that were legally built, as this was prohib-

---

[93] 'Antara Piagam Jakarta dan Tuntutan Penerapan Syari'at Islam' [online], available from http://www.kammimalang.tripod.com/syariat.html; accessed 24 July 2002.

[94] The event was a complicated one involving different forces. When a group of 'Amboneselooking' men burnt a motorcycle in front of a local mosque, the local Muslims thought that it was an attack by infidels on Muslims. FPI members were gathered from various places in Jakarta to help the local Muslims. G.J. Aditjondro, 'Guns, Pamphlets and Handie-Talkies', in *Violence in Indonesia*, eds. Inggrid Wessel and Georgia Wimhöfer (Hamburg: Abera Verlag, 2001), 111.

[95] Doulos is a Protestant Institute in East Jakarta. More explanation on this will be provided below.

[96] Rizieq Shihab, interview by author, Jakarta, 6 February 2002.

ited by Islam. However, he added, if the Christians did harm the Muslims, the latter should react accordingly.[97]

Christians acknowledged that there were efforts to Christianise. Franz Magnis-Suseno, a Catholic priest who is also lecturing at the Driyarkara Institute of Philosophy, for example, stated that even though Catholic and well-known Protestant Churches did not allow such activities, there were several small sects within Protestant churches that conducted Christianisation programs. These sects perceived both Muslims and Catholics as sinners. However, Magnis-Suseno rejected Muslim claims that Christians had employed financial or educational incentives to convert poor Muslims to Christianity. For him, Muslims who often cited the issue of Christianisation were only seeking to fuel hatred towards Christians.[98] In a similar way in 1990, the secretary of the PGI, J.M. Pattiasina, argued that the plan to Christianise Indonesia that was quoted and published by DDII was not correct and that the PGI had no such plan.[99]

There are some significant issues to be discussed here in relation Christianisation. These include the Inter-religious Consultation Forum (1967), church building (especially from the 1960s to the 1980s), the 1973 Marriage Bill, Christmas Celebrations (1981), the Draft on Religious Judicature Act (1989), and Christianisation efforts through education. The relation between these issues and Christianisation is discussed in each section below.

Inter-religious Consultation Forum

As discussed in Chapter Four, the government formed the Inter-religious Consultation Forum (*Wadah Musyawarah antar-Agama*) in November 1967. It has also been mentioned that the forum came with

---

[97] Rizieq Shihab, interview by author, Jakarta, 6 February 2002.

[98] Franz Magnis-Suseno, interview by author, Jakarta, 28 January 2002.

[99] Pattiasina's letter to *Media Dakwah* was published in the magazine on July 1990. The magazine commented that it was only quoted from the *Crescent International* that was circulated for two years and was never rejected by the PGI.

a proposal stating that the propagation of a religion should not be to enhance the number of its followers; rather it should be aimed at a better understanding of their religious teachings. In addition, the proposal recommended confining the propagation of religions to those who had not yet embraced one of the five religions; in other words '...not to make the religious believers a target for the spread of each others' religions'; a clause that was quoted from an official speech of President Soeharto at the meeting.[100]

Mohammad Natsir, M. Rasjidi (both DDII activists), and K.H. Masjkur from the Islamic side, as well as the delegation from the Hindus and the Buddhists, definitely agreed with the proposal. However, the Christians, represented by T.B. Simatupang, A.M. Tambunan (Protestants), and Ben Mang Reng Say (Catholic) bitterly opposed it.[101] Tambunan, for example, confirmed that Christians were to proclaim God's word to all nations by referring to texts in the Bible (Apostles 1:8; Mark 16:15). Therefore, Tambunan maintained that missionary activities could not be taken away from Christians, as this would violate God's decree. However, he underlined two things that according to him had been misunderstood by the Muslim community, namely the alleged efforts to Christianise Indonesia within a certain period of time and to conquer the Muslim world ('la conquete du monde Musulman'). The first was perceived by Tambunan as contradicting Christian teachings, as only God, not human beings, was capable of guiding people to Christianity. Similarly, Tambunan argued that the principle of the conquest of the Muslim world did not exist within the concept of

---

[100] The complete account of Soeharto's and Dahlan's speech was quoted in Natsir, *Islam dan Kristen di Indonesia*, 257-264.

[101] Simatupang restated his opinion at a session of the Working Group of the Council of Indonesian Churches (DGI) in 1978 at Palangka Raya, Kalimantan, that the 1967 meeting challenged this very task from God. He further stated that 'any efforts to limit this "mandate" from outside and amongst those of us who only perceive certain aspects of this "mandate", compels us to reflect more deeply and comprehensively about why we convey the Good News'; T.B. Simatupang, 'Menyampaikan Berita Kesukaan', in *Kehadiran Kristen dalam Perang, Revolusi dan Pembangunan* (Jakarta, BPK Gunung Mulia, 1986), 132.

Christian mission.[102] The situation at that time was well described by Rosihan Anwar, a journalist who was present when the meeting took place, as very tense. He explained that Simatupang, of the Protestant side, 'was fighting for his opinion like a tiger until his shirt was full of sweat'.[103]

In the forum, Natsir questioned why the harmonious relations that existed between Catholics and Protestants could not be extended to include the Muslims.[104] Natsir stated that it was not the attempt of each believer to convey God's message that had caused tense relations between Muslims and Christians. Rather, in contrast to Tambunan's argument on the conquest of the Muslim world, Natsir believed that the disharmonious relations between the two groups were caused by the activities of overseas missionaries who were targeting Indonesian Muslims within the frame of '*la conquete du monde Musulman*'. Natsir further maintained that Muslims believed that their religion was under threat because it was a target of a planned and expansive Christianisation program. Therefore, he requested that there should be a method that would guarantee multi-religious life in Indonesia without targeting other religious believers. Natsir argued that Muslims had their own code of ethics and therefore did not target other believers to embrace Islam.[105]

At the same forum, Rasjidi stated that Christianisation activities were conducted by Christians among Indonesian Muslims. He shared his own experience of being visited by two Christian missionaries who tried to convert him to Christianity. Moreover, he referred to a case in Yogyakarta in 1967 where an ex-Communist member who was in prison was approached by a Christian who offered him finan-

---

[102] 'Pidato Sambutan Dr A.M. Tambunan, S.H. pada Musyawarah Nasional Kerukunan dan Kebebasan Beragama', in *Pembinaan Kerukunan Hidup Umat Beragama*, 66-73.

[103] H. Rosihan Anwar, 'Prof. Dr. H.M. Rasjidi Pengungkap Gamblang Hubungan Antaragama di Indonesia', in *70 Tahun Prof. Dr. H.M. Rasjidi*, 156.

[104] Mohammad Natsir, *Mencari Modus Vivendi Antar Umat Beragama* (Jakarta: Media Dakwah, 1980), 16-17.

[105] Natsir, *Mencari Modus Vivendi*, 14-15; and Natsir, *Islam dan Kristen di Indonesia*, 211-214.

cial help for his family. This help, however, was conditional upon the agreement that the prisoner would embrace Christianity. Therefore, Rasjidi refuted Tambunan's argument that the concept of the conquest of the Islamic world did not exist. For Rasjidi, the concept was translated, especially in Indonesia, into a clear plan as written in Hendrik Kraemer's book *The Christian Message in a Non Christian World*. And it was against such a plan that the Christians rejected the proposal 'not to make the religious believers a target for the spread of each others' religions'.[106]

It is understandable that the Muslims in the inter-religious consultation forum were disappointed with the Christians for not being more conciliatory, considering that the proposal would benefit religious communities in general. The forum closed with no agreement among the participants regarding the proposal which included the clause 'not to make the religious believers a target for the spread of each others' religions'.[107] In response to the failure to achieve the agreement, Husein Umar argued that the reasons given by the Christians for rejecting the clause demonstrated how consistent they were when faced with values or a specific situation that they saw as weakening their position.[108] The proposal was not adopted as a government regulation. However, as stated in Chapter Four, in 1978 the government issued decree No. 70 (SK 70/1978), which contained guidance on religious propagation. This decree made the rejected proposal a government rule.

Polomka aptly described the Christians' fear if the proposal suggested at the forum was accepted. He stated that the Christians categorically rejected the proposal, arguing that it 'was identical with the spirit, if not the letter, of the "Jakarta Charter" which many Indonesians, both Christians and non-Christians, have opposed since the strug-

---

[106] Natsir, *Islam dan Kristen di Indonesia*, 272-273.

[107] The same proposal was re-discussed in 1970 and 1994 and was also rejected by the Christians on the same ground.

[108] Umar, 'Intoleransi Kaum Nasrani', 6.

gle for independence began'.[109] For DDII leaders and supporters, the event was a turning point, something that set the tone of Muslim-Christian relations for much of the New Order period. For them, Christians' insistence on the Inter-religious Consultation Forum in 1967 was proof of the efforts towards Christianisation cited many times in the magazine *Media Dakwah.*

The Issue of Church Buildings in Relation to Decree No. 01/BER/MDN-MAG/1969, Decree No. 70/1978, and Decree No. 77/1978

One issue that influenced relations between Muslims and Christians was the building of churches within Muslim compounds. The rapid growth of church buildings, especially from the second half of the 1960s to the 1970s, was more than supposition. For example, the number of Indonesian Baptist Churches (Gabungan Gereja-Gereja Baptis Indonesia/GGBI) increased significantly within ten years from 9 in 1960 to 34 in 1971.[110] Table 3 below gives a comparative picture of church and mosque construction in East Java over the seventeen-year period from 1973 to 1990. Table 4 shows a figure of the rapid growth of church members and denominations within the Protestant churches, especially between 1970 and 1990. Even though the construction of mosques increased rapidly and the number of Christian (Protestant) churches decreased quite significantly in 1990 (as shown in Table 3), one might argue that, considering the large number of Indonesian Muslims, it was reasonable that the government build more mosques than churches. Moreover, as shown in Table 4, the total denominations of Protestant churches increased almost 60% from 1970 to 1990.

---

[109] Peter Polomka, *Indonesia Since Sukarno* (Middlesex, England: Penguin Books, 1971), 184.
[110] Willis, *Indonesian Revival,* 180.

Table 3: Church and Mosque Constructions in East Java from 1973 to 1990[111]

	1973	1979	1984	1990
Mosque	15,574	17,750	20,648	25,655
Catholic churches	206	No data	No data	324
Protestant churches (including meeting halls)	1,330	2,308	No data	1,376

Table 4: Church Members and Denominations in mid 1900, 1970 and 1990 Indonesia[112]

	Mid 1900	Mid 1970	Mid 1990
Total affiliated members	563,050	12,316,542	22,275,190
Total denominations	25	171	270

Official data on the number of converts to Christianity from Islam are not available. This is understandable considering that the issue was very sensitive for the Indonesian community during the New Order period. However, Willis recorded that the majority of Christian growth amongst the Javanese since 1960 came from the *abangan.* Willis forwarded four reasons to explain the conversion, including the fact that

---

[111] Robert W. Hefner, 'Islamization and Democratization in Indonesia', in *Islam in an Era of Nation-States: Politics and Religious Renewal in Muslim Southeast Asia,* eds. Robert W. Hefner and Patricia Horvatich (Honolulu: University of Hawai'i Press, 1997), 88. Hefner took the data from various sources including Kantor Statistik dan Pemerintah Jawa Timur (East Java Statistic and Government Office), 1992.

[112] Barrett, Kurian, and Johnson, *World Christian Encyclopedia,* vol. 1, 377.

the *abangan* 'do not identify themselves with the *ummat*, and can therefore more easily move to another religion without being ostracized from their social group'. He further maintained that fewer converts had a *santri* background because they would experience 'personal crises, dissatisfaction in their spiritual lives' if they embraced Christianity.[113]

Muslims understood the rapid increase in church building, especially those built within Muslim compounds, as efforts by Christians to convert them to Christianity. Indeed, one of DDII's programs was to build mosques to counter the growth of churches and to strengthen Muslim belief through activities held at mosques. The *Media Dakwah* magazine of DDII continuously reported the alleged efforts of Christians to build churches in the areas where Muslims were the majority. One example was the building of a church in Simpang Kanan, Aceh. This area was renowned for its strong Islamic education. However, DDII claimed that the Christians, who formed 17.10% of the total population in the area, insisted on building a church in 1979. When the local government, based on complaints by some Muslims, ordered the Christians to stop the construction, they did not listen.[114] DDII also listed a more recent example of church construction in Karangasem, Situbondo (East Java) in 1991. The district, with a 97% Muslim population (at that time), was angered by the building of a Bethel church in the midst of a Muslim compound. DDII argued that the Muslims were angrier to learn that the local government, which in their view should have rejected the proposal, had given its approval for the construction. In addition, a few houses within the area were suspected of being utilised by Christians as prayer quarters. What made the Muslims in the area furious was the perception that within a distance of four kilometres there were six churches.[115]

---

[113] Willis, *Indonesian Revival*, 130-131.

[114] 'Maka Gereja pun Bermunculan', in *Fakta dan Data*, 73-74.

[115] 'Menggebunya Kristenisasi di Situbondo', in *Fakta dan Data*, 204-206.

According to Rasjidi, the Christians were enthusiastic in buying strategic land or houses from Muslims for inflated prices. If the Muslims showed no interest in selling, the missionaries would make use of people with no association to them to bring about the sales.[116] In addition, Rasjidi held that many churches were built 'in the midst of Muslim villages and rice fields, and in strategic corners of big towns, out of all proportion to the Christian presence in the area'.[117] Moreover, Hussein Umar argued that facts pointed at efforts by Christians to drive Muslims away from their religion, as shown by the rapid increase in the number of churches during the New Order government. This was coupled with the attitudes of certain Christian missionaries who did not obey the code of ethics in propagating their religion: 'By using the argument that every human being has the right to convert to other religions, these missionaries tried to convert Muslims to Christianity'.[118]

Mohammad Natsir believed that the Christians' continued actions in building churches within Muslim complexes had led to the destruction of churches in Meulaboh (1967), Makassar (1967), and Slipi, Jakarta (1969). When interviewed by a journalist from the Protestant-owned newspaper *Sinar Harapan*, Natsir stated that the burning of the churches in Makassar was only an effect of the Christianisation process.[119] In commenting on the destruction of the church in Slipi, Jakarta, he maintained that the Muslim's anger was firstly caused by the fact that there were already five churches within the area to cater for 350 Christians in the midst of 35,650 Muslims (at that time). Second, the Christians paid no attention to the instruction of the local governor of

---

[116] M. Rasjidi, 'The Ethical and Social Demands of Islam for a Modern Society with Special Consideration for the Moslems of Indonesia', paper presented in October 1968 in Tokyo, cited in M. Natsir, *Islam dan Kristen di Indonesia*, 245-246. See also M. Rasjidi, *Mengapa Aku Tetap Memeluk Agama Islam* (Jakarta: Hudaya, 1968), 15.

[117] H.M. Rasjidi, 'The Role of Christian Missions', 7. Reprinted from *International Review of Mission*, 65, no. 260 (1976) by *Media Dakwah* (no date).

[118] Hussein Umar, interview by author, Jakarta, 25 January 2002.

[119] Natsir, 'Kode Toleransi Beragama', in *Islam dan Kristen di Indonesia*, 208. See also Natsir, *Mencari Modus Vivendi*, 8.

Jakarta to discontinue building. Natsir realised that the destruction of these churches was illegal. However, he argued 'these illegal actions would not occur if the Christians adhered to the instruction of the local government to discontinue building'.[120]

Similarly, in regard to the destruction of several churches in Situbondo, East Java, in October 1996, Hussein Umar maintained that it was related to the illegal church construction by Christians in many areas of Indonesia. He argued that out of 33 churches that were burnt down, only three had permission (Izin Mendirikan Bangunan/IMB) from the local government.[121] However, Amien Rais, the chairman of Muhammadiyah, gave a rather different explanation for the riots in several areas of Indonesia, including Situbondo, Tasikmalaya (West Java) in December 1996, and in Singkawang (West Kalimantan) in December 1996. For Amien Rais, the riots were not religion-related. Rather, they were inflicted by the socio-economic deprivation suffered by grass roots people. Amien Rais believed that the number of poor people was increasing and the gap between the 'haves' and 'have nots' had risen significantly. It was in this condition that poor people were easily provoked to commit violent actions.[122]

The church building and other Christianisation efforts led some Muslims, including the DDII activists, to send a letter to Pope John Paul II when he visited Indonesia in October 1989.[123] The letter explained the history of Islam in Indonesia and the Muslims' concern about the Christians' abuse of *diakonia* (religious social welfare activities). Referring to the issue of church building, it stated that in villages where Christianisation was active, the missionaries built churches and chapels

---

[120] Natsir, 'Mohammad Natsir Mengajukan Tiga Saran untuk Tiga Pihak', in *Islam dan Kristen di Indonesia*, 238-239.

[121] Hussein Umar, interview by author, Jakarta 25 January 2002.

[122] Amien Rais, 'Ini Bukan Soal SARA, tapi Kesenjangan Sosial', *Forum Keadilan*, 27 January 1997, 94-98.

[123] Four people signed this letter: Mohammad Natsir, H.M. Rasjidi (both were DDII activists), K.H. Masykur (leading figure of Nahdhatul Ulama), and K.H. Rusli Abd. Wahib (Chairman of Perti).

without the permission of the local government. They further maintained that where Christians were afraid of being challenged by local Muslims, they would start by building houses then gradually transforming them into religious buildings. The letter appealed to the Pope to remind Catholics to be more tolerant of Muslims in order to maintain religious harmony amongst believers in Indonesia.[124]

Table 5: The number of churches damaged or burnt down in Indonesia from 1945–1997[125]

Period	Number	Average/year
1945-1954	0	0
1955-1964	2	0.2
1965-1974	46	4.6
1975-1984	891	8.9
1985-1994	32	13.2
1995-1997	89	44.5
Total	358	

The issue of church building re-emerged when the Doulos Institute of Theology at Cipayung, East Jakarta, was burnt down on 15 December 1999. This Protestant institution aimed at helping drug addicts and functioned as a prayer community centre. Regarding questions about the motives behind the torching, one scenario suggested that certain Muslim groups were angry that the Doulos Institute was using an unlicensed prayer house. According to the local people, it had attempted proselytising Muslims by offering them help, for example free medication, if they converted to their brand of Christianity.[126]

---

[124] See *Surat kepada Paus Yohannes Paulus II Agar Penyalahgunaan Diakonia Dihentikan* (Jakarta: DDII, 1989), 9-13, 21.

[125] Paul Tahalele and Thomas Santoso, eds., *Beginikah Kemerdekaan Kita?* (Surabaya: Forum Komunikasi Kristiani Surabaya, 1997), 39.

[126] 'Serangan Malam', *Tempo*, 26 December 1999, 28-29.

KISDI claimed that an investigation by a person named Hamdi and published in the *Jihad* tabloid in November 1999 revealed that the Doulos Institute, secretly as well as publicly, launched Christianisation programs. Based on this investigation and some internal publications by the Doulos Institute, KISDI leaders sent a letter to Police Headquarters (Kapolda) Metro Jaya, Jakarta, urging them to investigate the actors and motives behind Doulos. Although KISDI leaders regretted what had happened, they said that they 'could understand' (*dapat memahami*), and did not blame the Muslims who destroyed the building since they were provoked by the fact that the Doulos Institute carried on proselytising activities. KISDI stated that what inflamed the Muslims' hatred the most was the Doulos's attempt to label the Muslims as '*suku terasing*' (alien tribe), who had not been touched by the Bible.[127]

Nevertheless, KISDI rejected the accusation that only Muslims were behind the attack on Doulos. KISDI officials criticised arguments by some Muslim scholars, such as Djohan Efendi and Abdurrahman Wahid, that the attack was the result of Muslim hatred instilled by Muslim preachers on various occasions. Abdurrahman Wahid further argued that, in the last 40 years, the development of Islamic education and preaching had been based on hatred towards other religions. For that reason, he believed that Muslim attacks on churches and other religious institutions were the result of the misconceptions encouraged by Muslim preachers, ʿulamāʾ, and the like.[128]

Although one might disagree that Muslim animosity as ignited by the ʿulamāʾ was the sole and main reason for the attack on the Doulos Institute, there was some truth in Abdurrahman Wahid's remarks. In many Muslim schools throughout Indonesia and in many Friday sermons, teachers and ʿulamāʾ were quoting Qurʾānic verses to remind Muslims and students of the danger of Christians and

---

[127] KISDI, 'Yayasan Doulos, Duri dalam Daging Bangsa Indonesia', and 'Kasus Doulos: Surat untuk Kapolda Metro Jaya', *KISDI Menggugat (2)*, 41-46. See also, Husaini, *Gereja-Gereja Dibakar*, 48.

[128] Husaini, *Gereja-Gereja Dibakar*, 143.

Christianisation. The hatred towards Christians became widespread. Nevertheless, similar cases also occurred within Christian circles. For example, in 1999, a recording by Major General Theo Syafei, Military Commander of Udayana Region and a Protestant, was discovered. The recording revealed Theo's analysis of Muslim roles in Indonesian politics and concluded that Indonesian Islamic mass organisations were conspiring to establish an Islamic state. The cassette was clearly taped before the election of 1999, as it invoked Christians not to vote for sectarian parties (such as the National Mandate Party/ Partai Amanat Nasional, PAN, or National Awakening Party/Partai Kebangkitan Bangsa, PKB) in the election.[129] The recording provoked a lot of bigotry and provocation on Muslim and Christian sides.

From the Christian (both Catholic and Protestant) perspective, however, the explanation of the 'problem' of church building was quite different. Chapter Four has discussed the SK 70/1978 on propagating religion, and the SK 77/1978 on foreign aid to religious institutions in Indonesia. Soon after the issuing of these decrees, Christians strongly objected to them. As both decrees had no legal sanction, the Christians felt free to reject them. MAWI and DGI leaders questioned the reasons behind the issuance of the decrees as they believed that harmony between followers of different religions had largely been achieved. What angered the Christians the most was that under SK 70/1978 the propagation of religion could not be directed towards people who already had a religion; this was the proposal that had been firmly rejected by the Christians at the Inter-religious Consultation Forum in 1967. They further argued that this attempt to restrict the freedom to propagate religion contradicted the spirit of Pancasila and the 1945 Constitution. More importantly, Christianity teaches its followers to spread the religion to all human beings. Therefore, the Christians believed that this restriction on propagating religion

---

[129] 'Umat Islam Makin Galau' [online], available from http://www.gatra.com; accessed 20 January 1999.

contradicted the teachings of Jesus. After a very detailed scrutiny of the decrees, both DGI and MAWI firmly rejected them and urged the government to annul them.[130]

Because the above decrees had no legal sanction, Christians could not be prosecuted for going against them. However, it is important to note that even though Christians severely criticised and rejected the decrees, it did not mean that they were free to convert people to Christianity or to receive foreign aid, as government bureaucracy would try to prevent that. In a similar line, Christian criticism of decree 01/BER/MDN-MAG/1969, which regulated the building of prayer houses, did not leave them free to build churches. Franz Magnis-Suseno argued that the decree was issued without any consultation let alone agreement with the Christians. He further emphasised that with this decree it was very difficult for Christians to gain permission to build churches, and therefore they were frequently forced to use private dwellings as prayer houses, which often ignited tensions with Muslims.[131] For him, regular additional churches in every region should be seen as normal because of the increasing number of Catholics and Protestants who joined the urbanisation or transmigration programs. Magnis-Suseno further added that Christians actually had similar feelings about Islamisation. In the areas where Christians were the majority, there was anxiety that Muslims would try to convert them to the religion of Muhammad. He added that Muslims need not worry about the increasing number of Christians, since Muslims were the majority of the Indonesian population.[132]

Another response came from a Protestant, Natan Setiabudi, head of the PGI. He stated that it was important to note that, unlike mos-

---

[130] Sekretariat Umum Dewan Gereja-Gereja di Indonesia and Sekretariat Majelis Agung Waligereja Indonesia, *Tinjauan Mengenai Keputusan Menteri Agama No. 70 dan 77 Tahun 1978 dalam Rangka Penyelenggaraan Kebebasan Beragama dan Pemeliharaan Kerukunan Nasional* (Jakarta: DGI & MAWI, 1978).

[131] Franz Magnis-Suseno, 'SKB Itu Diskriminatif', *Gatra*, 1 February 1997, 40–41.

[132] Franz Magnis-Suseno, interview by author, Jakarta, 28 January 2002.

ques, Protestant churches had formal memberships. Therefore, it was important for these churches to have their own members, and to gain as many members as they could. In addition, there were 79 synods within the PGI, and other denominations outside the PGI. In contrast to the Catholics, these denominations had to have their own churches, and therefore the number of Protestant churches was very large. Natan admitted that PGI's decisions morally obliged Protestants, yet it had no rights to sanction those who did not follow government regulations, for example in church construction.[133] The Christians' continued rejection of the three decrees was quoted by exclusivist Muslims in explaining Christianisation.

The 1973 Marriage Bill and the Issue of Inter-religious Marriage

Another issue related to Muslim–Christian relations was the 1973 Marriage Bill (Rencana Undang-Undang Perkawinan). As discussed in Chapter Four, one of the points that angered the Muslims was article 11 (2), which stated 'The differences in nationality, ethnicity, country and place of origin, religion, faith and ancestry should not constitute an impediment to marriage'. While difference in nationality or ethnicity in a marriage was acceptable from the Islamic perspective, the difference in religion could not be tolerated, especially for Muslim women to marry non-Muslim men. Another point that became a source of Muslim outrage was article 2 (1), which stipulated 'Civil registration was necessary for the validity of Muslim marriage'. This point clearly contradicted the sharī'a which did not stipulate that civil registration was a condition of valid marriage. To some Muslims, accepting the above points and some other points (such as articles 62 on adopted children) would mean a rejection of Islam as a way of life.[134]

Tempo magazine reported that never in Indonesian history had a bill attracted so much attention from the society. Different Islamic

---

[133] Natan Setiabudi, interview by author, Jakarta, 27 February 2002.
[134] Azra, 'The Indonesian Marriage Law of 1974', 83.

organisations, including the Majelis Ulama Aceh, the Indonesian Islamic Youth (Generasi Muda Islam Indonesia/GMII), some Islamic student organisations (Pelajar Islam Indonesia/PII, Ikatan Pelajar Nahdhatul Ulama/IPNU, Ikatan Pelajar Putri Nahdhatul Ulama/IPPNU, and Ikatan Pelajar Muhammadiyah), and Muslim individuals rejected the Bill based on their belief that it contradicted Islamic teaching.[135] Anwar Harjono, for example, quoted the MUI's *fatwā* (see Chapter Four), arguing that inter-religious marriage was *harām* because the harm (*mafsadah*) of such a marriage outweighed its benefits (*maslahah*).[136] He also stated that Muslim rejection of the Marriage Bill was based purely on religion, not on politics. Even though he realised that the Garis-Garis Besar Haluan Negara (Broad Outlines of the State Policy/GBHN) stated the importance of having a national and uniform law within which every Indonesian citizen would be regulated, he maintained that such law could not be implemented in every aspect of life. He further stressed that, on the issue of family law, a national and uniform law could only regulate non-religious and non-cultural aspects of life (such as property or contract), not matters pertaining to religious aspects (such as marriage, divorce or inheritance).[137]

However, it was Rasjidi who was very active in rejecting the Marriage Bill. In his book *Kasus RUU Perkawinan dalam Hubungan Islam dan Kristen* (The Case of the Marriage Bill in its Relation to Muslim–Christian Relations), he firmly argued that inter-religious marriage was not allowed in Islam. He referred to a marriage in Solo Palace, Central Java, in June 1973, a few months before the Bill was debated. This was a marriage between Koes Supiah, a princess of the *Susuhunan* (Sultan) Pakubuwono XII, who was married to a Christian named Sylvanus, from Kalimantan. According to Rasjidi, the fact

---

[135] 'RUU Perkawinan, Aksi dan Reaksi', 6-8. See also Redaksi Panjimas, 'Dari Konseptor RUUP agar Diadili Hingga Demonstrasi Tak Ada Kalau Ada Komunikasi', *Panji Masyarakat*, 15 December 1973, 6.

[136] Anwar Harjono, 'Renungan Menjelang Ramadhan', *Media Dakwah*, March 1992, 6-7.

[137] 'RUU Perkawinan: Mencabut & Merubah', *Tempo*, 22 September 1973, 8-9.

that Koes Supiah was not allowed to marry her lover Abdullah Suwarna, a Muslim whom she had known for several years, but was allowed to marry a Christian, was proof of efforts to legalise inter-religious marriage. Rasjidi argued that there was a move to perceive inter-religious marriage as a normal practice, as later stipulated in the Marriage Bill. Rasjidi further stated that the Bill was nothing but an attempt to Christianise the 90% of Indonesians who were Muslims, and that it was 'a disguised Christianisation effort'. Although he admitted that not all Catholics or Protestants were willing to convert Muslims to Christianity, Rasjidi believed that there were Christian missionaries who supported the Bill in their attempts at Christianising Indonesian Muslims.[138]

The debates in parliament on the Marriage Bill continued in the newspapers, where both the Muslim and Christian sides defended their arguments. Rasjidi's opinion that the Bill was a disguised Christianisation effort was published in several newspapers, including *KAMI, Nusantara*, and *Abadi*, on 19 August 1973. On 12 December 1973, a Protestant-associated newspaper, *Sinar Harapan*, published a memorandum issued by the Komite Kesatuan Generasi Muda Indonesia (the Committee of Indonesian Youth) which stated that 'The state should not and could not impose the practice of religious teachings on its believers, including in terms of marriage'. In other words, the state should guarantee the freedom of its citizens to enter an inter-religious marriage.[139] In addition, the editorials of both *Kompas* (Catholic-owned)[140] and *Sinar Harapan*[141] newspapers examined the issue and argued that 'The religion-based law on marriage would pave the way for the implementation of other religion-based law on other aspects of life'. However, a more serious response came from a letter signed by S.A.E. Nababan

---

[138] H.M. Rasjidi, *Kasus RUU Perkawinan dalam Hubungan Islam dan Kristen* (Jakarta: Bulan Bintang, 1974), 9-12.

[139] 'Memorandum tentang RUU Perkawinan', *Sinar Harapan*, 12 December 1973.

[140] 'Para Penyusun UUD '45 Sudah beri Jalan Keluar', *Kompas*, 17 December 1973.

[141] 'Mengapa Suratkabar ini Begitu Getol Mengenai RUUP?', *Sinar Harapan*, 17 December 1973.

of the DGI and the secretary of the MAWI, Leo Soekoto SJ, dated 12 December 1973:

1. According to article 29 of the 1945 Constitution 'The state guaranteed to citizens the freedom to embrace their religion and to perform rituals according to their religion or belief.' This means that the freedom of choice constituted the most important thing in religion.

2. During the discussion on the Marriage Bill in the parliament, we were concerned that the state would not only guarantee the freedom of religion but would also impose the practice of religious law, at least concerning marriage.

3. We were hoping that every citizen would voluntarily go through a marriage ceremony according to their own religion. However if we considered that only marriages conducted according to one's own religion were valid, then many problems concerning religious freedom would arise.[142]

Large demonstrations against the Bill worried the New Order regime and therefore the government made fundamental changes to the Bill, which became Marriage Law No. 1/1974. Article 2 of the new formulation stipulated that 'A marriage is valid only if it satisfies the religious law of the spouses'. A.H. Johns stated that 'from several standpoints, the bill represents a milestone in the history of Islam in public life in Indonesia'.[143] Against this backdrop, the Perhimpunan Mahasiswa Katolik Republik Indonesia (Indonesian Catholic Student Association/PMKRI) released a statement arguing that the revised Bill deviated from the spirit of Pancasila and the 1945 Constitution in which

---

[142] 'Negara Perlu Berikan Ruang untuk Kawin Sah Menurut Hukum Negara', *Sinar Harapan*, 19 December 1973.

[143] Anthony H. Johns, 'Indonesia: Islam and Cultural Pluralism', in *Islam in Asia Religion, Politics, and Society*, ed. John L. Esposito (New York and Oxford: Oxford University Press, 1987), 219.

the freedom of religion was guaranteed. Moreover, the PMKRI criticised the new formulation, accusing the state through this revised Bill of forcing its citizens to perform their religious duty as a pre-requisite for a marriage.[144]

Rasjidi perceived the Christians' firm rejection of the revised Bill as opposition to Muslim family law and support for Christianisation. He further asserted that the 'Christians use every artifice to see that secular law prevails, which for the Muslims virtually means de-Islamisation of their collective life'.[145] What astonished Rasjidi the most was the perceived Christians' unwillingness to see the Muslims implementing Islamic law within their socio-political system. Rasjidi believed that the core of the Catholics' and Protestants' rejection of the Bill was their perception that religion must be prohibited from playing a determining role in the socio-political life of the Indonesian people.[146] Rasjidi's language here betrayed a deep suspicion and hostility towards Christians; he was basically accusing them of duplicity. Even though it was true that Christians did not want Islamic law implemented in Indonesia, to say that 'Christians use every artifice to see that secular law prevails' appears to be an exaggeration.

The issue of inter-religious marriage re-appeared several times in recent Indonesian history. As mentioned in Chapter Four, the issue was heatedly debated in 1992 when Munawir Sjadzali suggested an additional formulation to the Marriage Law of 1974, especially on the issue of inter-religious marriage. For Sjadzali, as Indonesia was heterogeneous society, the fact that inter-religious marriage was not allowed under the Marriage Law only paved the way for people of different faiths to live together outside marriage. For Muslims, who had felt relieved for 18 years after the issuance of the 1974 Marriage Law which stated that 'A marriage is valid only if it is conducted

---

[144] 'Dan Lahirlah UU Itu', 5–8.

[145] Rasjidi, 'The Role of Christian Missions', 19.

[146] Rasjidi, 'The Role of Christian Missions', 19–20.

according to one's own belief', Munawir's suggestion was quite appalling. Hussein Umar, for example, argued that Munawir's proposal was supported by some non-Muslims, especially Christians, who wanted to Christianise Muslims. For Hussein Umar, this was because, under the proposed change to the Marriage Law, Christian men could easily marry Muslim women to later convert them to Christianity.[147] Similarly, the Forum Ukhuwah (Brethren Forum) for discussing inter-religious marriage, and of which Anwar Harjono and Hussein Umar of DDII were members, wrote to the vice chairperson of the parliament on 20 February 1992 rejecting the proposal put forward by Munawir.[148]

The issue of inter-religious marriage concerned NU and Muhammadiyah organisations as well as MUI. NU was among the first to issue a *fatwā* in 1962 in its *Muktamar* (Summit Conference), which was reconfirmed in 1968 and 1989, prohibiting inter-religious marriage. The re-issuing of the *fatwā* in 1989 was seemingly based on the increasing practice of inter-religious marriage in Indonesia.[149] Muhammadiyah, in its *Tanwir* conference in Jakarta in January 1992, also argued that the 1974 Marriage Law clearly stated that inter-religious marriage was not allowed. This argument was apparently a response to Munawir's proposal. In a similar way, the MUI responded to this controversy by issuing guidelines for Muslims on marriage. Some other individuals as well as educational institutions, including IAINs, also severely criticised Munawir on this matter.[150]

Without aiming at a comprehensive discussion of inter-religious marriage after the fall of the New Order, it is worthy noting a recent case in

---

[147] 'UU Perkawinan Terancam Diubah', *Media Dakwah*, February 1992, 14–16.

[148] 'Forum Ukhuwah tentang Perkawinan Antaragama', *Media Dakwah*, April 1992, 14–15.

[149] Muhammad Ali, '*Fatwas* on Inter-Faith Marriage in Indonesia', *Studia Islamika* 9, no. 3 (2002): 11–13.

[150] These included lecturers of IAIN Surabaya, Harun Nasution of IAIN Jakarta, and Supreme Court member Bismar Siregar. See Darul Aqsha, Dick van der Meij, and Johan Hendrik Meuleman, *Islam in Indonesia: A Survey of Events and Developments from 1988 to March 1993* (Jakarta: INIS, 1995), 471–473.

order to analyse the exclusivist Muslims' perspectives on the issue. The problem of inter-religious marriage appeared again when marriages between Muslim women and non-Muslim men took place in 2002. In June 2002, the Radio 68H in Jakarta broadcast an interview with Zainun Kamal, a Muslim associated with the Jaringan Islam Liberal (Islamic Liberal Network/JIL), on inter-religious marriage. JIL is well-known as a network of young Indonesian Muslims that promotes pluralist and inclusivist interpretations of Islam, and was established in February 2001. In the interview, Zainun stated that the Qur'ānic verses did not explicitly prohibit a Muslim woman from marrying a non-Muslim man, even though a few (*sebagian*) *ᶜulamā'* maintained that it was prohibited (*ḥarām*).[151]

Zainun's view was severely criticised by various exclusivist Muslims. DDII argued that, because of the interview, some Muslim women in Batusangkar, West Sumatra, had married non-Muslim men.[152] In addition, Adian challenged Zainun's argument, saying that all *ᶜulamā'* were united in stating that it was *ḥarām* for a Muslim woman to marry a non-Muslim man. Quoting the opinion of Hamka, Adian believed that such a marriage was illegal and was seen as adultery (*zinā*) from the Islamic perspective.[153] Attempting to clarify Zainun's statement, Cholil Ridwan of KISDI argued that the former, in a discussion forum held on 26 August 2002, emphasised that he had never supported let alone encouraged Muslim women to marry non-Muslim men. Cholil reported that, on the contrary, Zainun had said that this kind of inter-religious marriage should be avoided (*jangan dilakukan*).[154]

Adian further added that inter-religious marriage in fact contradicted the Marriage Law of 1974, which stipulated that 'A marriage

---

[151] The interview was also published in 'Nikah Beda Agama' [online], available from http://www.islamlib.com/id/page.php?page=article&id=224; accessed 7 July 2002.

[152] 'Dialog "Kawin antar Agama"', *Media Dakwah*, September 2002, 13-14.

[153] Adian Husaini, 'Menyoal Perkawinan Beda Agama' [online], available from http://www.republika.co.id/cetak_detail.asp?id=94089&kat_id=217; accessed 13 September 2002.

[154] Cholil Ridwan, 'Pernikahan Antar Agama', *Media Dakwah*, September 2002, 3.

is valid only if it satisfies the religious law of the spouses'. Moreover, he argued that the law was strengthened by the *fatwā* on inter-religious marriage issued by the MUI in June 1980. Therefore, he was surprised to find that Indonesian society did not question inter-religious marriages between popular figures that were reported in the media, such as the marriage between Yuni Shara (a Muslim singer) and Henry Siahaan (a Christian). Even though Adian did not directly say that the inter-religious marriages he was discussing were efforts to Christianise Muslims, he noted that inter-religious marriage was permitted for Catholics if the Catholic partner agreed to make every effort to baptise their children and raise them as Christians.[155]

Participation in Christmas Celebrations and Imitating Muslim Traditions

Amongst the cultural issues that were perceived as potential factors in increasing tensions between Muslims and Christians was Muslim participation in Christmas celebrations. It was noted in Chapter Four that the MUI issued a *fatwā* prohibiting Muslims from attending such celebrations. While the prohibition was based on the argument that it was part of Christian prayer, Christians themselves were divided on its meaning. The Protestants as represented by S.A.E. Nababan (secretary of the DGI), stated that for them there was no separation between ritual and ceremonial activities. They acknowledged that there was prayer (Indonesian: *ibadat*) within the Christmas celebration (*perayaan Natal*). In contrast, J. Riberu of the MAWI stated that there was a separation between *ibadat* and *perayaan*. The prayer involved the attendance of a priest who conducted the service within a specific ceremony. In other words, the Catholics perceived Christmas celebrations not as part of prayer but as mere celebration.[156]

---

[155] Husaini, 'Menyoal Perkawinan Beda Agama'.

[156] 'Buya, Fatwa dan Kerukunan Beragama', *Tempo*, 30 May 1980, 14.

However, this issue concerned many Muslims in different areas of Indonesia. Based on the MUI *fatwā*, Adian held that Muslim participation in Christmas celebrations was prohibited (*harām*).[157] In addition, Hussein Umar disagreed with the claim that *Perayaan Natal Bersama* (Christmas celebration attended by the President and prominent figures of different religions), held annually at Balai Sidang Jakarta and broadcast by many TV channels, was proof of the existence of religious tolerance in Indonesia. Hussein Umar further maintained that the insistence of Christians on holding the *Perayaan Natal Bersama* affirmed the existence of the Christianisation process and Christian intention to violate Muslim beliefs. He further stressed that this meant that the Christians' intention was not only to secure more followers but to target Muslims for conversion.[158] It appears that Hussein Umar regarded almost any non-Muslim televised celebration as part of Christianisation efforts, and would be unwilling to regard this as simply a religious meeting or celebration.

Hussein Umar particularly criticised Abdurrahman Wahid (the former Indonesian President) who, during his presidential speech in the *Perayaan Natal Bersama*, addressed the Christians with *salām* (*assalāmuʿalaikum waraḥmatullāhi wabarakātuh*/May peace be with you and Allah's blessing and mercy to you). Hussein Umar believed that only Muslims could be addressed with the *salām*.[159] In this context, Adian quoted a ḥadīth by Imam Muslim stating that Muslims were prohibited from addressing the Jews and Christians with *salām*. Based on this ḥadīth Adian concluded that Christmas greetings to Christians were even more strongly prohibited, as the greetings carried the meaning of supporting the Christian celebration of the birth of Jesus as the Son of God, which contradicted Islamic belief.[160]

---

[157] Husaini, *Penyesatan Opini*, 10–11.

[158] Umar, 'Intoleransi Kaum Nasrani', 21–22.

[159] Umar, 'Intoleransi Kaum Nasrani', 21–22.

[160] Husaini, *Penyesatan Opini*, 10–11.

The emergence of the practice of *doa bersama* (prayer together between key figures of different faiths in order to ask God's guidance in overcoming national problems) has also worried some Muslims. Sumargono argued that the *doa bersama* had become a trend in Indonesia and pointed towards syncretism.[161] Moreover, Adian noted that, within two years from 1998 to 2000, there were at least 3 *doa bersama* activities and the practice was generally accepted by the ᶜ*ulamāʾ*. He firmly criticised the practice, arguing that *doa* (*duᶜāʾ*) was the essence of ᶜ*ibāda*, and its ritual was regulated in Islam. Therefore, as the *doa* was part of Islamic ritual, Muslims must not participate in *doa bersama* simply to be acknowledged for practising religious tolerance. Adian did not perceive the *doa bersama* as Christianisation, as the practice involved people of various faiths. However, he likened the practice to attending the *Perayaan Natal Bersama*, which had been interpreted by some as attempts at converting Muslims to Christianity.[162]

Exclusivist Muslims also believed that the Christians' deliberate efforts to imitate Muslim traditions constituted another element of tension between the two religious groups. For example, in the Christmas celebration in 1999, some TV stations broadcast a service from the Gereja Betawi at Kampung Sawah, Jakarta. Some Betawi people, native Jakartanese long known as pious Muslims but who had converted to Christianity, attended the service wearing traditional Betawi symbols which were claimed to have heavy Islamic identity. Hussein Umar argued that this imitation injured Muslim feelings. Moreover, the fact that many Betawi people had been converted to Christianity and this was exposed in the media inflicted Muslim animosity towards Christians.[163] Franz Magnis-Suseno, however, had a different perspective on the case of the Betawi people. He argued that the Bible did not perceive a certain culture as hegemonic, and therefore Christianity

---

[161] A. Sumargono, 'Ujian Berat', in KISDI, *KISDI Menggugat* (Jakarta: KISDI, 1999), 74.

[162] Husaini, *Penyesatan Opini*, 65-76.

[163] Umar, 'Intoleransi Kaum Nasrani', 21-22.

was always open to different cultures. He agreed that it was not wise to wear outfits identified as Islamic, such as the *jilbāb* (head scarf), but underlined that adoption of traditions was not meant as efforts to Christianise Muslims.[164]

Similarly, some Christian educational institutions imitated dress traditionally been worn by Muslims. At the Institute of Theology Ka-limatullah (a Protestant-based university in Jakarta), for instance, all the male lecturers and students wore *peci* (special style of cap) and the females wore *jilbāb*. Both types of headgear are generally perceived as portraying Islamic identity. This was perceived as 'an insult to Mus-lims' and angered the DDII activists. They believed that the existence of the institute was another clear example of proselytisation.[165]

Another example was the Institute of Theology Apostolos/STT Apostolos (a Protestant-based university) which aimed at 'training future church leaders who are capable of making theological dialogues with the Islamic world'.[166] One of the courses the institute offered was *tilāwatil Injīl* (reading the Gospel), in which the Gospel was read with the correct pronunciation. Rizieq argued that this was an insult to Muslims as the term used was a copy of the Islamic *tilāwatil Qu'rān*. Rizieq maintained that what triggered the Muslims' anger more was that the Apostolos published some books that carried Islamic headings, such as *Manasik Haji* (the Ritual of Pilgrimage/*ḥajj*), but contained criticism of Islamic teachings.[167]

The Religious Judicature Act Bill

The Religious Judicature Act Bill (Rencana Undang-Undang Peradilan Agama, thereafter will be cited as RUU-PA) was first proposed by Munawir

---

[164] Franz Magnis-Suseno, interview by author, Jakarta, 28 January 2002.

[165] Hussein Umar, interview by author, Jakarta, 25 January 2002. During the interview Umar showed the clipping that DDII had collected on the Institute of Theology Kalimatullah and other similar institutions.

[166] STT Apostolos brochure for 2000-2001 academic years.

[167] Rizieq Shihab, interview by author, Jakarta, 6 February 2002.

Sjadzali on 28 January 1989 in the plenary session of parliament. Munawir was the first Minister of Religious Affairs in Indonesian history to bring such a proposal before parliament. The proposal was later debated in June 1989. Munawir argued that the religious courts had existed in Indonesia since the early 1880s.[168] The lineage of the present Islamic courts in Indonesia can be traced to a Dutch Royal Decree of 1882 by which a system of Islamic tribunals called Priests' Councils (*priesterraden*) operated in Java and Madura alongside the existing ordinary courts in those areas. In 1937, a series of changes was applied to the courts in Java and Madura, which were renamed Penghulu Courts (*penghulugerecht*), to make them more efficient and produce more uniform decision-making. However, the colonial government limited the role of the Penghulu Courts to matters of marriage and divorce. A new development came in 1957 when the Indonesian government agreed to the formation of Islamic courts everywhere except Java, Madura, and South Kalimantan, where such a court already existed. The Islamic court was named Mahkamah Syariah (Pengadilan Agama) and had greater authority, including on matters of inheritance, marriage, and divorce.[169]

Therefore, for Munawir, the RUU-PA was to complement the existing religious courts.[170] Moreover, the RUU-PA was an attempt to implement decree 14/1970 on the regulation of judicial authority. Article 10 of the decree stated that the judicial authority was performed by the courts within the Civil Court, Religious Court, Military Court, and State Administrative Court (Peradilan Tata Usaha Negara/PTUN). Munawir argued that, out of these four courts, only the religious court was not regulated by a decree.[171]

---

[168] 'Peradilan Agama: Kebutuhan atau Kecemasan', *Tempo*, 24 June 1989, 24.

[169] Mark Cammack, 'Indonesia's 1989 Religious Judicature Act: Islamization of Indonesia or Indonesianization of Islam?', *Indonesia* 63 (April 1997): 144-148.

[170] 'Peradilan Agama: Kebutuhan atau Kecemasan', 24.

[171] 'Dari Piagam Jakarta ke Wawasan Nusantara', *Tempo*, 24 June 1989, 27.

The reactions from Catholics and Protestants to the proposed Bill were vociferous and deserve special analysis. A formal response from the PGI was sent to the parliament earlier on 10 May 1989. The letter expressed Protestants' anxiety should the RUU-PA be promulgated. One might wonder why the Protestants were very anxious given that the courts only had authority over Muslims. Nevertheless, they maintained that it was precisely the fact that Indonesians would have a separate law for its citizens that worried them. The letter further argued that Pancasila had been accepted as the only basis for the state and society, and if the RUU-PA were implemented it would disrupt the national consensus. PGI suggested that before the RUU-PA was heard in the parliament there needed to be a meeting of the existing religious institutions to create a national consensus to evaluate the RUU-PA.[172]

More serious responses came from the Catholics, who perceived that the stipulation of the RUU-PA was another step towards the establishment of an Islamic state. Franz Magnis-Suseno, for example, argued that the RUU-PA did not base itself on the 1945 Constitution, but on Islam. As a consequence, its validity as the national *undang-undang* (regulation) should be questioned. He further maintained that if the RUU-PA was passed it would weaken the authority of the state, as religion would be perceived as being above the state.[173] Father S. Widjojo, a Jesuit priest based in Yogyakarta, made a similar response. For him, the existence of the RUU-PA was a move towards the implementation of Islamic law. To support his argument, he referred to past events soon after independence when there were efforts on the Muslim side to establish an Islamic state. Furthermore, Widjojo maintained that the push to pass the RUU-PA was no different from the attempt at reviving the Jakarta Charter, which contradicted Pancasila. In other words, what concerned him most was that the existence of the RUU-PA demonstrated the discriminatory attitude of the government towards non-Muslims. As an alternative to the Bill, which he perceived as 'alien' to the majority

---

[172] 'Peradilan Agama: Kebutuhan atau Kecemasan', 25.

[173] Franz Magnis-Suseno, 'Seputar Rencana UU Peradilan Agama', *Hidup*, 25 June 1989, 25.

of Indonesians, Widjojo suggested the implementation of the *adat* (customary) law, which according to him was deeply rooted in Indonesian society.[174]

In commenting on Widjojo's firm statement that 'there is no tolerance to the Jakarta Charter' ('Tiada Toleransi untuk Piagam Jakarta', was adopted as the title of Widjojo's article), Natsir argued that both the Catholics and Protestants were very persistent in their intolerance of any regulation that would open up possibilities for Muslims to live according to Islamic teachings. In regard to the RUU-PA, Natsir believed that it would not cause any harm to non-Muslims, yet the Christians severely criticised it. Natsir further questioned Widjojo's suggestion that *adat* law would be more suitable for Indonesian Muslims than Islamic law. Natsir believed that the Christians were attempting to use their funds and forces to prevent the RUU-PA being promulgated, as could be seen from their efforts to publish the issues in their media, to question parliament on the validity of the Bill, and to lobby bureaucrats and key figures in the government.[175] One could conclude that Natsir's argument demonstrated his tendency to see things in a conspiratorial light.

For the DDII, attempts by the Christians to hinder the RUU-PA from being passed were seen as part of a long term strategy to eliminate Islamic aspirations since the Inter-religious Consultation Forum in 1967. In criticising the Christian media which supported objections to the RUU-PA, DDII stated that these media were biased and would only publish articles that were in favour of their view. For example, DDII claimed that *Kompas* refused to publish an article by

---

[174] S. Wijoyo, 'Antara Negara Agama dan Negara Pancasila', *Hidup*, 12 February 1989, 28–29, 50. See also his similar argument in 'Kesaktian Pancasila dalam Tantangan', *Hidup*, 5 March 1989, 40–41, and in 'Membahas RUU Peradilan Agama: Tiada Toleransi untuk Piagam Jakarta', *Hidup*, 2 July 1989, 23–26, 45. Some other Christian-owned newspapers supported the above-mentioned views in their editorials; for example, *Kompas*, 14 June 1989 and *Suara Pembaharuan*, 14 June 1989.

[175] M. Natsir, 'Tanpa Toleransi Tak-kan Ada Kerukunan', in *Fakta dan Data*, 44–49.

Rasjidi written in response to Franz Magnis-Suseno's piece published earlier by that newspaper.[176]

Hussein Umar shared Natsir's opinion that never before had the Christians been so united in bitterly opposing a regulation as they had been with the RUU-PA, which was seen by the Christians as benefiting the Muslims. He reasoned that in opposing the RUU-PA the Christians distorted Indonesian history and gave the wrong interpretation of the GBHN and Pancasila. For him, Widjojo's firm statement that 'There is no tolerance to the Jakarta Charter' proved the latter's objection towards Islamic law.[177] Hussein Umar added that Widjojo's statement that 'The RUU-PA was contradicting Pancasila as it did not adopt the Pancasila as its source of law' contradicted the National Conference on Church and Society's report of 1968, which said 'The Christian's belief accepted that the only source of laws was Jesus. He was also the source of Pancasila'.[178] It is worth noting that the facts that Widjojo was a Catholic and the National Conference was held by Protestants did not prevent Hussein Umar from making such a connection.

In addition to DDII's concern over the RUU-PA, Muhammadiyah was also very active in lobbying the government to pass the Bill. In a meeting with Soeharto, the Muhammadiyah team was advised by the President that the RUU-PA was a realisation of the government's protection of its citizens to freely practise their religious teachings. Soeharto clearly spelled out that for Muslims the implementation of the Islamic teachings involved more than praying, fasting, and alms giving. Therefore, Muhammadiyah maintained that the Christians should show their tolerance of their Muslim brothers.[179] The Bill was finally passed by President Soeharto as the Religious Judicature Act, and was designated Law No. 7/1989.

---

[176] 'Di mana Toleransi Mereka', *Media Dakwah*, August 1989, 7–10.

[177] Umar, 'Intoleransi Umat Nasrani', 12–13.

[178] S.A.E. Nababan, 'Laporan Konperensi Nasional Gereja dan Masyarakat', in *Panggilan Kristen dalam Pembangunan Masyarakat* (Jakarta: Badan Penerbit Kristen, 1968), 42.

[179] 'Menggugat Protes Naif', *Media Dakwah*, August 1989, 12–13.

Christianisation through Education

Chapter Four has discussed that the Christians, especially the Catholics, had debated the explanation of article 28 (2) of the Law on the National Education System No. 2/1989, which stated 'Teachers who teach religious studies have to be of the same religion as the subject he or she is teaching'. On 10 July 1990, the government issued four government regulations (*Peraturan Pemerintah*) in addition to the Law mentioned above, stated 'Students have the right to receive religious education according to their religion'. What stimulated debate was the statement of Fuad Hassan, Minister of Education and Culture at that time, in commenting on article 17 (2) of the government regulation, that religiously oriented schools would only be responsible for providing religious study in accordance with the religious orientation of the school.

This was good news for the Christians, who had consistently debated the Law on the National Education System No. 2/1989 because it meant that Christian educational institutions would not have to offer religious studies other than Christianity to their students. In contrast, for some Muslims, the Christians' refusal to provide religious education other than Christianity was perceived as Christianisation through education. Rizieq Shihab, for example, stated that in accepting the law on education the Islamic educational institutions had agreed to offer different religious education to their students according to their beliefs. He criticised the Christians' insistence on only offering Christianity to the non-Christian students at their schools. Rizieq further argued that this event had led him and FPI supporters to see the government as being incapable of handling many problems faced by Muslims, which had positioned Muslims to solve problems in their own way.[180] Also, Adian criticised the Christians' insistence on not providing Islamic studies for Muslim students at Christian schools. Adian maintained that on the basis of the argument that it was the

---

[180] Rizieq Shihab, interview by author, Jakarta, 6 February 2002.

schools' right whether or not to provide non-Christian studies, the Christian schools aimed at 'converting their Muslim students into Christianity'.[181]

This case also concerned KISDI, which issued a statement urging the Minister for Education and Culture, Wismoyo Arismunandar, to revise the Law, especially article 17 (2). In addition, KISDI urged non-Muslim schools to respect the rights of their students by providing religious studies according to the students' religions. More specifically to the Muslims, KISDI reminded them not to send their children to non-Muslim schools which did not provide Islamic studies because these schools would only target the students as converts.[182]

In addition to the controversial law on education, Christians were believed to have secretly spread their religious teachings through various textbooks. For instance, DDII noted that Intan Pariwara, a Christian affiliated publishing house based in Klaten, Yogyakarta, published books that were thought to have caused unease among school teachers. One example was a textbook on Pancasila in which students were asked to answer the following question: 'Sinta was a Muslim. She received an invitation to attend a Christmas celebration from her class mate. What should Sinta do?' Among the answers given and from which students were expected to choose was 'Sinta would come and congratulate her class mate'. DDII felt that this answer obviously contradicted Islamic teaching as expressed in the *fatwā* of the *culamā* dated on 7 March 1981 (see previous chapter).[183]

---

[181] Adian Husaini, interview by author, Jakarta 29 January 2002.

[182] 'Imbauan kepada Pemerintah RI: Revisi Sistem Pendidikan PP No. 29 Tahun 1990!' in *KISDI Menggugat*, 30–33. Recently there was a huge controversy surrounding the government's intention to impose a new law on the National Education System. Article 12 point 1 (a) stated that 'every student has the right to receive religious education according to their belief, and the teacher who teaches the subject should have the same religion as the student'. One of its implications was that Catholic schools would have to provide Muslim teachers to teach Islamic studies for Muslim students at their schools. Thousands of people, mainly Catholics and Protestants, went into Jakarta's streets to protest the Bill before it was stipulated. Nevertheless, the President signed the Law on 15 June 2003 and left the controversial article as it was.

[183] 'Kristenisasi Lewat Buku Pelajaran', in *Fakta dan Data*, 198-200.

Another alleged method of Christianisation was spotted by DDII in a survey conducted by a Christian student on 'Indonesian Muslim perceptions of the Bible'. Among the questions directed to Muslims was 'The Torah, Zabūr, Bible and Qur'ān were the words of God', to which they were expected to answer 'agree', 'partly agree', 'neutral', 'partly disagree', and 'disagree'. DDII saw this survey as a tricky attempt at distorting Muslim belief, because if they answered 'agree' to the question, it would mean that they accepted the Bible as it is, while in DDII's view the Bible as it exists now has been corrupted. However, a negative answer to the question would mean that Muslims disbelieved the Qur'ān as God's word.[184]

A more recent example of Christianisation claimed by the exclusivist Muslims was the establishment of the Apostolos Institute and schools under the management of Lippo, a business network owned by a Christian, James T. Riady, and which involved banking, supermarkets, shopping malls and insurance. The *Media Dakwah* examined Apostolos' presumed 'hidden agenda', which offered 40 credits in Islamic studies to its students. Hussein Umar claimed that attempts by Apostolos to Christianise Muslims should be seen as part of a long-term Christian mission campaign.[185] Similarly, DDII argued that James Riady had found a new way of converting Muslims to Christianity by offering scholarships for Muslim students to study at his institutions. It further asserted that some 26 schools had been opened in the area of Karawaci, Jakarta, and that every student had received around 1,179,000 rupiahs per year (approximately USD 150). It was the view of the DDII that once the students were enrolled and enjoying the facilities provided by the schools, they would be required by the schools to go to church.[186]

---

[184] 'Survey Cara Kristen', *Media Dakwah*, March 1992, 29.

[185] 'STT Apostolos Memang Wajib Diwaspadai', *Media Dakwah*, July 2002, 52-53.

[186] 'Antara Damai dan Kristenisasi', *Media Dakwah*, January 2002, 43-44.

A Brief Account of the Ambon Conflicts and Muslim–Christian Relations

Amongst recent issues closely related to Muslim–Christian relations was the Ambon conflicts. Without aiming at providing a complete picture of the conflicts, this study will highlight several important points to analyse the exclusivist Muslims' responses within the frame of Muslim–Christian relations. The Ambon conflicts started in January 1999. Much research has tried to shed light on the causes of the conflicts involving Muslims and Christians, and some have pointed to a 'minor' incident between a Muslim and a Christian over some money at a bus stop in Ambon as the main trigger for the first conflict.[187] Behind this trigger, however, some argued that the reasons for the conflicts dated back to the New Order, if not earlier. As discussed in Chapter Four, the New Order's policy on SARA benefited some Christians, including those who lived in the islands outside Java. In the case of Maluku, before Soeharto changed his policy on Muslims in 1990 with the establishment of the ICMI, all of its governors were Christians. However, since 1990 Muslims had started replacing the Christian political authority as governors of the island and in the regional bureaucracy. This created tense relations between Muslims and Christians.[188]

Van Klinken stated that the Ambon conflicts (there were many of violent incidents) could be grouped into two: the Ambon-related fighting in the south of Maluku province from early 1999 onwards, and the North Maluku fighting starting in the second half of 1999. By September 1999, it was estimated that 1,349 people had died in the Ambon area, and 2,004 had died in the North Maluku between October 1999 and March 2000. Worse still, the fatalities from the entire Maluku conflicts were estimated by the Catholic Bishop of Ambon at three to four thousand deaths by early 2000.[189] In this context, a valid question

---

[187] See for example, 'Tanah Air Mata Maluku', *Tempo*, 9 July 2000, 17.

[188] Gerry Van Klinken, 'What Caused the Ambon Violence?', *Inside Indonesia* (October–December, 1999): 16.

[189] Gerry Van Klinken, 'The Maluku Wars: Bringing Society Back In', *Indonesia* (April 2001): 2-3.

can be raised: 'Did religious animosity (between Muslims and Christians) cause the Ambon violence?' or, to be more precise, 'Are the reasons for the conflicts purely religious?' It seems that the answer is not an easy 'yes' or 'no'. Van Klinken suggested in an interesting analysis that the conflicts were triggered by 'pure bigotry':

> [The conflict] is based on the idea that people often identify with a particular religious community for quite worldly reasons. In Ambon at least, joining the Protestant or the Muslim community means being part of a network that not only worships God in a certain way but does practical things for its members—provide access to friends in powerful places for example, or protection when things get tough. These networks extend up the social ladder to influential circles in Jakarta.[190]

Amidst the uncertainty as to the causes of the conflicts, at least two things were clear. First, the number of victims had already reached thousands. Second, two religious communities were involved in the conflicts: Muslims and Christians. These two facts provided good reasons for people of both religious groups to support their communities and to seek refuge from their respective enemies.

The Exclusivists' Perspectives on the Ambon Conflicts

Laskar Jihad, more than any other exclusivist organisation discussed in this study, was concerned with the Ambon conflicts. Indeed, as stated above, the conflicts constituted the main reason for the establishment of this organisation. Laskar Jihad's disappointment at the national government did not originate only from the government's failure to comprehensively solve the national problem, especially the conflicts in Maluku. On the contrary, Laskar Jihad argued that, as early as the New Order period, Muslims had been disturbed by the Christianisation process

---

[190] Van Klinken, 'What Caused the Ambon Violence?', 15.

initiated by Catholic and Protestant churches and also that the government had failed to accomplish its role in banning such activities. During the reform period (*reformasi*) after the fall of Soeharto, Muslims faced another problem initiated by the Christian Separatist Movement (Gerakan Separatis Kristen). Part of Laskar Jihad's concern was their claim that this movement, in addition to its willingness to form a separate Negara Kristen Alifuru or Christian State of Alifuru (including West Papua, Maluku, Nusa Tenggara Timur and East Timor),[191] aimed at chasing Muslims out of their area and killing them. Laskar Jihad contended that the government had once again failed to protect Muslims from the separatist movement. Instead, the government (through the Penguasa Darurat Sipil/Civil Emergency Authority) was cooperating with the Republic of South Maluku to expel Muslims from Ambon:

> As a proof (that the government is cooperating with the Republik Maluku Selatan/RMS) the government has always had the same argument with the churches and the Christian community who are supporting the RMS that the RMS does not exist.[192]

KISDI released a statement dated 29 July 1999 that what had happened in Ambon was 'religious war' (*perang agama*) and not merely bloody violence involving different social groups. Quoting the Qur'ān 22:39–40, KISDI argued that the Muslims were the attacked, and therefore it urged the government to solve the situation by stopping the attacks. KISDI, claiming to have received some information from Muslims in Ambon, believed that the aggressors were the Christians and suspected that there were key Christian figures or organisations provoking the Christians in Ambon to fight the Muslims. This circum-

---

[191] Ja'far Umar Thalib, *Laskar Jihad Ahlus Sunnah wal Jama'ah: Mempelopori Perlawanan terhadap Kedurjanaan Hegemoni Salibis-Zionis Internasional di Indonesia* (Yogyakarta: DPP Forum Komunikasi Ahlus Sunna wal Jama'ah, 2001), 34-35. The problem is that Ja'far has never presented any credible evidence to substantiate this accusation.

[192] Ja'far Thalib, 'Pembelaan Negara Dijamin Undang-Undang' [online], available from http://www.laskarjihad.or.id; accessed 16 July, 2002.

stance was believed to be part of a Muslim cleansing policy within the eastern part of Indonesia.[193]

KISDI criticised statements by the former Indonesian President, B.J. Habibie, who stated that there was no religious war in Ambon as it involved only a small number of radical Muslims and Christians. KISDI argued that Habibie's statement was typical of the New Order method which had always attempted to hide real problems. KISDI further underlined that there was a fundamental problem in regard to the management of the relations between ethnic and religious groups in Indonesia. KISDI was even more irritated to hear the next president after Habibie, Abdurrahman Wahid, said that the Ambon conflicts had claimed only five persons, and that the trouble was inflicted by the New Order's policy which had made Muslims the 'golden boy' (*anak emas*).[194]

Laskar Jihad was also very critical of the existence of the Front Kedaulatan Maluku (Front of Moluccas Sovereignity/FKM), which they believed to have close ties to the Republic of South Maluku. Therefore, Laskar Jihad rejected the solution proposed by the Indonesian government to dissolve both Laskar Jihad and FKM in order to end the conflict in Maluku. For Laskar Jihad, the proposal to dissolve itself and FKM in one package meant that the government had equated Laskar Jihad and the separatist movement as the causes of violence in Ambon.[195]

A joint statement by some Muslim groups including DDII, KISDI, and FKASWJ stated that, having learnt from the situation in Ambon, they believed that there were some Christian military figures who were actively involved in hunting the Muslims out of Ambon, and even killing

---

[193] 'Ambon, Medan Jihad Kaum Muslim', in *KISDI Menggugat* (2), 31-35.

[194] 'KISDI Sesalkan Penjelasan Habibie tentang Kasus Ambon', and 'KISDI: Sikap Pihak Kristen Sudah Terlalu Jauh', in *KISDI Menggugat (2),* 5-6 and 56-59, respectively.

[195] 'Pernyataan Sikap Berkaitan dengan Upaya Paket Pembubaran FKM dan Rencana Penarikan Laskar Jihad dari Maluku oleh Pemerintah' [online], available from http://www.laskarjihad.or.id; accessed 16 July 2002.

them. In line with the argument of Laskar Jihad, these Muslim groups said that, based on the data they had gathered, these actions were closely related to the aim of Christians in the separatist movement, the FKM, to separate Ambon from the Indonesian state. These Muslim organisations urged the government to objectively understand the situation in Ambon and to learn from the experience of the separation of East Timor from Indonesia.[196]

The Inflammatory Rhetoric of the Laskar Jihad

Despite all the criticism directed at the national government on the Ambon conflicts, the current Indonesian President, Megawati Soekarno Putri, took action in the second week of May 2002 against both organisations. Alexander Manuputty, the leader of the FKM, and 16 of his followers were arrested by the Military District Police of Battalion XVI Pattimura on a charge of leading an attack on the government. Similarly, Ja'far Thalib was detained at Police Headquarters based on a speech that he delivered at a *tabligh akbar* at al-Fatah Mosque, Ambon, on 25 April 2002. He was charged with spreading mass provocative sentiment and inciting the attack on a Christian village in Ambon as well as with enmity and hostility towards the Indonesian President, according to articles 134 and 160 of the Indonesian Criminal Code.[197] Section 134 reads: 'Deliberate insult towards the President or Vice President will be punished by a maximum sentence of six years in gaol, or a 4,500 rupiah fine'. And section 160 reads: 'Whoever incites hatred orally or in writing which motivates the public to crime or opposes the authorities in violent ways, will face imprisonment of six years, or a 4,500 rupiah fine'. Part of Ja'far's speech was as follows:

---

[196] 'Seruan Bersama Tragedi Maluku', in *KISDI Menggugat* (2), 82–85. On 12 February 2002, the Malino II agreement was signed by 35 Muslim and 35 Christian delegates and government representatives, as a proposed solution to the Ambon conflicts. Laskar Jihad opposed to this agreement as part of the solution was to disband the existence of this organization in Ambon.

[197] 'Jafar Umar Thalib Resmi Tahanan Polisi' [online], available from http://www.kompas.com/kompas%2Dcetak/0205/06/utama/jafa01.htm; accessed 19 July 2002.

Oh Kapolda Sunarko (Head of District Police), please be afraid of God. If you realised that you would die you would feel disappointed for what you have done to the Muslims... Please remember (oh Christians) that the highest command is in Allah's hand. If you realised this you would repent of the dirty deeds that you have done (to the Muslims). For the Muslims whom I love and admire please make yourselves ready to face the disarmament that will be conducted by people commanded by those who place themselves as the RMS dogs (anjing-anjing RMS).[198]

Laskar Jihad supporters in their press release following the arrest argued that the Civil Emergency Authority in Maluku would receive money from the USA if they succeeded in catching Ja'far, as Ja'far's arrest was part of the US's grand scenario to 'cease the Islamic movements in Indonesia'.[199] They labelled the indictment of Ja'far irrelevant and malleable to the government's interest, and claimed that the arrest had been planned long before his speech.[200] Laskar Jihad further argued that the accusation directed at Ja'far of insulting the Indonesian government was irrational, since the tone of the entire speech was meant to fight the separatist movement in Maluku and to critically evaluate the government's action in Maluku based on his nationalism and religion. Laskar Jihad considered Ja'far Thalib's arrest as counter productive of any solution to the conflict and as a clear example of the government's inability to solve the problem.[201]

---

[198] 'Maklumat Perang Ustadz' [online], available from http://www.geocities. com/ambon67/noframe/photoy2knf.htm; accessed 16 July 2002.

[199] Abu Ismail, 'Ada Grand Design Sudutkan Umat Islam' [online], available from http://www.laskarjihad.or.id; accessed 19 July 2002.

[200] See Press Release [online], available from http://www.laskarjihad.or.id; accessed 8 June 2002.

[201] 'Pernyataan Sikap Berkaitan dengan penangkapan Ustadz Ja'far Umar Thalib oleh Kepolisian Republik Indonesia' [online], available from http://www.laskarjihad.or.id; accessed 20 July 2002.

Even though the press release by Laskar Jihad referred to the content of the speech, there was a dispute on its original draft. The above quoted speech was taken from *Ambon Berdarah Online*[202], which was known as the opponent website of *Laskar Jihad Online*. *Ambon Berdarah Online* stated that the speech was broadcast on Suara Perjuangan Muslim Maluku (SPMM) radio on 1–3 May 2002. Laskar Jihad itself did not place the speech in its website. However, from the content and the wording of the speech, it is highly possible that Ja'far was capable of saying such words. This may be compared to the Laskar Jihad unpublished recruitment document from 2000, which was written by Ja'far, and had the same inflammatory rhetoric as the speech quoted above.

A similar speech was delivered by Ja'far Thalib in a *tabligh akbar* held earlier at Baguala, Poka, Ambon, on 17 June 2001:

> On behalf of the Indonesian Muslims, we share the sadness at the loss of Indonesia's greatest people which was caused by the impertinence, insolence, and impudence of the Yon Gab of the Indonesian National Army (TNI) who have played their role as the RMS dogs (anjing-anjing piaraan RMS).[203]

In both speeches, Ja'far displayed his resentment towards Christians, especially in Maluku. His choice of the discourteous word 'anjing' (dogs) to refer to Christians warrants special examination, as the word indicates *najīs* or impure in the Islamic system. In many articles written by Laskar Jihad supporters, there is usually quite a sympathetic tone used in discussing the issue of how Muslims should relate to non-Muslims. For example, in discussing the rights of non-Muslims within an Islamic state, Muhammad Umar as-Sewed, the head of FKAWJ, stressed that the state would give non-Muslims the right

---

[202] 'Maklumat Perang Ustadz'.

[203] The speech was summarised by Khoyyin in 'Fatwa Mati untuk I Made Yasa', *Sabili*, 4 July 2001, 30.

to perform their religious duties. Quoting from several hadiths, as-Sewed argued that Islam was equal to justice and blessing, as even in the case of war the religion had formulated rules on how to fight its enemies.[204] Nevertheless, in practice, when addressing the Christians as a group, especially in the case of the conflicts in Maluku, the tone had changed and was sarcastic.

From the point of view of Laskar Jihad supporters, there seems to be an explanation of this changing attitude towards Christians. In many of their writings and interviews, the argument put forward to explain this change was a 'reciprocal attitude'. Within this, Laskar Jihad's contemptuous attitude towards Christians was a 'reaction' to what the Christians had done to them, rather than an 'action' initiated by Laskar Jihad. However, a different analysis can be developed on this matter. There is a high possibility that, when dealing with the Christians as a group or as a collective abstract, the prejudice regarding Christians emerged. This prejudice included the constructed image of Christians as having close ties with certain international organisations in proselytising Indonesian Muslims or as a separatist movement that wanted to establish a Christian state in Indonesia.

In line with the condemnation of Christians, Laskar Jihad supporters argued that Muslims had to be wary of the claim that the proportion of Indonesian Muslim had decreased significantly from 90% to 75%.[205] Realising the possible problem with the validity and accuracy of the claim, Laskar Jihad supporters contended that the decreasing number of Muslims was supported by the research findings of the Department of Religious Affairs on two things: the family planning program and the Christianisation process. Laskar Jihad argued that the family planning program targeted Muslim population

---

[204] Ustadz Muhammad Umar as-Sewed, 'Islam Sebagai Rahmat untuk Seluruh Alam' [online], available from http://www.laskarjihad.or.id; accessed 18 July 2002.

[205] The data were quoted from 'Anjloknya Dominasi Muslim Indonesia', Tabloid *Siar*, 18-24 November 1999, 14.

not the Christians. This policy, in turn, resulted in the rapid population growth of Christians as compared to Muslims.[206] In addition, they claimed that Christianisation activities were using more sophisticated means and methods without acknowledging the ethics of religious propagation. This alleged method included proselytising poorer Muslims with promises of financial help.[207]

The above argument on the significant decrease in the Muslim population deserves special examination. First, one has to question the survey method by Tabloid *SIAR*, if any, in calculating the percentage of Muslims and Christians. Closer examination reveals that *SIAR* did not actually hold its own survey, let alone a census, to come up with this unusual claim. It only mentioned that it received the information from an unknown source at the Central Statistics Bureau.[208] Second, as has been argued above in the case of the number of Indonesian Protestants, it was very possible that the 1990 survey by the Central Statistics Bureau, which showed that the Muslim population was 87.3%, was not precise. Nevertheless, other surveys that might provide a better result as compared to the BPS survey do not exist. Third, even if it was true that the number of Muslims targeted in the family program outweighed that of Christians, this could be regarded as reasonable considering that the number of Indonesian Muslims was much higher. The reason for targeting the Muslim majority could also be deemed reasonable considering that they were the poor in the society and therefore should be satisfied with smaller families. In addition these reasons, there is inconsistency in Laskar Jihad's argument that the Muslim population had decreased to 75%. For example, Laskar Jihad consistently asserted that the implementation of the *sharīʿa* in Indonesia was needed for the Muslim majority, which constituted more than 85% of the Indonesian population.

---

[206] Public Release 'Tantangan Bagi Umat Islam Atas Bahaya Kristenisasi' [online], available from http://www.laskarjihad.or.id; accessed 5 May 2002.

[207] Public Release 'Tantangan bagi Umat Islam'.

[208] 'Anjloknya Dominasi Muslim Indonesia', 14.

Concluding Remarks

The foregoing analysis showed that the exclusivist groups discussed in this study (DDII, KISDI, FPI and Laskar Jihad) differed in their degree of exclusiveness, their backgrounds and their concerns in regard to Muslim-Christian relations. However, these groups appear to have some characteristics in common, one of which is the view that salvation can only be achieved through the religion of Islam. The relations between the exclusivist Muslims and Christians have been coloured largely by disharmony, as can be found in the exclusivists' criticism in various writings and speeches. Their perspectives on Christians were to a significant extent related to perceptions of Christians developed in some classical Islamic theology and legal texts, even though no explicit connection was made to those texts. For example, the exclusivists held the view that Christianity underwent alteration. Moreover, the exclusivists criticise the concept of the Trinity in Christianity, arguing that the God of Muslims was different from that of the Christians because in Christianity God is described as having offspring. In addition, the exclusivists often justified their arguments on the basis of their literal reading of the Qur'ān. Some *tafsīr* references used by the exclusivists suggested that they did not apply a contextual method in understanding the Qur'ān.

During the New Order era, Muslim animosity towards Christians stemming from the colonial period intensified. The interviews conducted for this study showed that the exclusivists were troubled at the perceived ongoing Christianisation in Indonesia. The perceived Christianisation efforts included the Christians' rejection of the Inter-religious Consultation Forum's proposal, their construction of church buildings in Muslim compounds, and their support of the 1973 Marriage Bill the articles of which were seen as contradicting the *sharīʿa*. Further promotion of Christianity was perceived in attempts to urge Muslims to be involved in Christmas celebrations, in the imitation of Muslim traditions by wearing dress traditionally worn by Muslims, in the rejection of the proposed Religious Judicature Act seen as benefiting Muslims, and in the teaching of Christianity to non-Christian students.[]

6

The Inclusivist Muslims'
Viewpoints on
the Religious 'Other'

Introduction

This chapter explores the perspectives of the inclusivist Muslims on the religious 'other'. While the focus of the thesis is on Muslim–Christian relations, the fact that inclusivists often discuss Christianity or Christians within the context of other religions or religious believers should not be overlooked. Unlike the discussion on the exclusivist Muslims which focused on certain organisations, the analysis on the inclusivist Muslims in this chapter centres on some key figures and intellectuals who appear to have certain characteristics in common as discussed in Chapter One. The reason for this approach is that, for these intellectuals, the most important points are their ideas rather than any organisations. It is also important to note that because the approach of the inclusivists to issues of Muslim–Christians is different from that of the exclusivists, key issues discussed in this chapter will not always be the same as those discussed in Chapter Five.

The chapter has four sections. Section one looks at the birth of inclusive thought in Indonesia. The analysis includes the background of the renewal of Islamic thought and its relation to neo-modernism. The inclusivist perspectives on the religious 'other' will be discussed in section two. Various issues explored here include religious pluralism, the concept of *ahl al-kitāb*, and inter-religious marriage. Section three analyses the issue of Christianisation with an examination of the inclusivists' perspectives on the roots of disharmonious relations between Muslims and Christians. The last section examines the role of the inclusivists in the society by discussing some key institutions that support the inclusivist perspective in general, and on Muslim–Christian relations in particular.

The Birth of Inclusive Thought in Indonesia

Chapters Three and Four explained that since the Old Order and New Order periods, some Muslims were eager to make Islam the state ideology and religion. These efforts, including through the DI/TII movement, the rehabilitation of the Masyumi, and the revival of the Jakarta Charter, all failed. It is clear that the Indonesian government, especially the New Order, perceived political Islam as a serious threat to the continuity of a pluralistic Indonesian society, and made numerous attempts to limit, if not curtail, its activities. It was in such a situation that the renewal of Islamic thought (Gerakan Pembaruan Pemikiran Islam/GPPI) emerged as an answer to the chronic problem of the relations between Islam, both as an ideology and a set of values for Muslims, and the state.

The birth of inclusive thought in Indonesia cannot be detached from the GPPI since one of its main characteristics was inclusivism. The key figures of the GPPI realised that what was needed was an interpretation of the universal Islamic values into a set of specific political and socio-economic values for Indonesian society. In this context, the words 'reinterpret', 're-actualise', and '*ijthād*' are central. More importantly, the GPPI tried to avoid a textual approach to Islam and instead introduced a contextual understanding of the Islamic foundation texts, namely the Qur'ān and ḥadīth.

Background of the Renewal of Islamic Thought

The second half of the 1960s and the early 1970s witnessed the emergence of the GPPI in Indonesia. However, to discuss this emergence one needs to trace back to several events, such as the foundation of the Himpunan Mahasiswa Islam (Islamic Student Organisation/ HMI) as the most important university student organisation at that time, the psychological situation surrounding the mass killings of 1965-1966, and the politics of the New Order government, especially the SARA policy and the politics of modernisation.

The discussion of the Himpunan Mahasiswa Islam, which was established in 1947 in Yogyakarta, is important for at least two reasons. First, HMI promoted a new understanding of Islam by supporting a pluralistic approach to theology and politics; this approach laid the foundation for the GPPI in Indonesia. Second, although HMI never adopted the agenda for renewal as its official policy, some key figures of the GPPI, including Nurcholish Madjid (b. 1939), Djohan Effendi (b. 1939) and Ahmad Wahib (1942-1973), were leaders of this student organisation.

Chapters Three and Four have already discussed the Masyumi, which was banned by the Old Order government in 1960. Here it is important to analyse the relations between HMI and Masyumi. As noted by Nurcholish Madjid, at the beginning of the foundation of HMI Masyumi leaders were a little unhappy because they wanted the Gerakan Pemuda Islam Indonesia (Indonesian Young Muslims' Movement/ GPII) to be the only organisation for all Indonesian Muslim youth. A tense relationship between Masyumi and HMI developed in the following years and was marked by some major and minor conflicts.[1] Two are worth mentioning here. First, in 1953, the president of HMI, Dahlan Ranuwihardjo, held a large meeting at the University of Indonesia Jakarta which concluded that HMI supported the secular state, a

---

[1] Nurcholish Madjid, 'The Issue of Modernization among Muslims in Indonesia: From a Participant's Point of View', in *Readings on Islam in Southeast Asia*, eds. Ahmad Ibrahim, et al (Singapore: ISEAS, 1985), 381.

position that contradicted Masyumi's support for an Islamic state. Second, before the 1955 election, HMI angered Masyumi supporters with their decision to support all four Islamic political parties, namely Masyumi, NU, PSII and Perti.[2]

These two events triggered conflict between HMI and Masyumi. The Masyumi leaders criticised HMI's policy of accommodating Sukarno's political position as giving up its Islamic orientation. It is clear that both organisations had taken sharply distinctive positions; while HMI leaders were eager to work at almost any cost for the survival of the organisation, Masyumi held that 'It would be better to have martyrs for an ideology than to practice hypocrisy'.[3] The two examples underline features of HMI's political and ideological orientation. First, HMI was willing to compromise with the government for the sake of the survival of the organisation. On top of their statement that they supported the secular state, the HMI leaders were forced to accept the Political Manifesto (Manifesto Politik/Manipol) of the Sukarno government.[4] Nevertheless, HMI harvested what they had sacrificed in that their organisation was not outlawed by the government when Masyumi was banned. Second, HMI's support for all four Islamic political parties showed its independence. HMI's position of not readily taking any Islamic intellectual thinking for granted laid an important foundation for the birth of the GPPI in Indonesia.

The killings of 1965–1966 also played a role in supporting the emergence of the renewal of Islamic thought. Some members of the Islamic community, both of NU and Muhammadiyah backgrounds, were involved in the killings. This event left a deep memory within every Indonesian, especially and significantly for this discussion, the Muslim youth. These young Muslims, some of who were involved with HMI, were astonished

---

[2] Ahmad Wahib, *Pergolakan Pemikiran Islam: Catatan Harian Ahmad Wahib*, Eds. by Djohan Effendi and Ismed Natsir (Jakarta: LP3ES, 1988), 144-145

[3] Madjid, 'The Issue of Modernization', 382.

[4] The Political Manifesto was President Soekarno's speech of 17 August 1959, which constituted his central ideological theme.

at the Muslim belief that the act of killing people allied to Communism and the Communist party was part of *jihād*. This event brought them to question Islamic teachings, especially the concept of *jihād*, which in turn also facilitated them to reinterpret Islam beyond its literal meaning.[5]

The third element that gave an impetus to the birth of the GPPI was the politics of the New Order government, especially the SARA policy that restricted Muslims from participating in political organisations, and the policy of modernisation. Even though it appeared that Indonesia was a secular state, religion was not totally sidelined. The religious essence is visible in the Indonesian philosophy of state, Pancasila, whose first principle reads 'Belief in One God'. Moreover, as shown in Chapters Four and Five, the government passed some laws, including the 1974 Marriage Law and the Religious Judicature Act, which clearly had a religious flavour. The existence of the Majelis Ulama Indonesia was another example of how religion was not totally separate from the Indonesian state. However, it is also clear, as discussed in Chapter Four, that under the banner of the SARA policy the New Order state did not support any attempts at establishing a state based on religion. In this context, the Soeharto government wanted to keep at bay the idea of establishing an Islamic state as advocated by the exclusivist Muslims.

Under such circumstances some young Muslim intellectuals, including Usep Fathuddin and Utomo Danandjaja from the Pelajar Islam Indonesia (Indonesian Islam Students/PII), Ahmad Wahib, Dawam Rahardjo, and Djohan Effendi from the 'Limited Group' discussion circle in Yogyakarta, and Nurcholish Madjid from HMI Jakarta, tried to withdraw from participating in the political arena and instead occupied themselves with intellectual endeavours. As stated by Hefner based on interviews with these men, the attempt at developing the GPPI was meant as a long-term approach to neutralise 'military concerns while slowly deepening the roots of Islam in the nation as a

---

[5] See, for example, Djohan Effendi's explanation on the impact of the mass killing in the development of his thought, in Greg Barton, *Gagasan Islam Liberal di Indonesia: Pemikiran Neo-Modernisme Nurcholish Madjid, Djohan Effendi, Ahmad Wahib, dan Abdurrahman Wahid 1968-1980* (Jakarta: Paramadina, 1999), 181.

whole'.[6] For these young Muslims, 'There was still sufficient room to work within the system for changes beneficial to Muslim Indonesians'.[7] This new strategy was to a significant extent reflected in the approach by HMI leaders in avoiding direct conflict with the government and in trying to make the most of their restricted situation.

Soeharto's policy of modernisation also to a significant extent played a role in the birth of the GPPI. Within this policy, he aimed to transform Indonesians from an agricultural-traditional way of life to a modern-industrial one. As he became the Indonesian President amidst the political and economic turmoil left by the Old Order,[8] his main task was to develop a better economic and political system. In introducing a more pragmatic approach to solving the Indonesian economic and political problems within the frame of modernisation, Soeharto and his military-economist alliance felt that the politically influential Muslim leaders could be an impediment to bringing Indonesia out of its difficulties. This was because these Muslims might be keen to gear Indonesia to an ideologically-oriented political system as opposed to the regime's program-oriented system.[9] Hence it was also against such a backdrop that the renewal thought was introduced and developed. Among the groups that were enthusiastic to adopt modernisation was HMI.

Nurcholish Madjid: Key Figure of the Renewal of Islamic Thought

The discussion on Nurcholish Madjid as the person most widely associated with the GPPI does not suggest that before Nurcholish there were no discourses on, or no thinkers of, the renewal of Islamic thought. People like Sjech Muhammad Djamil Djambek (d. 1947) and Hadji Abdul Karim Amrullah (known as Hadji Rasul, d. 1945) also

---

[6] Robert W. Hefner, 'Islam, State and Civil Society: ICMI and the Struggle for the Indonesian Middle Class', *Indonesia* 56 (October 1993): 5.

[7] Hefner added that these young men believed that the cooperation with the military was not necessarily an evil thing. Hefner, 'Islamization and Democratization in Indonesia', 81.

[8] The inflation rate during the period 1964-1965 was 732%, and decreased slightly to 697% during 1965-1966; see, Arief Budiman, *Negara dan Pembangunan: Studi tentang Indonesia dan Korea Selatan* (Jakarta: Yayasan Padi dan Kapas, 1991), 48.

[9] Hassan, *Muslim Intellectual Responses*, 2.

promoted reform of religious thought pertaining to their era. Nevertheless, there is no doubt that Nurcholish and his renewal ideas played a very important role in the discussion on the GPPI in Indonesia during the New Order period.

Nurcholish was born into a Masyumi family. After finishing his elementary school in Jombang, East Java, he pursued his studies at the Pesantren Darul Ulum in the same province. From there Nurcholish went to Pondok Modern Gontor (Gontor modern *pesantren*) at 16. It was at Gontor that he developed his brilliant intellectual ability, as this *pesantren* had introduced a progressive orientation in studying Islam. Moreover, all students studying at Gontor were required to learn both Arabic and English. In 1961 Nurcholish went to Jakarta to study for his undergraduate degree at the State Institute of Islamic Studies Syarif Hidayatullah where he was awarded best scholar (*sarjana terbaik*) in his department in 1968.

In addition to his brilliant academic achievements, Nurcholish's involvement in HMI was also unusual. As stated, HMI was the most important student organisation and based its support on secular or non-religious institutions. Nurcholish was the president of HMI for two consecutive periods, 1966–1969 and 1969–1972. It is important to note that, before 1970, his views very much echoed Masyumi's. As Nurcholish himself clearly pointed out, during the early period of his presidency of HMI he had fought the issue of secularisation together with some Masyumi supporters. At this point, Nurcholish was even labeled as Natsir *muda* (the young Natsir, referring to Muhammad Natsir):

> When I was elected president of the HMI in 1966, the Masyumi leaders held out new hope for the HMI. Even though I was chosen at the expense of their candidate ... At first I was on the side of the Masyumi in almost everything. I joined the Masyumi intellectuals to fight the issue of secularization

discussed by Mochtar Lubis and Rosihan Anwar.[10] Most importantly, I joined the Masyumi leaders in their effort to rebuild their party.[11]

However, Nurcholish realised that it was impossible for the Masyumi to rehabilitate the party as some of its leaders were involved in the rebellion of the PRRI. In addition, the Masyumi's promotion of an Islamic state contradicted the Indonesian army's goal of a secular state. Nurcholish's in-depth interactions with the senior ex-Masyumi members finally led him to the conclusion that their socio-political ideas were not beneficial to the Muslim majority within the scheme of modernisation propagated by the New Order regime. He then started to focus his energy on developing the renewal of Islamic thought.[12]

Nurcholish's renewal ideas can be traced back to his *Nilai-nilai Dasar Perjuangan* (The Basic Values of Struggle/NDP), which was published in March 1969 and functioned as the ideological manual for HMI members. As stated by Nurcholish, the book, which was written after his journey to the Middle East, was a reflection of what he had learnt and experienced about Islamic ideology. Although at first glance the book was no more than a normative and standard description of Islamic teachings, closer scrutiny revealed that it advocated reform or change within the existing Islamic interpretation in Indonesia. However, as Nurcholish admitted, the reform that he proposed in the NDP was expressed in familiar terms and was supported by Qur'ānic verses so that it did not exite any harsh reaction from Muslim society.[13]

However, this was to change with a paper that Nurcholish delivered on 2 January 1970 at a meeting that was intended to be a closed

---

[10] Muchtar Lubis and Rosihan Anwar were prominent journalists of the Indonesian press who supported the notion of modernisation in their respective newspapers, *Indonesia Raya* and *Pedoman*. For a brief discussion on Nurcholish's encounter with these two scholars, see, Madjid,ʼ The Issue of Modernization', 380, 382.

[11] Madjid, 'The Issue of Modernization', 382. Italics are original.

[12] Madjid, 'The Issue of Modernization', 382.

[13] Madjid, 'The Issue of Modernization', 383-384.

and limited forum for Muslim students. The paper was entitled 'Keharusan Pembaharuan Pemikiran Islam dan Masalah Integrasi Umat' (The Necessity of Reforming Islamic Understanding and the Problem of Islamic Integration).[14] The content of the paper included a discussion of 'secularising', 'desacralising', and 'liberalising' Islamic thought and urged an Islamic renewal or reform (pembaruan), emphasising the need for an Islamic response to the challenges of the contemporary world. Realising that the strong Islamic orientation in Indonesia during that period was usually associated with opposition to the government, he felt obliged to define Islam inclusively. Nurcholish even explained his renewal ideas as a way out for Muslims in coping with the political situation of the New Order.[15] This was shown by, for example, his watchword 'Islam yes, Islamic party no', by which Nurcholish apparently tried to accept Pancasila while at the same time preparing a sound method for interpreting Islam. Indeed, Nurcholish was concerned that non-Muslims had responded positively to modernisation and had played a significant role within the national development program of the New Order government; a circumstance that could cause detriment to the Muslims themselves.

Nevertheless, the paper generated loud criticism from many Muslims, especially certain older ex-Masyumi leaders. Nurcholish was accused of advocating Westernisation and secularisation. It is surprising that the ex-Masyumi leaders refuted Nurcholish's idea. Upon closer examination it becomes apparent that these leaders were irritated by Nurcholish's proposition which described their movement as 'fossilized and obsolete, devoid of dynamism'.[16] Nurcholish's second paper, 'Reinvigorating Religious Understanding in the Indonesian

---

[14] Nurcholish Madjid, 'Keharusan Pembaharuan Pemikiran Islam dan Masalah Integrasi Umat', in Madjid, *Islam, Kemodernan, dan Keindonesiaan* (Bandung: Mizan, 1987), 204-214. In his writings, Nurcholish stated that the date of the meeting was 2 January 1970. However, some, such as Ahmad Wahib, cited the date as 3 January 1970; see Wahib, *Pergolakan Pemikiran Islam*, 166.

[15] Nurcholish Madjid, 'Menyambung Mata Rantai yang Hilang', in Nurcholish Madjid and Mohamad Roem, *Tidak Ada Negara Islam: Surat-Surat Politik Nurcholish Madjid-Mohamad Roem* (Jakarta: Penerbit Djambatan, 2000), 18.

[16] Madjid, 'Keharusan Pembaharuan Pemikiran Islam', 205.

Muslim Community', which was delivered in October 1972 and aimed at elaborating his thoughts, was just as severely criticised. In 1973, after Fazlur Rahman's[17] first visit to Indonesia, Nurcholish was invited to the University of Chicago for several months and later studied there from 1978 to 1984.

Nurcholish's ideas, however, continued to gain support, secretly and openly, from a wide range of Indonesian Muslims. In this respect, his thought may be seen as providing a theological basis for Muslims to respond positively to modernisation. Indeed, for many of them, his perspectives on Islam helped them to understanding of modernisation, and to take part in its process.[18] Since then, Nurcholish's renewal ideas, reflected mostly in his theological approach to social problems including democracy, justice, and religious pluralism, have been popular with and followed by many other Muslims.

For Nurcholish, the heavy emphasis Muslims placed on legal (fiqh-oriented) issues would curtail their analytical abilities in reading contemporary issues. During the early phase of the New Order government, the real issues were how to translate Islam in relation to political, socio-economic and cultural problems. Hence, what was needed was the reinterpretation of the Qur'ān and the application of ijtihād[19] without undervaluing the status of fiqh itself. This is to say that what was promoted by Nurcholish was a contextual approach to the Islamic foundation texts.[20] Nurcholish argued that fresh interpretation of the texts,

---

[17] Fazlur Rahman is a neo-modernist thinker from Pakistan. More on him will be discussed below.

[18] M. Dawam Rahardjo, 'Islam dan Modernisasi: Catatan atas Paham Sekularisasi Nurcholish Madjid', in Madjid, Islam, Kemodernan, dan Keindonesiaan, 29-31.

[19] The discussion on ijtihād in Madjid's thought can be found in many of his writings, some being 'Masalah Tradisi dan Inovasi Keislaman dalam Bidang Pemikiran, serta Tantangan dan Harapannya di Indonesia', in Islam Agama Kemanusiaan: Membangun Tradisi dan Visi Baru Islam, ed. M. Wahyuni Nafis (Jakarta: Paramadina, 1995), 58-65; 'Kontinuitas dan Kreativitas dalam memahami Pesan Agama', in Kehampaan Spiritual Masyarakat Modern: Respon dan Transformasi Nilai-Nilai Islam Menuju Masyarakat Madani, eds. M. Amin Akkas and Hasan M. Noer (Jakarta: Mediacita, 2000), 296-306.

[20] Madjid's promotion of his contextual approach to Islam can be seen in his writings, some being 'Konsep Asbab al-Nuzul, Relevansinya bagi Pandangan Historisis Segi-segi Tertentu Ajaran Keagamaan', in Kontekstualisasi Doktrin Islam dalam Sejarah, ed. Budhy Munawar-Rachman (Jakarta: Paramadina, 1994), 27.

especially the Qur'ān and ḥadīth, had to be accompanied by references
to the legacy of classical Islam. Hence, an in-depth knowledge of modern
thought as well as comprehension of classical Islamic scholarship was
the main feature of his thought. He often made references to the classical
Islamic works of, among others, Ibn Taymiyya.[21]

Nurcholish's main argument was explained in several but interconnected key terms, including 'liberalisation', 'secularisation', and
'desacralisation'. While this is not the place to discuss these issues at
length, it is important to briefly define these terms from Nurcholish's
perspective. For him, seeking values that were future-oriented required
a liberalisation process. This process needed other processes, including
'secularisation'. It is very clear that, for him, 'secularising' or 'secularisation' had to be differentiated from secularism. In Nurcholish's perspective, 'secularisation' was 'the "temporalising" of values which are in fact
worldly, and the freeing of the *umma* from the tendency to spiritualise
them'. Having defined the term 'secularisation', Nurcholish stated that
it had acquired a concrete meaning, i.e. 'desacralization of everything
other than that which truly possesses divine attributes, in other words,
the world'.[22]

Nurcholish's approach to Islam can be explained within the context
of the intellectual activity termed neo-modernism, which will be discussed in the next section. Some scholars, including Saeed and Barton,
agree on categorising Nurcholish as a neo-modernist.[23] Others have categorised him as a perennial thinker, who drew his ideas from other
perennial thinkers such as Frithjof Schuon and Seyyed Hussein Nasr.[24]

---

[21] Madjid admired Ibn Taymiyya very much and quoted the latter's works in numerous writings.
His Ph.D. thesis was also on Ibn Taymiyya and entitled 'Ibn Taymyya on Kalam and Falsafa'.

[22] Nurcholish Madjid, 'Keharusan Pembaharuan Pemikiran Islam', 206–207. The above quotations were taken from the English translation of the article in Charles Kurzman, ed., *Liberal
Islam: a Sourcebook* (New York and Oxford: Oxford University Press, 1998), 286.

[23] Abdullah Saeed, '*Ijtihād* and Innovation in Neo-Modernist Islamic Thought in Indonesia',
Islam and Christian-Muslim Relations 8, no. 3 (1997): 279–295; Barton, *Gagasan Islam Liberal
di Indonesia.*

[24] See, for instance, Komaruddin Hidayat, 'Schuon, Nasr dan Cak Nur', *Ulumul Qur'an 4*, no.
1 (1992): 84–86.

It is important to state, however, that not all inclusivist Muslims can be grouped as neo-modernist thinkers, nor that they fit all criteria of neo-modernism. Nurcholish has produced more comprehensive writings and expounded more of these writings to the public in comparison to other inclusivist Muslims of his generation, such as Djohan Effendi or Munawir Sjadzali, or even compared to the younger generation, such as Azyumardi Azra or Komaruddin Hidayat. The discussion on inclusivist thought below will to a significant extent refer to Nurcholish's writings.

Neo-modernism and Renewal of Islamic Thought in Indonesia

The renewal of Islamic thought (GPPI), especially as reflected by Nurcholish, was congruent with the ideas of neo-modernism. Saeed aptly described certain characteristics that were usually shared by the neo-modernists: the possession of a combination of traditional Islamic scholarship with modern Western education, the lack of dogmatism and *madhhab*ism, the subscription to a strong belief for fresh *ijtihād* (especially context-based *ijtihād*), and a firm belief that progress in society must be reflected in Islamic law.[25] Although not identical, these characteristics were also apparent within the GPPI. One can also see that neo-modernism was different from modernism, which in the Indonesian case was represented by Muhammadiyah.[26] Modernism emphasised certain issues that had become important in the West but then claimed that Islam had provided answers to those issues without providing a fully developed method of interpreting the Qur'ān. Neo-modernism, however, departed from the Qur'ān itself in its attempt at gaining guidance for the future.

The term neo-modernism was first coined by Fazlur Rahman (1919–1988), a well-known Muslim scholar who was born in what is now Pakistan and who taught for some years at the University of Chicago. In an article published in 1979, he divided the Islamic renewal movements into four categories: revivalist, modernist, neo-revivalist, and

---

[25] Saeed, '*Ijtihād* and Innovation', 279.

[26] See Chapter One for discussion on Muhammadiyah.

neo-modernist.[27] For the purpose of this study, the neo-modernist category with which Fazlur Rahman associated himself will be scrutinised. Fazlur Rahman argued that, in order to successfully face the modern world, Muslims should develop their self-confidence 'without either succumbing to the West blindly or negating it blindly', and 'to develop a sound methodology for studying the Qur'ān'.[28] In this context Fazlur Rahman proposed his method of Qur'ānic analysis which consisted of a double movement, in which the Qur'ān was first analysed in the present and then projected back to the time of its revelation. The second movement was in the opposite direction—from past to present.[29] Fazlur Rahman argued that any examination of the meaning of the Qur'ān must employ a historical approach since the Qur'ān 'is literally God's response through Muhammad's mind' to a historically specific setting.[30] He criticised Western Qur'ānic scholars, such as John Wansbrough, for abandoning the historical method in their approach to the Qur'ān, which had rendered them incapable of a coherent understanding of the text.[31]

At the same time, Fazlur Rahman claimed that Muslims themselves were afraid to offer views which differed from the received opinions. He further criticised their study for its lack of 'a genuine feel for the relevance of the Qur'ān today, which prevents presentation in terms adequate to the needs of contemporary man'.[32] The problem with most Muslim works on the subject, according to Fazlur Rahman, was that they took the Qur'ān verse by verse and explained it accordingly.

---

[27] For a complete view of this categorisation, see Fazlur Rahman, 'Islam: Past Influence and Present Challenge', in *Islam: Challenges and Opportunities*, eds. A.T. Welch and C. Pierre (Edinburgh: Edinburgh University Press, 1979), 315-330, especially 323-327.

[28] Rahman, 'Islam: Past Influence', 325.

[29] Fazlur Rahman, *Islam and Modernity: Transformation of an Intellectual Tradition* (Chicago: University of Chicago Press, 1982), 5. For further discussion on the 'double movement' method of *tafsīr* and its application, see Fazlur Rahman, 'Interpreting the Qur'ān', *Inquiry* 3, no. 5 (May 1986): 45-49. See also Fazlur Rahman, 'Translating the Qur'ān', *Religion and Literature 20* (1988): 23-30.

[30] Rahman, *Islam and Modernity*, 8.

[31] Fazlur Rahman, *Major Themes of the Qur'ān* (Minneapolis: Bibliotheca Islamica, 1994), xiii.

[32] Rahman, *Major Themes of the Qur'ān*, xii.

This procedure could not produce a cohesive outlook on life or the universe. Meanwhile, the topical arrangements of the Holy Book that have been produced by both Muslims and non-Muslims could not give a comprehensive answer to questions on the Qur'ānic concept of God, man or society.[33]

Fazlur Rahman realised that the need to understand the Qur'ān as a unity required a study of the views of the earliest Muslim generations, as well as of language, grammar, and style. However, he considered this need to be of secondary importance because 'the historical tradition will therefore be more an object of judgment for the new understanding than an aid to it, although this historical traditional product can undoubtedly yield insights'. The further effort that one had to make was the 'intellectual endeavor or jihād', technically called *ijtihād*, i.e. 'the effort to understand the meaning of a relevant text or precedent in the past, containing a rule, and to alter that rule by extending or restricting or otherwise modifying it in such a manner that a new situation can be subsumed under it by a new solution'.[34] The rather lengthy quote from Fazlur Rahman below is important to explain what he exactly meant by *ijtihād*:

> But this *ijtihād*, instead of being piecemeal and *ad hoc*, as it has been so far, must be systematic, comprehensive, and long range. Further, it must be understood that when one speaks of *ijtihād* one is not speaking of a single infallible act of some uniquely privileged mind that would show Muslims 'The Way' once and for all. To think that some paragon of virtue and knowledge is going to give a final *ijtihād* on all matters is not only naïve but extremely dangerous. *Ijtihād* must be a multiple effort of thinking minds—some naturally better than others,

---

[33] Rahman, *Major Themes of the Qur'an*, xi. Fazlur Rahman was very much convinced that this method would fail to grasp the general meaning of the Qur'ān behind the literal text itself, since its treatment of the subject could not yield 'an effective "weltanschauung" that was cohesive and meaningful for life as a whole'. Fazlur Rahman, *Islam*, 2nd ed. (Chicago: University of Chicago Press, 1979), 38-39.

[34] Rahman, *Islam and Modernity*, 7-8.

and some better than others in various areas—that confront each other in an open arena of debate, resulting eventually in an overall consensus.[35]

However, one might question whether the GPPI was directly influenced by Fazlur Rahman's neo-modernism. Saeed was correct in maintaining that Nurcholish, as one of the key figures of the GPPI, appeared to have been influenced by Fazlur Rahman. Nevertheless, there was no direct influence of Fazlur Rahman in the thinking of initiators of GPPI such as Nurcholish Madjid, Ahmad Wahib and Djohan Effendi even though it is clear from the above analysis that the renewal of Islamic thought shared the ideas and characteristics of neo-modernism. As mentioned, the GPPI emerged after the second half of the 1960s, and it was only in 1973 that Fazlur Rahman first visited Indonesia and had direct contact with people such as Nurcholish. This partly explains why, even though Nurcholish's method in interpreting the Qur'ān echoed that of Rahman, the latter's works were rarely quoted directly in Nurcholish's writings.[36] This, however, does not suggest that Fazlur Rahman's intellectual ability did not influence people like Nurcholish. As Barton argued, Fazlur Rahman clearly influenced Nurcholish, not by changing Nurcholish's frame of thought but by leading Nurcholish to study the classical heritage of Islamic thinking. It was Fazlur Rahman who encouraged Nurcholish to undertake Islamic studies and who supervised his research on Ibn Taymiyya.[37]

It is true that neo-modernism as such does not necessarily lead to inclusivism. Nevertheless, the characteristics of the neo-modernists, especially their lack of *madhhab*ism, their subscription to *ijtihād*, and their contextual method of interpreting the Qur'ān, facilitated their inclusive perspective. It is important to underline that the close relationship between the characteristics of the people involved in the

---

[35] Rahman, 'Islam: Past Influence', 325.

[36] One of Fazlur Rahman's works was directly cited by Nurcholish in the latter's 'Fazlur Rahman dan Rekonstruksi Etika al-Qur'an', *Islamika* 2 (1993): 23–28.

[37] Barton, *Gagasan Islam Liberal di Indonesia*, 447.

GPPI, the neo-modernists, and the inclusivists does not mean that the discussion on the inclusivist views of the religious 'other' will be restricted to those involved in the GPPI or the neo-modernists. As mentioned, this chapter will discuss the views of the inclusivists on the religious 'other' based on the criteria mentioned in Chapter One.

The Inclusivists on the Image of the Religious 'Other'

The GPPI that took place especially in the late 1960s and during the 1970s was carried on by like-minded younger generations. As stated in Chapter One on the definition and characteristics of the inclusivist Muslims, many Muslims could be included within this group even though they differed in their degree of inclusiveness and their concerns. Nevertheless, the examination on the inclusivist Muslim's perspectives here will focus on some significant figures in Muslim-Christian relations, who contributed to the discourse on inclusivism in Indonesia. These include Nurcholish Madjid and Budhy Munawar-Rachman (Paramadina); Azyumardi Azra, Quraish Shihab, Zainun Kamal, Komaruddin Hidayat (IAIN Jakarta); Ulil Abshar-Abdalla (Jaringan Islam Liberal and NU); and Amin Abdullah (IAIN Yogyakarta).

The Issue of Religious Pluralism

The general position of the inclusivists on religious pluralism was that plurality was a law of nature (*sunnatullāh*). Their view on this was mainly based on their reading of the Islamic foundation texts as well as some classical Islamic legal and theological texts. Amongst those who discussed the issue of religious pluralism were Nurcholish Madjid, Budhy Munawar-Rachman, and Azyumardi Azra. Nurcholish, for example, contended that the principle of religious pluralism was clearly explained in the Qur'ān:

> Verily, those who have attained to faith [in this divine writ], as well as those who follow the Jewish faith, and the Christians, and the Sabians—all who believe in God and the Last Day and do righteous deeds—shall have their reward with their Sustainer;

and no fear need they have, and neither shall they grieve (Q.S. 2:62).

Therefore, for Nurcholish, Muslims should reinterpret the basic concepts of religious freedom and pluralism as embodied in the Qur'ān and *sunna* and the early generations of Muslims.[38] He argued that the Qur'ānic perspective on religious pluralism emphasised that every religion had its right to exist, while underlining that the risk of following a certain religion was the responsibility of the follower. Nurcholish maintained that this perspective offered the hope for followers of all the existing religions that, because all religions strove to adhere to the same principle that there was only One Truth, they would gradually find their 'common platform' or *kalimatun sawā'*[39] as stated in the Qur'ān 3:64 cited above. As an example of the principle of *kalimatun sawā'*, Nurcholish stated that the Qur'ān as well as the *Injīl* urged human beings to firmly hold the doctrine of monotheism and not to take other human beings as God's adversaries. He further added that the similarities between Islamic and Christian teachings were not surprising if one thought that the origins of these teachings came from the same source, Almighty God. This was important, he emphasised, since few people who realised the existence of these similarities, be they Muslims or non-Muslims, thought about their implications.[40]

Nurcholish further elaborated his view on religious pluralism by stating that one of the beliefs deeply rooted within a Muslim's mind was that Islam was a universal religion for all human beings. Within this

---

[38] Nurcholish Madjid, 'Religious Pluralism and Islam: Experiences of Indonesia as a Nation State', Unpublished paper presented at the Institute of Asian Cultures (Tokyo, 28-30 January 1989), 20.

[39] Madjid, *Islam Agama Kemanusiaan*, 136-137. In the same way as he insisted on the importance of Muslims' understanding their own scripture to understand pluralism in the Indonesian context, Nurcholish often emphasised the significance of the concept of the 'common platform' *(kalimatun sawā')* in his works. See among others, 'Religious Tensions and Dialogues: The Dynamics of the Indonesian Nation Formation towards a 21st Century Society', Unpublished paper presented at the International Conference on Islam and the 21st Century (Leiden, 3-7 June 1996), 21-22.

[40] Madjid, *Islam Agama Kemanusiaan*, 137-142.

perspective, it was believed that human beings from the very beginning had accepted the doctrine of the One and Only God (*tawḥīd*), and as a consequence every human being was required to totally submit to God. Nurcholish believed that the essential and sincere query for the 'Truth' (*ḥanīf*) would naturally lead to a submissive or obedient (i.e. *islām* in its generic meaning) attitude towards the Truth itself; indeed, the best religion besides God is a tolerant and non-fanatical approach in searching for the Truth (*al-ḥanāfiyyat al-samḥaḥ*). He argued that the literal meaning of the word *al-dīn* ('submission' or 'obedience') also carried the same meaning as *al-islām*. For him, the authenticity of a religion depended on whether or not it promoted a submissive attitude to God (*al-islām*); based on this principle he labelled all authentic religions as esentially *al-islām*.[41]

Nurcholish's above argument on the meaning of *al-islām* was based on Ibn Taymiyya's explanation:[42]

> The (Arabic) term '*al-islām*' had the meaning of '*al-istislām*' (the submissive attitude) and '*al-inqiyād*' (obedience), and '*al-ikhlas*' (honesty)... Therefore within Islam there should be an attitude of submission to God, while abandoning the submissive attitude to others. This is the original meaning of the expression of '*Lā ilāha illa Allāh*.' If someone was submissive to God but at the same time submitted to others, that person would become a *mushrik*.

Nurcholish suggested that, considering the meaning of the term *al-islām*, other religious believers could also be called *muslimūn* for the

---

[41] Nurcholish explained this concept in numerous writings; see among others, 'Beberapa Renungan tentang Kehidupan Keagamaan di Indonesia untuk Generasi Mendatang', Paper presented at Taman Ismail Marzuki (Jakarta, 21 October 1992), 19-21; and 'Universalisme Islam dan Kosmopolitanisme Kebudayaan Islam', in his *Islam Doktrin dan Peradaban: Sebuah Telaah Kritis tentang Masalah Keimanan, Kemanusiaan dan Komoderenan*, 3rd ed. (Jakarta: Paramadina, 1995), 425-441.

[42] Nurcholish quoted from Ibn Taymiyya's *Kitāb al-Iqtidā' aṣ-Ṣirāt al-Mustaqīm Mukhālafat Aṣḥāb al-Jaḥīm* in 'Iman dan Kemajemukan Masyarakat: Antar Umat', *Islam Doktrin dan Peradaban*, 181.

same reason, as the Qur'ān 5:44 said that the Jewish who followed their religious belief in accordance with what had been taught by the 'pasrah' (muslimūn) prophet, they themselves were indeed muslimūn. He maintained that the religion brought by the Prophet Muhammad was named Islam, yet it was al-islām par excellence and stood besides the numerous al-islām religions that had preceded it. For Nurcholish, the Islamic teaching on religious pluralism discussed above had obviously urged human beings to follow the teachings of their respective religions without feeling threatened or guilty. He argued that an inclusivist attitude in perceiving other religions as well as religious believers had become imperative in a pluralistic society like Indonesia.[43]

On a similar line, Budhy Munawar-Rachman stated that the task of the prophets was to convey teachings about tawḥīd, and teachings about the necessity for humans to submit to and obey only Him alone. Therefore, based on this philosophy of tawḥīd, the Qur'ān taught the philosophy of religious plurality.[44] Budhy further stated that in understanding the concept of religious pluralism in Islam it was essential that one look at the use of the word 'path' in Islamic theology. In the Qur'ān, the word 'path' connoted many terms: ṣirāṭ, sabīl, sharīʿa, ṭarīqa, minhāj, mansak (plural: manāsik), and maslak (plural: sulūk), which all mean path, means, or method. This meant that these words or terms implied that there was not just one 'path of religion'.[45]

Budhy added that the implication of this idea of a plurality, of 'roads leading to God', was the need for a good understanding of the relationship between the religious communities as stated in the Qur'ān: 'All believers are but brethren. Hence, [whenever they are at odds,] make peace between your two brethren, and remain conscious of God, so

---

[43] Nurcholish Madjid 'Etika Beragama: dari Perbedaan Menuju Persamaaan', in Kehampaan Spiritual Masyarakat Modern, 5-8. The article was republished in Pluralitas Agama: Kerukunan dalam Keragaman, ed. Nur Achmad (Jakarta: Kompas, 2001), 1-8. This study refers to the latest publication.

[44] Budhy Munawar-Rachman, 'Teologi Islam mengenai Agama-Agama: Perspektif al-Qur'ān', in Islam Pluralis: Wacana Kesetaraan Kaum Beriman (Jakarta: Paramadina, 2001), 15.

[45] Munawar-Rachman, 'Teologi Islam mengenai Agama-Agama', 29.

that you might be graced with His mercy'.[46] For him, the fact that this verse ended with the prayer, 'that you might be graced with His mercy' emphasised that only those graced with mercy could accept other people. Budhy quoted the saying of a classical Muslim Sufi (mystic), Jalaluddin Rumi, to support his view:

> Although there are many ways, their goal is one. Do you not know that there are many paths to the Ka'bah? ... Hence, if what you are considering is the path, they are diverse and unlimited in number. However, if what you are considering is the goal, then they all lead to but one goal.[47]

Like Nurcholish, Budhy also underlined the importance of the Qur'ānic notion of the *kalimatun sawā'*, which emphasised that all could obtain 'salvation' as long as they believed in God, in the hereafter, and performed good deeds. Budhy added that the principle of *taqwā* (consciousness of God) as underlined in Islam was actually universal in nature. For him, it was here, in the argument of the universality of religious messages, that there emerged the meaning of the *fundamental sameness* of all the messages of God. The meaning of 'sameness' referred to the Qur'ānic term '*waṣiyyah*', namely 'an invitation to discover the foundations of belief', that is, a life attitude that was *ḥanīf*, as also mentioned in the following ḥadīth:[48]

> Ibn Abbas narrated that the Prophet was asked, 'Which religion is most loved by God?' The Prophet replied, 'A tolerant spirit of righteousness (*al-ḥanāfiyyat al-samḥaḥ*)' (Ḥadīth narrated by Imam Ahmad).

> Aishah narrated that the Messenger of God said: 'This day surely the Jews must know that in our religion there is

---

[46] Q.S. 49:10.

[47] Munawar-Rachman, 'Teologi Islam mengenai Agama-Agama', 30.

[48] Munawar-Rachman, 'Teologi Islam mengenai Agama-agama', 19-21.

openness. Verily I was sent with a tolerant spirit of righ-teousness (*al-ḥanāfiyyat al-samḥaḥ*)' (Ḥadīth narrated by Imam Ahmad).

In discussing religious pluralism, Azyumardi Azra maintained that Islam basically viewed human beings and humanity in a positive and optimistic way. He stated that, according to Islam, human beings originated from Adam and Ḥawā (Eve). Azyumardi further stated that human beings were born innocent (*fiṭrah*) and were endowed with the ability to inquire about the truth. This ability was designated as the attitude of *ḥanīf.* Based on the above view, Azyumardi held that religious pluralism was the law of nature and that Islam should not and could not be imposed on somebody. By referring to the Qur'ān 2:256 and 10:99, he underlined that, had God willed every human being would be created as *mu'min* (someone who had a faith):

> And [thus it is:] had thy Sustainer so willed, all those who live on earth would surely have attained to faith, all of them: dost thou, then, think that thou couldst compel people to believe (Q.S. 10:99).

> There shall be no coercion in matters of faith. Distinct has now become the right way from [the way of] error: hence, he who rejects the powers of evil and believes in God has indeed taken hold of a support most unfailing, which shall never give way: for God is all-hearing, all-knowing (Q.S. 2:256).

Hence, for Azyumardi, it was obvious that Islam admitted (*mengakui*) the right to exist of other religions and acknowledged (*membenarkan*) the rights of followers of these religions to observe their beliefs.[49] Quoting Isma'il alFaruqi and Lamya alFaruqi, Azyumardi argued that Islam 'has acknowledged as true the other religion's proph-

---

[49] Azyumardi Azra, *Konteks Berteologi di Indonesia* (Jakarta: Paramadina, 1999), 33-34.

ets and founders, its scripture and teaching'. Moreover, 'Islam teaches that the phenomenon of prophecy is universal', and that 'God has not differentiated between His messengers; that the prophets of all times and places have taught one and the same lesson—namely, that worship and service are due to God alone, and that evil must be avoided and the good pursued'.[50] Azyumardi realised that the Qur'ānic emphasis on the importance of developing a common platform between religious believers, especially on theological, doctrinal and ritual aspects, would be very difficult to achieve as it would enter the dangerous area of 'synctretism'. Hence, for him, the basis for the development of the common platform should depart from the ethical aspect of religions.[51]

While on the one hand there are Qur'ānic verses affirming religious pluralism, on the other hand there are also verses which might appear to be contradictory. An example of this is the Qur'ānic claim that it was the *khatam* (ending) of all the prophets and messengers and a *muṣaddiq* (truth maker), a *muhaymin* (preponderance), and a *furqān* (distinguisher of the good from the bad) of the deviations that had occurred among the followers of different faiths. Furthermore, the concept of religious pluralism is also challenged by some Qur'ānic verses, which seem to be quite harsh in addressing the followers of religions other than Islam, especially the Jews and Christians. For instance, in response to the call to the *kalimatun sawā'*, the Qur'ān states that the Jews and Christians rejected it and felt that they were the right people and only they could attain the truth:

> And they claim, 'None shall ever enter paradise unless he be a Jew'—or, 'a Christian'. Such are their wishful beliefs! Say: 'Produce an evidence for what you are claiming, if what you say is true!' Yea, indeed: everyone who surrenders his whole being unto God, and is a doer of good withal, shall have his reward with

---

[50] See, Isma'il R. alFaruqi and Lamya Lois alFaruqi, *The Cultural Atlas of Islam* (New York: Macmillan, 1986), 193.

[51] Azra, *Konteks Berteologi di Indonesia*, 36.

his Sustainer; and all such need have no fear, and neither shall they grieve (Q.S. 2:111-112).

In a similar line, within some classical Islamic texts, there are harsh expressions about other religious believers. Ibn Taymiyya, for example, wrote pamphlets against the maintenance or building of synagogues, and particularly of churches.[52] In his *Kitāb al-Iqtidā'* he thoroughly discussed and criticised certain religious concepts and practices held by both the Jews and Christians, such as monasticism (*rahbāniyya*) and the reverence for burial places or shrines. He stated that 'arrogance is the characteristic of the Jews, *shirk* of the Christians'.[53] In addition, he maintained that:

> The Jews simply deny that God abrogates precepts or sends forth a prophet bearing a *sharīʿa* which is different from that held hitherto, just as the Divine Word has it: 'The fools among them will say, "What has turned them from the *qibla* they observed formerly?"' (2:142) The Christians, on the other hand, arrogate to their learned and monks the right to establish new precepts and annul the old ones. That is why the Christians have not succeeded in formulating a permanent *sharīʿa.*[54]

It is interesting to note how the inclusivists interpreted such notions within their frame of thought. Budhy Munawar-Rachman, for example, argued that the Qur'ānic claim that it was the *khatam* of all messages was a theological view—which, because it was theological, was presented as a *claim of truth* that was unique to Islam. Budhy further asserted that the classical view which perceived the coming of the

---

[52] Moh. Ben Cheneb, 'Ibn Taimiya', in *The Shorter Encyclopaedia of Islam*, eds. H.A.R. Gibb and J.H. Kramers (Leiden: E.J. Brill, 1974), 152.

[53] Muhammad Umar Memon, *Ibn Taimiya's Struggle against Popular Religion* (The Hague: Mouton, 1976), 323.

[54] Memon, *Ibn Taimiya's Struggle*, 209.

Qur'ān as an abrogation (naskh) of the Holy Books that had come before it was not found in the Qur'ān itself.[55]

In addition to Budhy's attempt at reconciling this seemingly contradictory notion and to retain the inclusivist perspective of the Qur'an, Nurcholish Madjid commented on the Q.S. 2:111–112 quoted above. He argued that, generally speaking, the rejection was conveyed by the claim that The Jews and Christians were not be happy before the Prophet followed their religions. Nurcholish thought that this was logical considering that Prophet Muhammad brought a new religion which, for them, was perceived as a threat to their already established religion, Judaism and Christianity.[56] Therefore, for Nurcholish, it was precisely in this context that the Qur'ān reminded the Prophet:

> For, never will the Jews be pleased with thee, nor yet the Christians, unless thou follow their own creeds. Say: 'Behold, God's guidance is the only true guidance'. And, indeed, if thou shouldst follow their errant views after all the knowledge that has come unto thee, thou wouldst have none to protect thee from God, and none to bring thee succour (Q.S. 2:120).

Hence, in contrast to the exclusivists who often quoted the above verse as God's pronouncement or caution regarding the hidden agenda of the Jews and the Christians, Nurcholish perceived Q.S. 2:120 as a 'statement of the fact' concerning the reaction of these two religious followers towards the coming of Islam. For him, it was not a 'theological statement'.[57] This way of understanding the above quoted verse shows Nurcholish's inclusive perspective, as he attempted not to use the literal meaning of the verse to develop a harsh attitude towards other religious believers, in this case, Christians and Jews.

---

[55] Munawar-Rachman, 'Teologi Islam mengenai Agama-Agama', 24.

[56] Nurcholish Madjid, 'Wawasan al-Qur'an tentang Ahl al-Kitab' (Jakarta: Klub Kajian Agama Paramadina, 73/VII/1993), 8.

[57] Nurcholish Madjid, interview by author, Jakarta, 6 March 2002.

The above exploration leds one to question the limits of inclusivism, in so far as their view on religious pluralism was concerned. As mentioned in Chapter One, the inclusivists did not hold the view that all religions are the same. For most of them, the notion of religious pluralism as stated in the Qur'ān did not have to be interpreted as witnessing or accepting other religions as the same. As will be clear in the discussion on other issues below, for most of the inclusivists, Islam was the religion that offered a wider concept of religious pluralism than did other religions.

One example to show that the inclusivists did not position all religions at the same level was a polemic between Nurcholish and the Jesuit priest Franz Magnis-Suseno. In a public discussion in April 1995, Nurcholish quoted some new books by Christian scholars who proposed significantly different perspectives concerning Jesus' life and death as compared to the general Christian belief. For example, Nurcholish quoted the argument that Jesus did not die on the cross, that he married Maria Magdalena, had children, and managed to escape to Rome.[58] Magnis-Suseno, who first rang Nurcholish for clarification, wrote a letter to a number of key Indonesian Muslim and non-Muslim figures criticising Nurcholish's referral to those perceptions about Jesus. For Magnis-Suseno, this was hurtful to Christian feelings, because Nurcholish had insulted the most sacred aspects of Christianity.[59]

In responding to this criticism, Nurcholish, who thought that his clarification on the phone had been accepted by Magnis-Suseno, explained that the Qur'ānic perspective on Isa was quite different from that of the Bible. He further maintained that he was interested in any scholarly arguments that were proposed to support the Islamic views on the subject. In this context, Nurcholish supported the argument

---

[58] Barbara Thiering, *Jesus the Man* (Sydney: Doubleday, 1993), 544-545.

[59] This discussion was taken from private letters, the first sent by Franz Magnis-Suseno to Nurcholish Madjid dated 28 April 1995. Nurcholish wrote back to Magnis-Suseno on 3 May 1995, and the correspondence continued until 23 May 1995. Although these were private letters, they have been quoted significantly in different scholarly writings.

that Jesus was not crucified, which was also the Qur'ānic statement (Q.S. 4:157). Moreover, Nurcholish quoted another argument:

> [F]or Jesus to address God so directly as 'Father' does not necessarily mean he claimed to be his divine son in the Christian sense. Rather, it was a form of address often used by the Jewish holy man, the *nabi*, the *hasid*, or indeed anyone who felt he could enter into a direct dialogue with God.[60]

For Nurcholish, as a Muslim, his main interest in analysing such writings was that they could support the Qur'ānic perspective on Isa and on Christianity. Nevertheless, he underlined that he did not fully subscribe to the views stated in those books, as some arguments, for instance that Isa had children, was not part of core Islamic belief. Nurcholish further maintained that his interest in quoting those books was mainly intellectual, as it was presented in an intellectual forum. He underlined that he never intended to humiliate other religions, especially Christianity, which had been given a special place within Islam. In this context, it seems important to underline what Nurcholish stated during an interview that was conducted for this study. He argued that being an inclusivist did not mean being a neutral person. He maintained that as an inclusivist he had become a stronger believer in Islam because it was only this religion that possessed an inclusive perspective. Other religions, such as Christianity, had admitted the existence of other religions only very recently (in the case of Christianity, in 1962 with the Second Vatican Council). In addition, Nurcholish claimed that only Islam had the concept of *rukun iman* (pillars of faith), one of which required Muslims to believe in the existence of all the prophets and Holy Books sent by God.[61]

---

[60] Ian Wilson, *Jesus the Evidence* (London: Butler & Tanner, 1984), 89.

[61] Nurcholish Madjid, interview by author, Jakarta, 6 March 2002.

The Concept of Ahl al-Kitāb

The above examination on religious pluralism, al-dīn, al-islām, and kalimatun sawā' is closely related to the concept of ahl al-kitāb (People of the Book), which was explored at some length by some inclusivist Muslims. As a reflection of their perspective on religious pluralism, most inclusivists admitted the existence and rights of other religious believers, especially the ahl al-kitāb. Nevertheless, as will be seen below, the inclusivists differed as to which religious groups should be included within the categorisation of 'ahl al-kitāb' and as to whether other religious believers (especially Jews and Christians) as they exist today could be categorised as ahl al-kitāb.

Nurcholish, for example, contended that, before Islam, the concept of ahl al-kitāb did not exist. He further stated that, throughout the history of Islam, the concept gradually changed in line with the development of the Muslim communities. He admitted that the concept originally covered those who had different religious understandings of God as compared to Muslims, i.e. the Jews and the Christians. For Nurcholish, these differences, which were called shir'a (law system) and minhāj (way of life), were not essential as they referred to historical, social and cultural features.[62]

Nurcholish further argued that 'The importance of the concept of the "People of the Book" was that it contained the principle that the followers of those religions had the full right to exist and to freely practice their respective religion in any society'.[63] Quoting Muhammad Rashīd Riḍā, Nurcholish maintained that the concept of ahl al-kitāb was later extended to include the Zoroastrians, the Hindus and the Buddhists:

It was clear that the Qur'ān mentioned the followers of previous religions, the Ṣābi'īn and the Zoroastrians, and did not cite

---

[62] Nurcholish Madjid has elaborated this view on shir'ah and minhāj in some of his writings. See among others, Nurcholish Madjid, 'Klaim Kebenaran', in Cendekiawan & Religiusitas Masyarakat: Kolom-Kolom di Tabloid Tekad, ed. Budhy Munawar-Rachman (Jakarta: Tabloid Tekad & Paramadina, 1999), 60–61.

[63] Madjīd, 'Religious Pluralism and Islam', 17–18.

the Hindus, the Buddhists, and the Confucians, because the Ṣābi'īn and the Zoroastrians were known by the Arabs to whom the Qur'ān was originally revealed, and because the Ṣābi'īn and the Zoroastrians were living close to the Arabs in Iraq and Bahrain. [In addition,] the Arabs had not traveled to India, Japan and China, which would have enabled them to meet the followers of different religions. And the aim of the Qur'ān was accomplished by mentioning the religions that were known [to the Arabs], so that it would not give unfamiliar information by citing people unknown to the Arabs.[64]

Nurcholish's view on *ahl al-kitāb* was also shared by other inclusivist scholars including Zainun Kamal. Zainun stated that, etymologically, *ahl al-kitāb* meant 'people who have the book'. This could be understood as somebody who believed in one of the prophets and believed in a Holy Book. He underscored that, even though the Qur'ān generally mentioned the Jews and Christians within the context of *ahl al-kitāb*, many *tafsīrs* and Islamic history books did not confine the meaning to the two religious communities. The Jews and Christians were referred to and were famous only because they had a large number of followers.[65] Zainun, referring to Rashīd Riḍā's *Tafsīr al-Manār*, further asserted that, within the Indonesian context, the Hindus, Buddhist or Taoists were also regarded as *ahl al-kitāb* because they had Holy Books which were brought by different prophets. He underlined that what was meant by 'prophets' here was the bearers of moral orders, and therefore Sidharta Gautama, for example, could be regarded as a prophet who had brought a Holy Book.[66]

Zainun maintained that, as a consequence of this concept of *ahl al-kitāb*, Muslims had to admit their existence, and live together and

---

[64] Rashīd Riḍā, *Tafsīr al-Manār*, vol. 6 (Beirut: Dār al-Maʿrifah, no date), 188. Cited by Madjid, 'Etika Beragama', 7.

[65] Zainun Kamal, interview by author, Jakarta, 22 January 2002.

[66] Zainun Kamal, 'Penganut Budha dan Hindu adalah Ahli Kitab', in *Wajah Liberal Islam di Indonesia*, ed. Luthfi Assyaukanie (Jakarta: Jaringan Islam Liberal, 2002), 144.

cooperate with them. Therefore, for him, Islam taught the Muslims to be tolerant and open to the *ahl al-kitāb*. He admitted that amongst the *ahl al-kitāb* there were people who were hostile to the Muslims. However, for Zainun, this phenomenon was to be found in every religious society. It was in this context that the Qur'ān stated: 'There were differences amongst the People of the Book' (*laisū sawā'an min ahl al-kitāb*). In responding to the argument that the *ahl al-kitāb* today were different from those described in the Qur'ān, Zainun argued that the Christians, for example, had deviated from their religion from the 4th century C.E. and that their Holy Book had undergone changes before the coming of Islam in the 7th century C.E. Moreover, the Qur'ān stated that the Christians believed in the Trinity, which meant that at the time the Qur'ān was revealed Christian belief had already deviated from its original teachings. Hence for Zainun, the term *ahl al-kitāb* was a valid expression for the followers of different religions mentioned above.[67]

The Qur'ānic request that Muslims should be tolerant to the *ahl al-kitāb* was also underlined by Quraish Shihab, an expert on *tafsīr* in Indonesia. He argued that there were positive tones among the verses that mentioned the *ahl al-kitāb*, despite the Qur'ānic acknowledgment that there were differences in terms of belief. Quraish referred to Qur'ān 3:64 to argue that the Holy Book urged Muslims to find a common platform with the *ahl al-kitāb*. Moreover, he maintained that criticism directed at the *ahl al-kitāb* was delivered in a subtle way, as stated in the following verse:[68]

> Say: 'O followers of earlier revelation! Do you find fault with us for no other reason than that we believe in God [alone], and in that which He has bestowed from on high upon us as well as that which He has bestowed aforetime?—or [is it only] because most of you are iniquitous? (Q.S. 5:59).

---

[67] Kamal, 'Penganut Budha dan Hindu', 145-147

[68] M. Quraish Shihab, 'Wawasan al-Qur'an tentang Ahl al-Kitab' (Jakarta: Klub Kajian Agama Paramadina, 73/VII/1993), 3.

Both Quraish and Nurcholish emphasised that God reminded Muslims not to argue with the *ahl al-kitāb*, unless in a positive manner. This, they argued, was urged in the Qur'ān:

> And do not argue with the followers of earlier revelation otherwise than in a most kindly manner—unless it be such of them as are bent on evildoing—and say: 'We believe in that which has been bestowed from on high upon us, as well as that which has been bestowed upon you: for our God and your God is one and the same, and it is unto Him that We [all] surrender ourselves' (Q.S. 29:46).

In a very similar way, Budhy Munawar-Rachman stated that the concept of the People of the Book in Islam had given certain recognition to the followers of other religions who had a Holy Book by giving them the freedom to carry out the teachings of their respective religions. He further asserted that the term *ahl al-kitāb* was specific to the followers of religions other than Islam who did not acknowledge the prophethood of Muhammad and his teachings, but who had a belief in God. Also, in the Qur'ān, the Jews and Christians had a special position, and in fact were guaranteed the right to practise their religion in safety. Furthermore, according to the Qur'ān, the essence of the teachings revealed to all the prophets and messengers was the same. Because of this, it was indeed true that all the communities of believers in God's religions were but one community.[69]

An interesting view regarding the position of *ahl al-kitāb* was also put forward by Ibn Taymiyya:

> Indeed the *ahl al-kitāb* was not the *mushrik*. This was in accordance with the words of God in the Qur'ān (Q.S. 22:17). If it was argued that God attributed *shirk* to the *ahl al-kitāb* in His words (Q.S. 9:31), it meant that they had committed the act of *shirk* and that it was an act which was not ordained by

---

[69] Munawar-Rachman, 'Teologi Islam Mengenai Agama-Agama', 27-28.

God; [however] it should be differentiated from attributing them as *mushrik* [persons who committed the act of *shirk*],[70] since the origin of their religion was in accordance with other holy books that taught the concept of the oneness of God (*tawḥid*), and not the teaching of *shirk*.[71]

Furthermore, Ibn Taymiyya quoted a *ḥadīth* that Pophet Muhammad urged the Muslims to treat the Zoroastrians as they treated the *ahl al-kitāb*:

> That was why Prophet Muhammad said of the Zoroastrians, 'Please carry out the *sunna* towards them [the Zoroastrians] as you do towards the *ahl al-kitāb*', and he realised a peaceful relationship with the people of Bahrain amongst whom were the Zoroastrians, and all the caliphs as well as the *ᶜulamāʾ* had agreed on this matter.[72]

Nurcholish's frequent references to Ibn Taymiyya, in this context on the *ahl al-kitāb*, deserve special analysis. As mentioned in Chapter Two, Ibn Taymiyya, who was claimed by Nurcholish as his source of inspiration and as the pioneer of Islamic renewal, was a disciple of the Hanbali tradition, which was renowned for its traditional approach to the Islamic foundation texts. In addition, Ibn Taymiyya was also well-known for his attempt to negate the sciences of the ancients (*al-ᶜulūm al-awāʾil* or *al-ᶜulūm al-qudamāʾ*) in general, and Greek logic in particular.[73] This position was perceived by some as supporting an exclusivist perspective.

---

[70] Nurcholish's explanation on this issue will be provided in Chapter Seven.

[71] Ibn Taymiyya, *Aḥkam al-Zawāj* (Beirut: Dār al-Kutub al-ᶜIlmiyyah, 1988), 188–189.

[72] Ibn Taymiyya, *Minhaj al-Sunna*, vol. 8 (n.p, 1986), 516.

[73] Ibn Taymiyya wrote a special book on this subject, *Jahd al-Qarīḥah fī Tajrīd al-Naṣīḥah*. The English translation is by Wael B. Hallaq, *Ibn Taymiyya against the Greek Logicians* (Oxford: Clarendon Press, 1993). The term *al-ᶜulūm al-awāʾil* is generally used within the Islamic philosophy, especially in the debates on 'appropriation' of the Greek sciences into the Islamic sciences. See for example, Ignaz Goldziher, 'The Attitude of Orthodox Islam toward the Ancient Sciences', in *Studies on Islam*, ed. Merlin L. Swartz (New York: Oxford University Press, 1981), 185–215.

Therefore, one might ask how Ibn Taymiyya could be pictured as the promoter of an inclusivist perspective on Muslim-Christian relations, as claimed by Nurcholish. On closer examination, there are reasons that might be used to support this claim. First of all, some scholars argued that even though the Hanbalis applied a traditional approach to Islam *ijtihād* remained alive amongst them. In addition, the Hanbali leaders often refused to recognise the *ijmāʿ* tradition of the living community on principle.[74] Second, although belonging to the Hanbali tradition, Ibn Taymiyya 'did not follow all its opinions blindly but considered himself a *mudjtahid fi 'l-madhhab*'. It was also argued that, in line with the Hanbali leaders' principles mentioned above, on some points Ibn Taymiyya rejected *taqlīd* and even *ijmāʿ*.[75] Third, while Ibn Taymiyya's rebuttal of the *al-ʿulūm al-awāʾil* and rationalisation supported the exclusivist perspective to some extent, he was actually proposing the concept of *ijtihād*, which to a considerable degree became the concern of the inclusivists. Therefore, it seems that based on these reasons and on Ibn Taymiyya's view on *ahl al-kitāb* discussed above, people such as Nurcholish found a way of categorising Ibn Taymiyya as an inclusivist.

Nevertheless, are the above arguments sound enough to justify Nurcholish's claim that Ibn Taymiyya was promoting an inclusivist view in terms of religious pluralism? There are two different answers to be found within Ibn Taymiyya's writings. On one hand, his argument that the Zoroastrians should be treated as the *ahl al-kitāb* and that the *ahl al-kitāb* were not *mushrik* might lead to the claim that Ibn Taymiyya promoted an inclusivist view on religious pluralism. On the other hand, and this is stronger than the first, Ibn Taymiyya through his writings often positioned himself as a fierce opponent of non-Muslims. He, for example, argued that God commanded Prophet Muhammad 'to follow the *sharīʿa* and not the fancies (*ahwāʾ*) of the ignorant'. He elabo-

---

[74] Marshall Hodgson, *The Venture of Islam*, vol. 3 (Chicago and London: The University of Chicago Press, 1974), 160.

[75] Cheneb, 'Ibn Taimiya', 152.

rated that the term 'their fancies'[76] in Q.S 2:120 referred to 'the fancies of the parties of men who deny part of the Revelation. They include Jews and Christians and others who reject the Koran'.[77] Ibn Taymiyya stated:

> Note the use of the phrase 'their religion' and the negative attitude to 'their fancies': The infidels will not be pleased with anything short of unconditional conforming of their religion. The warning applies to any such compliance, be it limited or extensive. It is, moreover, well known that assimilating elements of their faith is a way of assimilating, or coming dangerously close to assimilating, their fancies.[78]

In contrast to the inclusivist tone of the Qur'ānic verses on *ahl al-kitāb*, there are also critiques directed towards this group within the Qur'ān. It is important to discuss how the inclusivists interpreted such verses. According to Quraish Shihab, for example, most of the Qur'ānic critiques on the *ahl al-kitāb* were actually directed to the Jews and not to the Christians. From the very beginning of Islamic history, the Jews, who lived close to the Muslim community, and Christians, who lived in a more remote area, displayed different attitudes towards Muslims. The King of Ethiopia, who was a Christian, for example, gave a safe place to the Muslims who migrated (*hijra*) to the area. Quraish further argued that quite the opposite attitude was shown by the Jews, who could not bear that Prophet Muhammad was not a member of their community and that he had shiften their influence within Medina. Hence, the context of the criticism directed towards the Jews was their hostile attitudes to the Muslims, which emerged from

---

[76] Mohammad Asad did not translate the word '*ahwā'ahum*' in this verse as 'their fancies'. Instead, he translated it as 'their errant views'.

[77] Ibn Taymiyya, *Kitāb al-Iqtidā' aṣ-Ṣirāt al-Mustaqīm Mukhālafat Aṣḥāb al-Jaḥīm*, 2 vols. (Riyadh: Dār al-Aṣōmah, 1998). The above quotation was taken from the English translation of the book by Memon, *Ibn Taimiya's Struggle*, 100.

[78] Memon, *Ibn Taimiya's Struggle*, 100.

political and economic reasons. It was in this context that the Qur'ān stated:[79]

> Thou wilt surely find that, of all people, the most hostile to those who believe [in this divine writ] are the Jews as well as those who are bent on ascribing divinity to aught beside God; and thou wilt surely find that, of all people, they who say, 'Behold, we are Christians', come closest to feeling affection for those who believe [in this divine writ]: this is so because there are priests and monks among them, and because these are not given to arrogance (Q.S. 5:82).

In light of the above, Quraish noted that the Qur'ānic verses which prohibited Muslims from appointing Jews and Christians as their leaders (awliyā) had to be understood in the context of ahl al-kitāb described above. Referring to Q.S. 3:118,[80] Quraish maintained that the verse was revealed in relation to the attitudes of the Bani Quraizah of the Jewish community, who had betrayed their agreement with Prophet Muhammad. Quoting Rashīd Riḍā, Quraish argued that the prohibition on appointing Jews and Christians as leaders of the Muslim community was valid only if they fought the Muslims or intended to do so.[81]

On Inter-religious Marriage

Closely related to the concept of ahl al-kitāb was the issue of inter-religious marriage. The position of Muslims in general was that it was permissible for a Muslim man to marry an ahl al-kitāb woman. However, the inclusivists differed in the degree of their inclusivism

---

[79] Shihab, 'Wawasan al-Qur'an tentang Ahl al-Kitab', 3-7.

[80] Q.S. 3:118 reads: 'O you who have attained to faith! Do not take for your bosom-friends people who are not of your kind. They spare no effort to corrupt you; they would love to see you in distress. Vehement hatred has already come into the open from out of their mouths, but what their hearts conceal is yet worse. We have indeed made the signs [thereof] clear unto you, if you would but use your reason'.

[81] Shihab, 'Wawasan al-Qur'an tentang Ahl al-Kitab', 7.

regarding this. Some held the view that the permission was for Muslim men to marry only Jewish and Christian women. Others argued that men could marry women who had been vouchsafed revelation. Some inclusivists went even further, arguing that marriage between a Muslim woman and non-Muslim man was also possible within Islam.

Quraish Shihab said that, even though Muslims generally agreed that a Muslim man was permitted to marry an *ahl al-kitāb* woman, he realised there were opinions that prohibited such a marriage, for example that forwarded by the Prophet's Companion Abdullah bin Umar, who considered the *ahl al-kitāb* as *mushrik* (polytheists). Nevertheless, Quraish argued that this perception contradicted the perceptions and practices of other companions including Caliph Uthman and Ibn Abbas. Moreover, he maintained that, in some Qur'ānic verses, the word *al-mushrikīn* was put side by side with the word *ahl al-kitāb* using the connecting word *wauw*, meaning 'and'. For Quraish, this was a clear distinction by the Qur'ān, as the word *wauw* functioned as a connection between two different things. He realised that there were various reasons for people to prohibit such a marriage, including the fear that the harmony of family life would be challenged if the spouse adhered to a different religion. However, from the Qur'ānic point of view and based on the practice of the Companions of the prophet (*ṣaḥāba*), marriage between a Muslim man and an *ahl al-kitāb* woman was *ḥalāl*.[82]

Zainun argued that the regulation stated by the Qur'ān on interreligious marriage was clearly stated in the following verse:

> Today, all the good things of life have been made lawful to you... And [lawful to you are], in wedlock, women from among those who have been vouchsafed revelation before your time—provided that you give them dowers, taking them in honest wedlock, not in fornication, nor as secret love-companions ... (Q.S. 5:5).

---

[82] Shihab, 'Wawasan al-Qur'an tentang Ahl al-kitāb', 15-16.

Therefore, for Zainun, the marriage between a Muslim man and a non-Muslim woman was permitted in Islam. Parallel with his view on *ahl al-kitāb*, he went further to underline that the above-quoted verse did not actually limit the permission for Muslim men to marry only *ahl al-kitāb* women, traditionally perceived as referring to Jews and Christians; it also stated that it was lawful to marry women from among those who had been vouchsafed revelation (*alladhīna ūtū al-kitāb*). He emphasised that in Islamic history there were many cases where the *ṣaḥāba* (referring to male friends) were married to *ahl al-kitāb* women. He gave a more recent example by referring to his lecturer in Egypt who had married a non-Muslim woman.[83]

However, the reverse, which was marriage between a Muslim woman and a non-Muslim man, was disputed amongst the *ᶜulamā'*, as this circumstance was not clearly stated in the Qur'ān. Nevertheless, Zainun maintain that a marriage between a Muslim woman and a non-Muslim man was not explicitly prohibited in the Qur'ān, even though a few (*sebagian*) *ᶜulamā'* maintained that it was prohibited (*harām*).[84] He argued that in the present time different circumstances surrounding male-female relations had emerged, and that the *ijtihād* concerning inter-religious marriage should be reviewed. In commenting on the *ḥadīth* which stated that there should be four criteria for a person to marry another person, namely religion, beauty, wealth, and descent, he maintained that religion here should be understood as good morality or values. Therefore, the Prophet had actually suggested that a person should marry someone of good morality.

As mentioned in Chapter Five, Zainun Kamal was reported by Cholil Ridwan of KISDI who said that Zainun never supported let alone promoted marriage between a Muslim woman and a non-Muslim man. This was understood by Cholil as inconsistency with an earlier statement published on the Jaringan Islam Liberal website. Never-

---

[83] Kamal, 'Nikah Beda Agama' [online]; accessed 7 July 2002.
[84] Kamal, 'Nikah Beda Agama' [online]; accessed 7 July 2002.

theless, from his writings and interview statements that were gathered during the course of this study, it is safe to argue that Zainun was consistent in his perspective that marriage between a Muslim woman and a non-Muslim man was not explicitly prohibited in the Qur'ān. The statement cited by Cholil that such marriage should be avoided (if it was correctly cited), however, should not be understood to mean that the former did not agree with inter-religious marriage. In one interview, Zainun said 'The arguments that I have forwarded concerning the *ahl al-kitāb* were not mine but instead they belonged to the *ʿulamāʾ*. It is true, however, that I supported their views for the sake of a peaceful Islam'.[85] It seems that Zainun shared the view of many other scholars, such as Quraish Shihab, that the harmony of family life could be threatened if spouses adhered to different religions.

While Nurcholish Madjid was productive in his opinions on the *ahl al-kitāb*, his perspective on marriage between Muslims and *ahl al-kitāb* is barely to be found in his writings. Nurcholish was very inclusive in extending the definition of *ahl al-kitāb* to include the Zoroastrians, the Hindus and the Buddhists; therefore his own circumstance was interesting when his daughter, Nadia Madjid, was to marry a New York Jew, David Bychkov, in September 2001. Nurcholish's high admiration regarding the position of *ahl al-kitāb* in Islam, and his own argument that Jews who followed their religious belief in accordance with what had been taught by the '*pasrah*' (*muslim*) prophet were indeed *muslimūn*, did not extend to giving his daughter freedom to marry a Jewish man.

Some reasons can be cited to explain Nurcholish's perspective. First, for him, the Qur'ānic concept was clear that a Muslim man might marry a woman of the *ahl al-kitāb*, but not vice versa. In a private letter to his daughter on 13 August 2001, he insisted that Bychkov had to embrace Islam as a requirement to marry her. Second, Nurcholish reasoned that if she married the Jewish man, 'Ninety-nine percent of

---

[85] Zainun Kamal, interview by author, Jakarta, 22 January 2002.

Islamic scholars will argue that your marriage is unlawful; and it is a great sin, one of the greatest sins in Islam after *shirk*, rebelling against parents, kill other human beings, and destroy the environment'. In an interview with *Gatra* magazine, Nurcholish explained that in the matter of marriage he followed the *madhhab* of the 'traditionalist', in which the marriage had to have *ijāb qabūl* (offer and acceptance), *walī* (male relative legally responsible for the bride), *mahr* (dowry) and witnesses. He even added that the marriage had to proceed with *khutbah nikāḥ* (sermon delivered following the *ijab qabūl*). Nurcholish argued that in the case of his daughter, 'All the *sharīʿa* requirements for the marriage were fulfilled' (*seluruh aturan syariat Islam dalam pernikahan itu sudah terpenuhi*).[86] Third, Nurcholish's firm attitude that his daughter could only marry Bychkov provided he became a Muslim must also be explained within Nurcholish's position as a key Muslim figure in Indonesia whose actions were often copied by other Muslims. Even though he did not voice this concern, it seemed that Nurcholish felt the need to argue along the lines of the majority of the *ʿulamāʾ* on the issue of inter-religious marriage in order to avoid controversy.

Christianisation and Roots of Disharmony between Muslims and Christians

In understanding Christianisation and the background of Muslim–Christians relations that were sometimes coloured by disharmony, the inclusivists' approach was quite different as compared to the exclusivists. Their perspective in understanding the religious 'other' prevented the inclusivists from easily being discriminative and judgemental towards Christians. The data gathered below were mainly from interviews.

---

[86] Nurcholish Madjid sent a copy of his personal letters to Nadia Madjid to *Media Dakwah* after the magazine published the news of the wedding in April 2002. The interview was published in 'Kontroversi Perkawinan Putri Cak Nur', *Gatra* 22 (20 April 2002).

On Christianisation

Whereas exclusivist Muslims were very irritated by Christianisation and discussed the issue in much detail, the inclusivists responded to it in general and not case by case. Phenomena perceived as Christianisation, such as church building, educations, or the RUUPA was not a concern for them. Instead, the inclusivists in many cases attempted to understand the background of these efforts and the more fundamental problems within the relations between Muslims and Christians.

When asked about the proselytising activities conducted by Christians, Komaruddin Hidayat, for example, argued that one had to trace the background of Christian attitudes towards Muslims to the New Order period, even to the colonial era in Indonesia, as the relationship between Islam and Christianity in Indonesia could not be separated from the historical background of the coming of Christianity to the area. For him, because Christianity in Indonesia came through the West it therefore created a political stigma; Islam was seen as a fighting symbol of the *pribumi,* and Christianity was a symbol of colonial religion. This circumstance was unfortunate because in Indonesia the image of Christianity was contaminated by the colonialist image. In Komaruddin's perspective, this had created hatred on the Muslims' part towards Christians. Therefore, Muslims were suspicious of Christian activities and suspected them of attempting to convert Muslims to Christianity.[87]

In addition, Komaruddin argued that there was evidence that the media was very biased in their reports on conflicts involving Muslims and Christians. Media that supported Muslims would blame the Christians, and vice versa. He believed that this added ammunition to the already inflamed conflicts. Furthermore, there was professional third party intervention which played one group off against the other. Komaruddin believed that the conflicts involving Muslims and Christians in some areas of Indonesia were no longer based on religious matters; on the contrary, they stemmed from hatred. Also, even though

---

[87] Komaruddin Hidayat, interview by author, Jakarta, 24 January 2002.

people realised that it was not a matter of religion, their understanding of the concept of citizenship was very minimal. Komaruddin concluded that, in conflict involving Muslims and Christians, religion was (mis)used to mobilise the masses. For him, the source of the conflict was not polemic (*pendapat*) but more related to income or economic status (*pendapatan*).[88]

Similarly, Nurcholish Madjid attempted to trace the historical background of Muslim–Christian relations. He maintained that, after the mass killing in 1965–1967, a number of Muslims were suspected by other Muslims of having aligned with the Communist Party (PKI) and were thus alienated, if not violated. Because the government ordered Indonesians to embrace one of the five existing religions, these alienated Muslims tried to find an alternative by embracing Christianity because the Christians welcomed them more than their fellow Muslims did. In addition, Nurcholish held that some key positions within Soeharto's cabinet that were given to Christians had added to the hatred within Muslims' minds, even though this was not the Christians' fault. These circumstances had given the Christians the opening to advance their agenda, including building many churches, even though their adherents were small in number. However, Nurcholish underlined that this was not the Christians' fault. For him, the Christianisation process was a sociological phenomenon that happened by accident and not by deliberation.[89]

In understanding the problem of the imitation of Muslim traditions and attending Christmas celebrations, which were believed by the exclusivists to increase tensions between Muslims and Christians, Abdurrahman Wahid took a different line. As discussed in Chapter Five, the exclusivist Muslims would not direct the *salām* towards non-Muslims. Abdurrahman Wahid, however, argued that within Indonesian

---

[88] Komaruddin Hidayat, interview by author, Jakarta, 24 January 2002.

[89] Komaruddin Hidayat, interview by author, Jakarta, 24 January 2002; and Nurcholish Madjid, interview by author, Jakarta, 6 March 2002.

history Islam and other religions had long been acculturated. Therefore, for him, it was not surprising that some religious rituals within Indonesian Islam were taken from other religions, such as the *selametan* (commemoration for the dead) on the 3rd, 7th, 40th and 1000th days for family members that had passed away. He further stressed that Christianity in Indonesia was also heavily influenced by Islam, so strongly that some Christians recited the *salām* in speeches or official addresses. Abdurrahman Wahid perceived this as normal since Islam was the religion of the majority of the Indonesian population. He underlined that this had also happened to the Muslim minority in America: when they greeted their fellow Americans, they said 'good morning' or 'good evening' and not *salām*.[90]

In addition, on the issue of attending Christmas celebrations Abdurrahman Wahid criticised the *fatwā* by the MUI. In an article published in 1981, he maintained that the problem with this *fatwā* was the unclear function of the *ᶜulamā'* within the MUI. In his view, the function of the MUI was only as 'a facilitator between the government and the Muslims and not as an authoritative body that could issue a religious regulation on behalf of the Muslims'. For him, the *fatwā* had created other questions: 'Would there be other *fatawā* issued concerning the love relations between Muslims and non-Muslims? Would the MUI issue a *fatwā* prohibiting non-Muslims going to the houses of Muslims?' Abdurrahman Wahid suggested that the MUI should deal with more fundamental issues faced by Indonesian society, including Islamic perspectives on the problems of poverty, justice, and education, rather than occupying themselves with issues such as Christmas celebrations.[91]

---

[90] Abdurrahman Wahid, 'Toleransi dan Batasnya', in *Membangun Demokrasi*, ed. Zaini S Al-Raef (Bandung: Remaja Rosdakarya, 1999), 66-67.

[91] Abdurrahman Wahid, 'Fatwa Natal, Ujung, dan Pangkal', *Tempo* (26 May 1981). The article was republished in *Melawan Melalui Lelucon*, eds. Mustafa Ismail, et al. (Jakarta: Pusat Data dan Analisa Tempo, 2000), 26-27.

As mentioned in Chapter Three, the Christians had rejected the inclusion of the Jakarta Charter in the Preamble of the 1945 Constitution and had responded negatively to later attempts at reviving the Charter. However, Ulil Abshar-Abdalla did not consider this rejection as proof of Christian antipathy towards Muslims, as understood by some Muslims. For him, the fact that Christians were fond of people like Nurcholish Madjid or Abdurrahman Wahid was enough to explain that the Christians disliked other Muslims who interpreted Islam in an exclusive way.[92]

Roots of Disharmony

In line with Ulil's contention that the basic reason for the disharmonious relations between Muslims and Christians was the 'unfair' proselytising from both the Christian and Muslim sides, Azyumardi Azra noted six causes of conflicts among the followers of Islam and Christianity that could be generated by followers of either religion: (1) circulation of publications containing plans for religious expansion and for discrediting particular religions; (2) aggressive expansion of religious propagation; (3) unlicensed prayer houses; (4) adoption of certain government regulations considered to discriminate against certain religions; (5) public display of religious rituals; and (6) mutual suspicions relating to the issue of the position of religion in Indonesia. Azyumardi, however, admitted that this approach did not address the fact that some riots were internal conflicts that tended to involve particular sects within Islam and Christianity in Indonesia.[93]

Even though some inclusivists forwarded the argument that Christianisation efforts were not solely the Christians' fault, Azyumardi underlined the unfair proselytising activities by certain Christians as one of the causes of the disharmony between Muslims and Christians.

---

[92] Ulil Abshar-Abdalla, interview by author, Jakarta, 6 March 2002.

[93] Azyumardi Azra, 'Islam and Christianity in Indonesia: The Roots of Conflict and Hostility', in *Religion and Culture in Asia-Pacific: Violence or Healing?*, ed. J.A. Camilleri (Melbourne: Vista Publication, 2001), 85–90.

One case was the existence of the Apostolos and Kalimatullah Institutes of Theology. Azyumardi asserted that, in addition to their missions and activities which had caused discomfort amongst Muslims, the Apostolos Institute named certain IAIN Jakarta's lecturers in their brochures to legitimise their claim of formal cooperation with the Islamic institute. Azyumardi, as the rector of IAIN Jakarta, underlined that this was not true as his institution had never had any formal cooperation with the Protestant body. The second case was Christianisation within the IAIN Jakarta by way of meditation classes. Azyumardi pointed to a Christian missionary named Yohannes Iwan who was claimed to have attempted to Christianise the IAIN Jakarta's students by persuading them to criticise Islamic belief. Among Yohannes' teaching was that ʿIed al-Aḍha (butchering animals as religious offerings) was a day of mass-killing. The students were also asked to cite Christian prayers before starting meditation classes.[94] Azyumardi maintained that these activities were capable of aggravating Muslim–Christian tensions.[95]

The inclusivists' different approach to Christianisation led to further questions on the recommendations they would put for better relations between Muslims and Christians. As can be seen from Nurcholish's writings, he insisted that the Qurʾānic concept of religious pluralism and ahl al-kitāb needed to be well understood and implemented in daily life. Nevertheless, Komaruddin Hidayat maintained that theological efforts to solve tense relations between Muslims and Christians should not be perceived as the main effort. For him, the problem of Indonesian society started with the faulty political management of the New Order, and conflicts involving Muslims and Christians occured because there was no rule of law or justice. Therefore, in Komaruddin's view, to solve the problem one should start with upholding justice, legal supremacy and democracy: 'A clean and strong government should be created and thus any conflict that

---

[94] IAIN Jakarta Students, 'Kristenisasi dan Penipuan Gaya Baru (Melalui Bela Diri dan Pengobatan)', Unpublished report, 27 February 2002.

[95] Azyumardi Azra, interview by author, Jakarta, 4 March 2002.

emerges will be solved rationally and not ethnically or based on religion'. He further explained:

> To solve the conflicts involving Muslims and Christians, political parties and NGOs have to build the paradigm of the nation-state and not citizenship; civility and not communalism. We have to develop a discourse on democracy, clean government, transparency, and accountability as areas shared by all the community. To other religious or ethnic communities we have to show our commitment to universal values, but internally we can show our ethnic or religious identities. We have to articulate Islam in such a way that can be shared by all human beings.[96]

Amin Abdullah proposed a different approach. Because he assumed that certain approaches to the study of religion could contribute to violence between religious followers, his approach in solving disharmonious relations between Muslims and Christians was through reformation of religious studies. Amin emphasised that religion had two important dimensions: theological-normative and historio-cultural. Within Indonesian society, it would be dangerous to emphasise the sacred dimension and to ignore the historio-cultural element, as had commonly been the practice of the study of religion. Therefore, for him, in a heterogeneous society like Indonesia, an inclusive, open-ended philosophical approach was needed. Amin called this the fundamental-philosophical method (al-falsafa al-ūlā), which should be differentiated from the philosophical-theological approach (al-ʿilm al-ilāhī). He believed that the former approach was capable of clarifying the dispute concerning text (doctrinal-theological) and reality (cultural-sociological). This method had also facilitated the fusion of the sacred and profane in contemporary religious discourse.[97]

---

[96] Komaruddin Hidayat, interview by author, Jakarta, 24 January 2002.

[97] Amin Abdullah, *Rekonstruksi Metodologi Studi Agama dalam Masyarakat Multikultural dan Multirelijius* (Yogyakarta: IAIN Sunan Kalijaga, 2000), 2-10.

The Role of the Inclusivists in Indonesian Society

Support for inclusivist thought can be seen in the existence of certain institutions, either directly or indirectly. Below is the discussion on some important institutions that support inclusivist thought, including NGOs concerned with interfaith dialogue, and the State Institute of Islamic Studies, in different areas of Indonesia.

Non-Government Organisations on Interfaith Dialogue

Some Indonesian intellectuals, especially Muslim and Christian, realised the need to open a dialogue between religious groups by establishing non-government organisations (NGOs) concerned with the issue. Since the end of the 1980s, some manifestations of interfaith dialogue, in particular involving Muslims and Christians, have emerged. The emergence of these NGOs was not a coincidence, as towards the end of the 1980s and in early 1990s Muslims started to gain self-confidence, especially with the establishment of the Association of Indonesian Muslim Intellectuals (ICMI) in 1990.[98] It is worth noting that this interfaith dialogue did not necessarily assume that the main cause of the inter-religious tension was theological. In the same way, these institutions did not necessarily support or imitate the state-sponsored efforts on inter-religious dialogue discussed above.

Among the first NGOs was the Paramadina Foundation (Yayasan Paramadina) established on 31 October 1986 with Nurcholish Madjid as its key figure. Other important figures at Paramadina, especially at its inception, included Usep Fathuddin, Utomo Dananjaya, Komaruddin Hidayat, and Budhy Munawar-Rachman. Paramadina is a centre for seminars, courses and dialogues on religion and society. It has three important characteristics, namely independence, openness and culture orientation. First, it was not affiliated with any socio-political organisation, be it in Indonesia or overseas. Hence it was oriented towards 'truth' and humanity. Second, Paramadina was an open forum for people of different

---

[98] On the discussion on ICMI see Chapter Four.

religious and cultural backgrounds to openly and democratically discuss religious and social issues. It held a belief that what one considered as 'truth' was in fact relative and was therefore open to examination. Third, it was culture-oriented in the sense that Paramadina did not focus its programs on practical political issues. In addition, Paramadina held the principle that the future of Islam rested in the hands of liberal Islam, and therefore introduced a 'liberal' interpretation of Islam in which the values of human rights, democracy, pluralism, and feminism were highly regarded.[99]

Paramadina, in accord with the aim of its designers, who were mostly business men, was established as a medium for 'urban' Muslims to discuss, analyse and scrutinise Islamic teachings. This medium was clearly created to cater for the Muslim professionals who needed Islamic responses to problems they encountered in modern life, such as business ethics and banking. Therefore, the target of this institution was the urban middle class and upper class Muslims as the trendsetters within Indonesian society. As such, it was hoped that if they could gain a deep and wide understanding of Islam, their policies would be coloured by their rich comprehension of the religion. Hence, although Paramadina was not formally called an interfaith dialogue institution, its approach to Islam helped to promote religious tolerance amongst different believers.[100] Nurcholish Madjid believed that the tolerance he promoted through the activities at Paramadina should be based on deliberation and not accident. He further maintained his emphasis that 'Tolerance is not a problem of procedure but it is a problem of belief. Even though it is bitter, we have to go on with the

---

[99] Paramadina, *Pandangan Dasar Yayasan Wakaf Paramadina* (Jakarta, no date).

[100] Periodically Paramadina conducts short courses which run for three and a half months ranging from Arabic, Introduction to Islamic Studies, to the theoretical comprehension of Islamic mystics (sufism). The aim of these courses is to give a comprehensive and fair understanding of Islam so that participants can develop an understanding of different ideologies within Islam, as well as to develop a comprehension towards other religions.

process. The bitterness is short term and the sweetness will be gained in the long term period'.[101]

Paramadina conducted courses including Qur'ānic studies, Islamic mysticism, and Islam and the problem of modern society. In addition, it developed a monthly forum to discuss contemporary issues on Islam held at a four-star hotel in Jakarta. In the field of publication, Paramadina published two journals in 1998 and 1999, and some books. Among the books touching on the issue of Muslim–Christian relations in particular, and religious pluralism in general, were, Budhy Munawar-Rachman, *Islam Pluralis: Wacana Kesetaraan Kaum Beriman*; George B. Grose and Benyamin J. Hubbard, *Tiga Agama Satu Tuhan* (translated from *Three Religions One God*), Alwi Shihab, *Islam Inklusif*, and Azyumardi Azra, *Konteks Berteologi di Indonesia*.

Another institution for inter-religious dialogue is INTERFIDEI (Institute for Inter-Faith Dialogue in Indonesia), founded in 1992 by the Protestant, Th. Sumartana (d. 2003). Other figures involved in INTER-FIDEI are Elga Sarapung and Djohan Effendi. The Indonesian name for this institution, DIAN (*Dialog Antariman*) signifies an important meaning. Sumartana chose the word '*iman*', meaning faith, to stress the common concerns of individual believers, instead of '*agama*', meaning religion, which focuses on institutionalised religion. INTERFIDEI holds monthly inter-religious discussions concentrating on the formulation of spirituality for the modern era. It also pays significant attention to social actions focusing on human rights and other humanitarian aid.[102] The focus on humanitarian aid does not necessarily exclude theological dialogue from INTERFIDEI's programs. Sumartana was well aware of the history of both Muslim–Christian conflict and political, economic and hegemonic conflict, especially in Indonesia. INTERFIDEI's activities, the-

---

[101] Nurcholish Madjid, interview by author, Jakarta, 6 March 2002.

[102] INTERFIDEI, *DIAN/INTERFIDEI* (Yogyakarta: INTERFIDEI Secretariat, no date).

refore, include theological relations, communication between leaders, institutional relations, and joint action.[103]

MADIA (Masyarakat Dialog Antar Agama/Society for Inter-Religious Dialogue) was established in November 1995 by people of different religious backgrounds with a similar hope for sincere, honest, open and critical inter-religious dialogue.[104] The prominent members of MADIA included the Catholic Jesuit priest Sandyawan Sumardi, Amanda Suharnoko and Sutrisno. The background of its establishment was their concern that the interaction between various religions were being coloured by 'mutual suspicion, chauvinism, condescension, traumatic conflicts and exclusive and arrogant theologies'. For the members of MADIA, the dialogue between religions was imperative. This means that each believer had to be ready to critically examine, and if necessary to reformulate, their religion as a result of dialogue between different religions and faiths. After the Situbondo (East Java) riots of 1996 in which several churches were burnt down, the dialogues developed at MADIA became more socially-oriented. Indeed, this was the first time that MADIA entered the world of politics.

MADIA is open to participation by people of any religious or spiritual background. Among the Muslim figures that were involved at MADIA were Budhy Munawar-Rachman, Djohan Effendi, Komaruddin Hidayat, and Ulil Abshar-Abdalla. Some Catholic figures included Ignatius Ismartono, while Protestant figures included Martin Lukito Sinaga. It is interesting to note a unique feature of MADIA: prayers for opening and closing meetings were conducted according to the religion or spiritual belief of the host venue. In short, in MADIA, diversity in belief or religion was highly valued.

---

[103] Th. Sumartana, 'SARA: An Unfinished Process of Social Integration?', Unpublished paper presented at the International Seminar on Religious Plurality and Nationalism in Indonesia (Leiden, 26-27 November, 1997), 18.

[104] The discussion on MADIA below was taken from a leaflet published by MADIA, *An Experiment Named MADIA* (Jakarta: MADIA Secretariat, no date).

Jaringan Islam Liberal (Liberal Islamic Network/JIL) was formed in March 2001 by some young Muslims (born mainly in the late 1960s or early 1970s), who were concerned with the emergence of literalist Muslims (those who interpreted Islam in a textual way). JIL placed a heavy emphasis on the importance of *ijtihād*, believing that this was the major principle that would enable Islam to exist in different contexts, and attempted to interpret Islam based on the religio-ethical spirit of the Qur'ān and *sunna*. For JIL, any religious interpretation was 'relative' because interpretation was a 'product of human activity', which was confined to a certain time and place and should be 'open', as any kind of interpretation always had the possibility of being right or wrong. In addition, JIL based itself on a pluralistic view since a religious interpretation, in one way or another, was a reflection of the interpreter's need within a certain time and place.[105]

Ulil Abshar-Abdalla, one of the key figures of JIL, as well as other figures including Goenawan Mohamad, Luthfie Assyaukanie, Ihsan Ali-Fauzi, Nong Daral Mahmada, Hamid Basyaib and Ahmad Sahal, stated that JIL was concerned with the fact that radical Islam was growing in Indonesia, whereas liberal Islam had been 'unorganized, weak-seeming, not militant, not resistant and unassertive in giving voice to its perspectives'.[106] Therefore, JIL had responded to this by running programs including seminars and discussions on Islam, talk shows on *68 H* Radio, establishing a website, and publishing books. Two books that were recently published were *Wajah Liberal Islam di Indonesia* (The Face of Liberal Islam in Indonesia/2002) and *Syariat Islam: Pandangan Muslim Liberal* (Islamic Sharīᶜa: The Perspective of Liberal Muslims/2003).

ICRP (Indonesian Conference on Religion and Peace) was founded in 2001 and also aimed at religious dialogue and peace relations

---

[105] 'Program Jaringan Islam Liberal' [online], available from http://www.islamlib. com; accessed 14 November 2002.

[106] Linda Christanty, 'Is There a Rainbow in Islam?', Quoted from *Latitude* magazine, July 2003.

between followers of different faiths, especially Muslims and Christians. Indeed, some of ICRP members were also actively involved in MADIA. Chaired by Djohan Effendi, this forum conducted activities in several areas of Indonesia, focusing on three aspects: doctrinal dialogues, socio-political issues, and humanitarian help.[107] At the doctrinal level, ICRP developed a 'liberal' interpretation of religion which emphasised the transcendent unity of religions. According to Ulil of ICRP, one of the most crucial problems surrounding Muslim–Christian relations was both the unfair proselytising efforts by the Christians and the *daʿwa* activities of the Muslims. He pointed to the emergence of the evangelical denominations within the Protestant circles outside the PGI as an obvious example of unfair proselytising activities. However, Ulil criticised some Muslims who tended to generalise the issue of Christianisation rather than distinguish case by case. This tendency was shown, for instance, by the writings on Christianisation activities published in the *Media Dakwah* as journalistic reportage without appropriately interviewing the primary sources behind the events reported.[108] In addition, Ulil referred to the protest against the building of St Ignatius Church at Banjardowo, Semarang, Central Java. The committee for the church building maintained that they had followed the procedures prescribed by the local government. However, on 12 February 2002, a group of Muslims named Forum Umat Islam Semarang (Islamic Community Forum of Semarang) approached the local government urging the cancellation of the church building.[109]

Efforts by these non-government organisations on religious dialogue have succeeded to a significant extent. In contrast to government efforts on the same issue, the activities of these NGOs were more sincerely directed towards better relations between religious groups.

---

[107] This information was gathered from the interviews with Ignatius Sumartono, S.J., Jakarta, 29 January 2002, and Ulil Absar-Abdalla, 6 March 2002, as well as from some brochures.

[108] Ulil Abshar-Abdalla, interview by author, Jakarta, 6 March 2002.

[109] 'Pembangunan Gereja Diprotes', and 'Proyek Gereja Sesuai Prosedur', *Suara Merdeka* 12 and 13 February 2002, respectively. There were no following reports on this case.

More importantly, their efforts at religious dialogue were conducted not solely in response to an already-inflamed situation between different religious believers. Rather, they were aimed at educating people on the importance of religious tolerance.

State Institute of Islamic Studies (IAIN)

Among the important institutions that have supported the inclusivist view is the State Institute of Islamic Studies, which has 14 branches in different parts of Indonesia. It is not an exaggeration that some hold the view that one of the most effective approaches to developing a culture of religious tolerance in a country such as Indonesia, where Muslims are the majority, is by reforming the education of its leaders.[110] It is in this context that IAIN has played an important role.

IAIN Yogyakarta and Jakarta were later developments of Perguruan Tinggi Agama Islam Negeri (State Islamic Higher Learning Institute/PTAIN) and Akademi Dinas Ilmu Agama (Religious Studies Academy), which merged in 1960. The PTAIN and ADIA had different purposes: whereas the former aimed at producing Islamic Studies graduates who could provide, among others, religious instruction in schools or religious activities for Indonesian Muslims, the latter was intended for government officials to learn Islam in order to later develop teacher training in schools.[111] In line with the discussion in Chapter Four, the establishment of IAIN should not be detached from the New Order agenda of weakening Muslim political activity by introducing a modern interpretation of Islam. As mentioned in the discussion on Mukti Ali above, as Minister of Religious Affairs (1971–1977) he was given the task by the New Order government to reform IAIN. The task was then continued by his successors Alamsyah Ratu perwiranegara (1977–1982), Munawir Sjadzali (1983–1988), and Tarmizi Taher (1994–1998).

---

[110] Abdullah Saeed, 'Towards Religious Tolerance through Reform in Islamic Education: The Case of the State Institute of Islamic Studies of Indonesia', *Indonesia and the Malay World* 27, no. 79 (1999): 177.

[111] Saeed, 'Towards Religious Tolerance', 182.

In line with the emergence of the renewal of Islamic thought in the 1970s, the reform of the IAIN started by Mukti Ali, and the appointment of Harun Nasution as the rector of IAIN Jakarta, there were other significant changes in terms of the approach to Islamic Studies. Azyumardi Azra noted some trends within Islamic Studies at the IAIN over the past two decades. Among the important trends was the *non-madhhab* approach in which the method applied in studying Islamic law, theology or sufism did not favour a particular line of thought. Azyumardi claimed that the result of this *non-madhhab* approach was the weakening of sectarianism within the IAIN milieu and within Muslim society in general. Another significant trend was the shift from a normative approach to Islamic studies to more historical, sociological and empirical approaches. With this new trend, IAIN students were expected to better understand the reality within which they lived.[112] It is also within this approach that a more tolerant Islam was to be introduced.

Since 1990, IAIN lecturers from all over Indonesia went to pursue their Masters and Doctoral degrees at the Institute of Islamic Studies, McGill University, Montreal Canada, under the first phase of the Indonesia Canada Islamic Higher Education Project (ICIHEP). This was a joint project of professional development for the teaching staff, administrative personnel and library facilities of the State Institute of Islamic Studies system of Indonesia. A further purpose of the project was to increase the participation of women in teaching and managerial roles. The project focused on the IAINs Jakarta and Yogyakarta, which functioned as feeder sites for the rest of the system. The second phase of the project ran from 1995 to 2000, and by the end of this phase 91 Muslim lecturers from different cities across Indonesia had completed their studies at McGill University. Having learnt modern approaches to Islamic studies in these institutions and some other Western in-

---

[112] Azyumardi Azra, 'Studi-Studi Agama di Perguruan Tinggi Agama Islam Negeri', in *Pendidikan Islam: Tradisi dan Modernisasi Menuju Milenium Baru* (Jakarta: Logos, 2000), 169-174.

stitutions, IAIN lecturers were expected to introduce modern and tolerant approaches to Islamic Studies, which was very significant in promoting harmonious relations between religious believers, including Muslims and Christians.

Concluding Remarks

The relations between inclusivist Muslims and Christians are coloured largely by harmony. The discussion on the inclusivists centred on some key figures and intellectuals rather than on organisations because of the importance of their ideas. They too differ in their degree of inclusiveness, in their backgrounds and in their concerns on Muslim-Christian relations. Nevertheless, in general the inclusivists appear to have certain characteristics in common, among the most significant of which is the belief that salvation is also possible outside Islam. Even though it is not the intention of this thesis to argue that inclusivist viewpoints were merely based solely on theological notions, the examination of their perspectives shows that their method of interpreting theological texts had a special and significant role in their perspectives on Muslim-Christian relations. The inclusivists held the view that plurality was the law of nature (*sunnatullāh*), and therefore Muslims should reinterpret the basic concepts of religious freedom and pluralism as embodied in the Qur'ān and *sunna* and the early generation of Muslims. Within this view, all religions were perceived to adhere to the same principle of One Truth; therefore they would gradually find their 'common platform' or *kalimatun sawā'*. This view was reflected in the inclusivists' perspectives on other issues, including inter-religous marriage.

However, the birth of inclusive thought in Indonesia should not be detached from the political situation of the early New Order era. The inclusivists learnt from the New Order government's harsh attitude towards political Islam, and therefore devoted themselves to intellectual activism. Based on their inclusivist perspective in understanding Islamic teachings on the religious 'other', and on their efforts to accommodate government policies on issues pertaining to religion, the inclusivists relationship with Christians tended to be more harmonious as compared to that of the exclusivists. This choice of attitude towards Christians had two implications. First, it kindled critiques from some Muslims, especially exclusivists, that the inclusivists had contributed significantly to a political compromise between Islam and the New Order's policies. Conversely, the inclusivists criticised the hostile attitudes towards Christians on the part of the exclusivists. This will be discussed in the next chapter.[]

7

Mutual Critiques between the Exclusivists and Inclusivists

Introduction

Chapters Five and Six discussed the perspectives of the exclusivist and inclusivist Muslims on the religious 'other' with a special emphasis on Christians within the context of Muslim-Christian relations. This chapter explores how the exclusivists and inclusivists perceived each other, focusing on the extent to which they rejected or accepted their respective positions on some of the key issues discussed in those two chapters. However, before discussing this subject, it is important to note that comments and critiques directed towards each other by the exclusivists and inclusivists were not always related to their perspectives on Muslim-Christian relations. More general issues, such as the method applied in understanding Islam, were also in the spotlight. These more general issues are also discussed in this chapter in so far as they explain the positions of exclusivists and inclusivists on Muslim-Christian relations. This chapter has two sections. Section one examines the exclusivists' perspectives on the inclusivists. The inclusivists' criticisms of the exclusivists are analysed in Section two.

Exclusivists' Perspectives on the Inclusivists

It is important to note that of the four exclusivist groups discussed in this study, DDII and KISDI were more productive in their comments and criticisms towards the inclusivists than were FPI and Laskar Jihad. Moreover, these exclusivist groups often directed their critiques at liberal Islam, which included the examination of the key inclusivist figures' thoughts, therefore this kind of criticism is also scrutinised. There were also significant critiques and comments directed at the inclusivists' thought on Muslim-Christian relations from individuals who in one way or another were related to the exclusivists, including Daud Rasyid,[1] and therefore are included in this section. Important issues put forward by the exclusivists included the renewal of Islamic thought and inclusivist theological perspectives, Christianity and Christianisation, and the *ahl al-kitāb*.

The Renewal Movement and Inclusivist Theological Perspectives

The exclusivists severely criticised the renewal of Islamic thought (Gerakan Pembaruan Keagamaan Islam) and inclusivist theological perspectives. Key issues raised were the alleged link between the inclusivists and the Jews and Christians, the assumption that the inclusivists tended to weaken Muslims' faith by giving new and deviant interpretations of the Islamic foundation texts, and the inclusivists' lack of concern about the issue of Christianisation.

Chapter Six discussed the background of the renewal thought and the role that its key figures, including Nurcholish Madjid, played in the development of Islamic thinking in Indonesia. As mentioned, after delivering his paper 'Reinvigorating Religious Understanding in the Indonesian Muslim Community' in October 1972, Nurcholish was in-

---

[1] Daud Rasyid is a lecturer at the State Institute of Islamic Studies Jakarta and a fierce opponent of Nurcholish Madjid. Although not formally a member of one of the exclusivist organisations discussed in this study, Daud Rasyid had a close relationship with DDII and his views on the inclusivist Muslims showed a striking resemblance to those of DDII. Therefore, Daud Rasyid's critiques on the inclusivists, especially on Nurcholish's views on *ahl al-kitāb*, would be quite significant in further explaining the exclusivist's perspectives.

vited for several months to the University of Chicago, where he later pursued his doctoral degree from 1978 to 1984. This cooled criticisms directed towards him for a while until he delivered another paper on 21 October 1992 called 'Some Reflections on Religious Life in Indonesia for the Coming Generations'. One of its topics was the differences between God (with a capital G) and god, which provoked a huge debate amongst the exclusivists. It is important to note that, for most of the exclusivists, the renewal of Islamic thought was almost identical with Nurcholish Madjid and hence it was towards him, more than anybody else, that the critiques were directed.

In its special edition on Nurcholish Madjid released soon after the 1992 paper, the *Media Dakwah* labelled Nurcholish's mode of thinking as Gerakan Pembaruan Keagamaan (Religious Renewal Movement), abbreviated to GPK to alter the more common name of the Gerakan Pembaruan Pemikiran Islam (GPPI). It seems that the term Gerakan Pembaruan Keagamaan was deliberately chosen, as its abbreviation, GPK, referred to the earlier well-known Gerakan Pengacau Keamanan (Security Disorder Movement), a term used by the New Order government for any movements that challenged its authority. Indeed, it was the perception of the *Media Dakwah* and DDII that Nurcholish's renewal thought was causing disturbances to Muslim thought.[2] DDII claimed that the renewal of Islamic thought was parallel with the New Order agenda to eliminate political Islam. In addition, DDII believed that Nurcholish's intellectuality had been used as a means to position the Muslims at the periphery within Indonesian political discourse. More importantly, Nurcholish was claimed to have said 'The Qur'ān was not relevant with the progress of the modern era' and to have questioned the success of the Prophet's mission. This caused anger within the exclusivist groups.[3]

---

[2] *Media Dakwah*, December 1992, 41–52.

[3] 'Nabi Gagal Menjalankan Missinya? (Menguji Pemikiran Nurcholish)', *Media Dakwah*, December 1992, 41.

It is difficult to locate DDII's claim within Nurcholish's numerous writings, and DDII's assertion did not reflect Nurcholish's perspective in general. The statement closest to this claim was Nurcholish's discussion on the *Salaf*. Nurcholish started by describing the situation following the Prophet's death and then discussed the authority of the *Salaf* on matters pertaining to religion. He posted an assumption that 'The *Salaf* were those who really understood their religious teachings and performed their religious duties'. He further forwarded a note in a form of question: 'So, if that was not what the *Salaf* really did, who else would do so? Or do we claim that they, if not the Prophet himself, failed (to convey his message)?[4]

The perception that the renewal of Islamic thought, specifically Nurcholish's perspective, was leading Muslim society into danger was widely held within the DDII, as can be seen in the articles published at *Media Dakwah*. In addition to the special report mentioned above, in its edition of August 1993, for example, the magazine analysed and criticised William Liddle (a well-known scholar of Indonesia), and argued that he had attempted to support Nurcholish and the GPK when they were severely criticised by different Muslim groups. In commenting on Liddle's visit to Jakarta in mid 1993 and his effort to meet several key Muslim figures, *Media Dakwah* argued that it was 'The reflection of his concern for the fate of the renewal figures and their *"imam"* [leader], Nurcholish Madjid, who is now deemed to be just part of history'.[5]

In addition to the special edition of *Media Dakwah*, a book on *Menggugat Gerakan Pembaruan Keagamaan* (Charging the Religious Renewal Movement), which echoed the exclusivist perspectives, was

---

[4] Madjid, *Islam, Doktrin dan Peradaban*, 380.

[5] 'William Liddle Mau Mengulang Sejarah Lama Memecah Belah Umat', *Media Dakwah*, August 1993, 41.

published.[6] The book severely criticised Nurcholish's thought and assessed the thought of Dawam Rahardjo, Zainun Kamal, and Atho Mudzhar. It reported that on 1 February 1993 a meeting was held at the As-Syafi'iyah Mosque in Jakarta at which some in the audience severely criticised Nurcholish's thought and even demanded that he be brought to justice for advocating a view that was considered 'controversial'. Indeed, the mass gathering was held as a forum to protect Muslim belief from the dangerous efforts of the GPPI.[7]

Following DDII, Adian Husaini criticised those who praised Nurcholish as if 'he could do no wrong'. This was strengthened by some ᶜulamāʾ, such as Hamam Ja'far of the Pesantren Pabelan, Magelang, Central Java, who called Nurcholish 'a walking library'. In contrast, Adian said that, after reading Nurcholish's various writings, he believed that Nurcholish was a duplicate of the Jesuits and orientalists. Moreover, Adian claimed that Nurcholish's wish that Islamic teaching be secularised was also an aspiration of the Jews and Christians. For Adian, Nurcholish's statements that secularisation was in line with Qur'ānic verses had in reality distorted the meaning of the Scripture. Adian further criticised William Liddle, 'Who perceived that Nurcholish Madjid's obsession was to persuade Indonesian Muslims to hold a rational, tolerant and secular[8] Islam'. However, Adian's view of the renewal thought as such was not widely held within KISDI, or to say the least it did not become the main concern of this organisation.

In addition to the exclusivists' critiques of the renewal of Islamic thought and Nurcholish, they also criticised ideas propagated by the inclusivists in general. The exclusivists believed that theological ideas promoted by the inclusivists, such as religious pluralism, were absurd

---

[6] Lukman Hakiem, ed., *Menggugat Gerakan Pembaruan Keagamaan: Debat Besar 'Pembaruan Islam'* (Jakarta: Lembaga Studi Informasi Pembangunan, 1995). The Lembaga Studi Informasi Pembangunan (Institute for the Study of Information and Development/LSIP) was chaired by Ridwan Saidi, who was the secretary of the HMI during Nurcholish Madjid's leadership. This institute seemed to have characteristics of the exclusivist groups. However, no other books were published by this institute and it appears that it was dissolved after its first publication.

[7] 'Cak Nur Tak Bisa Dijatuhi Sanksi', in *Menggugat Gerakan Pembaruan Keagamaan*, 374-376.

[8] Husaini, 'Nurcholish Madjid Sekularisasi Tiada Henti', 38-39.

and could destroy Islamic belief. Rizieq Shihab, for example, maintained that some Muslims put too much emphasis on the role of reason. He further argued that the inclusivists, as represented by the Islamic Liberal Network (JIL), considered anything that could not be comprehended by reason as irrational. This, for him, contradicted Islamic teaching, because in Islam some things were beyond reason and Muslims needed only to believe them (*imān*).[9] Laskar Jihad, too, severely criticised the Islamic Liberal Network and inclusivist ideas in general. Eko Rahardjo, for example, argued that Laskar Jihad sought to prevent Muslims from being influenced by liberal Islam, as this brand of Islam deviated from Islamic teaching. In doing so, Laskar Jihad collaborated with some Muslims, including Ja'far Thalib and Adian Husaini, to prevent lay Muslims from being influenced by liberal Islamic thought.[10] However, as FPI was mainly concerned with fighting against immoral activities, and Laskar Jihad was preoccupied with the Muslims' fate in Ambon, critiques towards the inclusivists were not part of their top agenda.

DDII made a similar criticism of the liberal group. In its special edition on pluralist and liberal Islam, *Media Dakwah* stated that JIL had peculiar ideas (*ide-ide yang aneh*) concerning Islam. First, it stated that JIL argued that the substance of Islam was more important than its label. DDII criticised this statement, arguing that in Islam there was no separation between substance and label. Second, the magazine quoted JIL's argument that the Qur'ān needed to be reinterpreted to respond to changes in contemporary times. DDII firmly held that Islam was always up to date and did not need reinterpretation. Third, it claimed that JIL maintained that human beings always had the potential to misinterpret God's messages, and therefore Muslims should be more open towards different interpretations. DDII emphasised that one could only be open to other interpretations on matters that had not been decided by Islamic law. For example, on prayer,

---

[9] Rizieq Shihab, interview by author, Jakarta, 6 February 2002.
[10] Eko Rahardjo, interview by author, Jakarta, 5 February 2002.

other interpretations were unacceptable because the matter had been decided by the *sharīʿa* as *wājib* (it had to be performed). Fourth, the magazine quoted JIL's view that there would be no need to establish an Islamic state in Indonesia. DDII countered that the majority of Indonesian Muslims wanted the implementation of the *sharīʿa* at individual, social and state levels.[11]

Even though it was mainly concerned with the Ambon conflicts, when the inclusivist touched on the issue of religious tolerance within the context of the conflicts Laskar Jihad felt compelled to state its position. Its bulletin, *Laskar Jihad*, criticised Budhy Munawar-Rachman, who allegedly stated that the Ambon conflicts were proof that religious tolerance was fading away in Indonesia. Budhy's reference to the lack of religious tolerance, which positioned religious followers as the offenders, was severely criticised, as Laskar Jihad believed that it was the Christians who had initiated the conflicts. The bulletin further denounced the inclusivist Muslims, 'Who were busy discussing the theories of liberal, radical, inclusivist, exclusivist, and pluralist Islam within air conditioned rooms, earning money from the discussion without any real attempts at saving their fellow Muslims who were dying in Maluku'.[12]

Adian Husaini also criticised Budhy's inclusivist view that tolerance between religious believers would only be achieved provided the followers of different religions developed an inclusivist perspective. In Adian's understanding, Budhy was promoting the doctrine of *persamaan agama* (syncretism), which might lead people to doubt their own religion.[13] Adian pointed to an example of Ahmad Wahib's diary, which stated: 'I do not know whether God would have the heart to send both of my fathers [referring to Father H.C. Stolk and Father

[11] 'Jaringan Islam Liberal di Indonesia', *Media Dakwah*, March 2002, 54–55.

[12] Sanihu Munir, 'Koreksi terhadap Kelompok Kajian Utan Kayu ("Islam" Liberal)', *Buletin Laskar Jihad Ahlus Sunnah Wal Jamaah* 16, 2002, 4–5.

[13] Husaini, *Penyesatan Opini*, 35.

Willenborg of the Jesuit Order in Yogyakarta] into Hell. I hope not'.[14] Adian further underlined that, in day to day life, the propagators of the inclusivist perspective were not honest with themselves because they still embraced an organised religion and did not dare, for example, to ask their family that when they died they did not need to be buried in an Islamic way.[15]

The animosity towards the inclusivists, especially towards Abdurrahman Wahid, was also broadly held by the supporters of KISDI. Amongst the open letters and press releases published by KISDI, there were severe critiques of Abdurrahman Wahid's tendency to blame 'a certain group of Muslims' without clarifying which group he had in mind. KISDI argued that Abdurrahman Wahid had continuously hurt Muslims' feelings by making statements blaming them for the burning of the Protestant Institute of Doulos. KISDI was also very angry with Abdurrahman Wahid's frequent references to the 'right wing Islam' or 'vicious Islam' (Islam Galak) as the mastermind behind several violent events, while at the same time defending the Christian minority.[16]

Whereas, according to Abdurrahman Wahid, 'The Doulos Institute was a pure social organisation that was only involved in humanitarian activities and was not at all involved in any other activities such as politics or Christianisation', Adian Husaini firmly believed that it was involved in Christianisation efforts. Adian maintained that Abdurrahman Wahid's defence of Christians did not and would not solve the problem of Muslim-Christian relations because he had been unfair on the matter.[17] In attempting to understand Abdurrahman Wahid's views, Adian stated that, at first glance, Abdurrahman Wahid's insistence on defending the Christians showed that he was supporting the weak in society. However, Adian questioned the notion that Christians were the weak in

---

[14] Husaini, Penyesatan Opini, 32.

[15] Husaini, Penyesatan Opini, 25-27.

[16] 'Kasus Maluku: Gus Dur Sudah Terlalu Lama Menyakiti Hati Umat Islam MPR Harus Segera Bertindak', in KISDI Menggugat 2, 89-94.

[17] Adian Husaini, Gus Dur Kau Mau Kemana? Telaah Kritis atas Pemikiran dan Politik Kegamaan Presiden Abdurrahman Wahid (Jakarta: DEA Press, 2000), 110-115.

Indonesia, as during the New Order period they were powerful because they were close to Soeharto. In addition, in the field of business, Christians were also more powerful than Muslims. Therefore, for Adian, the argument that Abdurrahman Wahid had defended the Christians because they were weak was incorrect.[18]

In the case of the renewal of Islamic thought and Nurcholish's thought, DDII severely criticised the theological perspectives of the inclusivists. For example, there was a widely-held belief within the DDII and reflected in their magazine that the inclusivists had propagated the idea of syncretism, which had been earlier developed by a Jewish organisation named the 'Freemansonry'. This organisation was based in the United States of America and had established a theosophy forum in Indonesia called Nederlandsch Indische Theosofische Vereeniging (East Indies Theosophy Forum/NITV), which was a branch of its head office in Madras, India. The *Media Dakwah* quoted an article published in *Liberty* magazine dated 1946, in which Annie Bessant, the leader of the NITV in Indonesia, was said to make statements that were deemed identical to Nurcholish's opinions. It quoted from the *Liberty*: 'Only after a person had understood God and themselves would they be able to help solve the problems of modern society'.[19] The *Media Dakwah* then compared Bessant's account with part of Nurcholish's paper that he delivered in October 1992 and in which he said: 'We have to be aware of our own responsibility to God in understanding the religious teachings without allowing the existence of clerical authority, because Islam does not acknowledge the clerical system'.[20] For DDII, the fact that Nurcholish's thoughts resembled Jewish perspectives was not surprising as the Jewish had been propagating their thought in Indonesia. DDII further stated that Nurcholish's thought did not reflect Islamic teachings and was very close to that of the Freemansonry.[21]

---

[18] Husaini, *Gus Dur Kau Mau Kemana?* 113.

[19] *Liberty*, 15 October 1946, 38–41. The above quotation was taken from *Media Dakwah*, December 1992, 44–45.

[20] 'Nurcholish Madjid dan Annie Bessant', *Media Dakwah*, December 1992, 44–45.

[21] '"Penyerahan Diri" Yes, Islam "No"?', *Media Dakwah*, December 1992, 47.

In addition, DDII criticised the inclusivists' lack of concern on the issue of Christianisation. Hussein Umăr, for example, was critical of 'some groups of Muslims (such as those who developed the *Jaringan Islam Liberal*) who were too elitist, and did not want to see what had happened at the grass roots level'. He contrasted this with the thinking of Mohamad Roem or H.M. Rasjidi, who were 'moderate' in their understanding of Islam yet still concerned with the problem of Christianisation.[22] DDII supporters were even angrier to learn of Abdurrahman Wahid's involvement as honorary member of the Laskar Kristus (the Jesus Soldiers), into which he was inaugurated on 28 January 2002 at Manado University, Minahasa, North Sulawesi. According to the secretary of the Laskar Kristus, Abdurrahman Wahid was inaugurated as a member of the organisation because his perspectives were in line with the mission of the Laskar Kristus, namely to create true friendships regardless of race, religion, or ethnicity.[23] What concerned DDII most was the task that was given to Abdurrahman Wahid, as a member of this organisation, to challenge any attempt at implementing the Jakarta Charter and to protect the Christians in Java.[24] DDII's hatred towards Abdurrahman Wahid was reflected in some of its publications. In its May 2001 edition, for instance, the *Media Dakwah* reported that some 2,500 Christians supported his holding the presidency during the second memorandum of the People's Representative Council held in April 2001. This was seen as reflecting Abdurrahman Wahid's close relationship with Christians.[25]

Ahl al-Kitāb

In commenting on Nurcholish's paper 'Some Reflections on Religious Life in Indonesia for the Coming Generations', Daud Rasyid claimed that Nurcholish argued that all religions (including Islam, Judaism,

---

[22] Hussein Umar, interview by author, Jakarta, 25 January 2002.

[23] 'Abdurrahman Wahid Jadi Anggota Kehormatan Laskar Kristus', *Koran Tempo*, 29 January 2002.

[24] Hussein Umar, interview by author, Jakarta, 25 January 2002.

[25] 'Jihad Ngawur Pendukung Gus Dur', *Media Dakwah*, May 2001, 41–45.

Christianity, Hinduism, and Buddhism) were equal because believers outside Islam could be categorised as the *ahl-al-kitāb*. Daud Rasyid held that Nurcholish's perspective was strange and had never occurred in the literature of Islam.[26] Daud Rasyid further questioned Nurcholish's reference to the words of ʿAbdul-Ḥamīd Ḥakīm, an *ʿulamā'* claimed by Nurcholish to be an important reform figure in West Sumatra. According to Nurcholish, ʿAbdul-Ḥamīd Ḥakīm stated that Rashīd Riḍā argued that those included in the category of *ahl al-kitāb* were not only Jews, Christians, and Magians, but also Hindus, Buddhists, followers of Chinese and Japanese religions, and others. Daud Rasyid believed that this unusual and surprising statement was clearly a great untruth attributed by Nurcholish to Riḍā.[27]

Daud Rasyid expressed regret that Nurcholish did not verify the legitimacy of the information that he quoted. He claimed that Nurcholish only had *'tawakkal'* (trust and passive acceptance) in his quote and lacked the critical attitude that he called for in criticising others. For Daud Rasyid, Nurcholish should have asked if it was true that Riḍā had expressed such an opinion. He further asserted: 'If it was true, in what book did he say those words? And if there was one, could that opinion be justified according to the standard of the Qur'ān, the *sunna* and the mainstream *ʿulamā'* throughout history?' Referring to volume 2 of Riḍā's largest work *Tafsīr al-Manār*, Daud Rasyid asserted that he could not locate a single word that expressed Nurcholish's claim. In contrast, Daud Rasyid argued that Riḍā had honestly said that there were different opinions as to whether or not the Magians had a Holy Book. Daud Rasyid added that the Jews and Christians were viewed as *'mushrik'* by some *ʿulamā'*, and amongst whom was Ibn Umar, the son of Caliph Umar ibn Khattab, who was seen as an authoritative scholar of *fiqh* and *uṣūl al-fiqh* because of his precise and rational *ijtihād*.[28]

---

[26] Daud Rasyid, 'Kesesatan Dikemas dengan Gaya Ilmiah', in *Menggugat Gerakan Pembaruan Keagamaan*, 102.

[27] Rasyid, 'Kesesatan Dikemas dengan Gaya Ilmiah', 103.

[28] Rasyid, 'Kesesatan Dikemas dengan Gaya Ilmiah', 103-104.

As mentioned, Nurcholish Madjid often made references to the classical Islamic works of Ibn Taymiyya. In a similar line to Daud Rasyid, Adian Husaini also criticised Nurcholish's reference to Ibn Taymiyya. In some of his writings, Nurcholish had stated that, according to Ibn Taymiyya, most of the content of the Holy Books that came before Islam was still valid and only sections with stories (such as the coming of the Prophet Muhammad) and with phrases that contained commands had been changed.[29] According to Adian, Ibn Taymiyya explained at length that the *ahl al-kitāb* had altered and changed 'most' (*sebagian besar*)[30] of the content and meaning of the Torah and *Injīl* before the coming of Prophet Muhammad. Therefore, in Adian's perspective, Nurcholish had incorrectly portrayed Ibn Taymiyya.[31]

It is interesting to analyse the perspectives of Adian and Nurcholish on Ibn Taymiyya and the validity of the Scriptures that came before Islam. Interestingly, both referred to the same book and the same volume of Ibn Taymiyya's *al-Jawāb al-Ṣaḥīḥ li man Baddala Dīn al-Masīḥ*. The phrase quoted by Adian was '*wa shahida ᶜalaihim bi annahum ḥarrafū kathīran min maᶜaniya al-taurāti wa al-injīli qabla nubuwwatihi*' (and the Prophet witnessed that the ahl al-kitāb had altered many of the meanings of the Torah and Injil before his prophethood).[32] Adian firmly held that Nurcholish's contention on the validity of the content of pre-Islamic Scriptures was incorrect. On closer examination, it becomes clear that Nurcholish's reference to Ibn Taymiyya does not contradict Adian's statement that there were alterations and changes to those Scriptures. However, Nurcholish affirmed Ibn Taymiyya's argument that these changes, albeit numerous as argued by Adian, were made only within the sections

---

[29] See, for example, Nurcholish Madjid, 'Beberapa Renungan tentang Kehidupan Keagamaan', 15.

[30] Adian Husaini had translated the word *kastīran* as 'most', whereas some other *mufasssir* translated the word as 'many'. See for example Shihab, 'Wawasan Al-Qur'an tentang Ahl al-Kitab', 4.

[31] Adian Husaini, 'Islam Pluralis, Nurcholish dan Ibnu Taimiyah', *Media Dakwah*, March 2002, 44.

[32] Ibn Taymiyya, *Al-Jawāb al-Ṣaḥīḥ*, vol. 1, 387.

on stories and commands (*wa innamā buddilat baʿḍu alfāẓi al-kha-bariyyāt wa baʿḍu maʿānī al-amriyyāt*).[33]

On the condemnation of the *ahl al-kitāb* as *mushrikīn* (polythe-ists), Adian also claimed that Nurcholish had wrongly presented Ibn Taymiyya's opinion. As stated in Chapter Six, Nurcholish argued that according to Ibn Taymiyya in his *al-Aḥkam al-Zawāj* the *ahl al-kitāb* was not *mushrikīn* (*inna ahla al-kitābi lam yadkhulū fi al-mushrikīna*). Adian maintained that this statement contradicted Ibn Taymiyya's as-sertion 'The *ahl al-kitāb* had committed the act of *shirk*'. Hence, ac-cording to Adian, Nurcholish's reference to Ibn Taymiyya was not accu-rate.[34] Nurcholish explained in his interview that Ibn Taymiyya did not identify the *ahl al-kitāb* with *mushrikīn (isim fāʿil* or active noun), which refers to a permanent identity, yet admitted that the People of the Book were *yushrik*, i.e. they committed the act of *shirk*, which referred only to a temporary activity. Nurcholish added that the Qur'ān did not men-tion the *ahl al-kitāb* as *mushrikīn*; it described them only as having committed the act of *shirk*.[35]

It is important to note that Adian did in fact quote Ibn Taymiyya's explanation that the *ahl al-kitāb* committed the act of *shirk* but were not categorised as *mushrikīn*. Hence it should have been obvious to Adian that, according to Ibn Taymiyya and Nurcholish, the label '*mush-rikīn*' was more unsympathetic as compared to '*yushrik*.' Therefore, Adian's contention is puzzling that Nurcholish had failed to quote the last part of Ibn Taymiyya's sentence '*Wa al-ismu awkadu min al-fiʿli*' (and the re-ference to *mushrikūn*[36] [*bi al-ismi*] was stronger than that to the act of *shirk* [*bi al-fiʿli*]).[37] In Adian's view, Nurcholish failed to quote this part of the sentence in order to show his readers that Islam did have an

---

[33] Ibn Taymiyya, *Al-Jawāb al-Ṣaḥīḥ*, vol. 2, 18, and quoted by Madjid in 'Beberapa Renungan tentang Kehidupan Keagamaan', 15, n. 43 and 44.

[34] Husaini, 'Islam Pluralis, Nurcholish dan Ibnu Taimiyah', 45.

[35] Nurcholish Madjid, interview by author, Jakarta, 6 March 2002. See also Madjid, 'Wawasan Al-Qur'an tentang Ahl al-Kitab', 13-15.

[36] Husaini, 'Islam Pluralis, Nurcholish dan Ibnu Taimiyah', 45.

[37] Ibn Taymiyya, *Aḥkam al-Zawāj*, 189.

inclusivist perspective on *ahl al-kitāb*.[38] This in fact contradicted Adian's own quotation of Ibn Taymiyya's view mentioned above that the *ahl al-kitāb* committed to the act of *shirk* but were not categorised as *mushrikīn*.

Inclusivists 'Responses to the Exclusivists' Perspectives

The other side of the picture is that it is very difficult to find inclusivist writings on the exclusivists or their thought. In interviews conducted for this study with several key inclusivist figures, there was a tendency not to respond to the exclusivists' critiques directed against them. Amongst the reasons they gave to explain this was that the critiques were generally 'emotional' and 'personal', and therefore did not need to be countered. This reason was closely in line with Nurcholish's explanation as to why he did not respond to critiques directed towards the renewal of Islamic thought, and more specifically to his thought, during the first half of the 1970s.[39] Therefore, it seems that the inclusivists' silence towards the critiques directed at them by the exclusivists was a reflection of their disagreement with the exclusivists' method and approach.

In general, the inclusivists held the view that the exclusivists approached Islam from a very narrow perspective. Komaruddin Hidayat, for example, maintained that the exclusivist Muslims had reduced the meaning of the *sharīʿa* to *fiqh*, and therefore every aspect of life was judged by *fiqh*. For Komaruddin, *sharīʿa* should be interpreted in its wider meaning in which the role of *ijtihād* is central.[40] Moreover, Zainun Kamal asserted that the exclusivists were very subjective and reluctant to accept counter arguments from non-Muslims or from fellow Muslims with different understandings of Islam.[41]

---

[38] Husaini, 'Islam Pluralis, Nurcholish dan Ibnu Taimiyah', 45.

[39] Nurcholish stated his argument for not responding to critiques directed at him in a letter to Mohamad Roem dated 29 March 1983, which was later published in *Tidak Ada Negara Islam*, 22-23.

[40] Komaruddin Hidayat, interview by author, Jakarta, 24 January 2002.

[41] Zainun Kamal, interview by author, Jakarta, 22 January 2002.

Nurcholish expressed concern that the exclusivists usually quoted more Qur'ānic verses that had a bitter tone in addressing other believers, to the neglect of many sympathetic verses directed at them. He gave an example of verse 3:112, which states that the *ahl al-kitāb* is over-shadowed by ignominy.[42] However, Nurcholish argued that the verse went to say: '... *illā biḥablin min Allāh wa ḥablin min an-nās'* (save when they bind themselves again in a bond with God and a bond with men). He explained that the word *'illā'* in the above verse meant 'exception' (*istithna*), and therefore it was obvious to him that the Qur'ān did not generalise the *ahl al-kitāb* as people who were overshadowed by humiliation. However, Nurcholish regretted that this verse and other similar verses with a more sympathetic tone towards other religious believers were never quoted by the exclusivists.[43]

In a similar line, Zainun stated that the exclusivists always quoted certain Qur'ānic verses, such as verse 2:120, as the explanation of conflict between Muslims and Christians. For him this approach was dangerous as it did not do justice to the whole spirit of the Qur'ān, and would only turn Muslims and non-Muslims away from Islam. Zainun further argued that the exclusivists were people who were not happy and contented in their political and economic life and therefore tried to blame others for their circumstances. Moreover, he stated that some exclusivists did not understand Islamic teachings and thus blindly followed others. Referring to the Laskar Jihad and FPI, Zainun believed that these organisations would not survive for long as they had no clear agenda or programs. In contrast to the exclusivists' thinking, he believed that Muslims needed to develop an inclusivist approach to Islam.[44]

---

[42] Q.S. 3: 112 said: 'Overshadowed by ignominy are they wherever they may be, save [when they bind themselves again] in a bond with God and a bond with men; for they have earned the burden of God's condemnation, and are overshadowed by humiliation: all this [has befallen them] because they persisted in denying the truth of God's message and in slaying the prophets against all right: all this, because they rebelled [against God], and persisted in transgressing the bounds of what is right'.

[43] Nurcholish Madjid, interview by author, Jakarta, 6 March 2002.

[44] Zainun Kamal, interview by author, Jakarta, 22 January 2002.

Ulil Abshar-Abdalla shared Zainun's argument that Indonesian Muslims needed to develop an inclusivist perspective on theology. Ulil criticised the argument by the exclusivists that the inclusivist perspective might encourage people to turn away from Islam (*murtad*). On the contrary, he held that if Islam was not interpreted in an inclusivist way it would be portrayed as a 'cruel' religion and there would be sufficient ground for people to abandon their faith. According to Ulil, the exclusivists' method of interpreting the Islamic foundation texts was based on the assumption that Muslims were under siege or at war. For him, a textual and contextual interpretation of Islam was needed. In commenting on the violent attacks carried out by the FPI, Ulil argued that violence could not be tolerated because, according to Islamic teachings, combating disobedience (*kemunkaran*) and violation of God's law (*kemaksiatan*) should also be based on ethics. He further maintained that Islam did not need to be defended by violence because this would stop the disobedience for a very short time only. For him, the best solution to the problem was to establish crisis centres in which the government, business people and society could work together to eliminate violence.[45]

Despite all their critiques directed towards the exclusivists, the inclusivists generally accepted that developing an inclusivist perspective would not produce an instant result. Nurcholish, for example, compared it to planting a crop. He firmly believed that the concept of tolerance that existed in Indonesia had happened only by accident and was not deliberately developed, and therefore would not have a deep impact on many people. Nurcholish argued that what he wanted to emphasise was that tolerance was not a matter of a 'procedure' but a matter of 'belief'. Therefore, for him, even its socialisation was bitter and lengthy, it should be continued. Nurcholish believed that 'The bitterness will only stay for a short time but in the long run we will enjoy the result'.[46] It was also in this context that the existence of Paramadina as an institution for developing inclusivist thought was deemed im-

---

[45] 'Polisi Moral di Rimba Metropolitan', 46.

[46] Nurcholish Madjid, interview by author, Jakarta, 6 March 2002.

portant, even though it might take a while before people would accept its ideas.[47]

In commenting on the exclusivists' approach to the question of *ahl al-kitāb*, Zainun argued that they had misread the sources consulted by the inclusivists. As mentioned, Daud Rasyid referred to volume 2 of Rashīd Riḍā's *Tafsīr al-Manār* and argued that Nurcholish's quotation of Riḍā was incorrect. In response to this, Zainun contended that Daud Rasyid should have checked a different volume of *Tafsīr al-Manār* to locate Nurcholish's reference to Riḍā.[48] Indeed, a closer examination of Riḍā's *tafsīr* reveals that he did say that the *ahl al-kitāb* included Jews and Christians, as well as Hindus, Buddhists, and followers of Chinese and Japanese religions.[49] Zainun argued that this opinion was also quoted about half a century previously by a great *ʿulamā'* of West Sumatra, ʿAbdul Ḥamīd Ḥakīm, in his book *al-Muʿīn al-Mubīn*.[50]

Zainun further maintained that Daud Rasyid was wrong in his criticism that Nurcholish's perspective was aberrant and had never before occurred in the literature of Islam, because other Muslim scholars, including al-Baghdādī, Abu Hanifah and al-Mawdudi, shared this opinion. What angered Zainun most was Daud Rasyid's accusation that people who held different opinions from his were sinful. For Zainun, it was acceptable to have different opinions but it was not acceptable to accuse someone who had different perspectives as sinful. Hence, for Zainun, it was Daud Rasyid's view that was strange.[51]

---

[47] Zainun Kamal, interview by author, Jakarta, 22 January 2002.

[48] Neither Daud Rasyid nor Zainun Kamal mentioned the edition of the *Tafsīr al-Manār* that they quoted. Zainun suggested Daud Rasyid should refer to volume 4 of Riḍā's work. This study found Zainun's reference in volume 6 of *Tafsīr al-Manār*.

[49] Rashīd Riḍā, *Tafsīr al-Manār*, vol. 6, 188. See Chapter Six for the full quote of this statement by Rashīd Riḍā.

[50] Zainun Kamal, 'Kritik Sealmamater atas Kritik Daud Rasyid', in *Menggugat Gerakan Pembaruan Keagamaan,* 223–225.

[51] Kamal, 'Kritik Sealmamater', 224–225.

Concluding Remarks

The exclusivists' main criticism of the inclusivists was the latter's approach to Islam, particularly through the renewal of Islamic thought as promoted by Nurcholish Madjid. The exclusivists held the view that the interpretation of Islam offered by the inclusivists would endanger Muslim belief. It is clear that, amongst the exclusivist groups, DDII and KISDI were the organisations most outspoken in their disappointment and disapproval. In contrast, the inclusivists hardly spoke a word critical of the exclusivists. This lack of criticism might be explained in two ways. First, as people attempting to promote religious tolerance, the inclusivists seemed to accept different perspectives in understanding Islam and therefore tried to accept criticism directed to them by the exclusivists. Second, as intellectual Muslims, the inclusivists did not feel they should resort to the exclusivists' critical methods and approaches.[]

8

Conclusion

Studies conducted on Muslim–Christian relations in Indonesia have tended to focus on certain conflict involving both religious communities, and on the religious aspects of the relations. In addition, those studies do not pay particular attention to different views within Islam and Christianity or to the historical and theological backgrounds of such views, and therefore failed to understand the complexities of Muslim–Christian relations. This study is an attempt to investigate the perspectives of the exclusivist and inclusivist Muslims on Muslim–Christian relations in Indonesia, especially during the New Order period (1965–1998). It found that there is no uniform view within Muslim communities on Muslim–Christian relations or Christianity. It also argued that theological perceptions and some New Order policies played the most determining roles in shaping the exclusivist and inclusivist Muslims' viewpoints on the relationship between Muslims and Christians. The study documented the development and the complexities of the relationship between Muslims and Christians in Indonesia.

Theological and Legal Perceptions of the Religious 'Other' in Classical Islam. Investigation of various classical theological and legal texts revealed that there are different perspectives in regard to the religious 'other'. In speaking about the Christians, as part of the religious 'other', some classical jurists, such as al-Māwardī and Ibn Rushd, argued that in certain aspects Christians were not seen as equal to Muslims and therefore did not enjoy the same rights as did Muslims. As discussed in Chapter 2, Christians, for instance, had to pay the protection tax (*jizya*) to the state. Moreover, they were not permitted to erect higher buildings than Muslims and had to distinguish their appearance from Muslims by wearing different clothes. In addition, some classical Muslim theologians, such as Ibn Taymiyya and Ibn Ḥazm, maintained that Christianity was a corrupted religion and that the Gospels (*Injīl*) had undergone some changes to their meanings (*taḥrīf*) and some alterations to their wording (*tabdīl*) before the time of Prophet Muhammad. One point of criticism by some classical Muslim theologians was the Trinity (*tathlīth*). Many of them held the view that this doctrine was against Islamic teachings, as Prophet Isa was not the son of God, and also that the doctrine was irreconcilable with sound reason. Even though by the 20th century the themes surrounding Muslim–Christian relations differed from those of the classical period, some themes of classical tradition, such as the distortion of Christianity and the greeting of Christians, remain alive for exclusivist Muslims in Indonesia today.

Government Policy on Muslim–Christian Relations. Examination of the government policy on Muslim–Christian relations shows that from the Dutch colonial period onwards, the policies of successive governments affected the relationship between Muslims and Christians in different ways. During the Dutch regime, Christian missionary schools, churches, hospitals and orphanages received generous subsidies from the government as compared to that given to Islamic institutions. This treatment was deeply resented by some Muslims, who identified the

Dutch as Christians and Christians as colonists. As discussed in Chapter 3, animosity towards Christians was seen as early as the 20th century in some Muslim writings. Some apologetic and polemic works on the side of Muslims, such as by A.D. Haanie and M. Natsir, criticised Christianity and Christians to counter similar works published by Christians on Islam.

By the time the Indonesians were approaching the independence, the Islamic groups (*kelompok Islam*) on the one hand, and the nationalist groups (*kelompok nasionalis*) including Christians, nationalists, and nominal Muslims/*abangan* on the other, were in dispute on the philosophical basis of the Indonesian state. When it was decided that the Indonesian state was to be based on Pancasila, the Islamic groups were disappointed. Furthermore, some Muslims saw that Christianisation efforts were ongoing and were alarmed at the growing number of Christians, especially by the mid-1960s. However, Muslim unease did not seem to concern Sukarno, who was heavily occupied with problems within the newly-born state. Hence, animosity towards Christians that had been felt since the colonial period was exacerbated during the Old Order by Christian involvement in rejecting the Jakarta Charter and in converting Muslims to Christianity.

With the shift of presidency from Sukarno to Soeharto, Muslim–Christian relations changed dramatically. Soeharto intentionally and carefully controlled Indonesians based on the policy of SARA, under which any discussion of ethnicity, religion, race and inter-group relations was banned. Within the scheme of SARA, two important moves were taken: to exploit the Chinese, who were mainly Christians, and to weaken Islamic political power. The government, for example, gave the Chinese an important role in the Indonesian economy while at the same time concealing its business cooperation with them from the public. This led the *pribumi*, who were mainly Muslims, to channel their anger towards the Chinese. Furthermore, the New Order government suppressed any tendency of political Islam. To advance this, the regime fused the Islamic political parties in 1973 and forced all socio-political organisations to declare Pancasila as their sole ideology in 1984. With the alleged-support from Christians, the government introduced policies unpopular to some Muslims, such as the Marriage Bill of 1973, which was perceived as contradicting the *sharīʿa*. These elements of SARA policy caused tense relations between Muslims and Christians.

In the late 1980s and early 1990s, Soeharto turned his attention to Muslims. This was marked by his support for the establishment of the Association of Indonesian Muslim Intellectuals (ICMI). Nevertheless, this did not automatically ease the tense relations between Muslims and Christians, as some Christians continued to enjoy various privileges from the regime. As shown in the number of military personnel and the portfolios of economic affairs within the New Order cabinet, the domination of *abangan* and non-Muslims, especially Christians, was apparent. This was worsened by the perceived dramatic increase in the Christian population and in missionary activities through social services such as education and medicine. State-sponsored attempts at inter-religious dialogue to ease tensions between religious believers, especially Muslims and Christians, did not reach their targets as the regime was shown to have its own agenda in facilitating these dialogues.

Exclusivist and Inclusivist on Muslim–Christian Relations. The exclusivists and inclusivists look at the relations between Muslims and Christians in a different way as they have different backgrounds. The exclusivist groups discussed in this study (DDII, KISDI, FPI and Laskar Jihad) differ in their degree of exclusiveness, their backgrounds and their concerns in regard to Muslim–Christian relations. For example, DDII, the oldest exclusivist Muslim organisation discussed in this study which was established to respond to the problems of Muslim–Christian relations, has more concerns on the subject. However, these groups appear to have some characteristics in common, one of which is the view that salvation can only be achieved through the religion of Islam.

The relations between the exclusivist Muslims and Christians have been coloured largely by disharmony, as can be found in the exclusivists' criticism in various writings and speeches. The study examined the concerns of the exclusivists in order to identify the background to their attitudes. It found that their concerns could be grouped into two categories: theological and socio-economic-political. Theologically speaking, the exclusivists held the view that Christianity underwent alteration. Their argument is found, for example, in articles by DDII and Laskar Jihad leaders. Moreover, the exclusivists criticised the concept of the Trinity in Christianity, arguing that the God of Muslims was different from that of the Christians because in Christianity God is described as having offspring.

With this perception in mind, they were troubled at the perceived ongoing Christianisation in Indonesia. All exclusivist groups in the study stated the view that it was the Christianisation activities that had torn apart the relationship between Muslims and Christians. The perceived Christianisation efforts included the Christians' rejection of the Inter-religious Consultation Forum's proposal 'not to make the religious believers a target for the spread of each others' religions', their construction of church buildings in Muslim compounds, and their support of the 1973 Marriage Bill the articles of which were seen as contradicting the *sharī'a*. Further promotion of Christianity was perceived in attempts to urge Muslims to be involved in Christmas celebrations, in the imitation of Muslim traditions by wearing dress traditionally worn by Muslims, in the rejection of the proposed Religious Judicature Act seen as benefiting Muslims, and in the teaching of Christianity to non-Christian students.

The discussion in this study on the inclusivists centred on some key figures and intellectuals rather than on organisations because of the importance of their ideas. They too differ in their degree of inclusiveness, in their backgrounds and in their concerns on Muslim–Christian relations. Nevertheless, in general the inclusivists appear to have certain characteristics in common, among the most significant of which is the belief that salvation is also possible outside Islam.

The relations between inclusivist Muslims and Christians are coloured largely by harmony. Investigation into the concerns of the inclusivists revealed that socio-political and theological reasons were behind their attitudes. First, with the New Order's restriction to Muslims from participating in political organisations, a group of young Muslim intellectuals tried to withdraw from the political arena and engage instead in intellectual exercises. This laid an important foundation for the reform of Islamic thinking in Indonesia, which is characterised mainly by inclusivism.

Second, the inclusivists, including Nurcholish Madjid and Budhy Munawar-Rachman, held the view that plurality was the law of nature (*sunnatullāh*), and therefore Muslims should reinterpret the basic concepts of religious freedom and pluralism as embodied in the Qur'ān and *sunna* and the early generation of Muslims. Within this view, all religions were perceived to adhere to the same principle of One Truth; therefore they would gradually find their 'common platform' or *kalimatun sawā*'. As a reflection of their perspective on religious pluralism, most inclusivists admitted the existence and rights of other religious believers, especially the *ahl al-kitāb*. One issue related to the *ahl al-kitāb* which concerned the inclusivists was inter-religious marriage. The inclusivists differed in their degree of inclusivism in regard to marriage between Muslims and the *ahl al-kitāb*. Some thought that Muslim men were permitted to marry only Jewish and Christian women; others, including Nurcholish, argued that Muslim men could marry women who had been vouchsafed revelation. Some inclusivists, such as Zainun Kamal, went even further, arguing that marriage between a Muslim woman and non-Muslim man was also possible within Islam.

The exclusivists and inclusivists mutually criticise each other. Nevertheless, it is the exclusivists who are more adamant in uttering their criticism to the inclusivists through articles in their media or sermons in mosques. Three of their important critiques are the belief that the inclusivists have established a link with Jews and Christians, the assumption that inclusivism weakens Muslim faith by giving new interpretations to the Islamic foundation texts which deviate from the accepted views, and the inclusivists' lack of concern about Christianisation. In contrast, the inclusivists tend not to criticise or respond to critiques directed at them by the exclusivists, as they consider these to be emotional or personal.

Although this study has discussed the perspectives of prominent Catholic and Protestant leaders on the issue of Muslim–Christian relations, a thorough exploration was not within its scope. Therefore, further research on the Catholic and Protestant perspectives on Muslim–Christian relations is needed in order to present a complete picture of relations from both sides, Muslims and Christians, based on which proposals for improving relations can be considered.[]

Selected
Bibliography

1. Books, Journal Articles, and Papers

Abdullah, Amin. *Rekonstruksi Metodologi Studi Agama dalam Masyarakat Multikultural dan Multirelijius.* Yogyakarta: IAIN Sunan Kalijaga, 2000.

Aditjondro, G.J. Guns, Pamphlets and Handie-Talkies'. In *Violence in Indonesia.* Edited by Inggrid Wessel and Georgia Wimhöfer. Hamburg: Abera Verlag, 2001: 100–128.

Algadri, Hamid. *Dutch Policy against Islam and Indonesians of Arab Descent in Indonesia.* Jakarta: LP3ES, 1994.

Ali, Abdullah Yusuf *The Holy Qur'an: Text, Translation and Commentary.* Beirut, Lebanon: Dar al-Arabia, 1938.

Ali, Muhammad. '*Fatwas* on Inter-Faith Marriage in Indonesia'. *Studia Islamika* 9, no. 3 (2002): 1–33.

Ananda, Endang Basri, ed. *70 Tahun Prof. Dr. H.M. Rasjidi.* Jakarta: Pelita, 1985.

Anawati, G. 'An Assessment of the Christian–Islamic Dialogue'. In *The Vatican, Islam, and the Middle East*. Edited by Kail C. Ellis. Syracuse: Syracuse University Press, 1987: 51-68.

Anderson, Benedict. R.O'G. 'Current Data on the Indonesian Military Elite'. *Indonesia* 48 (October 1989): 65-96.

_____and Ruth T. McVey. *A Preliminary Analysis of the October 1, 1965, Coup in Indonesia*. Ithaca, N.Y.: Modern Indonesia Project, Cornell University, 1971.

Anshari, E. Saifuddin. *Piagam Jakarta 22 Juni 1945*. Jakarta: Rajawali, 1981.

Al-Anshari, Zakariyya. *Fatḥ al-Wahhāb bī Sharḥ Tanqīḥ al-Lubab*. Beyrūt: Dār al-Kutub al-ᶜIlmiyyah, 1998.

alFaruqi, Isma'il R. and Lamya Lois alFaruqi. *The Cultural Atlas of Islam*. New York: Macmillan, 1986.

Aqsha, Darul, Dick van der Meij, and Johan Hendrik Meuleman. *Islam in Indonesia: A Survey of Events and Developments from 1988 to March 1993*. Jakarta: INIS, 1995.

Arnaldez, R. "Ibn Ḥazm." In *The Encyclopaedia of Islam*. New edition. Edited by Bernard Lewis et al. Leiden: E.J. Brill, 1971.

Asad, Muhammad. *The Message of the Qur'ān*. Gibraltar: Dar al-Andalus, 1980.

Aziz, Muhammad Abdul. *Japan's Colonialism and Indonesia*. The Hague: Martinus Nijhoff, 1955.

Azra, Azyumardi. *Konteks Berteologi di Indonesia*. Jakarta: Paramadina, 1999.

_____. 'Studi-Studi Agama di Perguruan Tinggi Agama Islam Negeri'. In *Pendidikan Islam: Tradisi dan Modernisasi Menuju Milenium Baru*. Jakarta: Logos, 2000: 169-174.

_____. 'Islam and Christianity in Indonesia: The Roots of Conflict and Hostility'. In *Religion and Culture in Asia-Pacific: Violence or Healing?* Edited by J.A. Camilleri. Melbourne: Vista Publication, 2001: 85-90.

_____. 'The Indonesian Marriage Law of 1974: An Institutionalization of the *Shari'a* for Social Changes'. In *Shari'a and Politics in Modern Indonesia.* Edited by Arskal Salim and Azyumardi Azra. Singapore: ISEAS, 2003: 76-95.

Bakker, F.L. *Tuhan Yesus dalam Agama Islam.* Jakarta: BPK Gunung Mulia, 1957.

Bakry, Hasbullah. *Nabi Isa dalam al-Qur'an dan Nabi Muhammad dalam Bijbel.* Fourth Edition. Jakarta: Melati Offset, 1974.

Barret, David B., ed. *World Christian Encyclopedia: A Comparative Study of Churches and Religions in the Modern World AD 1900-2000.* Nairobi: Oxford University Press, 1982.

_____, George T. Kurian, and Todd M. Johnson. *World Christian Encyclopedia: A Comparative Survey of Churches and Religions in the Modern World.* Vol. 1. Second Edition. Nairobi: Oxford University Press, 2001.

Barton, Greg. *Gagasan Islam Liberal di Indonesia: Pemikiran Neo-Modernisme Nurcholish Madjid, Djohan Effendi, Ahmad Wahib, dan Abdurrahman Wahid 1968-1980.* Jakarta: Paramadina, 1999.

Benda, Harry J. *The Crescent and the Rising Sun: Indonesian Islam under the Japanese Occupation 1942-1945.* The Hague: W. Van Hoeve, 1958.

_____. 'Christian Snouck Horgronje and the Foundations of Dutch Islamic Policy in Indonesia'. In *Continuity and Change in Southeast Asia: Collected Journal Articles of Harry J. Benda.* Edited by A. Suddard. New Haven, Connecticut: Yale University Southeast Asia Studies, 1972: 83-92.

Biro Pusat Statistik. *Sensus Penduduk 1971.* Jakarta: BPS, March 1975.

_____. *Hasil Sensus Penduduk 1990*. Jakarta: BPS, 1990.

Boland, B.J. *The Struggle of Islam in Modern Indonesia*. The Hague: Martinus Nijhoff, 1982.

Bresnan, John. *Managing Indonesia: The Modern Political Economy*. New York: Columbia University Press, 1993.

Budiman, Arief. *Negara dan Pembangunan: Studi tentang Indonesia dan Korea Selatan*. Jakarta: Yayasan Padi dan Kapas, 1991.

Cammack, Mark. 'Indonesia's 1989 Religious Judicature Act: Islamization of Indonesia or Indonesianization of Islam?'. *Indonesia* 63 (April 1997): 143–168.

Chauvel, Richard. *Nationalists, Soldiers and Separatists: The Ambonese Islands from Colonialism to Revolt 1880-1950*. Leiden: KITLV Press, 1990.

Cheneb, Moh. Ben. 'Ibn Taimiya'. In *The Shorter Encyclopaedia of Islam*. Edited by H.A.R. Gibb and J.H. Kramers. Leiden: E.J. Brill, 1974.

Cooley, Frank L. *Indonesia: Church & Society*. New York: Friendship Press, 1968.

Coppel, Charles, A. *Indonesian Chinese in Crisis*. Kuala Lumpur and Melbourne: Oxford University Press, 1983.

Crouch, Harold. *The Army and Politics in Indonesia*. Revised Edition. Ithaca: Cornell University Press, 1988.

Dewan Dakwah Islamiyah Indonesia. *Anggaran Dasar & Perobahan dan Penambahan Akta*. Jakarta: DDII, 1967.

_____. *Surat kepada Paus Yohannes Paulus II Agar Penyalahgunaan Diakonia Dihentikan*. Jakarta: DDII, 1989.

Dewan Gereja-Gereja di Indonesia, Sekretariat Umum and Sekretariat Majelis Agung Waligereja Indonesia. *Tinjauan Mengenai Keputusan Menteri Agama No. 70 dan 77 Tahun 1978 dalam Rangka Penyelenggaraan Kebebasan Beragama dan Pemeliharaan Kerukunan Nasional*. Jakarta: DGI & MAWI, 1978.

The Editors. 'Current Data on the Indonesian Military Elite: July 1, 1989–January 1, 1992'. *Indonesia* 53 (April 1992): 93–136.

Effendi, Djohan. 'Dialog Antar-Agama: Bisakah Melahirkan Teologi Kerukunan?'. In *Agama dan Tantangan Zaman: Pilihan Artikel Prisma 1975-1984*. Jakarta: LP3ES, 1985: 168–178.

Esposito, John L, ed. *Islam in Asia: Religion, Politics, and Society*. Oxford: Oxford University Press, 1987.

Fealy, Greg. 'Inside the Laskar Jihad: An Interview with the Leader of a New, Radical and Militant Sect'. *Inside Indonesia* 65 (January–March 2001): 28–29.

Feillard, Andrée. *NU vis-à-vis Negara: Pencarian Isi, Bentuk dan Makna*. Yogyakarta: LKiS, 1999.

Feith, Herbert. *The Decline of Constitutional Democracy in Indonesia*. Ithaca and London: Cornell University Press, 1962.

———. 'The End of the Indonesian Rebellion'. *Pacific Affairs* 36, no. 1 (Spring, 1963): 32–46.

———and Lance Castles, eds. *Indonesian Political Thinking 1945-1965*. Ithaca and London: Cornell University Press, 1970.

Gautama, Sudargo and R.N. Hornick. *An Introduction to Indonesian Law: Unity and Diversity*. Bandung: Alumni, 1974.

Geertz, Clifford. *Religion of Java*. New York: Glencoe, 1960.

Goldziher, Ignaz. 'The Attitude of Orthodox Islam toward the Ancient Sciences'. In *Studies on Islam*. Edited by Merlin L. Swartz. New York: Oxford University Press, 1981: 185–215.

Haanie, A.D. *Islam Menentang Kraemer*. Yogyakarta and Pekalongan: Penyiaran Islam, 1929.

Haddad, Yvonne Yazbeck and Wadi Z. Haddad, eds. *Christian-Muslim Encounters*. Gainesville: University of Florida, 1988.

Hadikusuma, Djarnawi. *Sekitar Perjanjian Lama, Perjanjian Baru*. Fourth Edition. Yogyakarta: Pimpinan Pusat Muhammadiyah, no date.

Hakiem, Lukman, ed. *Fakta & Data: Usaha-usaha Kristenisasi di Indonesia*. Jakarta: Media Dakwah, 1991.

_____. *Perjalanan Mencari Keadilan dan Persatuan: Biografi Dr. Anwar Harjono, SH*. Jakarta: Media Dakwah, 1993.

_____, ed. *Menggugat Gerakan Pembaruan Keagamaan: Debat Besar 'Pembaruan Islam'*. Jakarta: Lembaga Studi Informasi Pembangunan, 1995.

Hallaq, Wael B. *Ibn Taymiyya against the Greek Logicians*. Oxford: Clarendon Press, 1993.

Hamka, Rusydi. *Pribadi dan Martabat Buya Prof. Dr. Hamka*. Jakarta: Pustaka Panjimas, 1983.

Hasan, Ahmad. *Analogical Reasoning in Islamic Jurisprudence: A Study of the Juridical Principle of Qiyas*. Islamabad, Pakistan: Islamic Research Institute, 1986.

Hasan, Noorhaidi. 'Faith and Politics: The Rise of the Laskar Jihad in the Era of Transition in Indonesia'. *Indonesia* 73 (April 2003): 145–169.

Hassan, Muhammad Kamal. *Muslim Intellectual Responses to 'New Order' Modernization in Indonesia*. Kuala Lumpur: Dewan Bahasa dan Pustaka, 1982.

Hasyim, Umar. *Toleransi dan Kemerdekaan dalam Islam Sebagai Dasar Menuju Dialog dan Kerukunan Antar Agama*. Surabaya: Bina Ilmu, 1977.

Hatta, Mohammad. *Sekitar Proklamasi 17 Agustus 1945*. Jakarta: Tintamas, 1970.

Hauken, A. SJ. *Ensiklopedi Populer tentang Gereja Katolik di Indonesia*. Jakarta: Yayasan Cipta Loka Caraka, 1989.

Hefner, Robert W. 'Islam, State and Civil Society: ICMI and the Struggle for the Indonesian Middle Class'. *Indonesia* 56 (October 1993): 1-35.

_____. 'Print Islam: Mass Media and Ideological Rivalries among Indonesian Muslims'. *Indonesia* 64 (October 1997): 77-103.

_____. 'Islamization and Democratization in Indonesia'. In *Islam in an Era of Nation-States: Politics and Religious Renewal in Muslim Southeast Asia.* Edited by Robert W. Hefner and Patricia Horvatich. Honolulu: University of Hawai'i Press, 1997: 75-127.

_____. *Civil Islam: Muslims and Democratization in Indonesia.* Princeton and Oxford: Princeton University Press, 2000.

Heryanto, Ariel. 'Ethnic Identities and Erasure: Chinese Indonesians in Public Culture'. In *Southeast Asian Identities.* Edited by J.S. Kahn. Singapore: ISEAS, 1998: 95-114.

Hidayat, Komaruddin. 'Schoun, Nasr dan Cak Nur'. *Ulumul Qur'an* 4, no. 1 (1993): 84-86.

Hodgson, Marshall. *The Venture of Islam.* Vol. 3. Chicago: University of Chicago Press, 1974.

Hosen, Nadirsyah. '*Fatwa* and Politics in Indonesia'. In *Shari'a and Politics in Modern Indonesia:* 168-180.

Husaini, Adian. *Gereja-Gereja Dibakar: Membedah Akar Konflik SARA di Indonesia.* Jakarta: DEA Press, 2000.

_____. *Gus Dur Kau Mau Kemana? Telaah Kritis atas Pemikiran dan Politik Kegamaan Presiden Abdurrahman Wahid.* Jakarta: DEA Press, 2000.

_____. *Penyesatan Opini: Sebuah Rekayasa Mengubah Citra.* Jakarta: Gema Insani Press, 2002.

Husin, Asna. 'Philosophical and Sociological Aspects of *Da'wah:* A Study of Dewan Dakwah Islamiyah Indonesia'. Ph.D. diss., Columbia University, 1998.

Ibn Ḥazm, Abī Muḥammad ᶜAlī ibn Aḥmad al-Maᶜrūf. *Al-Fiṣāl fī al-Milal wa-al-Aḥwā' al-Niḥāl.* Vol. 1. Bayrut: Dār al-Kutub al-ᶜIlmiyyah, 1996.

Ibn Rushd, Abu al-Walīd Muḥammad. *The Distinguished Jurist's Primer: A Translation of Bidāyat al-Mujtahid.* Translated by Imran A.K. Nyazee. 2 Vols. Reading, UK: Centre for Muslim Contribution to Civilization, 1994.

_____. *Aḥkam al-Zawāj.* Beyrūt: Dār al-Kutub al-ᶜIlmiyyah, 1988.

_____. *Al-Jawāb al-Ṣaḥīh li man Baddala Dīn al-Masīh,* Edited by Majdī Qāsim. 4 Vols. Jeddah: Maktabat al-Balad al-Amīn, 1993.

_____. *Kitāb al-Iqtidā' aṣ-Ṣirāt al-Mustaqīm Mukhālafat Aṣḥāb al-Jaḥīm.* 2 Vols. Riyadh: Dār al-Aṣōmah, 1998.

'The Incident of Makassar on October 1, 1967: Attempts to Repair the Crack in the Indonesian Image of Tolerance?'. *Review of Indonesian and Malayan Affairs* 1, no. 4 (December 1967): 20–32.

Isa, Zubaidah. 'Printing and Publishing in Indonesia: 1602–1970'. Ph.D. diss., Indiana University, 1972.

Jackson, Karl D. 'Bureaucratic Polity: A Theoretical Framework for the Analysis of Power and Communications in Indonesia'. In *Political Power and Communications in Indonesia.* Edited by Karl D. Jackson and Lucian W. Pye. Los Angeles: University of California Press, 1978: 3–22.

Jenkins, David. *Suharto and His Generals: Indonesian Military Politics 1975–1983.* Ithaca: Cornell Modern Indonesia Project, 1984.

John Paul II. *Crossing the Threshold of Hope.* Translated by Jenny and Martha McPhee. New York: Alfred A. Knopf Publisher, 1994.

Johns, Anthony H. 'Indonesia: Islam and Cultural Pluralism'. In *Islam in Asia: Religion, Politics, and Society.* Edited by John L. Esposito. New York and Oxford: Oxford University Press, 1987: 202–229.

Jones, Gavin W. 'Religion and Education in Indonesia'. *Indonesia* 22 (October 1976): 19–56.

Ka'bah, Rifyal. *Christian Presence in Indonesia: A View of Christian-Muslim Relations*. Leicester: The Islamic Foundation, 1985.

Kahin, George McTurnan. *Nationalism and Revolution in Indonesia*. Ithaca: Cornell University Press, 1952.

Kahn, Joel S. and F. Loh Kok Wah, eds. *Fragmented Vision: Culture and Politics in Contemporary Malaysia*. Sydney: Allen & Unwin, 1992.

Kamal, Zainun. 'Penganut Budha dan Hindu adalah Ahli Kitab'. In *Wajah Liberal Islam di Indonesia*. Edited by Luthfi Assyaukanie. Jakarta: Jaringan Islam Liberal, 2002: 143-147.

Katz, June S. and Ronald S. Katz. 'The New Indonesian Marriage Law: A Mirror of Indonesia's Political, Cultural, and Legal System'. *The American Journal of Comparative Law* 23 (1975): 653-681.

KISDI. *KISDI Menggugat*. Jakarta: KISDI, 1999.

_____. *KISDI Menggugat (2) Upaya Melawan Kezaliman dan Kemungkaran*. Jakarta: KISDI, 2002.

Kraemer, Hendrik. *Agama Islam*. Third Edition. Jakarta: Badan Penerbit Kristen, 1952.

Kurasawa, Aiko. *Mobilisasi dan Kontrol: Studi tentang Perubahan Sosial di Pedesaan Jawa 1942-1945*. Jakarta: Rasindo, 1993.

Kurzman, Charles, ed. *Liberal Islam: a Sourcebook*. New York and Oxford: Oxford University Press, 1998.

Lee, Oey Hong. *Indonesia Facing the 1980s: A Political Analysis*. Hull, England: Published for South-East Asia Research Group by Europress, [pref. 1979].

Lev, Daniel S. *Islamic Courts in Indonesia: A Study in the Political Bases of Legal Institution*. Berkeley: University of California Press, 1972.

Liddle, R. William. 'Participation and the Political Parties'. In *Political Power and Communications in Indonesia*. Edited by Karl D.

Jackson and Lucian W. Pye. Los Angeles: University of California Press, 1978: 171-195.

_____. 'Indonesia in 1987: The New Order at the Height of Its Power'. *Asian Survey* 28, no. 2 (February 1988): 180-191.

_____. 'The Islamic Turn in Indonesia: A Political Explanation'. *The Journal of Asian Studies* 55, no. 3 (August 1996): 613-634.

_____. 'Media Dakwah Scripturalism: One Form of Islamic Political Thought and Action in New Order Indonesia'. In *Toward a New Paradigm: Recent Developments in Indonesian Islamic Thought*. Edited by Mark R. Woodward. Tempe: Arizona State University, 1996: 323-356.

_____. 'Regime: The New Order.' In *Indonesia Beyond Suharto*. Edited by Donald K. Emerson. Armonk, New York: M.E. Sharpe, 1999: 39-70.

Lowry, Robert *The Armed Forces of Indonesia*. New South Wales, Australia: Allen & Unwin, 1996.

Macdougall, John A. 'Patterns of Military Control in the Indonesian Higher Central Bureaucracy'. *Indonesia* 33 (April 1982): 89-121.

Madjid, Nurcholish. 'The Issue of Modernization among Muslims in Indonesia: From a Participant's Point of View'. In *Readings on Islam in Southeast Asia*. Edited by Ahmad Ibrahim, et al. Singapore: ISEAS, 1985.

_____. *Islam Kemodernan dan Keindonesiaan*. Bandung: Mizan, 1987.

_____. 'Religious Pluralism and Islam: Experiences of Indonesia as a Nation State'. Unpublished paper presented at Institute of Asian Cultures. Tokyo, 28-30 January 1989.

_____. *Islam, Doktrin dan Peradaban: Sebuah Telaah Kritis tentang Masalah Keimanan, Kemanusiaan dan Komodernan*. Third Edition. Jakarta: Paramadina, 1995.

_____. 'Fazlur Rahman dan Rekonstruksi Etika al-Qur'an'. *Islamika* 2 (1993): 23–28.

_____. *Wawasan Al-Qur'an tentang Ahl Al-Kitab.* Jakarta: Klub Kajian Agama Paramadina, 73/VII/1993.

_____. 'Beberapa Renungan tentang Kehidupan Keagamaan untuk Generasi Mendatang'. Paper presented at Taman Ismail Marzuki. Jakarta, 21 October 1992.

_____. *Kontekstualisasi Doktrin Islam dalam Sejarah.* Edited by Budhy Munawar-Rachman. Jakarta: Paramadina, 1994.

_____. *Islam Agama Kemanusiaan.* Edited by M. Wahyuni Nafis. Jakarta: Paramadina, 1995.

_____. 'Religious Tensions and Dialogues: The Dynamics of the Indonesian Nation Formation Towards a 21st Century Society'. Unpublished paper presented at the International Conference on Islam and the 21st Century. Leiden, 3–7 June 1996.

_____. *Cendekiawan & Religiusitas Masyarakat: Kolom-Kolom di Tabloid Tekad.* Edited by Budhy Munawar-Rachman. Jakarta: Tabloid Tekad & Paramadina, 1999.

_____. *Kehampaan Spiritual Masyarakat Modern: Respons dan Transformasi Nilai-Nilai Islam Menuju Masyarakat Madani.* Edited by M. Amin Akkas and Hasan M. Noer. Jakarta: Mediacita, 2000.

_____and Mohamad Roem. *Tidak Ada Negara Islam: Surat-Surat Politik Nurcholish Madjid–Mohamad Roem.* Jakarta: Penerbit Djambatan, 2000.

Mahendra, Yusril Ihza. 'Combining Activism and Intellectualism: The Biography of Mohammad Natsir'. *Studia Islamika* 2, no. 1 (1995): 111-147.

Majelis Ulama DKI Jakarta. *Seruan Tentang Perkawinan Antar Agama.* Jakarta: MUI Jakarta, 1986.

Majelis Ulama Indonesia. *Kumpulan Fatwa Majelis Ulama Indonesia.* Jakarta: Pustaka Panjimas, 1984.

Mālik ibn Anas. *Al-Muwatta: The First Formulation of Islamic Law.* Translated by Aisha Abdurrahman Bewley. London and New York: Kegan Paul International, 1989.

Māwardī, ᶜAlī ibn Muḥammad al-. *Al-Aḥkām al-Sulṭāniyya wa al-Wilāyāt al-Dīniyya.* Cairo: Maṭbaᶜah Musṭafā al-Bābī al-Halabī wa Aulādah, 1973.

McVey, Ruth. 'The Post-Revolutionary Transformation of the Indonesian Army'. *Indonesia* 11 (April 1971): 131–176.

Mehden, Fred von der. *Religion and Nationalism in Southeast Asia.* Madison: University of Wisconsin, 1963.

Memon, Muhammad Umar. *Ibn Taimiya's Struggle against Popular Religion.* The Hague: Mouton, 1976.

Mody, Nawaz B. *Indonesia under Suharto.* New York: APT Books Inc., 1987.

Moertopo, Ali. *Strategi Politik Nasional.* Jakarta: CSIS, 1974.

_____. *Agama Bukan untuk Dipolitikkan.* Jakarta: Departemen Penerangan RI, 1980.

_____. *Strategi Pembangunan Nasional.* Jakarta: CSIS, 1981.

Mudzhar, Mohammad Atho. *Fatwas of the Council of Indonesia Ulama: A Study of Islamic Legal Thought in Indonesia 1975-1988.* Jakarta: INIS, 1993.

Munawar-Rachman, Budhy. *Islam Pluralis: Wacana Kesetaraan Kaum Beriman.* Jakarta: Paramadina, 2001.

Munhanif, Ali. 'Islam and the Struggle for Religious Pluralism in Indonesia; A Political Reading of the Religious Thought of Mukti Ali'. *Studia Islamika* 3, no. 1 (1996): 79–126.

Muskens, M.P.M. *Partner in Nation Building: The Catholic Church in Indonesia.* Aachen: Missio Aktuell Verlag, 1979.

Nababan, S.A.E. 'Laporan Konperensi Nasional Gereja dan Masyarakat'. In *Panggilan Kristen dalam Pembangunan Masyarakat*. Jakarta: Badan Penerbit Kristen, 1968.

Natsir, Mohammad. *Islam dan Kristen di Indonesia*. Jakarta: Media Dakwah, 1980.

_____. *Mencari Modus Vivendi Antar Umat Beragama*. Jakarta: Media Dakwah, 1980.

Neill, Stephen. *History of Christian Missions*. Harmondsworth, Middlesex: Penguin, 1964.

Nieuwenhuijze, van C.A.O. *Aspects of Islam in Post-Colonial Indonesia*. The Hague: W. van Hoeve, 1958.

Noer, Deliar. *The Modernist Muslim Movement in Indonesia 1900-1942*. London and New York: Oxford University Press, 1973.

_____. *Administration of Islam in Indonesia*. Ithaca, New York: Cornell University Monograph Series, 1978.

Polomka, Peter. *Indonesia Since Sukarno*. Middlesex, England: Penguin Books, 1971.

Quṭb, Sayyid. *Fī Dhilālil Qur'ān*. Vol. 1. Beyrūt: Dār Al-Shuruq, 1993.

Rahman, Fazlur. *Islam*. Second Edition. Chicago: University of Chicago Press, 1979.

_____. 'Islam: Past Influence and Present Challenge'. In *Islam: Challenges and Opportunities*. Edited by A.T. Welch and C. Pierre. Edinburgh: Edinburgh University Press, 1979: 315-330.

_____. *Islam and Modernity: Transformation of an Intellectual Tradition*. Chicago: University of Chicago Press, 1982.

_____. 'Interpreting the Qur'an'. *Inquiry* 3, no. 5 (May 1986): 45-49.

_____. 'Translating the Qur'an'. *Religion and Literature* 20 (1988): 23-30.

_____. *Major Themes of the Qur'an*. Minneapolis, MN: Bibliotheca Islamica, 1994.

Rasjidi, M. *Mengapa Aku Tetap Memeluk Agama Islam.* Jakarta: Hudaya, 1968.

_____. *Kasus RUU Perkawinan dalam Hubungan Islam dan Kristen.* Jakarta: Bulan Bintang, 1974.

_____. 'The Role of Christian Mission'. Reprinted from *International Review of Mission* 65, no. 260 (October 1976) by Media Dakwah, no date.

Ricklefs, Merle. C. *A History of Modern Indonesia since c. 1200.* Third edition. Stanford, California: Stanford University Press, 2001.

Riḍā, Rashīd. *Tafsīr al-Manār.* Vols. 4 & 6 . Beyrūt: Dār al-Maʿrifah, no date.

Roberts, Nancy R. 'Reopening the Muslim-Christian Dialogue of the 13-14ᵗʰ Centuries: Critical Reflections on Ibn Taymiyyah's Response to Christianity in *Al-Jawāb al-Ṣaḥīḥ li man Baddala Dīn al-Masīḥ*'. *Muslim World* 86, nos. 3–4 (July–October 1996): 342–366.

Robinson, Neal. *Christ in Islam and Christianity: The Representation of Jesus in the Qur'ān and the Classical Muslim Commentaries.* London: Macmillan, 1991.

Ropi, Ismatu. 'Depicting the Other Faith: A Bibliographical Survey of Indonesian Muslim Polemics on Christianity'. *Studia Islamika* 6, no. 1 (1999): 79–120.

Saeed, Abdullah. 'Religious Reconciliation in Indonesia "Legalist-Exclusivists" vs. "Contextualist-Inclusivists"'. Unpublished paper.

_____. '*Ijtihād* and Innovation in Neo-Modernist Islamic Thought in Indonesia'. *Islam and Christian–Muslim Relations* 8, no. 3 (1997): 279–295.

_____. 'Rethinking Citizenship Rights of Non-Muslims in an Islamic State: Rashīd al-Ghannūshī's Contribution to the Evolving Debate'. *Islam and Christian–Muslim Relations* 10, no. 3 (1999): 307–323.

_____. 'Towards Religious Tolerance through Reform in Islamic Education: The Case of the State Institute of Islamic Studies of Indonesia'. *Indonesia and the Malay World* 27, no. 79 (1999): 177–191.

_____. 'The Charge of Distortion of Jewish and Christian Scriptures'. *Muslim World* 92 (Fall 2002): 419–436.

Said, Salim. 'Suharto's Armed Forces: Building a Power Base in New Order Indonesia, 1966–1998'. *Asian Survey* 38, no. 6 (June 1998): 535–552.

Salam, Solichin. *Partai Muslimin Indonesia.* Jakarta: Lembaga Penyelidikan Islam, 1970.

Salim, Arskal and Azyumardi Azra, eds. *Shari'a and Politics in Modern Indonesia.* Singapore: ISEAS, 2003.

Samson, Allan. 'Indonesia 1972: The Solidification of Military Control'. *Asian Survey* 13, no. 2 (February 1973): 127–139.

_____. 'Army and Islam in Indonesia'. *Pacific Affairs* 44, no. 4 (Winter 1971–1972): 545–565.

_____. 'Islam in Indonesian Politics'. *Asian Survey* 8, no. 12 (December 1968): 1001–1017.

Ṣanᶜānī, al-. *Subul al-Salām: Sharh Bulūgh al-Marām min Jamiᶜ Adillat al-Aḥkām.* Vol. 4. Beyrūt: Dār al-Jīl, 1982.

Saripudin, ed. *Negara Sekuler: Sebuah Polemik.* Jakarta: Putra Berdikari Bangsa, 2000.

Schissel, Gregory A. 'The Quest for Common Ground: The Roman Catholic Church and Islam after the Second Vatican Council'. Ph.D. diss., Harvard University, 1998.

Schwarz, Adam. *A Nation in Waiting: Indonesia in the 1990s.* New South Wales, Australia: Allen & Unwin, 1994.

Secretariatus Pro non-Christianis. *Guidelines for a Dialogue between Muslims and Christians.* Rome: Secretariat for Non-Christians, 1969.

Shepard, William. 'Secularists, Traditionalists and Islamists in South-east Asia: a Paradigm Revisited'. Unpublished paper presented at the Conference on Islam, Civil Society and Development in Southeast Asia. University of Melbourne, 11-12 July 1998.

Shihab, Alwi. *Membendung Arus: Respons Gerakan Muhammadiyah terhadap Penetrasi Misi Kristen di Indonesia.* Bandung: Mizan, 1998.

Shihab, M. Quraish. *Wawasan al-Qur'an tentang Ahl al-Kitab.* Jakarta: Klub Kajian Agama Paramadina, 73/VII/ 1993.

Shihab, Rizieq. *Dialog Piagam Jakarta.* Jakarta: Pustaka Ibnu Sidah, 2000.

Siddiqui, Ataullah. *Christian–Muslim Dialogue in the Twentieth Century.* London: Macmillan Press Ltd., 1997.

Simatupang, T.B. *Kehadiran Kristen Dalam Perang, Revolusi dan Pembangunan.* Jakarta, BPK Gunung Mulia, 1986.

Somers, Mary F. *Peranakan Chinese Politics in Indonesia.* Ithaca: Cornell University, 1964.

SRS, Herdi. 'Forum Demokrasi (Democratic Forum): An Intellectuals' Response to the State and Political Islam'. *Studia Islamika* 2, no. 4 (1995): 161-182.

Steenbrink, Karel A. *Dutch Colonialism and the Indonesian Islam: Contacts and Conflicts 1596-1950.* Translated by J. Steenbrink and H. Jansen. Amsterdam: Rodopi, 1993.

_____. 'Muslim–Christian Relations in the *Pancasila* State of Indonesia'. *Muslim World* 88, nos. 3-4 (1998): 320-352.

_____. 'The Pancasila Ideology and an Indonesian Muslim Theology of Religions'. In *Muslim Perceptions of Other Religions: A Historical Survey.* Edited by J. Waardenburg. New York and Oxford: Oxford University Press, 1999: 280-296.

Sudjangi. *Pembinaan Kerukunan Hidup Umat Beragama: 50 Tahun Kemerdekaan Republik Indonesia*. Jakarta: Departemen Agama RI, 1995/1996.

_____. *Kompilasi Peraturan Perundang-undangan Kerukunan Hidup Umat Beragama*. Jakarta: Departemen Agama RI, 1997/1998.

Sumartana, 'SARA: An Unfinished Process of Social Integration?'. Unpublished paper presented at The International Seminar on Religious Plurality and Nationalism in Indonesia. Leiden: 26-27 November 1997.

Suminto, H. Aqib. *Politik Islam Hindia Belanda*. Jakarta: LP3ES, 1985.

Suryadinata, Leo. *The Chinese Minority in Indonesia*. Singapore: Chopmen Enterprises, 1978.

_____. *Political Parties and the 1982 General Elections in Indonesia*. Singapore: ISEAS, 1982.

_____. *The Ethnic Chinese Issue and National Integration in Indonesia*. Singapore: ISEAS, 1999.

Tahalele, Paul and Thomas Santoso. *Beginikah Kemerdekaan Kita?*. Surabaya: Forum Komunikasi Kristiani Indonesia, 1997.

Taher, Tarmizi. *Aspiring for the Middle Path: Religious Harmony in Indonesia*. Jakarta: CENSIS, 1997.

Taylor, Michael H. 'The Role of Religion in Society'. In *Christians and Muslims in the Commonwealth*. Edited by Anthony O'Mahony and Ataullah Siddiqui. London: Altajir World of Islam Trust, 2001: 42-63.

Thalib, Ja'far Umar. *Laskar Jihad Ahlus Sunnah wal Jama'ah: Mempelopori Perlawanan terhadap Kedurjanaan Hegemoni Salibis-Zionis Internasional di Indonesia*. (Yogyakarta: DPP Forum Komunikasi Ahlus Sunna wal Jama'ah, 2001).

Thiering, Barbara. *Jesus the Man*. Sydney: Doubleday, 1993.

Tritton, A.S. *The Caliphs and Their Non-Muslim Subjects: A Critical Study of the Covenant of ᶜUmar*. Second Edition. London: Frank Cass and Co, 1970.

van der Kroef, Justus Maria. *Dutch Colonial Policy in Indonesia 1900-1941*. Ph.D. diss., Columbia University, 1950.

van Klinken, Gerry. 'What Caused the Ambon Violence?'. *Inside Indonesia* (October–December, 1999): 15-16.

_____. 'The Maluku Wars: Bringing Society Back In'. *Indonesia* (April 2001): 1-25.

Wahib, Ahmad. *Pergolakan Pemikiran Islam: Catatan Harian Ahmad Wahib*. Edited by Djohan Effendi and Ismed Natsir. Jakarta: LP3ES, 1988.

Wahid, Abdurrahman. 'Toleransi dan Batasnya'. In *Membangun Demokrasi*. Edited by Zaini S Al-Raef. Bandung: Remaja Rosdakarya, 1999: 65-67.

_____. 'Fatwa Natal, Ujung, dan Pangkal'. In *Melawan Melalui Lelucon*. Edited by Mustafa Ismail, et al. Jakarta: Pusat Data dan Analisa Tempo, 2000: 26-27.

Ward, K.E. *The Foundation of the Partai Muslimin Indonesia*. Ithaca, New York: Cornell University Press, 1970.

_____. *The 1971 Election in Indonesia: An East Java Case Study*. Clayton, Australia: Centre on Southeast Asian Studies Monash University, 1974.

Wardy, Bisjron A. *Memahami Kegiatan Nasrani*. Yogyakarta: Muhammadiyah, 1964.

Weber, Max. *Economy and Society: An Outline of Interpretive Sociology*. Edited by G. Roth and C. Wittich. Vol. 1. Berkeley and Los Angeles: University of California Press, 1978.

Willis, A.T. *Indonesian Revival: Why Two Million Came to Christ?* California: William Carey Library, 1977.

Willmott, Donald E. *The National Status of the Chinese in Indonesia.* Revised Edition. Ithaca, N.Y.: Cornell University, 1961.

Wilson, Ian. *Jesus the Evidence.* London: Butler & Tanner, 1984.

Woodward, Mark R., ed. *Toward a New Paradigm: Recent Developments in Indonesian Islamic Thought.* Tempe: Arizona State University, Program for Southeast Asian Studies, 1996.

Yamin, Muhammad. *Naskah Persiapan Undang-Undang Dasar 1945.* 3 Vols. Jakarta: Yayasan Prapantja, 1959-1960.

Ye'or, Bat. *The Dhimmi: Jews and Christians under Islam.* Rutherford, N.J: Fairleigh Dickinson, 1985.

Yewangoe, A.A. 'Gereja di Era Reformasi'. In *Gereja dan Reformasi.* Edited by Victor Silaen. Jakarta: Yakoma PGI, 1999: 16-35.

Zwemer, Samuel M. *Across the World of Islam.* New York: F.H. Revell, 1929.

2. Magazines and Newspapers

'Abdurrahman Wahid Jadi Anggota Kehormatan Laskar Kristus'. *Koran Tempo*, 29 January 2002.

Amien Rais. 'Ini Bukan Soal SARA, tapi Kesenjangan Sosial'. *Forum Keadilan*, 27 January 1997, 94-98.

'Ancaman Bagi yang Kafir dan yang Kufar'. *Forum Keadilan*, 14 December 1998, 32-36.

'Anjloknya Dominasi Muslim Indonesia'. *Tabloid Siar*, 18-24 November 1999, 14.

'Antara Damai dan Kristenisasi'. *Media Dakwah*, January 2002, 43-44.

'Arswendo' and 'Setelah "Kagum 5 Juta" Itu Diumumkan'. *Tempo*, 27 October 1990, 27-30.

'Babi atau Bukan Itulah Soalnya'. *Tempo*, 5 November 1988, 72-75.

'Buya, Fatwa dan Kerukunan Beragama'. *Tempo*, 30 May 1980, 12-14.

Christanty, Linda. "Is There a Rainbow in Islam?" Quoted from *Latitude* magazine, July 2003.

'Dan Lahirlah UU Itu dengan Afdruk Kilat'. *Tempo*, 29 December 1973, 5-8.

'Dari Konseptor RUUP agar Diadili Hingga Demonstrasi Tak Ada Kalau Ada Komunikasi'. *Panji Masyarakat*, 15 December 1973.

'Dari Perkara Priok dan Bom BCA'. *Tempo*, 19 January 1985, 12-13.

'Dari Piagam Jakarta ke Wawasan Nusantara'. *Tempo*, 24 June 1989, 27.

'Dialog "Kawin antar Agama"'. *Media Dakwah*, September 2002, 13-14.

'Dialog tentang Nabi Isa'. *Media Dakwah*, June 2001, 57.

'Dicari Partner Bonafide'. *Tempo*, 14 March 1991, 68.

'Dimana Toleransi Mereka'. *Media Dakwah*, August 1989, 7-10.

'Forum Ukhuwah tentang Perkawinan Antaragama'. *Media Dakwah*, April 1992, 14-15.

Harjono, Anwar. 'Renungan Menjelang Ramadhan'. *Media Dakwah*, March 1992, 6-7.

'Hukum Rajam Sah, Mengapa Dipersoalkan?'. *Media Dakwah*, June 2001, 41-55.

'Huru-Hara di Tanjung Priok'. *Tempo*, 22 September 1984, 12-15.

Husaini, Adian. 'Rajam, Siapa Takut?'. *Media Dakwah*, June 2001, 41.

_____. 'Islam Pluralis, Nurcholish dan Ibnu Taimiyah'. *Media Dakwah*, March 2002, 44-46.

_____. 'Nurcholish Madjid Sekularisasi Tiada Henti'. *Suara Hidayatullah*, March 2002, 38-39.

'Jaringan Islam Liberal di Indonesia'. *Media Dakwah*, March 2002, 54-55.

'Jihad Ngawur Pendukung Gus Dur'. *Media Dakwah*, May 2001, 41-45.

'Kontroversi Perkawinan Putri Cak Nur'. *Gatra*, 15 April 2002.

Leifer, Michael. 'Suharto's Pilgrimage to Mecca: Is There a Subplot?'. *International Herald Tribune*, 21 June 1991.

Magnis-Suseno, Franz. 'Seputar Rencana UU Peradilan Agama'. *Hidup*, 25 June 1989, 24-25.

_____. 'SKB Itu Diskriminatif'. *Gatra*, 1 February 1997, 40-41.

'Memorandum tentang RUU Perkawinan'. *Sinar Harapan*, 12 December 1973.

'Mengapa Suratkabar ini Begitu Getol Mengenai RUUP?. *Sinar Harapan*, 17 December 1973.

'Mengapa Takut Syariat Islam'. *Media Dakwah*, July 2002, 42-43.

'Mengenang "Abdullah" Teladan dalam Kesadaran Hukum'. *Media Dakwah*, June 2001, 6-7.

'Menggugat Protes Naif'. *Media Dakwah*, August 1989, 12-13.

Munir, Sanihu. 'Koreksi terhadap Kelompok Kajian Utan Kayu ("Islam" Liberal)'. *Buletin Laskar Jihad Ahlus Sunnah Wal Jamaah* 16, 2002, 4-5.

'Nabi Gagal Menjalankan Missinya? (Menguji Pemikiran Nurcholish)'. *Media* Dakwah, December 1992, 41.

'Negara Perlu Berikan Ruang untuk Kawin Sah Menurut Hukum Negara'. *Sinar Harapan*, 19 December 1973.

'Nurcholish Madjid dan Annie Bessant'. *Media Dakwah*, December 1992, 44-45.

'Para Penyusun UUD '45 Sudah beri Jalan Keluar'. *Kompas*, 17 December 1973.

'Pembangunan Gereja Diprotes', and 'Proyek Gereja Sesuai Prosedur'. *Suara Merdeka* 12 and 13 February 2002.

'"Penyerahan Diri" Yes, Islam "No"?' *Media Dakwah*, December 1992, 47.

'Peradilan Agama: Kebutuhan atau Kecemasan'. *Tempo*, 24 June 1989, 24.

'Polisi Moral di Rimba Metropolitan'. *Tempo*, 23 January 2000, 44-45.

Ridwan, Cholil. 'Pernikahan Antar Agama'. *Media Dakwah*, September 2002, 3.

'RUU Perkawinan: Aksi dan Reaksi'. *Tempo*, 8 September 1973, 10.

'RUU Perkawinan: Mencabut & Merubah'. *Tempo*, 22 September 1973, 8-9.

Scott, Margaret. 'Suharto Writes His Last Chapter'. *The New York Times Magazine*, 2 June 1991.

'Serangan Malam'. *Tempo*, 26 December 1999, 28-29.

'STT Apostolos Memang Wajib Diwaspadai'. *Media Dakwah*, July 2002, 52-53.

'Survey Cara Kristen'. *Media Dakwah*, March 1992, 29.

'Syariat Islam Diadili, Umat Islam Bergolak'. *Media Dakwah*, June 2001, 50-51.

'Tak Cukup dengan Ucapan Terima Kasih'. *Tempo*, 10 March 1990, 22-23.

'Tanah Air Mata Maluku'. *Tempo*, 9 July 2000, 17.

Thalib, Ja'far Umar, 'Goenawan Merajam Syariah'. *Buletin Laskar Jihad Ahlus Sunnah Wal Jamaah* 13, 2002, 4-6.

_____. 'Syariah Merajam Goenawan'. *Buletin Laskar Jihad Ahlus Sunnah Wal Jamaah* 14, 2002, 5-6.

Umar, Hussein. 'Perjuangan Menegakkan Syariat Islam'. *Media Dakwah*, July 2002, 6-7.

'UU Perkawinan Terancam Diubah'. *Media Dakwah*, February 1992, 14-16.

Widjojo, S. 'Antara Negara Agama dan Negara Pancasila'. *Hidup*, 12 February 1989, 28-29, 50.

_____. 'Kesaktian Pancasila dalam Tantangan'. *Hidup*, 5 March 1989, 40-41.

_____. 'UU Sistem Pendidikan Nasional Ditandatangani'. *Hidup*, 5 March 1989, 24-25.

_____. 'Membahas RUU Peradilan Agama: Tiada Toleransi untuk Piagam Jakarta'. *Hidup*, 2 July 1989, 23-26, 45.

'William Liddle Mau Mengulang Sejarah Lama Memecah Belah Umat'. *Media Dakwah*, August 1993, 41.

3. Interviews

Abshar-Abdalla, Ulil. Interview by author. Jakarta, 6 March 2002.

Azra, Azyumardi. Interview by author. Jakarta, 4 March 2002.

Hidayat, Komaruddin. Interview by author. Jakarta, 24 January 2002

Husaini, Adian. Interview by author. Jakarta, 29 January 2002.

Kamal, Zainun. Interview by author. Jakarta, 22 January 2002

Madjid, Nurcholish. Interview by author. Jakarta, 6 March 2002

Magnis-Suseno, Franz. Interview by author. Jakarta, 28 January 2002.

Rahardjo, Eko. Interview by author. Jakarta, 5 February 2002.

Setiabudi, Natan. Interview by author. Jakarta, 27 February, 2002

Shihab, Rizieq. Interview by author. Jakarta, 6 February 2002.

Sumartono, Ignatius, S.J. Interview by author. Jakarta, 29 January 2002.

Umar, Hussein. Interview by author. Jakarta 25 January 2002

4. Internet Resources

Anglican Communion. Available from http://www.anglicancommunion.org. Accessed 15 July 2003.

International Crisis Group. 'Indonesia: Violence and Radical Muslims' [online]. Available from http://www.crisisweb.org/projects/asia/indonesia/reports/ A400455_ 10102001.pdf. Accessed 20 October 2001.

Paul VI. *Lumen Gentium*, chapter 2, no.16 [online]. Available from http://www.vatican.va/archive/hist_councils/ii_vatican_council/documents/vat-ii_const_ 19641121_ lumen-gentium_en.html. Accessed 29 March 2003.

_____. *Nostra Aetate*, no. 3 [online]. Available from http://www.vatican.va/archive /hist_councils/ii_vatican_council/documents/vat-ii_decl_19651028_nostra-aetate_ en.html. Accessed 29 March 2003.

World Conference on Religion and Peace. Available from http://www.wcrp.org/. Accessed 15 July 2003.

World Faiths Development Dialogue. Available from http://www.wfdd.org.uk/. Accessed 15 July 2003.

Detikcom. 'Pembubaran Laskar Jihad Tak Terkait Bom Bali' [online]. Available from http://www.detik.com; accessed 7 November 2002

Kompas. 'Laskar Front Pembela Islam Dibekukan' [online]. Available from http://www.kompas.com/kompas-cetak/0211/07/utama/clas01.htm. Accessed 7 November 2002.

_____. 'Pembubaran Laskar Jihad Bukan Tekanan Pemerintah' [online]. Available from http://www.kompas.com/kompas-cetak/0210/17/daerah/pemb19.htm. Accessed 9 November 2002.

Laskar Jihad. 'Laskar Jihad Troopers' [online]. Available from http://www.laskarjihad.or.id/english/article/ljtroopers.htm. Accessed 18 May 2001.

_____. Laskar Jihad Online. Available at http://www.laskarjihad.or.id.

Pikiran Rakyat. 'Alasan Pembubaran Laskar Jihad' [online]. Available from http://www.pikiran-rakyat.com/cetak/1002/17/0106. Accessed 7 November 2002.

'Antara Piagam Jakarta dan Tuntutan Penerapan Syari'at Islam' [online], available from http://www.kammimalang.tripod.com/syariat.html; accessed 24 July 2002.

'Umat Islam Makin Galau' [online], available from http://www.gatra.com; accessed 20 January 1999.

Islam Liberal. http://www.islamlib.com/id/page.php?page=article&id=224; accessed 7 July 2002.

http://www.islamlib.com

Adian Husaini, 'Menyoal Perkawinan Beda Agama' [online], available from http://www.republika.co.id/cetak_detail.asp?id=-94089&kat_id=217; accessed 13 September 2002.

'Maklumat Perang Ustadz' [online], available from http://www.-geocities.com/ambon67/noframe/photoy2knf.htm; accessed 16 July 2002.

5. Brochures and reports

INTERFIDEI. *DIAN/INTERFIDEI.* Yogyakarta: INTERFIDEI Secretariat, no date.

MADIA. *An Experiment Named MADIA.* Jakarta: MADIA Secretariat, no date.

Paramadina. *Pandangan Dasar Yayasan Wakaf Paramadina.* Jakarta, no date.

IAIN Jakarta Students. 'Kristenisasi dan Penipuan Gaya Baru (Melalui Bela Diri dan Pengobatan)'. Unpublished report, 27 February 2002.

STT Apostolos. Brochure of 2000-2001 academic years.

Tamam, Buchari. *Laporan Kegiatan DDII Pusat Selama 24 Tahun pada Tasyakur 24 Tahun DDII.* Jakarta: Dewan Dakwah, 1991.

Appendix 1

Joint decree of the Ministers of Religious and Internal Affairs
Number 01/ber/mdn-mag/1969

on

The implementation of government mandates for ensuring law and
order and the effective administration of religious development
and worship by religious followers

The Ministers of Religious and Internal Affairs

CONSIDERING:

a. that the State ensures the freedom of every citizen to follow his/
    her own religion and conduct worship according to that religion and
    faith;

b. that the Government has the task of providing leadership and aid
    to facilitate efforts to develop religion in accordance with the

teachings of each religion, and to monitor such efforts so that each citizen develops and implements the teachings of his/her religion effectively, orderly and in a harmonious environment;

c. that the Government has the responsibility to protect all efforts by religious followers to develop their religion and worship in its name provided such activities do not contravene the law and do not disturb public peace and order;

d. that in order to achieve the above, there must be standards relating to the implementation of Government mandates for ensuring law and order and the effective administration of religious development and worship by religious followers.

RECALLING:

1. Articles 17(3) and 29 of the 1945 Constitution;
2. Decision of the People's Consultative Assembly of the Republic of Indonesia Number XXVII/MPRS/1966;
3. Statute Number 18 of the year 1965;
4. Government Regulation Number 27 of the year 1956;
5. Presidential Decree Number 319 of the year 1968;

RULES AS FOLLOWS

TO GIVE ASSENT TO:

The Joint Decree of the Ministers of Religious and Internal Affairs on the Implementation of Government Mandates for Ensuring Law and Order and the Effective Administration of Religious Development and Worship by Religious Followers.

ARTICLE 1

The District Head (*Kepala Daerah*) must allow all efforts to propagate religions and to conduct worship by their followers, provided such activities do not contravene the law and do not disturb public peace and order.

ARTICLE 2

1. The District Head is to show leadership and to monitor the propagation and worship of religions by their followers in order that such activities:

a. do not incite division between religious followers;

b. are not accompanied by intimidation, bribes, force, or threats of any kind;

c. do not violate the law or public peace and order.

2. In implementing the mandate aforementioned in section 1 of this Article, the District Head is to be aided by, and given use of the mechanisms of, the Local Head of the Department of Religious Affairs.

ARTICLE 3

1. The Local Head of the Department of Religious Affairs is to lead, direct and monitor those who conduct religion instruction or sermons in places of worship, in a way which advances the unification of all community groups and mutual understanding among followers of different religions.

2. The Local Head of the Department of Religious Affairs is to endeavour to ensure that all religious instruction refrains from attacking or ridiculing other religions.

ARTICLE 4

1. The establishment of any place of worship requires permission of the District Head or a government official to whom he/she has delegated authority for the granting of such permission.

2. The District Head or official as described above in Section 1 of this Article may give the aforementioned permission after considering:

a. the opinion of the Local Head of the Department of Religious Affairs;

b. the plans of the proposed establishment;

c. local conditions and circumstances.

3. If required, the District Head or relevant official may request the opinions of local religious organisations and leaders.

ARTICLE 5

1. If conflict or opposition between religious followers is caused by religious propagation, instruction or sermons, or the establishment of a place of worship, the District Head must immediately provide a fair and unbiased resolution.

2. If the aforementioned conflict or opposition gives rise to criminal actions, resolution must be left to the authoritative law enforcement mechanisms, and must be based on law.

3. Other religious issues that arise and are resolved by the Local Head of the Department of Religious Affairs must be reported immediately to the local District Head.

ARTICLE 6

This Decree is shall enter into force from the date it is given assent.

Assented to at: Jakarta

Date: 13 September 1969

MINISTER OF INTERNAL AFFAIRS: Amir Machmud

MINISTER OF RELIGIOUS AFFAIRS: K.H. Moh. Dahlan

Appendix 2

Decree of the Minister of Religious Affairs of the Republic of
Indonesia
Number 70 of the year 1978
on
A guide for propagating religions

The Minister of Religious Affairs

CONSIDERING:

e. that religious harmony is an unconditional requirement for national
    unification and unity, as well as for the strengthening of national
    stability and security;

f. that in strengthening religious harmony the government has a
    responsibility to protect efforts to develop and propagate reli-
    gions;

g. that by virtue of this, a guide must be formulated relating to the propagation of religion.

RECALLING:

1. Articles 17(3) and 29 of the 1945 Constitution;
2. Decision of the People's Consultative Assembly of the Republic of Indonesia Number IV/MPR/1978;
3. Presidential Decrees Number 44 and Number 45 of the year 1974;
4. Decree of the Minister of Religious Affairs Number 18 of the year 1975 (Amended);

WITH REGARD TO:

a. Instruction of the President of the Republic of Indonesia on 24 May 1978.

RULES AS FOLLOWS

TO GIVE ASSENT TO:

The Decree of the Minister of Religious Affairs on A Guide for Propagating Religion.

FIRSTLY:

In order to foster national stability and uphold religious harmony, the development and propagation of religions must be carried out in the spirit of harmony, thoughtfulness, doing unto others as one would have them do unto oneself (*tepo seliro*), and mutual respect between religious followers in accordance with the essence of Pancasila.

SECONDLY:

The propagation of a religion is prohibited if:

a. it is directed at people who already have another religion;
b. it employs the use of bribes—materials, money, clothes, food and drink, drugs, etc.—in order to persuade people to adopt a particular faith;

c. it is carried out by the distribution of pamphlets, bulletins, magazines, books and the like in areas or dwellings of people who already have another religion;

d. it is carried out by approaching, under any pretext whatsoever, the private residences of people who already have another religion.

THIRDLY:

If a religion, developed or propagated in the manner described in the aforementioned second ruling, disturbs religious harmony, action will be taken pursuant to the relevant laws in force.

FORTHLY:

The entire Department of Religious Affairs, including its regional bodies, is hereby given the mandate of overseeing the implementation of this Decree and conducting constant consultation and co-ordination with the Government and local community leaders.

FIFTHLY:

This Decree is shall enter into force from the date it is given assent.

Assented to at: Jakarta

Date: 1 August 1978

MINISTER OF RELIGIOUS AFFAIRS: H. Alamsjah Ratu Perwiranegara

Appendix 3

**Decree of the Minister of Religious Affairs
of the Republic of Indonesia
Number 77 of the year 1978
on
Foreign aid to religious institutions in Indonesia**

The Minister of Religious Affairs

CONSIDERING:

h. that in strengthening national unification, unity, stability and defence, religious life must be constructed and directed towards strengthening intra-and inter-religious harmony as well as harmony between religious followers and the Government;

i. that foreign aid to religious institutions in Indonesia must be organised and directed towards avoiding any negative consequences which may disturb national unification and unity, intra-

and inter-religious harmony, as well as the increasingly solid national stability and defence.

RECALLING:

6. Articles 17(3) and 29 of the 1945 Constitution;

7. Decision of the People's Consultative Assembly of the Republic of Indonesia Number IV/MPR/1978 on the Guidelines for the Future Direction of the Nation;

8. Presidential Decrees Number 44 and Number 45 of the year 1974 on Points regarding Departmental Design and the Plan for Departmental Design;

9. Decree of the Minister of Religious Affairs Number 18 of the year 1975 on the Organisational Plan and Working Scheme of the Department of Religious Affairs (Amended);

10. Decree of the Minister of Religious Affairs Number 22 of the year 1978 on Considerations and Recommendations in regard to Foreign Nationals who Conduct Religious Activities in Indonesia.

WITH REGARD TO:

b. the Seven Motions of the Third Development Cabinet

c. Instruction of the President of the Republic of Indonesia on 14 May 1978.

d. the Outcome of Discussions between the Minister of Religious Affairs and the Commander for the Restoration of Peace, Security and Order (*Pangkopkamtib*) on 20 May 1978.

RULES AS FOLLOWS

TO GIVE ASSENT TO:

The Decree of the Minister of Religious Affairs on Foreign Aid to Religious Institutions in Indonesia.

ARTICLE 1

The definitions in this Decree are as follows:

a. Foreign Aid is any form of aid which originates from foreign countries in the form of personnel, materials and/or finances given by foreign governments, organisations or individuals to Religious Organisations or individuals in Indonesia with any purpose relating to, or suspected of relating to, the construction, development and propagation of religions in Indonesia;

b. Religious Organisations are organisations, groups, institutional bodies and other forms of religious organisation which aim to develop and propagate religions which are institutionally managed by the Government's Department of Religious Affairs.

ARTICLE 2

Foreign Aid as intended by Article 1(a) of this Decree may only be carried out after the consent or recommendation of the Minister for Religious Affairs.

ARTICLE 3

1. In the construction, development, propagation and leadership of religion in Indonesia, the use of foreign personnel must be limited.

2. Foreign nationals in Indonesia whose primary purpose for being in Indonesia is not related to religion may, after obtaining permission from the Minister of Religious Affairs or one of his/her officials, carry out incidental religious activities and nothing more.

3. Religious Organisations as intended by Article 1(b) of this Decree may use foreign nationals to carry out religious activities after obtaining permission from the Minister of Religious Affairs.

4. Religious Organisations as intended by Article 1(b) of this Decree must carry out educational and training programs with the aim of replacing such aforementioned foreign personnel with Indonesian nationals within a specified time.

5. The educational and training programs aforementioned in Section 4 of this Article must be implemented within six months of the assent of this Decree and must be completed within two years of their initial implementation.

ARTICLE 4

In regard to Religious Organisations which receive Foreign Aid that does not satisfy the requirements of Article 2 and Article 3 Sections 3, 4, and 5 of this Decree, and foreign nationals who breach Article 3 Section 2 of this Decree, action may be taken pursuant to the relevant laws in force.

ARTICLE 5

The Director-General of the Council for Islam and Hajj Affairs (*Bimas Islam dan Urusan Haji*), the Director-General of the Protestant Christian Council (*Bimas Kristen Protestan*), the Director-General of the Catholic Council (*Bimas Katolik*), and the Director of the Hindu and Buddhist Council (*Bimas Hindu dan Buddha*) (all under the auspices of the Department of Religious Affairs), in addition to the Head of the Regional Office of the Department of Religious Affairs, must implement this Decree and take any required action. These officials must also issue reports on the implementation of this Decree.

ARTICLE 6

1. Everything in contradiction to this Decree is hereby declared invalid.
2. Matters that have not yet been settled in this Decree will be dealt with in further detail by the Minister for Religious Affairs.

ARTICLE 7

This Decree is shall enter into force from the date it is given assent.

Assented to at: Jakarta

Date: 15 August 1978

MINISTER OF RELIGIOUS AFFIARS: H. Alamsjah Ratu Perwiranegara

Appendix 4

Decree of the Minister of Religious Affairs
Number 35 of the year 1980
on
The inter-faith conciliation council

The Minister for Religious Affairs

CONSIDERING:

That to advance harmony amongst fellow religious followers, for the creation of national unity according to the unity and unification prescribed by Pancasila and the 1945 Constitution, for the implementation of the Guide to the Comprehension and Implementation of Pancasila (Pedoman Penghayatan dan Pengamalan Pancasila), and mutual responsibility for the application of the Broad Outlines of the State Policy (Garis-garis Besar Halauan Negara), an Inter-faith Conciliation

Council is required. This Council will act as a forum for consultation and communication between religious leaders/figures and also between religious leaders/figures and the Government.

RECALLING:

5. Articles 17(3) and 29 of the 1945 Constitution;

6. Decision of the People's Consultative Assembly of the Republic of Indonesia Number II/MPR/1978 on a Guide to the Comprehension and Implementation of Pancasila;

7. Decision of the People's Consultative Assembly of the Republic of Indonesia Number II/MPR/1978 on the Broad Outlines of the State Policy;

8. Presidential Decree Number 44 of the year 1974 on Points regarding Departmental Design;

9. Presidential Decree Number 44 of the year 1974 on the Plan for Departmental Design at Annex 14. Presidential Decree Number 30 of the year 1978, Presidential Decree Number 47 of the year 1979, and Presidential Decree Number 22 of the year 1980 on Amendments to Annex 14 of the Presidential Decree Number 45 of the year 1974.

10. Joint Decree of the Ministers of Religious and Internal Affairs Number 1 (for both Ministers) of the year 1979 on Correct Methods relating to the Propagation of Religion and to Foreign Aid for Religious Institutions in Indonesia, which incorporates Decree of the Minister of Religious Affairs Number 70 of the year 1978 on A Guide to Propagating Religions and Decree of the Minister of Religious Affairs Number 77 of the year 1978 on Foreign Aid to Religious Institutions in Indonesia.

WITH REGARD TO:

The Summary of the Monitoring and Technical Discussion Meeting between Officials of the Department of Religious Affairs and Representatives of the Religious Congresses for the formation of an Inter-faith Conciliation Council, 17-18 October 1979; the Operational Assembly of 13-14 February 1980, the Operational Assembly of 17 March 1980, the Operational Assembly of 17-18 July 1980, and the Summit of 30 June 1980 in Jakarta.

RULES AS FOLLOWS

TO GIVE ASSENT TO:

The Decree of the Minister of Religious Affairs on the Inter-faith Conciliation Council.

FIRSTLY:

The INTER-FAITH CONCILIATION COUNCIL is hereby formed, as agreed upon by the Representatives of the Religious Congresses and Officials of Department of Religious Affairs at the Summit of 30 June 1980 in Jakarta. The BASIC GUIDE agreed upon at the Summit will be taken as an Annex to this Decree.

SECONDLY:

The funds for the implementation of this Decree will be issued under the Budget of the Department of Religious Affairs.

THIRDLY:

This Decree is shall enter into force from the date it is given assent.

Assented to at: Jakarta

Date: 30 June 1980

MINISTER OF RELIGIOUS AFFIRS: H. Alamsjah Ratu Perwiranegara

Annex to the Decree of the Minister of Religious Affairs
Number 35 of the year 1980

on

A basic guide for the inter-faith conciliation council

WITH THE MERCY OF THE ONE AND ONLY GOD

The Religious Congresses of Indonesia, that is:

1. The Council of the *Ulamā'* of Indonesia (MUI);
2. The Council of Indonesian Churches (DGI);
3. The Indonesian Catholic Bishops' Conference (MAWI);
4. The Association of Indonesian Hindu Dharma (PHDP);
5. The Council of Indonesian Buddhist (WALUBI);

Agree:

That in order to advance harmony between fellow followers of religion for the achievement of national unity and unification based on Pancasila, the 1945 Constitution, the implementation of the Guide to the Comprehension and Implementation of Pancasila, and the application of the Broad Outlines of the State Policy, a Conciliation Council is required to act as a forum for consultation and communication between religious leaders/figures in Indonesia. The Council will function according to the following standards:

ARTICLE 1: STATUS

The Conciliation Council, a forum for consultation and communication between religious leaders and figures is:

a. A council or forum for religious leaders/figures to discuss mutual responsibility and co-operation amongst citizens of different religious, based on Pancasila and the 1945 Constitution in an effort to increase our unification, unity and wholeness as a nation, and to implement the Guide to the Comprehension and Implementation of Pancasila and the Broad Outlines of the State Policy.

b. A council or forum for religious leaders/figures to discuss co-operation with the Government in relation to implementing the Guide to the Comprehension and Implementation of Pancasila, the Broad Outlines of the State Policy, and other government standards, particularly those relating to religious matters.

ARTICLE 2: NAME

The Conciliation Council, this forum for consultation and communication, is to be called the INTER-FAITH CONCILIATION COUNCIL or abbreviated to the CONCILIATION COUNCIL.

ARTICLE 3: FORM

1. The Conciliation Council will take the form of assemblies to be held on an *ad hoc* basis, at the request of either the Minister of Religious Affairs or one or more of the Religious Congresses.

2. These assemblies may be:

   a. a meeting between representatives from the Religious Congresses;

   b. a meeting between representatives from the Religious Congresses and the Government.

ARTICLE 4: SCHEMA

1. The Conciliation Council comprises of:

   a. assemblies

   b. a Secretariat.

2. The assemblies of the Conciliation Council are to be of the following kinds:

   a. a Comprehensive Assembly, which is attended by representatives from the Religious Congresses and the Minister of

Religious Affairs (or another representative from the Department of Religious Affairs);

b. an Operational Assembly, which is attended by the Secretariat and liaisons from the Religious Congresses or by people delegated by the Comprehensive Assembly.

3. Upon the request of the Conciliation Council, advisers from the Government, Governmental Institutions, Community Institutions and individuals may participate in the Comprehensive Assembly or the Operational Assembly on an *ad hoc* basis.

4. The Department of Religious Affairs is to arrange a Secretariat and facilities for the Conciliation Council.

5. Each Religious Assembly is to appoint one of its representatives to become the Liaison between the Religious Congresses and the Department of Religious Affairs, and to support the Secretariat of the Conciliation Council.

ARTICLE 5: OPERATION PLAN

1. Decisions reached by the Conciliation Council are to be based on conciliation (*musyawarah*) with the aim of achieving a consensus (*mufakat*), and in the instance of a consensus not being reached, the issue in question is to be postponed and then re-discussed after being sufficient time to settle.

2. The Comprehensive Assembly is to discuss issues of primary concern, which are to be prepared in advance by the Operational Assembly.

3. The Operational Assembly is charged with the tasks of:

a. preparing issues for discussion in Comprehensive Assembly;

b. discussing issues of detail at the discretion of the Comprehensive Assembly.

4. The Secretariat of the Conciliation Council is to administer anything required by the Comprehensive Assembly or the Operational Assembly.

ARTICLE 6: AUTHORITY

1. The Conciliation Council may discuss anything regarding mutual responsibility and co-operation among the followers of different religions, and with the Government, provided it is based on Pancasila and the 1945 Constitution, the advancement of the unification, unity and wholeness of the nation and the implementation of the Guide to the Comprehension and Implementation of Pancasila, the Broad Outlines of the State Policy, and other measures for unity provided by the Government, especially those relating to religion.

2. The decisions reached by the Conciliation Council are agreements with a morally binding value and are to be taken as suggestions or recommendations for the Government, the Religious Congresses and society at large.

ARTICLE 7: OTHER

Other pressing matters are to be dealt with by mutual consensus at a later date.

Jakarta, 30 June 1980.

Congress Representatives

1. The Council of the *ʿUlamā'* of Indonesia (MUI)
   K.H.M. Syukri Ghazali: General Chair
   Drs. H. Mas'udi: General Secretary
2. The Council of Indonesian Churches (DGI)
   Prof. Dr. P.D. Latuihamallo: Chair
   Dr. S.A.E. Nababan: General Secretary
3. The Indonesian Catholic Bishops' Conference (MAWI)
   Mgr. Drs. F.X. Hadisumarto O. Carm
   Mgr. Drs. Ig. Harsana Pr.: Chair of the Inter-faith Committee.

4. The Association of Indonesian Hindu Dharma (PHDP)
   Drs. Ida Bagus Oka Puniatmadja: Chair I
   I Wayan Surpha: General Secretary
5. The Council of Indonesian Buddhist (WALUBI)
   Soeparto Hs.: General Chair
   Ir. T. Soekarno: Secretary-General Department of Religious Affairs
   Drs. H. Kafrawi, MA: Secretary-General

Index

12 November 1991, incident, 134
1945 Constitution, 124, 166, 169, 177, 196
1974 Marriage Law, 203
    and the Religious Judicature Act, 230
68 H Radio, 274

abangan, 71, 89, 92, 111, 116-120, 190-191
Abbas, Abdul, 78
ᶜAbd al-Rahman ibn ᶜAwf, 46
Abd. Yadi, 161
Abduh, Muhammad, 32
Abdullah bin Umar, 260
Abdullah, 172, 175, 177
Abdullah, Amin, 241, 269
Abdulrahim, Imaduddin, 114
Abraham, 52
ABRI (Angkatan Bersenjata Republik Indonesia), 99
abrogation (*naskh*), 249

Abshar-Abdalla, Ulil, 241, 267, 273, 275, 295
Abu Hanifa, 47, 48, 296
Abū Hurayra, 50
Action Committee of Indonesian Students, *see* KAMI
Adam, 246
adat (customary) law, 211
Advent Hospital, 122
al-Aḥkam al-Zawāj, 292
ahl al-dhimma (non-Muslim protec), 43, 45, 47
ahl al-kitāb (People of the Book), 39, 43, 45-49, 137-138, 157-160, 227, 253-262, 281, 290-294, 296
    the concept of, 252
Ahlus Sunnah wal-Jama'ah, 155
Aishah, 245
Ali, Mukti, 130-131, 133, 276-277

Ali-Fauzi, Ihsan, 274
aliran kepercayaan, 90
Amanda Suharnoko, 273
Ambon
    conflict, 36, 144, 216, 286
    violence, 217
al-amru bi al-maʿrūf wa al-nahyu ʿan al-munkar, 152
ʿan la taʿbudū illā-allāh, 159
Andrew, 41
Anglican Communion, 56
Anglican Consultative Council, 55
animists, 95, 98
anti-Semitism, 149
anti-vice campaign (*Gerakan Anti Maksiat*), 152, 184
Anwar, Rosihan, 187
apologetic, 68
Apostolos, 208, 215, 268
Institute, 215
ʿaqīdah, 163
Arab, 94
Arabic language, 121
Archbishop of Canterbury, 54
Arismunandar, Wismoyo, 214
Armed Forces, 100, 113
Army Strategic Reserve Command, *see* Kostrad
Aryūsiyya, 43
Asad, Muhammad, 159, 168, 179
asas-tunggal, 107
Asj'ari, Hasjim, 33, 77
assalāmu ʿalaykum, 49
Assembly Sessions, 76
Assimilation Program, 95-96
Association of Indonesian Buddhist Scholars, *see* KCBI
Association of Indonesian Hindu Dharma *see* PHDP

Association of Indonesian Muslim Intellectuals, *see* ICMI
Association of the Islamic Convocation, 57
Assyaukanie, Luthfie, 274
atheism, 57
Atmowiloto, Arswendo, 125
Al-Azhar University, 146
Azra, Azyumardi, 37, 237, 241, 246-247, 267, 272, 277

bāligh, 46
Baasyir, Abubakar, 169
al-Baghdādī, 296
Bahrain, 253, 256
Bakin, 117
Bakker, F.L., 84
Bakrie, Aburizal, 116
Bali bombing, 153, 156
banking, 271
Banū Taghlab', 47
Baptist Church, 136-137, 148
Barton, 236, 240
Basri, Hasan, 116
Basyaib, Hamid, 274
Basyir, Achmad Azhar, 116
Belief in God (*ketuhanan*), 73, 75, 124, 230
Benda, 72
Berber, 46
Bethel church, 191
Bethesda, 122
Bible, 161, 215, 250
Biblical criticism, 84
Bidāyat al-Mujtahid, 48
bidʿa (innovation), 32
BMI (Bank Muamalat Indonesia), 116
Boland, 87-88, 131
Bosnia, 149
BPS (Biro Pusat Statistik), 182, 224

BPUPKI (Badan Usaha Penyelidik Persiapan Kemerdekaan Indonesia), 73
Bresnan, 110
Al-Būliqāniyya, 43
Buddhism, 55, 290
Buddhist, 98, 252-253, 262, 296
Budi Pekerti, 112
Buletin Dakwah, 152
business ethics, 271
Bychkov, David, 262-263

Carolus Hospital, 122
Catholic, 27, 32, 66, 83, 109
    Church, 54, 82
    Party, 77
Central Statistics Bureau, *see* BPS
Charitas Hospital, 122
Chasbullah, Wahab, 33
China, 253
Chinese, 94-95, 296
    anti — demonstrations, 99
Christian, 30-31, 241-242, 247-249, 252, 255, 258-259, 267, 279, 281, 290
    missionaries, 63
    missionary, 83
    separatist movement, 218
Christianisation, 60, 63, 65, 71, 83, 144, 148-149, 163-165, 180, 182, 185, 187, 192-193, 196, 206-207, 213, 215, 223-225, 227, 263-264, 281, 289
    efforts, 33
Christianise, 180
Christianity, 95, 249, 251, 267, 281, 290
Christmas Celebrations, 185, 207
churches, 248
    building, 264
    Congress, 164

Civil Court, 209
Civil Emergency Authority, 221
classical Islamic scholarship, 236
classical Islamic works, 236
Coen, Jan Pieterszoon, 61
colonialist image, 264
common platform or *kalimatun sawā',* 242
Communism, 93, 99, 127, 230
Communist Party, *see* PKI
Communist, 98, 112, 129
    ex —, 121
Companions of the prophet (*ṣaḥāba*), 260
Conference of Catholic Bishops of Indonesia, 136
Confucianism, 55
Confucians, 253
consciousness of God, 245
Constituent Assembly, 77
Consultative Council of Indonesian Muslims, *see* Masyumi
contextual approach, 235
contextual method, 240
contextual understanding, 227
contextualist-inclusivists, 28
contradictions (*munāqaḍat*), 41
Council of Churches, 107
Council of Indonesian Buddhist, *see* Walubi
Council of Indonesian Churches, *see* PGI
Council of the the *ʿUlamā'* of Indonesia, *see* MUI
CRC (Cipta Loka Caraka), 125
criminal law (*ḥudūd*), 171
crucifixion of Jesus, 86
CSIS (Centre for Strategic and International Studies), 111-113
culture-oriented, 271

Dachlan, K.H.M., 129
Da'wah, 147
Dahlan, Ahmad, 32
Danandjaja, Utomo, 230, 270
Darul Ulum, Pesantren, 232
DDII (Dewan Dakwah Islamiyah Indonesia),
    36-37, 143-144, 146-148, 157, 159-
    161, 177-178, 180, 185, 189, 191,
    204, 211, 214-215, 219, 225, 281-
    283, 288-289, 297
De Britto, High Schools, 123
democracy, 235, 268
Denny J.A., 176
Department of Defence and Security, 117
Department of Home Affairs, 117
Department of Religious Affairs, 129,
    131-132, 223
Departments of Information, Social Affairs,
    Religion, Foreign Affairs and Jus-
    tice, 117
depoliticising Muslims, 107
desacralising, 234
desacralization, 236
destructive actions, 184
detestable heretics, 61
DGI (Dewan Gereja-Gereja di Indonesia),
    82, 133, 196, 205
dhimmīs, 44-45, 58
DI (Darul Islam)/TII (Tentara Islam Indo-
    nesia), 78, 101, 103
    and PRII, 81
    movement, 227
al-dīn ('submission' or 'obedience'), 243,
    252
diakonia, 193
DIAN, 272
Dioma, 125
disobedience (*kemunkaran*), 295

divine attributes, 236
divinity of Jesus, 85
Djajadiningrat, Husein, 74, 77
Djambek, Sjech Muhammad Djamil, 231
Djarnawi, 86-87
doa bersama, 207
dogmatism, 237
Doulos Institute of Theology, 184, 194-195
DPR (Dewan Perwakilan Rakyat), 168
Draft on Religious Judicature Act, 185
Driyarkara, Sekolah Tinggi Filsafat, 131,
    185
Dutch, 72, 94-95
    colonial period, 59
    Colonial Policy, 60
    favouritism towards Christians, 66
    policies, 59

early generations of Muslims, 242
East Java Christian Church, 83, 120
Efendi, Djohan, 115, 195, 228, 230, 237,
    240, 272-273, 275
ethnic Chinese, 93
Europeans, 94
exception, 294
exclusivists, 29
    Muslims, 29
extra ecclesia nulla salus' (there is no
    salvation outside the church), 61

Fachruddin, A.R., 66
Faculty of Veterinary Science at Bogor
    Institute of Agriculture, 150
Al-Faruqi, Isma'il, 246
fascism, 72
fasting, 121
Fathuddin, Usep, 230, 270
fatwā, 139-140, 206, 266

FCHI (Forum Cendekiawan Hindu Indo-
nesia), 115
Fī Dhilālil Qur'ān, 163
final religion, 30
fiqh, 290, 293
    status of —, 235
*Al-Fiṣal fi al-Milal wa-al-Ahwā' wa-al-
Niḥal*, 41
fiṭrah (innocent), 246
Five-Year Plan, 97
FKAWJ, 155-156, 219
FKM (Front Kedaulatan Maluku), 219-220
Foreign Orientals, 94
Forum Demokrasi, 115
Forum for Indonesian Hindu Scholars, *see*
    FCHI
Forum Komunikasi Ahlus Sunnah wal-
    Jama'ah (Communication Forum of
    Those Who Upheld Customs Based
    on the Practice and Authority of the
    Prophet Muhammad and his Com-
    panions), 154
Forum Umat Islam Semarang (Islamic Com-
    munity Forum of Semarang), 275
Fourth Development Cabinet, 118
FPI (Front Pembela Islam), 36-37, 143,
    151-153, 157, 167, 171, 183-184, 213,
    225, 281, 285, 294-295
Freemansonry, 288
Front of Moluccas Sovereignity, *see* FKM
fundamental sameness, 245
fundamentalist Islam, 93
fundamental-philosophical method (*al-fal-
    safa al-ūlā*), 269
furqān (distinguisher of the good from the
    bad), 247

G 30 S/PKI, 90, 101
Gatra, 263

Gautama, Sidharta, 253
GBHN (Garis-Garis Besar Haluan Negara),
    212
Gerakan Pembaruan Keagamaan (Reli-
    gious Renewal Movement), 282
Gerakan Pemuda Islam Indonesia, 89
Gerakan Pengacau Keamanan (Security
    Disorder Movement), 282
Gerakan Persaudaraan Muslim Indo-
    nesia, 176
Gerakan Separatis Kristen, 218
GGBI (Gabungan Gereja-Gereja Baptis
    Indonesia), 82, 189
GMII, 199
God, 161
    (with a capital G) and god, 282
goeroe ordonnantie (teacher ordinance),
    66
Golkar (Golongan Karya), 104-105, 107
Gontor, Pondok Modern, 232
good evening, 266
good morning, 266
Gospels (*Injīl*), 41, 85-86, 208
GPPI (Gerakan Pembaruan Pemikiran
    Islam), 227-232-233, 237, 240, 281-
    282, 284, 297
grammar, 239
Greek, 256
Grose, George B., 272
Guided Democracy, 81
Gunung Maria Hospital, 122
Gunung Mulia, Badan Penerbit Kristen
    (BPK), 124

Ḥakīm, ᶜAbdul Ḥamīd, 290-296
ḥanīf, 245-246
ḥarām, 261
Ḥawā (Eve), 246

ḥadīth, 227
ḥalāl, 260
al-ḥanāfiyyat al-samḥaḥ, 243, 245-246
Haanie, A.D., 68-69
Habibie, B.J., 114, 219
Hadikusumo, Ki Bagus, 74
Hadji Rasul, 231
hajj (pilgrimage), 115
Hamka, 137, 139, 204
Hanbali, 256-257
Hanbalite, 40
Harahap, Burhanuddin, 81
Harjono, Anwar, 146, 149, 199, 203
Harthoorn, Samuel E., 64-65
Hasbullah, 85-86
Hasjim, Wahid, 74
Hassan, Ahmad, 146
Hatta, Muhammad, 75-76
Haz, Hamzah, 184
Hazeu, Godard Arend, 65
Hefner, 230
Henry Siahaan, 205
Hermanu, 110
Hidayat, Komaruddin, 237, 241, 264, 268,
    270, 273, 293
Hindu, 95, 98, 252-253, 262, 290, 296
Hinduism, 55, 290
historical
    approach, 238
    traditional, 239
Hizbullah (Army of Allah), 72
HMI (Himpunan Mahasiswa Islam), 150,
    228-229, 231-232
    Jakarta, 230
hukum keluarga (family law), 177
Humardani, Sudjono, 111
Hurgronje, Snouck, 63

Husaini, Adian, 37, 150, 162, 164-166,
    175, 178, 180-182, 204-207, 213,
    284-289, 291-292

IAIN (Institut Agama Islam Negeri), 131,
    276
    Jakarta, 170, 268, 277
    Yogyakarta, 276
Ibn Abbas, 50, 260
Ibn al-Subkhi, 165
Ibn Hazm, 40-42
Ibn Qayyim al-Jawziyya, 44
Ibn Rushd, 46-48
Ibn Taymiyya, 40, 42, 44, 50, 236, 240,
    243, 248, 255-257, 290-293
Ibrahim, Saikh, 65
ICIHEP (Indonesia Canada Islamic Higher
    Education Project), 277
ICMI (Ikatan Cendekiawan Muslim Indo-
    nesia), 114-115, 216
ICRP (Indonesian Conference on Religion
    and Peace), 274
ideologically-oriented political system, 231
Idris, Fahmi, 116
ʿIed al-Aḍha, 268
Ignatius Church, St, 275
Ihya'us Sunnah, 155
ijāb qabūl, 263
ʿijmā, 257
ijthād, 29, 31, 45, 227, 235, 237, 239-240,
    257, 274, 290, 293
    context-based, 237
Imlek, 96
Inclusivism, 227, 240
inclusivists, 29, 279
    Muslims, 31
India, 253
Indian, 94

Indonesia, 230
Indonesian Baptist Churches, *see* GGBI
Indonesian Catholic Student Association,
    see PMKRI
Indonesian Communist Party, *see* PKI
Indonesian Council of Bishops/MAWI, 82,
    133, 196, 205
Indonesian Council of Churches, 128
Indonesian Democratic Party, *see* PDI
Indonesian Islamic State, *see* NII
Indonesian Muslim Party, *see* PMI
Indonesian Nationalist Party, *see* PNI
Indonesian University, 150
Injīl (Gospel), 39-41, 242
al-inqiyād, 243
Institute of Theology apostolos, 208
Intan Pariwara, 214
intellectual endeavor, 239
Interfaith Dialogue, 270, 272
INTERFIDEI, 272
International Institute of Islamic Thought
    and Civilization, 150
Inter-religious Consultation, 158
Inter-religious marriage, 198, 203, 227,
    259
IPNU, 199
IPPNU, 199
Iraq, 253
Isa, Prophet, 40, 85, 162, 251
Almasih di dalam al-Qur'an dan Hadits,
    161
ISKA (Ikatan Sarjana Katolik Indonesia),
    115
islām dīn wa dawla, 179
islām raḥmatan li al-ᶜālamīn, 169
Islam Inklusif, 272
Islam Menentang Kraemer, 68
*Islam Pluralis: Wacana Kesetaraan Kaum
    Beriman*, 272

Islam, 52, 55, 168, 243, 252, 267, 289
    and the problem of modern society,
        272
    and the state, 30
    Galak, 287
    in its generic meaning, 243
    par excellence, 244
    yes, Islamic party no, 234
Islamic University Jakarta, 146
Islamic, 73, 242
    army (*Hizbullah*), 79
    banking, 178
    boarding schools (*pesantren*), 148
    courts, 209
    fanaticism, 63
    group, 71
    ideology, 233
    law, 177, 210, 212
    mysticism, 272
    state, 87-88, 171, 174-175, 210, 229-
        230, 233
    theology, 244
Islamisation, 65, 171
Israelites, 85
issues, 237
    of Christianisation, 180
al-istislām, 243
Iwan, Yohannes, 268

Ja'far, Hamam, 284
Jakarta, 62
    Charter, 60, 72-73, 77, 87, 166, 168,
        170-171, 175, 178-180, 183, 188, 210-
        212, 227, 267, 289
Japan, 253
Japanese, 72, 296
Javanese, 190
*Al-Jawāb al-Ṣaḥīh li man Baddala Dīn
    al-Masīḥ*, 40

Jayabaya University, 150
  Foundation, 176
Jesuit Order, 287
Jesus Christ, 52, 55, 86, 161
Jewish, 241, 244
Jews, 69, 245, 247-249, 252, 255, 258-
  259, 262, 281, 290
jihād, 155, 195, 230, 239
JIL (Jaringan Islam Liberal), 204, 261,
  274, 285, 289
jizya (tribute), 45-46
John Paul II, Pope, 53, 193
John XXIII, Pope, 51, 82
John, 40-41, 85-86
Johns, A.H., 201
Journal *Studiën*, 70
Judaism, 85, 249, 289
justice, 235, 268

Ka'bah, 245
kāfirūn, 163
kaʿba, 106
Kalimatullah, Institutes of Theology, 268
kalimatun sawā', 245, 247, 252, 278
Kamal, Zainun, 37, 204, 241, 253-254,
  260-262, 284, 293-294, 296
KAMI (Komite Aksi Mahasiswa Indo-
  nesia), 128, 200
Kanisius, 125
Kantor Urusan Agama (Office for Religious
  Affairs), 72, 77
Karo Batak Protestant Church, 83, 120
Kartosuwirjo, 79-80
Kashmir, 149
KCBI (Keluarga Cendekiawan Buddhis
  Indonesia), 115
kebatinan, 103

Keharusan Pembaharuan Pemikiran Islam
  dan Masalah Integrasi Umat (The
  Necessity of Reforming Islamic
  Understanding and the Problem of
  Islamic Integration), 234
Kesatuan Aksi Pengganyangan Gerakan
  September Tiga Puluh, 122
Ketapang incident, 184
Khan, Inamullah, 56
kharaj, 45
khatam (ending), 247
khurafāt (superstition), 32
khutbah nikāḥ, 263
King of Ethiopia, 258
King, The Nan, 97
KISDI (Komite Indonesia untuk Solidaritas
  Dunia Islam), 36-37, 143, 149-151,
  162-163, 174, 176-177, 181-182,
  195, 214, 218-219, 225, 261, 281,
  284, 287, 297
Kitāb al-Iqtidā', 248
Komando Pastor, 125
Komite Kesatuan Generasi Muda Indo-
  nesia, 200
Kompas, 125, 200, 211
Kompas-Gramedia, Kelompok (Kompas-
  Gramedia Group), 125
Konteks Berteologi di Indonesia, 272
Kopkamtib (Komando Pemulihan Ke-
  amanan dan Ketertiban), 111
Korps Mubalig Jakarta, 150
Kostrad (Komando Cadangan Strategis
  Angkatan Darat), 90
Kraemer, Hendrik, 68-69, 188

Lā ilāha illa Allāh, 243
al-Lāt, 69
Lambeth Conference, 55-56

Laskar
  Jihad, 36-37, 143, 154-157, 161-162,
    171-172, 174, 177, 217-223, 225,
    281, 285-286, 294
  Kristus, 289
Latuharhary, 78
law
  of nature (*sunnatullāh*), 241, 278
  on the National Education System, 213
legacy of classical Islam, 236
legal
  (*fiqh*-oriented) issues, 235
  supremacy, 268
legalist-exclusivists, 28
lemak babi, 126
liberal interpretation of Islam, 271
Liberal Islamic Network, *see* JIL
liberalisation, 236
  process, 236
liberalising, 234
Liberty, 288
Liddle, William, 28, 283-284
Liong, Liem Sioe, 97
LIPIA, 154
literal meaning, 230
Luke, 40-41, 85-86

Ma'arif, Syafii, 178
*madhhab*ism, 237, 240
MADIA (Masyarakat Dialog Antar Agama),
  273
Madjid, Nurcholish, 37, 114, 178, 228, 230-
    233, 240-242, 244, 249-251, 255-
    257, 262-263, 270-271, 281, 288-
    294, 297
al-Madkhali, Syaikh Rabi' ibn Hadi, 156
Magdalena, Maria, 250
Magians, 45-46, 290

Magnis-Suseno, Franz, 185, 197, 207, 210,
  212, 250
Mahendra, Yusril Ihza, 147, 150
Mahkamah Syariah, 209
Mahmada, Nong Daral, 274
Mahmud, Amir, 105
Mahometan religion, 62
mahr, 263
Majelis Wali Gereja Indonesia, 82
Malay, 98
Malaysia, 176
Malik ibn Anas, 45, 48, 50
Maluku, 286
manāsik, 244
Manado University, 289
Manasik Haji, 208
al-*Manat*, 69
Mangunbahan, 127-128
manhaj, 168
Manifesto Politik (Political Manifesto), 229
mansak, 244
Manuputty, Alexander, 220
al-Maqdūniyya, 43
Maramis, A.A., 75
Mardjono, Hartono, 118
Mark, 40-41, 85-86
Marriage Bill for Indonesian Muslims,
    109, 185, 199, *see also* RUU Per-
    nikahan Umat Islam
Marriage, 225
  Law, 108-109
  Law of 1974, 204
Mary, 52
Maryam, 41
Masjkur, K.H., 186
Masjumi-Socialist Party of Indonesia, 101
maslak, 244

mass killing
  in 1965–1967, 265
  of 1965–1966, 228-229
Master Plan Pembangunan Bangsa (Master Plan for the Development of the Nation), 111- 113
Masyumi (Majelis Syuro Muslimin Indonesia), 72, 80-82, 100, 103, 105, 144, 147, 227-229, 232-233
  ex –, 234
Matthew, 40-41, 85-86
Al-Mawardi, 44-45
Al-Mawdudi, 166, 296
McGill University, 277
meanings (taḥrīf), 40
Mecca, 69
Media Dakwah, 28, 172, 181, 189, 191, 215, 275, 282-283, 285, 288-289
Medina, 258
Megawati Soekarno Putri, 220
Memahami Kegiatan Nasrani, 86
Menggugat Gerakan Pembaruan Keagamaan (Charging the Religious Renewal Movement), 283
Messiah, 162
MIAI (Majlisul Islamil A'laa Indonesia), 80
Military, 209
Mindanao, 149
minhāj (way of life), 244, 252
Minister
  for Education and Culture, 214
  of International Affairs, 183
  of Religious Affairs, 135, 138, 146, 183, 209
Ministry of Education, Training and Religion, 78
Ministry of Religious Affairs, 78, 88, 130, 133

Mintaredja, H.M. Safaat, 102
missionary, 120
modern
  industrial, 231
  thought, 236
  world, 238
modernisation, 233-235
modernism, 237
modernist, 237
Moertopo, Ali, 104-107, 110-113
Mohamad, Goenawan, 172, 274
Mohamedans, 52
Moluccan islands, 67
monotheism, 242
Montini, Cardinal, 51
Moorish religion, 62
Mooy, Adrianus, 119
moral campaign, 184
MPR (Majelis Permusyawaratan Rakyat), 168-169
mu'min, 246
al-Muʿīn al-Mubīn, 296
mudjtahid fi 'l-madhhab', 257
Mudzhar, Atho, 138, 284
Muhammad ibn Abd al-Wahhab, 151
Muhammad ibn Saud University, 151
Muhammad Saw., Prophet, 40, 52, 68-69, 125-126, 128, 151, 178-179, 197, 244, 249, 255-259, 291
Muhammad, Fadel, 116
Muhammad, Mar'ie, 122, 128
Muhammadiyah, 32-34, 68, 74, 80, 86, 136, 138, 178, 203, 212, 229, 237
muhaymīn (preponderance), 247
MUI (Majelis Ulama Indonesia), 116, 133, 135, 137-140, 203, 205-206, 230, 266
Munawar-Rachman, Budhy, 241, 244, 248, 255, 270, 272-273, 286

Al-Munawwarah mosque, 144
Muqbil ibn Hadi al-Wadi'i, Syaikh, 154
Murdani, Benny, 110-111, 113-114, 117-118
Murdaya, Hartati, 183-184
musaddiq (truth maker), 247
mushrik, 243, 255-257, 260
al-mushrikīn, 260, 292
Muslim Students Association, *see* HMI
Muslims, 27, 54, 265
   World League, 56
   youth, 229
muslimūn, 243-244
Musyawarah Antar Agama (Inter-religious
   Consultation Forum), 129, 189, 211,
   225
al-Muwaṭṭa', 45, 48
Muzadi, Hasyim, 178

Nababan, S.A.E., 200, 205
*Nabi Isa dalam al-Qur'an dan Nabi
   Muhammad dalam Bijbel* (Jesus
   Christ in the Qur'ān and Muhamad
   in the Bible), 84
Nahdhatul Ulama, 32-34, 72, 74, 77, 80-
   81, 89, 103-107, 122, 136, 203, 229
Nasr, Seyyed Hussein, 236
Nasution, A.H., 90
Nasution, Harun, 277
Nasution, Yunan, 146
National Education System Law, 123
National Intelligence Coordinative Body
   (Badan Koordinasi Intelijen Negara
   /Bakin), 110
nationalist group, 71
Natives, 94

Natsir, Mohammad, 70-71, 79-81, 100,
   145-146, 149, 158, 160, 186-187,
   192, 211-212
   muda, 232
   young, 232
Nederlandsch Indische Theosofische
   Vereeniging (East Indies Theosophy
   Forum/NITV), 288
Negara Kristen Alifuru, 218
neo-modernism, 227, 236-237, 240
neo-modernist, 28, 236, 238, 241
   thinkers, 237
neo-revivalist, 237
neutral person, 251
New Heavens and a New Earth, 87
New Order, 27-28, 34-36, 59-60, 91-96,
   99, 104-105, 109-110, 112, 117, 120,
   130, 139, 141, 147, 180, 189-190,
   192, 216, 219, 225, 227-228, 230,
   232-235, 268, 276, 278-279, 282,
   288
New Testament, 85-87
NIFCON (Network for Interfaith Concerns),
   56
NII (Negara Islam Indonesia), 79
Nilai-Nilai Dasar Perjuangan, 233
niṣāb, 47
Noer, Deliar, 88, 115
nominal Muslims, 63, 95
non-madhhab approach, 277
non-*pribumi*, 96, 98
Nurdin, Rusjad, 146
Nurul Iman mosque, 113
Nusantara, 200

Obor, 125
Old and New Testaments, 39, 86
Old Order, 60, 71, 103, 227-228, 231

Old Testament, 86-87
Onck's, Van, 85
One and Only God (tawḥīd), 243
One Truth, 242
Oneness of God (tawḥīd), 43, 85
Operational Command for the Restoration
    of Security and Order, see Kopkamtib

pagans (mushrikūn), 70
Pahud, Charles Ferdinand (Colonial Minis-
    ter), 64
Pakubuwono XII, 199
PAM Swakarsa, 152
PAN (Partai Amanat Nasional), 196
Pancasila, 87, 100, 103, 107, 110, 112, 124,
    171, 210, 212, 214, 234
Panji Masjarakat, 83
Panti Rapih Hospitals, 122
Paraclete (al-Bāriqlīṭ), 43
Paramadina, Foundation, 178, 270-271295
Parkindo (Partai Kristen Indonesia), 104
Parmusi (Partai Muslimin Indonesia
    Indonesian Muslim Party), 86, 102,
    107
Partai Bulan Bintang, 150
Partai Katolik Indonesia (Indonesian
    Catholic Party), 125
pasrah (muslim), 262
path, 244
    of religion, 244
Pattiasina, J.M., 185
Paul VI, 51
PCID (Pontifical Council for Inter-religious
    Dialogue), 54
PDI (Partai Demokrasi Indonesia), 106-107
Pembela Islam, 70
Pemuda Muhammadiyah, 126
Penghulu Courts, 209

People's Consultative Assembly, see MPR
Perayaan Natal Bersama, 139, 206
perennial thinker, 236
Perguruan Tinggi Agama Islam Negeri,
    276
persamaan agama (syncretism), 286
Persis (Persatuan Islam), 70, 146, 154
Perti (Persatuan Tarbiyah Islamiyah), 104
Petra Christian University, 123
PGI (Persatuan Gereja-Gereja Indonesia),
    123, 181, 197, 199, 210, 275
PHDP (Parisada Hindu Dharma Pusat),
    133
Piagam Madinah, 175
PIKI (Persatuan Inteligensia Kristen
    Indonesia), 115
PKB (Partai Kebangkitan Bangsa), 196
PKI (Partai Komunis Indonesia), 81, 99,
    105, 120, 230, 265
    Revolt, 101
PKI (Partai Komunis Indonesia), 90, 103
pluralistic
    approach, 228
    society, 244
PMI (Partai Muslimin Indonesia), 101
PMKRI (Perhimpunan Mahasiswa Katolik
    Republik Indonesia), 120, 201-202
PNI (Partai Nasionalis Indonesia), 89
polemic, 68
policy of modernisation, 230
politics of modernisation, 228
polygamy, 127
PPIM (Pusat Pengkajian Islam dan Masya-
    rakat), 170
PPKI, 75-76
PPP (Partai Persatuan Pembangunan),
    106-107, 110
pragmatic approach, 231

Prawiranegara, Syafruddin, 81
Prawiro, Radius, 118-119
Prawoto, Mangkusasmito, 100-101
prayer, 121
Preamble of the 1945 Constitution, 267
Preparatory Work for Indonesian Independence, 73
Prevention of the Mistreatment of Religion, 90
pribumi, 96, 98-99
problem of christianisation, 137
program-oriented system, 231
Protestant, 27, 32, 66, 83, 109, 181, 187
    Institute of Doulos, 287
Protestantism, 183
PRRI (Pemerintah Revolusioner Republik Indonesia), 78-81, 100, 103
    rebellion of the —, 233
PSII (Partai Sarikat Islam Indonesia), 80-81, 104

qiyās (analogy), 164
awlawī, 163, 165
Qur'ān, 29, 31, 39, 41, 161, 175, 215, 227, 238, 247, 255, 274, 278, 285, 294
    and ḥadīth, 236
    reinterpretation of the, 235
    studies, 272
Qutb, Sayyid, 163, 165-166

radical Islamist, 28
Rahardjo, Dawam, 114, 230, 280
Rahardjo, Eko, 174, 285
Rahman, Fazlur, 235, 237-238, 240
Rais, Amien, 193
rajam, 171-172, 175
Ramaḍān fasting, 144
Ranuwihardjo, Dahlan, 228

Rasjidi, H.M., 146, 149, 186, 188, 192, 199-200, 202, 212, 289
Rasyid, Daud, 281, 289-290, 296
Ratuperwiranegara, Alamsyah, 133-134, 276
re-actualise, 227
Reading, 125
reality (cultural-sociological), 269
reform (*pembaruan*), 234
    period (*reformasi*), 218
reinterpret, 227
Reinvigorating Religious Understanding in the Indonesian Muslim Community, 234, 281
religio-ethical, 274
Religious, 209
    expansion, 267
    Judicature Act, 212, 225
    pluralism, 40, 227, 235, 241-242, 244, 246-247, 250, 257
    plurality, 244
    propagation, 188
    syncretism (*penyamaan agama*), 162
    war (*perang agama*), 218
Rencana Undang-Undang Perkawinan, 108
Renville Agreement, 79
Republika, 176
respected heretics, 60
revivalist, 237
Riady, James T., 215
Riberu, J., 205
Riḍā, Rashīd, 252-253, 259, 290, 296
Ridwan, Cholil, 204, 261-262
right wing Islam, 287
RMS (Republik Maluku Selatan), 76, 221
roads leading to God, 244
Roem, Mohamad, 100, 102, 289

Roman Catholicism, 52
rukun iman, 251
Rumi, Jalaluddin, 245
RUU Pokok-Pokok Perkawinan, 108
RUU-PA, 209-211, 264

Ṣābi'īn, 252-253
ṣirāṭ, 244
sabīl, 244
Sabians, 241
Sabili, 172
Saeed, 236-237, 240
Sahal, Ahmad, 274
Saksi, 172
salām, 266
    towards, 265
Salaf, 283
Salafi-Wahhabi, 155
Salafy, 151, 155
Sanata Dharma Catholic University, 123
Santa Cruz, 134
Santo Thomas Catholic High School, 123
santri, 116-119, 191
SARA, 92-93, 216
    policy, 36, 99, 107, 110, 113, 117, 120,
    127, 141, 228, 230
Sarapung, Elga, 272
Satya Wacana Christian University, 123
Say, Ben Mang Reng, 77, 186
Schumann, Olaf, 61
Schuon, Frithjof, 236
sciences of the ancients (al-ʿulūm al-awā'il
    or al-ʿulūm al-qudamā'), 256
scripturalist, 28
Second Vatican Council, 53, 251
secular state, 73, 87, 228-230, 233
secularisation, 232, 234, 236
secularising, 234, 236

secularism, 236
Sekitar Perjanjian Lama dan Perjanjian
    Baru (The Old and New Testament),
    86
Sekretariat Bersama Golongan Karya, 104
Setiabudi, Natan, 197
Shafiʿi school, 33
Al-Shafii, 47
Shafiite ʿulamā', 50
Shara, Yuni, 205
sharīʿa, 30-31, 109, 168-171, 244, 248, 286,
    293
Shepard, 28
Shihab, Alwi, 272
Shihab, Habieb Muhammad Rizieq, 36-
    37, 151-153, 167, 169- 171, 177-
    179, 183-184, 208, 213, 285
Shihab, Quraish, 241, 254-255, 258-259,
    262
shirʿa (law system), 252
shirk, 164, 255-256, 263, 292
SIAR, Tabloid, 224
Silalahi, Harry Tjan, 122
Simatupang, T.B., 186-187
Simon, 41
Simon, Gottfried, 64
Sinar Harapan, 192, 200
singular loyalty (monoloyalitas), 105
Situbondo (East Java) riots of 1996, 273
Sjadzali, Munawir, 134, 138, 202-203, 209,
    237, 276
Sjahrir, 146
Society for Inter-Religious Dialogue, see
    MADIA
Soeharto, 27, 90, 92-93, 95-96, 99-102,
    106, 113-117, 128-129, 132, 135,
    137, 141, 176, 186, 212, 218, 230-
    231, 265, 288

Soekoto SJ, Leo, 201
Soemitro, 105
Soerjadjaya, William, 97
Some Reflections on Religious Life in Indonesia for the Coming Generations, 282, 289
Son of God, 42
Soumokil, Dr., 76
spirit, 274
State Administrative Court, 209
Steenbrink, Karel, 60-61
Stella Duce, High Schools, 123
Stolk, H.C., 286
A Study of History, 86-87
style, 239
Suara Hidayatullah, 172
Subchan, Z.E. 122
substantialist, 28
Sudharmono, 114
Sudomo, 111
Sukarno, 71, 73, 75-77, 79, 81-82, 88-89, 91-92, 100, 122, 127, 229
    and Islam, 87
suluk, 244
Sumardi, Sandyawan, 273
Sumargono, Ahmad, 150, 176, 207
Sumarlin, Johannes, 118-119
Sumartana, Th., 272
Sunarko, Kapolda, 221
sunna, 29, 31, 242, 274, 278
Susanto, Tri, 126
Sutiyoso, 152
Sutrisno, 273
Sutrisno, Try, 114
Suwarna, Abdullah, 200
Syafei, Theo, 196
As-Syafi'iyah Mosque, 284

Syariat Islam: Pandangan Muslim Liberal, 274
Syarif Hidayatullah, State Institute of Islamic Studies, 232
synagogues, 248
syncretism, 207

ṭarīqa, 244
tabligh akbar, 222
tafsīr, 165
    al-Manār, 253, 290, 296
    bi al-ma'thūr, 168
taḥrīf, 84, 160
Taher, Tarmizi, 134, 181, 276
Tambunan, A.M., 186, 188
Tanjung Priok
    event, 113
    Jakarta, 109
Taoism, 55
Taoists, 253
taqlīd, 257
taqwā, 245
tathlīth (Trinity), 42
tawakkal (trust and passive acceptance), 290
tawḥīd, 57, 244
Taylor, Michael, 57
Tebu Ireng, Pesantren, 77
Tempo, 172, 198
temporalising of values, 236
Ten Berg, J.J., 70-71
tendency to spiritualise, 236
text (doctrinal-theological), 269
textual approach, 227
Thalib, Ja'far Umar, 36, 152, 155, 172-173, 175, 221-222, 285
Al-Thawri, 47

theological
    approach, 235
    basis, 235
    doctrinal and ritual aspects, 247
    view, 248
Third Development Cabinet, 117
Tiga Agama Satu Tuhan, 272
TII (Indonesian Islamic Army), 78
tilāwatil
    Injīl, 208
    Qu'rān, 208
Torah, 40-41, 215
Toynbee, Arnold, 86-87
transcendent unity of religions, 275
tricky theological concept, 85
Trinity (*tathlīth*), 39-40, 84-85, 57, 225
Truth (*ḥaniῆ*), 243
Tuhan Yesus dalam Agama Islam, 84
tujuh kata (seven words), 74
turn away from Islam (*Murtad*), 295

ᶜ*ulamā'*, 33, 261, 266
al-ᶜulūm al-awā'il, 257
Umar ibn Khattab, Caliph, 46, 290
Umar, Husein, 37, 147, 149, 177, 188, 192-
    193, 203, 206-207, 212, 215, 289
Umar, Muhammad, 222
umma, 236
United Development Party, *see* PPP
United States, 30
universal
    Islamic values, 227
    religion, 242
University of Chicago, 235, 237, 282
University of Indonesia, 228
untruths (*akādhīb*), 41
urban Muslims, 271
Ursula High Schools, St, 123

uṣūl al-fiqh (Islamic legal theory), 151, 290
US's grand scenario, 221
al-ᶜUzza, 69

Van Klinken, 217
Vatican and Pontifical Council for Inter-
    Religious Dialogue, 57
Vatican Secretariat for Non-Christian
    Religions, 54
vicious Islam, 287
violation of God's law (*kemaksiatan*), 295
Voetius, Gisbertus, 61
von der Mehden, Fred, 64

wājib, 286
Wadah Musyawarah antar Agama (Con-
    sultation Forum), 185
Wadah Musyawarah Antar Umat Ber-
    agama (Inter-religious Council), 133
Wadah Musyawarah Antar Umat Ber-
    agama, 134
Wahhabism, 151
Wahib, Ahmad, 228, 230, 240, 286
Wahid, Abdurrahman, 115, 195, 206, 219,
    265-266, 287-289
Wajah Liberal Islam di Indonesia, 274
Walean, Robert Paul, 161
walī, 263
Walubi (Perwalian Umat Buddha Indo-
    nesia), 133, 183
Wanandi, Sofyan (Liem Bian Kie), 111
Wansbrough, John, 238
Wardy, Bisjron, 86
waṣiyyah, 245
WCRP (World Conference on Religion and
    Peace), 57
West, 93
Westernisation, 234

WFDD (World Faiths Development Dialogue), 57
Widjojo, Father, 124
Widjojo, S., 210-211
Willis, A.T., 82
Wirjosandjojo, Sukiman, 80-81
Wongsonegoro, 74
wordings (*tabdīl*), 40
World Council, 164
  of Churches, 55-56
World Muslim Congress, 56

Yafie, Ali, 116
Yahya, 41

Yahya, Hasyim, 164
Yani, Achmad, 90
Yayasan Dewan Dakwah Islamiyah Indonesia, 145
Yewangoe, A.A., 181-182
yushrik, 292

Zabūr, 215
zakāt, 45-47
zindiq, 69
Zionism, 57
Zoroastrians, 252, 256-257, 262
Zuhri, Saifuddin, 77
Zwemer, Samuel, 64